CW01021424

A VISION

The Way of the Dream

Anthony Lunt was an advanced student of the psychiatrist R.D. Laing from 1982 until Laing's death in 1989. His first book, *Apollo versus the Echomaker: A Laingian Approach to Psychotherapy, Dreams and Shamanism* (Element Books 1990), was reviewed in the *Journal of the Society for Existential Analysis* as "essential reading." Gradually, Anthony and his wife, Anna, began to receive on-going instruction through their dreams: the educative process that underlay all of the highest civilizations in antiquity. That educative process is now the focus of his work. Anthony lives in Caversham with Anna, who is a poet.

AVISION

The Way of the Dream

Anthony Lunt

The author may be contacted in writing at: 10 St. Anne's Road, Caversham, Reading, Berkshire, RG4 7PA, United Kingdom.

ISBN-10: 1453788980
EAN-13: 9781453788981

Published by Anthony Lunt.
Printed by CreateSpace, a part of the Amazon group of companies.
Cover illustration by Sheridan Lunt: maze with Egyptian hieroglyph of five-pointed star.

This book presents a path for spiritual development. It is not intended as an alternative to psychiatric or psychotherapeutic treatment. A person in need of such treatment should consult a suitable practitioner.

Under no circumstances should one act upon a dream instruction that involves harm to oneself or others. The author expressly disclaims liability for any consequences that may arise from a reader acting upon a dream instruction.

For Anna and our children

When I was fifteen, I learnt that an eleven-year-old boy who lived across the road from me, who had been a brilliant pupil at his primary school, feared that he would do less well when he went on to Reading Boys' Grammar School. The reason for this was that he believed his success to be entirely due to his having sat next to an extraordinary girl and that, without her, his own abilities would fail to flourish. As it turned out, that girl was to become my wife. By the time the reader has completed Chapter One, they will be quite clear that I could not possibly have written this book without Anna's inspiring contribution. That contribution included her dreams, her insights and an endless mutual exploration of all the questions that, over the past thirteen years, the process of writing *Avision* raised. It needs to be said, too, that Anna has been a tireless and invaluable editor and typer of the manuscript. I count myself as being the most fortunate of men to have been blessed with such a companion through life.

CONTENTS

Introduction: The Ancient Tradition 1

Chapter One: The Original Religion 9

Chapter Two: The Law 25

Chapter Three: God and the Dream 36

Chapter Four: The Requirement 47

Chapter Five: Reconnection 52

Chapter Six: The Sphinx 60

Chapter Seven: The Otherworld 69

Chapter Eight: Restoration 81

Chapter Nine: Resonance 90

Chapter Ten: The Earth Womb 117

Chapter Eleven: The Phallus 131

Chapter Twelve: The Imminent and the Manifest 144

Chapter Thirteen: The Green Jewel 174

Chapter Fourteen: The Serpent 201

Chapter Fifteen: The Temple 245

Chapter Sixteen: The Present 271

Chapter Seventeen: Conclusion 283

References 299

Acknowledgements 344

INTRODUCTION

The Ancient Tradition

This book is about the ancient and universal tradition of receiving instruction through dreams.

My interest in the Dream was ignited when I was twenty by a trilogy of television programmes that Laurens van der Post had made about the life of C.G. Jung. I say ignited because Jung and the Dream exploded into my life at that point and changed the course of it forever. That was in 1972. I abandoned my career as a musician and, by 1977, completed my initial training as a psychotherapist. Subsequently, in 1982, I became an advanced student of the psychiatrist R.D. Laing. My training with Laing was brought to a close by his death in the autumn of 1989. At this critical juncture, I was again deeply affected by Laurens van der Post. He had agreed to be interviewed by me for the journal *International Minds* after I had sent him an article of mine on the potter Bernard Leach – the great bridge between East and West – that had been published in the first issue. The journal, which was designed to bring psychological insight into international relations, included contributions from major academic and political figures.

When, shortly before Christmas, we met to get to know each other, Laurens told me that he had ceased giving interviews but that my article had led him to change his mind because he believed that I would listen to what he had to say. It became clear that he had something of great importance to convey, something he had previously found no-one would take seriously. He revealed what that was when I interviewed him on Boxing Day: "And so I think, as very often happens in life, when life itself feels imperilled, somehow out of it comes the saving element. Somehow this process always breaks through with one individual – although many contribute. The window into this elemental area was opened by Freud, by his work on dreams and by his showing that the key to the door of what we need is the Dream. And then Jung carried it further. The saving thing in life is there! In the long-run, I back the Dream."[1] The printed word cannot convey the manner in which this was said – the deep sense of knowing drawn from a lifetime of contemplation.

That the Dream can provide the solution to the political ills of the world does not fit into the conceptual framework of contemporary politics. But in his statement Laurens was in effect arguing for a return to the primacy of the Dream in the affairs of Man that had existed in earlier times. For, as Robert J. White stated in his preface to the *Oneirocritica* by Artemidorus, "In a sense, Freud, Jung, and others were not so much innovators as restorers, since they were reassigning to dreams and dream-readings the importance that they had held in antiquity, and which they had lost in more recent centuries. Assyrians, Egyptians, Hebrews, Greeks and Romans (to mention only the Mediterranean world) were all profoundly convinced of the significance of man's dreams. Indeed, the gravest personal, political, and economic decisions often rested upon their interpretation."[2] As the philosopher Peter Kingsley observes in his outstanding work of scholarship *In The Dark Places of Wisdom*, the thought of society receiving its laws through dreams is so far removed from conventional notions of reality that many people find it difficult to grasp how that could once have been so.[3]

In antiquity, pre-eminent among those philosophers now known as the pre-Socratics was Parmenides, who has been called the father of Western logic. This appellation indicates the extraordinary determining influence that Parmenides in particular and the pre-Socratics in general exerted upon the development of Western civilization and, hence, their relevance for us today. The influence of the pre-Socratics is of such an order that, in the words of Giorgio de Santillana, "as our own awareness of history builds up, we cannot help realizing that it is those ancients who have dealt out all the ideas that Western thought has played with ever since."[4] (Santillana wrote this whilst recognising that high science — such as that which existed in ancient Egypt — far anteceded and heavily influenced the Greek civilization.)

Plato, recognising the importance of, and being deeply influenced by, the seminal contribution that Parmenides had made to Western thought, wished to be seen as Parmenides' successor.[5] Yet, the revelations provided by recent archaeological evidence concerning Parmenides have been suppressed because they reveal that the pre-Socratic view of what it is to be a human being and philosopher was very different from that held today[6] and, indeed, in key respects, to that presented by Plato.

The evidence reveals that Parmenides was a law-giver who received the laws from the Dream and that, in common with other pre-Socratics, the Dream was both his guide through life and the means by which he healed others.[7] It was because of the understanding they received through their dreams that the pre-Socratics were known as 'the wise'.[8]

The fact that the seeds of Western civilization were sown by the Dream[9] and that philosophers were experts at tending to that process is so antithetical to the conventional world view that the truth about the pre-Socratics has been refashioned to make it consistent with the rationalist outlook of mainstream academia.[10] Such was the wisdom of the pre-Socratics that they knew their way of life would be misrepresented and their teaching would be fragmented and distorted. They would also have known that, at any time, the Dream can simply re-present everything that has been lost.

In the *Oxford English Dictionary*, the first definition of 'philosopher' is "A lover of wisdom; one who devotes himself to the search of fundamental truth." and the second is "An adept in occult science... a diviner of dreams." We are told that in Middle English the second definition was often not separable from the first "the notions being popularly identified."[11]

This shows that what Kingsley has described was a living element of the culture of England and demonstrates the partiality of the modern notion of what it is to be a philosopher.

The identification in Middle English of a philosopher with a diviner of dreams is an indication of the enduring influence of Druidism in Britain. Caesar made reference to the Druids as teachers held in great honour. Dion Chrysostom recorded: "they concern themselves with divination and all branches of wisdom";[12] whilst Diodorus Siculus explains that the title 'Druid' means 'one who is very knowledgeable'. "The knowledge he seeks visits him in a dream of revelation... When he awakes, he finds himself in possession of the understanding he sought."[13] It is immediately obvious that this description of the Druids corresponds to Kingsley's account of the pre-Socratics. The Dream was the vehicle upon which they journeyed through life. Yet, the Dream as they knew it is virtually neglected in the West today, even though "all the ideas that Western thought has played with" since the pre-Socratics were given to them in dreams and visions. In contrast, the contemporary Tibetan lama Tenzin Wangyal Rinpoche states: "there is nothing more real than dream."[14] He describes how "Most Tibetans – high spiritual masters and simple ordinary people – consider dreams to be a potential source of both the most profound spiritual knowledge and of guidance for everyday life."[15] I shall, throughout this book, provide examples of other cultures in which the ancient tradition has survived to the present day.

Knowledge of the significance of the Dream is a part of every child's birthright. It is the most essential element of their intellectual heritage – a heritage which is no longer bequeathed to the majority of children. In the West, we are taught Pythagoras' theorem, but not "how important dreams and dream-divination were considered to be by early Pythagoreans as a means of providing them with knowledge, teaching and guidance"[16] or that Pythagoras "deprecated things opposed to... visions in dreams in particular."[17] We are not even told that Pythagoras held that "Through numbers... he was able to worship and commune with the divine."[18]

It will, of course, be argued that mathematics and geometry are taught in schools as pure disciplines and that these, in association with the sciences, have advanced beyond concern with religious and spiritual issues. This, however, was not the view of Albert Einstein who stated "I assert that the cosmic religious experience is the strongest and the noblest driving force behind scientific research."[19] "The basis of all scientific work is the conviction that the world is an ordered and comprehensive entity, which is a religious sentiment. My religious feeling is a humble amazement at the order revealed in the small patch of reality to which our feeble intelligence is equal."[20] "I see a pattern. But my imagination cannot picture the maker of that pattern... The human mind is unable to conceive of the four dimensions. How can it conceive of a God, before whom a thousand years and a thousand dimensions are as one?"[21]

There was no doubt in the minds of the pre-Socratics that they were in direct contact with 'the maker of the pattern' through their dreams. In this, they were not alone since, as Kelly Bulkeley writes, "Virtually every religious tradition in history, from cultures all over the world, has offered an explanation of dreaming that refers in some way to God, the Divine, or to some other transpersonal power or spiritual realm. On this point there is a broad historical and cross-cultural consensus: dreaming has its ultimate roots in religious powers and realities."[22] It is understandable, then, that "The Pythagorean curriculum was designed with a single underlying purpose, to bring the lives of men and women into harmony with the divine."[23] For some readers, these ideas will create a stumbling block. However, a great deal hinges upon what one understands by the terms 'God' or 'the Divine'. One could equally speak of the 'Tao'. Indeed, I cite the scientific humanist Oliver Reiser using the term 'God' as a central reference in his system of thought. I will demonstrate that, whatever term one chooses to use, there is good reason to conclude that the pre-Socratics were right.

It was said of the pre-Socratic Cretan philosopher Epimenides that he learnt all he knew through the Dream. Epimenides was famed for having acquired, through that education, the ability to heal entire populations of cities.[24]

I do not doubt for one moment that what was said about Epimenides' ability to heal the populations of cities was true. There are certain irreducible truths – about the Earth on which we stand, the universe within which we are housed and Man's part within the whole – that inhere in the depths of every human being. A civilization can only endure and flourish to the extent it is concordant with, and gives due recognition to, those truths. When this is so, what is within and what is without are in alignment. In so far as a civilization fails to fulfil this condition, which is in fact an obligation, there are observable consequences that result from each distortion of the truth. As the Egyptologist R.A. Schwaller de Lubicz states, "The principle of harmony is cosmic law, the voice of God. Whatever the disorder caused by man or natural accident, Nature, if left to her own devices, will reestablish order by means of affinity, the consciousness innate in all things."[25] The means that Nature uses to put everything in order again in the consciousness of Man is the Dream. For, through the Dream, Life itself directs the attention of each person to that which they should be addressing for the benefit of themselves and of the whole.

Epimenides was also one of the great law-givers of Crete who received the laws through their dreams.[26] It is clear that the view derived from modern science, that the experience of an individual must be replicable by others if it is to be judged to have general validity, was not held in ancient times so far as the Dream was concerned. Then, the philosophy of an individual or the code of conduct of a whole nation could be determined by a single dream.

Epimenides' role as a law-giver was a natural outgrowth of the Dream being his teacher. The experience of being taught by the Dream is as available now as it was in ancient times. It is not the Dream that has changed, but Man's attitude towards, and understanding of, the Dream. One can see this reflected in the English language. The word 'avision' is defined within the *O.E.D.* as, in the first instance, "A vision or dream" and, in the second, a "Warning or monition (given in a dream)"[27] – the original meaning of 'monition' being "Instruction, direction".[28] Since 'avis', which is the root of 'avision', means "Advice, advise",[29] I am using the term 'avision' to denote advice which is received through a dream or vision. The *O.E.D.* records that the word 'avision' is now obsolete. It is my intention to restore this noble word to common usage and, in the process, to re-establish an awareness of why avision was known to be essential for the survival and well-being of human society.

The experience of avision brings one directly into the territory of the ancient Mysteries for, as Joscelyn Godwin explains, "The Greater Mysteries, or higher grades of initiation, were conducted individually rather than collectively. The initiations of Isis were given to those priests or laity selected by the goddess through having had significant dreams. Sometimes the dream itself might be the initiation."[30] This is of particular relevance because the Mysteries "point the way to the true goal of human existence."[31] The Mysteries appear in the dreams of today, as they have always done, irrespective of whether or not the issues concerned have been marginalized by society. As a consequence of the guidance that my wife, Anna, and I have received through our dreams, I have, over the years, been in a position to help numerous psychotherapists who have consulted me with regard to dreams (both their own and those of their patients) which they could not understand. Much that has been impenetrable to them has touched upon the Mysteries.

As I only have a limited amount of time for individual consultations, my purpose in writing this book is to enable all those who are interested to experience the benefits of avision. Keeping at the forefront of my mind the difficulties which the psychotherapists encountered before they consulted me, I realized that I could best assist the reader by providing examples of the dream instructions received by Anna and myself. The reader will then gain a clearer sense of how the process of avision unfolds.

Tenzin Wangyal Rinpoche relates "There are numerous examples in the Tibetan tradition of practitioners who received teachings in dreams. Often the dreams come in sequence, each night's dream starting where the previous night's dream ends, and in this way transmitting entire, detailed teachings until a precise and appropriate point of completion is reached, at which point the dreams stop. Volumes of teachings have been 'discovered' this way, including many of the practices that Tibetans have been doing for centuries. This is what we call 'mind treasure'... The teachings are inherent in the foundational wisdom that any culture can eventually access. They are not only Buddhist or Bön teachings; they are teachings for all humans."[32]

If humanity is to meet the challenges presented in the years ahead, contemporary society must return to the Way of the Dream. This is the message that Laurens van der Post sought to impart nearly twenty years ago. Although his doing so made no obvious difference to the world, it made a very great difference to me. To date, modern Man has acted from a position of imbalance: virtually ignoring avision, relying instead upon the limited understanding of his intellect; the consequence of which has been increasing disharmony within society and the environment. There seems little chance that the 'powers that be' will respond to Laurens' call to "back the Dream". And, so, it is up to each individual to determine for themselves whether they wish to follow in the footsteps of Parmenides and Pythagoras and play their part within the universe as Nature intended.

CHAPTER ONE

The Original Religion

In March of 1989, the year after we first met but before we had developed an intimate relationship, Anna had an extraordinarily vivid dream. I mention this dream, even though it is not obviously instructional in the way that the dreams which follow are, because it was the seed from which the later dreams evolved:

> Anthony and I are holding hands, climbing the spiral staircase of an ivory tower. I am leading the way, clad in a sumptuous white gown; Anthony is attired in black. The atmosphere is magical. We are laughing with joy. Reaching the top of the tower, we come out onto a balcony beneath a pale, full moon. Waiting there are Pegasus and the Unicorn. We watch as they both leap from the balcony. For a moment, they fly – and, then, dive down into the sea below, where they transform into dolphins.

We felt a deep sense of awe when we contemplated the sublime ambience of the dream and its mystical imagery. However, although it was evident that Anna's dream referred to the relationship between us and that a process of transformation was explicitly depicted, it was not at all obvious to either of us what was signified by her leading the way of ascent to Pegasus and the Unicorn. Such obscurity of meaning often occurs when a dream is predictive. Then, the dream might only make sense to the dreamer after the predicted event has occurred. For this reason, a great deal of insight comes with hindsight.

Here, I should mention that the sequence of our dreams does not always chart a straight course. Despite this, having experimented with a number of ways of presenting our experience of avision, I found that by far the best approach was to arrange our dreams in the sequence in which they were dreamt; although, because some dreams concern issues which we only began to understand many years later, chronological order is not always adhered to. At this point, I will say no more in order that the reader can get a sense of how our understanding slowly developed with each new dream instruction.

The next dream I shall recount was also one of Anna's which came in August of 1990:

> I am talking with Anthony. These words come into my mind:
> "The more intimate,
> The more infinite."

Looking back, I find it remarkable that this dream encapsulated so concisely the essence of our path ahead.

In contrast to the patriarchal traditions, we were being shown that our relationship is intrinsic to our spiritual development. This message was under-laid by the use of pairing. The pair, which had been represented by Anna and myself and, then, by Pegasus and the Unicorn, both as themselves and as the two dolphins, was now presented as a rhyming couplet. It was only several years later that we learnt that Pegasus is a symbol of divine poetic inspiration[1] and, hence, that the appearance of Pegasus in the first dream was predictive of a poetical form being utilized in the second. Particularly affecting for us was the discovery that Pegasus is not simply a source of poetry, but of poetry as a vehicle for attaining the infinite – that "the rider of

Pegasus could *figuratively* 'fly through the air, to reach the heavens'."[2] Wendy Doniger O'Flaherty specifically relates this flight to the Dream: "Pegasus himself is a dream figure; he is the winged horse who carries the hero into his dream in many myths."[3] Barbara Walker notes that the cult of Pegasus may have originated in Egypt, at the site of a sacred spring in Abydos called Pega.[4] Abydos was a major dream centre in antiquity; its links with avision are revealed by the ancient Egyptian word 'peg' meaning 'to explain' and 'to unfold'.[5] Curiously, both of these meanings apply to Anna's dream instruction, as it explains the unfolding from the intimate to the infinite. One can go further and say that it is a succinct, totally Pegasean commentary on the previous dream. One might even say that it functions as a caption to the earlier dream, since it relates that it is through greater intimacy that we can ascend to the Pegasean heights. A. Leo Oppenheim records that, in the ancient Near East, the creativeness of a poet "can derive its authenticity and legitimation only from the fact that his opus reflects faithfully its prototype in heaven which was revealed to him either in a dream or through a specific and special divine intervention."[6]

When, in 2007, I obtained a copy of the contributions to the first international Colloquium on the Dream (held in France in 1962), I was delighted to find, in a paper by Henry Corbin entitled 'The Visionary Dream in Islamic Spirituality', an account of the thirteenth century Sufi Rūzbehān whose teaching is an exemplification of the instruction "The more intimate, The more infinite". "Rūzbehān is certainly one of Iran's greatest mystics. His doctrine is characterized by a complete asceticism of love which puts an end to the opposition established by traditional asceticism between human love and divine love. For Rūzbehān there is but one love, but one text, the meaning of which must be learned. In his beautiful book, entitled *Jasmin of Love's Faithful*, Rūzbehān expressly distinguishes between those he calls the 'pious devotees', whose spiritual experience did not have its origin in human love, and those he calls the 'intimates', the faithful of love, who have been initiated by a human love that was for them the beginning of the spiritual way. Let it be especially noted that no 'conversion' is involved here, no passing from a human object to a divine object (God is not an object), but that a transformation takes place within the loving subject: the unity of the Contemplator and the Contemplated announces itself in the ecstatic agitation of the soul when it is exposed to human beauty experienced as the mystery of a supreme theophany, that is to say, in the ecstasy of the soul that perceives the prophetic meaning of beauty."[7]

Anna and I began to live together towards the end of 1990, some months after the publication of my first book, *Apollo versus the Echomaker*. Inspired by Anna's dream concerning the intimate and the infinite, we realized that we needed to retreat from social activity for a period of time and, also, to put our books to one side in order to explore the truth of life entirely through our own experience. As a result of this, we began to reconsider the validity of the acquired knowledge that we had received through our education and reading. Time passed and, then, in September of 1991, Anna dreamt:

> I am in a bed-chamber in an ancient palace – perhaps in Turkey or Arabia. I have woken in the night. It is dark, but the light of the full moon illuminates the room, which is circular with a domed ceiling. The moonlight is streaming in through huge arched windows that have no glass panes. The room is sparsely furnished, though there are luxurious Persian rugs on the floor and I am in a very large bed with silken sheets and covers. Anthony is asleep beside me. In the shadows stands a wizened old man. I feel he is a nomadic wise man and that he is well over a hundred years old. I get out of bed and walk over to him. Then he speaks, saying "There is no need to play music. What you are seeking can only be found in silence."

Having put aside our books, we were now being advised to put aside our music as well. I can't say that this instruction was altogether welcome, since listening to our records and C.D.s was very important to us. Even so, we began to consider why we had been told that we didn't need to play music. We gradually became aware of the extent to which playing recordings took us out of the present and back into the past associations those recordings had for us. And this raised a particular issue for me as some of the music that we played had been recorded by classical musicians I had known personally, a few of whom had been major influences on my development, who had since died. I realized that these recordings kept them alive for me; whereas, in the natural order of things, when they died, the glorious sounds they made ceased with them, lost except to the world of memory. Recordings helped me to avoid this experience of loss and its painful contribution to the ongoing movement of life. It became apparent, too, that all music took us out of our mental world into the imagination and emotional world of the composer. We found that, whilst this can be enriching when experienced occasionally through a live performance, music, especially recorded music, functioned in effect as an eddy that impeded our focusing upon the natural flow. And, so, we increasingly immersed ourselves in extended periods of silence. What I have described in a few sentences actually took us a few years to work through.

It eventually dawned on us that our ascending the ivory tower in Anna's first dream had pointed to our going into retreat; and that Anna leading the way had indicated that she would lead with the guidance from her dreams. We could then see that the spiral staircase symbolized the yearly cycle of dreams which were to be the means by which we would ascend. In contrast to this symbolism, the instruction "There is no need to play music. What you are seeking can only be found in silence." can be understood immediately in its own terms. It is not in need of any interpretation, but is simply to be acted upon.

This type of instructional dream is an established part of Western religious heritage. For instance, in the Christian tradition, it is said of the Three Wise Men "And being warned of God in a dream that they should not return to Herod, they departed into their own country another way. And when they were departed, behold, the angel of the Lord appeared to Joseph in a dream, saying, Arise, and take the young child and his mother and flee into Egypt, and be thou there until I bring thee word: for Herod will seek the young child to destroy him. When he arose, he took the young child and his mother by night and departed into Egypt: And was there until the death of Herod."(Matthew 2:12-15) At this critical juncture in the life of Christ, the key to survival is the Dream. One is left in no doubt that when the wisest of men have such a dream they act upon it with complete fidelity to the dream instruction. In this, the compilers of the gospel were recording a tradition of avision which goes back into the depths of time. One may well wonder what happened to that tradition so far as Christianity is concerned. I shall answer that question later in this book.

With regard to contemporary psychotherapy, White was right to say that "In a sense, Freud, Jung, and others were not so much innovators as restorers since they were reassigning to dreams and dream-readings the importance that they had held in antiquity." However, it is only 'in a sense' that this was true of Freud because with regard to avision he did precisely the opposite. It was a central tenet of Freud's approach to dreams that "We must not concern ourselves with what the dream appears to tell us, whether it is intelligible or absurd, clear or confused, since it cannot possibly be the unconscious material we are in search of."[8] In taking this stance, Freud ruled out the possibility of benefitting from avision.

I had, in 1987, realized that Freud's approach created an obstacle to my being able to relate to the Dream; and, so, I was free from his influence by the time Anna (who was unaware of Freud's views) dreamt the lines "The more intimate, The more infinite." The effect upon us of combining this guidance with the instruction that "What you are seeking can only be found in silence." was the development of a deep sense of fellowship in silence out of which emerged an increasing sensitivity to the changing moods of Nature. It was within this context that, towards the end of 1991, I dreamt:

> I have come from the time of the Buddha, with whom I was associated. I am shocked to realize that something which was then regarded as fundamental to the practice of the Buddha is no longer even mentioned.

This was the first dream of mine in which the issue of reincarnation was explicitly mentioned. Until then, I had not formed any definite views on the subject. Now, I began to see how our shared experience of silence had taken me back to the way of being I had known in an earlier life.

Before proceeding, I wish to emphasise that the texts which I cite in association with our dreams were, in virtually all cases, unknown to us when we had the dreams in question.

The decisive time in the life of the Buddha was the night upon which he gained enlightenment. In the ancient *Pali Canon* it is recalled "Five dreams now appeared to the Bodhisatta." "It was the night before his attainment of enlightenment; and the dreams were a premonition that he was about to attain his goal."[9] The Buddha recounts that on the following night, after he had stilled his mind through meditation, "I inclined my mind to the knowledge of recollection of past lives... 'I was there so-named, of such a race, with such appearance, such food, such experience of pleasure and pain, such a life term; and passing away thence, I reappeared elsewhere, and there too I was so-named, of such a race, with such an appearance, such experience of pleasure and pain, such a life term; passing away thence I reappeared here' – thus with details and particulars I recollected my manifold past life. This was the first true knowledge attained by me."[10] There is a correspondence between the focus of my first dream in this sequence being upon a past life in which I was associated with the Buddha and the Buddha saying that the first knowledge he attained was about his past lives. This correspondence, which was created by the Dream, is of particular interest because it was said of Pythagoras, who himself placed such a high value upon avision, that *"he made the starting-point of education the reminiscence of the previous lives which souls lived through before entering the bodies in which they happened to be living."*[11] The reader may well find that a past life issue initiates their own experience of avision. This has certainly been the case for a significant number of people who have consulted me.

In April of 1992, Anna had the following dream:

Anthony gives me a beautiful pack of Tarot cards. They contain a set of bird cards. The birds, painted in white, silver and gold, are raised to appear three-dimensional. I am particularly drawn to the heron. As I look at the card, I notice a dove flying around the room. I go to tell Anthony, who is in the next room. He is opening a letter.

The letter reads "Believe in the stars and that they directly affect everything that happens to us."

We awoke early and, after discussing the dream, decided to go for a walk just before sunrise. It was a cold, misty morning. The mist was so dense that we could barely see ahead for more than a few yards. Suddenly, as we turned into a riverside park, we could just make out a heron feeding by a miniature waterfall. It was the first heron that either of us could remember seeing. It seemed that we had been transported into a Chinese scroll painting. Somehow, we had walked into Anna's dream and the magical beauty of the dream spread like the dawn into our waking life. We found ourselves in the land of the soul, where the dream bird that Anna was drawn towards, that was raised to appear three-dimensional, became the very bird that was standing before us.

This experience is at odds with Freud's view that dreams are determined by the activities of the day prior to the dream – which he called "the day's residues" – and by unresolved disturbances from one's childhood. Patricia Cox Miller, in her book *Dreams in Late Antiquity*, writes in a footnote "Commenting on the difference between Freud and Artemidorus [second century A.D.] regarding the temporal referentiality of dreams, Winkler remarks that 'Artemidorus' soul is looking to the immediate future, Freud's to the distant past,' and he observes further that 'at times one may wonder which is the stranger supposition – that the unconscious mind is aware of momentous changes in the offing or that it is obsessed with the remote events of one's childhood; Plutarch argues from the strangeness of our powers of memory to the reasonableness of precognition'."[12]

It is, of course, the case that many dreams do make reference to past events. However, one of the differences between Freud and Jung was that Jung, like Artemidorus (whose *Oneirocritica* Jung had studied in depth), observed that dreams were equally determined by future events – this, Jung called "the prospective function". Cox Miller provides an account of how "In the particular case of oneiromancy,

Stoics understood dreams as signs of a reality into which the present would flow. Thus dreams were predictive of the future – not merely predictive but deeply revelatory of the flow in time of configurations embedded in the present."[13] Through our experience, our attention was being directed towards this profound relationship between the Dream and the unfolding of events in material reality – to the very heart of the mystery of life. The Tarot card in Anna's dream was emblematic of this relationship. Luther Martin could have been describing what the Tarot card represented when he wrote that for the Stoics and Artemidorus "divination by dreams was 'a literate reading of the objective signs of the world as ordered by the syntax of fate'."[14]

Cox Miller describes how, in Cicero's *De divinatione*, his brother Quintus argues that "things happen by fate, which is defined as 'an orderly series of causes in which the cause is linked to cause and from each cause an effect is produced'."[15] One element of what was so important to us about Anna's dream and its relation to the experience that followed it was our realizing that, as Quintus understood, "If there were a person insightful enough to perceive the connections that join cause to cause, that person would know what the future will be because the passage of time is 'like the uncoiling of a rope: it creates nothing new but produces each event in its order'."[16]

Again, I am indebted to Cox Miller for pointing out that "George Steiner has coined the striking phrase 'hieroglyphics of futurity' to characterize antiquity's understanding of dreams as an imagistic language."[17] The application of this phrase is particularly apt with regard to Anna's dream, since, in ancient Egypt, a heron symbolized the Word of God – itself a term for the Dream. As Rundle Clark said, the phoenix – with which the heron was identified – "embodies the original Logos, the Word or declaration of destiny which mediates between the divine mind and created things."[18] To mention this is to go beyond the understanding that we had at the time. But, not to mention it would be to fail to give one of the most essential, and in some ways the most uncanny, element of the experience its due.

Freud observed that dreams are often multidetermined – by which he meant that they have more than one meaning. The same holds true for life in general. There can be layer upon layer of significance within a single event. We were astonished to discover that in ancient Egypt the heron had itself denoted precisely the experience that we were presented with. Furthermore, the manifestation of the heron as the phoenix epitomized "the appearance of light and life out of the original darkness and chaos."[19] This again corresponds to the pattern of our experience, which began in darkness and within which the appearance of light was a central element, with the process of illumination being both physical and mental. In the Heliopolitan Myth of Creation, creation commences when the heron appears on a raised mound and delivers the message of Life.[20] In our experience, the heron, by appearing before us after Anna had dreamt of it, delivered that message simply through its appearance. We were shown that this element of the Egyptian myth was revelatory of a truth which can be witnessed in our own age.

On 10th July 1993, the year following my dream of my Buddhist past life, Anna dreamt:

> There is a Buddhist monk, wearing dark red robes, meditating under Caversham Bridge. He is sitting in the lotus position on the surface of the water.

We had no idea what this dream might mean. Then, precisely a year to the day later, on 10th July 1994, we unexpectedly received an invitation to attend a Buddhist service to be held that afternoon in Caversham (where we live). Despite being in retreat, we decided to accept the invitation because of our dreams relating to Buddhism. The service was conducted by Lama Thupten Nyima, who was dressed in the dark red robes of a Tibetan monk, just as in Anna's dream. Afterwards, it was arranged for us to meet Lama Thupten alone in the early hours of the following morning. At this meeting, he told us that, while meditating on the day before the service, he had had a vision of a couple whom he had known in a previous life and that, upon our entering the room where the service was held, he had immediately recognised us as being that couple. So, Anna's dream of the year before had represented Lama Thupten meditating on the flow which was to bring him into contact with us again. As a result of our meeting with Lama Thupten, we were privileged to be introduced to an extraordinary Tibetan nun, Anila Pema Zangmo, with whom we and Lama Thupten engaged in a particularly clarifying conversation upon the subject of reincarnation. During our discussion, Lama Thupten expressed his opinion that Anna and I are directly instructed by the Buddha through our dreams.

In the sequence of our dreams which I have mentioned so far, there is a perceptible relationship between the dreams and subsequent events. The pattern began with Anna's dream of the ivory tower, which indicated that her leading us step by step would include the use of poetical means. This was realized when she dreamt the lines "The more intimate, The more infinite." In Anna's dream of the heron, there was a direct and almost immediate connection between the dream image of the heron and the live heron that we caught sight of shortly after we awoke. Then, we moved from the position of my having dreamt of being associated with the Buddha in a past life, via Anna's dream of the meditating Buddhist monk, to our being recognised by a Buddhist monk with whom we had been associated in a past life. We were observing ever-widening ripples radiating from the Dream.

Our meeting Lama Thupten led to discussions with other high lamas. However, at the end of these we were still no closer to understanding what it was that was fundamental to the practice of the Buddha that is now no longer even mentioned. But we had, through a vision, begun to be taken into the mysterious territory that Philostratus described as "divination by means of dreams, which is the divinest and most godlike of human faculties."[21]

In August of 1993, a month after her dream of the meditating Buddhist monk, Anna had another dream which anticipated Lama Thupten saying that he had known us as a couple in a past life:

Anthony and I are moving together through the cosmos, through space and time. These words come into my mind:

19

> "Harnessed to one another,
> As Earth and Moon,
> Through measureless depths
> And countless unfoldings we move
> In undulating dance
> While songs of love
> Flow from our hearts."

This beautiful dream is both a summary and a development of the dreams which preceded it. Our ascending the spiral staircase in the dream of the ivory tower is now amplified into our spiralling together through the cosmos. In the same way, the Pegasean couplet has developed into a substantial verse, which is itself an amplification of Anna's second dream. In that dream, as in this, words come into her mind while we are together. And here, too, the statement "The more intimate, The more infinite." has been extended into our being "Harnessed to one another... Through measureless depths." The "undulating dance" makes reference to a dream of Anna's from 1992 which we were only able to fully understand several years later and which, for that reason, I shall discuss in due course. The "songs of love" demonstrate that the instruction "There is no need to play music." does not mean that there is no place for music in our lives. The songs are not learnt, but flow naturally from the heart. The "countless unfoldings" are our countless lives. Our journeying together is presented within a context of our having travelled together over aeons. It is also a movement back through those immeasurable periods of time. I would add that, as Peter Russell has stated, "the spiral is crucial to Nature; it is the signature of the universe... We have both inferred and direct proof that the spiral is the preferred shape of creation."[22]

The movement back through time was epitomized in a dream of Anna's a few months later, in November 1993:

> I am shown that Love is the original religion and am given these words for a love poem:
> "Our altar
> One another"

20

The guidance provided by the Dream, that Love is the original religion, is completely at odds with the established notion that earliest Man was by nature brutish and uncivilized. However, as Riane Eisler states, "most of what we have learned to think of as our cultural evolution has in fact been interpretation... It has consisted of conclusions drawn from fragmentary data interpreted to conform to the traditional model of our cultural evolution as a linear progression from 'primitive man' to so-called 'civilized man', who, despite their many differences, shared a common preoccupation with conquering, killing, and dominating."[23] "the social organization and belief systems of these early centers of civilization were very different from how we have been taught society always has been – and by implication always will be – structured. To begin with, these early cradles of civilization seem to have been remarkably peaceful."[24] "The original direction in the mainstream of our cultural evolution was toward partnership but... following a period of chaos and almost total cultural disruption, there occurred a fundamental social shift."[25] "Contrary to what we have been taught of the Neolithic or first agrarian civilizations as male-dominant and highly violent, these were generally peaceful societies that traded extensively with their neighbors rather than killing or plundering to acquire wealth. Thanks to far more scientific and extensive archeological excavations, we also know that in these highly creative societies women held important social positions as priestesses, craftspeople, and elders of matrilineal clans. Moreover, these were generally equalitarian societies, where, as Mellaart writes, there are no signs of major differences in status based on sex."[26]

One can see from Eisler's account how the dream provided us with an antidote to the pervasive influence of patriarchy upon "the traditional model of our cultural evolution." This ability of the Dream is discussed in the account of avision presented by Iamblichos in his work *The Egyptian Mysteries*. There, he states that, when one has divine dreams, one "receives from them... a power and a capacity of knowing which reasons intelligently both of things that were and things that will be... [and] restores to order many things among men which were discordant and disorderly."[27] The ability of the Dream to provide "a view of every period of time"[28] and, in so doing, to restore the understanding which existed when life was lived as Nature intended was cogently summarized by Lao Tzu in the phrase "Turning back is how the way moves."[29] Lao Tzu noted that "The ability to know the beginning of antiquity Is called the thread running through the way."[30] Thus, he counselled "Let your wheels move only along old ruts."[31] In the ancient Egyptian Mysteries, "turning back" was referred to as 'returning to the First Time'. It was this faculty of the Dream which lay at the heart of the inherent conservatism of the ancient Egyptian civilization. In the prologue to his *Book of Wisdom*, which is the oldest known book in the world, the revered ancient Egyptian sage and statesman Ptah-Hotep, having reached a great age, requested of his pharaoh, Isesi, permission to nurture a 'spiritual son'. He asked "Let me pass on to him the words of those who know how to listen, the instructions of the ancestors, the guides, who, long ago, listened to the divine powers."[32]

The scientist and philosopher Charles Musès (one of the most brilliant minds of the twentieth century, who was a world authority on the scientific foundations of the ancient wisdom traditions and the light they can provide for modern science), in one of his most important scientific publications, wrote of "the fundamental reality of love as ultimate power."[33] Musès defined 'love' as the "universal symbiotic power of cosmic process"[34] – that is, the universal power by which everything in the Universe lives together. Elsewhere, he explained how the celebrated physician and alchemist Paracelsus and his great contemporary Cornelius Agrippa, who had "received their mantle and conceptual tools from a tradition that may be traced back to earliest times,"[35] both realized that the purpose of alchemy was not the Faustian ambition to master and manipulate nature which had preoccupied them in their younger years,[36] but "the *conscious* leading by man to higher ground of the forces that comprise his own nature, thus resulting finally in an actual metamorphosis of human nature far in advance of the pace set by ordinary experience;"[37] and that "The basis of this highest power... is that so profound yet deceptively simple power of Love."[38] Thus, at its height, alchemy was rooted "in natural operations and processes amenable to the law of Love-transmutation which extend throughout nature."[39] Musès laments: "Unfortunately the history of science since their time has shown that for the most part it has tended to follow the road and goals of the early rather than the mature Paracelsus and Agrippa."[40]

By means of a vision, Anna was instructed about the religion of the First Time – the religion of Love. There was no mention of religious worship in any conventional sense. When receiving dream instruction on a subject such as religion, about which one may have fixed opinions or, at least, an established viewpoint, it is essential that one should, as Ptah-Hotep emphasised, "know how to listen." This means, as Iamblichos counsels, that "it is necessary that thou shouldst prefer the true meaning of dreams before thy own notions."[41]

It is noticeable that the lines:

"Our altar
One another"

are entirely concordant with the earlier instruction:

"The more intimate,
The more infinite."

The emphasis in both dreams is upon our present existence: the loving way in which we interact with each other being the means to fulfil our sacred obligation and attain our spiritual goals.

In her dream, Anna was given the lines "Our altar One another" for a poem, so she felt charged with the task of composing verse to contain them. Her poem, which was written on the day of the dream, comprises the elements of our everyday experience, taking as its theme her dream instructions that our relationship be the focus of our religious life:

We worship within the temple
Of truth eternal,
Whose gateways are the twilight arcs

23

Of dawn and dusk,
Whose spire
Natural desire.

Our altar
One another;
Our sacrament
Love, dance, feast,
With passion: pure
Communion with Nature.

Eisler could have been commenting on Anna's poem when she stated that for the Neolithic peoples there were no "sharp polarities"[42] between spirituality and Nature. Eisler goes on to say "We also know from a number of contemporary tribal societies that the separation between nature and spirituality is not universal. The way tribal people think of nature is generally in spiritual terms."[43]

All of our subsequent understanding was built upon our having been told that Love is the original religion and that we should make our altar one another. This was a natural starting point, since the relationship between a couple is the foundation of a family and the family is the foundation of society. In saying this, I do not mean to imply that a person must be in a relationship in order to benefit from avision. (Our dreams also tell of some lives in which we pursued a solitary, or relatively solitary, existence because only one of us had incarnated.) Each person's path is different and we have all to wait to see in which direction the Dream guides us.

Four days after Anna had written her poem, the themes of love and reincarnation were continued in a dream within a dream which was to be a portent of things to come:

Anthony and I find ourselves in a past life which can only be entered through a dream state. We spend some time there. Afterwards, we reflect upon the fact that we are deeply in love and can both clearly remember being deeply in love in the past life, even though memories are not supposed to be carried over.

24

CHAPTER TWO

The Law

In September of 1994, Anna dreamt:

> Anthony and I go to visit a school in the countryside where we
> may send our children. The school is a mansion set in enormous
> grounds. Elephants and giraffes are roaming in the gardens. We are
> invited to stay for dinner. Soup is served to us in ancient Egyptian
> glazed bowls that have pillars on the inside painted with garlands
> of green leaves and blue flowers. It crosses my mind that food from
> ancient times is concealed behind the pillars and we shall imbibe it
> with our soup.

Anna and I were certain that the food from ancient times which we
were to imbibe was to be understood metaphorically. Upon consulting
the *O.E.D.*, we found this to be in keeping with the use, within the
dream, of 'imbibe' because the word means both "To drink (liquid)"
and, from earlier usage, "To drink in, absorb or assimilate (knowledge,
ideas, etc.); to take into one's mind or moral system."[1] Regarded in
this light, it makes complete sense that the dream was set within the
environs of a school. Thus, the possibility was being presented by the
Dream of our assimilating knowledge and ideas from ancient Egypt.

Anna's awareness, within her dream, of ancient Egyptian knowledge being concealed parallels my awareness, in my dream, of a practice of the Buddha which is no longer even mentioned.

An ancient Egyptian name for Egypt was 'Mer',[2] a word which also meant 'Love'.[3] There is, therefore, a remarkable continuity between Anna's dream of the ancient Egyptian bowls and her dreams on Love which preceded it. As a consequence of our being told that Love is the original religion, we realized that, in naming their land 'Mer', the ancient Egyptians were indicating that their culture was once an embodiment of the religion of the First Time. It is probable that the choice of the name was a result of dream instructions about Love akin to those given to Anna. There is reason to think this since, as stated in the *British Museum Dictionary of Ancient Egypt*, "Dreams played an important role in Egyptian culture, principally because they were thought to serve as a means of communicating the will of the gods."[4]

Anna later identified the flowers painted onto the pillars inside the bowls as being representations of the blue lotus, which are described in the *British Museum Dictionary of Ancient Egypt* as being "symbolic of rebirth."[5] We could then see that the theme of reincarnation, which had appeared in our earlier dreams, was now, upon Anna's dreaming of ancient Egypt, represented by means of a symbol from that culture.

Having dreamt, in September of 1994, of an ancient symbol of rebirth, Anna then had the following dream in November of that year:

> Anthony is standing behind me. I twice turn my head back towards him and say the word 'recense'. This word has been coined to denote the relationship between one's present life and one's past life, especially during the early part of one's present life.

We found that 'recense' means "To survey, review, revise."[6] Both 'review' and 'revise' mean "To see or behold, to look at, again."[7] In Anna's dream, the beholding again is enacted by her looking back at me twice. As, in the dream, the gesture of looking back specifically represented reviewing a past life, this dream opened our minds to considering the influence that our past life experience had exerted upon our earlier development in this life.

It is usual for people in the West to regard the issue of reincarnation as a matter of belief and to assume that there is no evidence to support such an idea. However, claims of past life memories have been extensively studied; and the leading specialist in the world, Dr. Ian Stevenson, medical school psychiatrist at the University of Virginia, argues that "*some* of the cases do much more than suggest reincarnation; they seem to me to furnish considerable evidence for it."[8] Carl Sagan, the sceptical bastion of the American scientific establishment, expressed himself more strongly, stating that reincarnation can be the *only* explanation for such cases.[9]

Walker points out that "reincarnation was the standard belief of all the ancient nations... not only in the Orient but throughout pagan Europe."[10] It is not always appreciated that this applied to ancient Egypt where, as Lucie Lamy reports, "Many are the texts alluding to reincarnation, either overtly or implicitly through such locutions as 'renewal of life' or 'repetition of births'."[11] Thus, in Anna's sequence of dreams, the guidance concerning 'recense' is an instance of our assimilating knowledge from ancient Egypt. Furthermore, it is consistent with the blue lotus being a symbol of rebirth that this knowledge concerns reincarnation.

The move in the West away from a recognition and understanding of the process of reincarnation was not, as is often believed, due to a natural superseding of 'primitive' ideas over time, but rather to a specific edict issued in the year 553 by the Second Council of Constantinople, that was later enforced by the Inquisition, in which it was decreed "Whosoever shall support the mythical doctrine of the pre-existence of the soul and the consequent wonderful opinion of its return, let him be anathema."[12] Charles Freeman has demonstrated that the Catholic Church obtained the power to impose such a ruling through a political move that had been made by the emperor

Theodosius in an attempt to stabilize the crumbling Roman Empire. This move had "defined the Church... [and] provided the legal framework within which Christianity had been given dominance over paganism."[13] In 380, despite Christians comprising only a tiny minority of the Latin-speaking West,[14] Theodosius had issued an edict, that was first announced to the people of Constantinople and then, the following year, made law for "the whole world",[15] in which he proclaimed "It is Our will that all peoples ruled by the administration of Our Clemency shall practice that religion which the divine Peter the Apostle transmitted to the Romans... we shall believe in the single deity of the Father, the Son and the Holy Ghost under the concept of equal majesty and of the Holy Trinity. We command that persons who follow this rule shall embrace the name of catholic Christians. The rest, however, whom We judge demented and insane, shall carry the infamy of heretical dogmas... they shall be smitten first by Divine Vengeance, and secondly by the retribution of hostility which We shall assume in accordance with the Divine Judgement."[16] In so doing, Theodosius had gone against the Edict of Toleration, decreed by the emperor Constantine in 330, promising "that no one whatsoever should be denied freedom to devote himself either to the cult of the Christians or to such religion as he deems best suited for himself.";[17] a policy which had been reiterated in 364 by the court orator Themistius, himself a pagan, in his address to the Christian emperor Jovian: "It seems that you must be aware that a king cannot compel his subjects in everything... there are some matters which have escaped compulsion... for example the whole question of virtue, and above all, reverence for the divine."[18]

The word 'pagan' is derived from the Latin 'paganus' meaning 'villager or rustic'. In Christian Latin, 'pagan' denoted "'heathen' as opposed to Christian or Jewish, indicating the fact that the ancient idolatry lingered on in the rural villages and hamlets after Christianity had been generally accepted in the towns and cities of the Roman Empire."[19] However, this definition, which characterizes a pagan as a peasant, does not convey the experience of the fifth century philosopher Synesius who defined a Hellene – a Greek pagan – as one "able to associate with men on the basis of a knowledge of all worthwhile literature."[20] In the *O.E.D.*, it is stated that the word 'heathen' is generally assumed to be derived from the Gothic for 'heath'.[21] But it has also been suggested that 'heathen' derives from the Germanic 'heiden' meaning 'that which is hidden' because "the pagan people continued their rites in secret."[22] To counter this activity, in 392, Theodosius issued a new law by which "Not only was any activity associated with pagan rites suppressed, but any symbol of paganism, even in domestic shrines, was banned. The pagan gods were reclassified as evil spirits. Local officials were given widespread powers to enter homes to search out offending material."[23] The effect of these measures was, to use Freeman's evocative phrase, "the closing of the Western mind." By this, Freeman meant the cessation of "the tradition of rational thought"[24] founded upon the application of deductive proof and inductive reasoning. (This tradition was only reclaimed in the seventeenth century.) I would argue that even more devastating was the loss of the ancient tradition of natural wisdom which had been so essential to Parmenides, Pythagoras and those others who had played such a determining role in the development of the application of rational thought.

Returning to Iamblichos' statement that, when one has divine dreams, one "receives from them... a power and a capacity of knowing which reasons intelligently both of things that were and things that will be... [and] restores to order many things among men which were discordant and disorderly", this process can be observed in the sequence of dream instruction given to Anna. There, the Dream circumnavigated the discord and disorder which still affects the world today as a consequence of Theodosius' political strategies; and it did so by informing us that Love is the original religion, that our altar should be one another and that reincarnation is a reality to be embraced and assimilated into our understanding of ourselves.

There is a stark contrast between the dissonance that arose in this chapter upon mention of the edicts of Theodosius and the pervasive sense of peace and harmony in Anna's dreams on the subject of Love.

The subtle emanation from those dreams had a transmuting effect which was exquisitely portrayed in a dream of mine from that time:

> Anna appears as a beautiful white dove that is consuming lilac blossom. I watch as she becomes imbued with the colour of the flowers she is feeding upon.

It will be remembered that, in her dream of the heron, Anna came to tell me that, while looking at the card she was drawn to, she had noticed a dove flying around the room. The dove was, in India, a symbol of Love in all its manifestations; in Greece, the totem of Aphrodite[25] and the symbol of Sophia, the spirit of Female Wisdom;[26] and, in ancient Egypt, a symbol of Isis, into whose Mysteries one was initiated through dreams. As the messenger bird, the dove is the conveyor of divine wisdom. It is in this sense that Anna was portrayed as a dove in my dream, since she conveyed to me wisdom concerning Love in all its manifestations. The lilac, then, was representative of the Dream itself. It seems to me that this blossom was chosen because its name provides a play on words which indicates that the Dream, as 'lie-lack', is the flower of truth.

From 1st January 1995, I began to have numerous dreams which were instructional. It appeared that this outflow of dreams had been instigated by our decision to marry that year – again, emphasising the link between Love and the Dream. Early in the year, we learned by chance that the ancient Egyptian civilization had been founded upon the Law of Maat; Maat being a goddess who was the personification of the principles of truth, justice and harmony. Then, in May, I had a dream in which:

> I am told that there is something about the Law of Maat which I do not understand.

And, a few days later, I dreamt:

> The elephant god Ganesh tells me that he is going to instruct me in the Law of Maat. He impresses upon me that I must tell Anna my dream and then says "Consider the relation between 'thought' and 'ought'."

There are two instructions contained within this dream. The first is that I tell my dream to Anna. We had been sharing our dreams for many years, but it was now made clear that it is a requirement of the Law of Maat that we do so. In this way our relationship is brought into harmony with the natural order. One can understand then why the ancient Egyptian name for the dream oracle, 'Tep Re', also meant 'the base of a triangle'.[27] I was particularly delighted to learn this because, long before, I had used the imagery of the two points of the base of a triangle as the best possible depiction of our discussing our different perspectives on the same experience. We had come to see that our respective dreams function as co-ordinates by which we are able to orient ourselves within the panoply of existence.

I remember how moved I was when I read that, in many of the native tribes of North America, relating an experience of avision was the most important moment of a person's life. When a tribal member, of any age and either gender, was blessed with a significant dream, it was their sacred responsibility to enact that dream, in the form of a dance, before all the assembled people of their tribe. Since it concerned the destiny of all, complete fidelity to the dream was their deepest obligation; and conveying every nuance and subtle feeling their highest achievement. Amongst those people, avision was held to be so essential that a man, no matter how brave, was not considered to be fully a man until he had had a significant dream or vision. In his account of three hundred and fifty dreams collected over a period of a hundred and fifty years from the tribes of the Great Plains, Lee Irwin comments that in such a society "The shared structures of social life provide a malleable context for the gradual transformation of the collective as a result of the visionary encounter."[28]

Anna and I were not born into such a society so we had to be shown, through avision, how the Dream required us to relate to it. Our first guidance in this regard came from Ganesh – the remover of obstacles at the start of an endeavour. His impressing upon me that I should tell Anna my dream was itself a 'thought' which contained an 'ought'.

We concluded that, as I had been instructed within a dream to ensure I told my dream to Anna, the word 'thought' referred to thoughts which appear in dreams rather than to those one has in the waking state. And, hence, that Ganesh was telling us to consider what light a dream instruction throws upon our conduct in our everyday life, pointing out that the main part of that guidance consists of a moral obligation to think or act in a certain way – that, with regard to avision, 'thought' is 'thou ought'.

Through the combination of my being instructed to tell Anna my dream and to consider the relation between 'thought' and 'ought', I realized that 'conscious' is the soul mate of 'conscience', since both literally mean "To know together."[29] This demonstrates that the relationship between oneself and another was once understood to be the context within which each individual could increase their consciousness and develop their conscience.

The guidance in my dream is a development of that provided in Anna's of August 1990 which began "I am talking with Anthony" and ended with the words "The more intimate, The more infinite." I say this because 'intimate' refers to "the inmost thoughts or feelings; proceeding from, concerning, or affecting one's inmost self"; and 'to intimate' is "To make known" or "to communicate (knowledge)." To communicate 'intimately' is to do so "in a way that involves or effects a very close connexion or union." By emphasising the requirement for us to share our dreams, Ganesh was providing guidance as to how we could achieve intimacy at the deepest level of our being. Furthermore, by focusing our attention upon the 'ought' contained within the dream 'thought', he was instructing us about what is most 'intimate' in the adjectival sense of "Pertaining to or connected with the inmost nature or fundamental character of a thing; essential; intrinsic."[30] Through the instruction that I tell Anna my dream, we were being initiated by Ganesh into the central mystery of Man's existence – a mystery which was conveyed in the ancient Egyptian language through the relationship between 'uhem', meaning 'to tell a dream', and 'uhem ankh', meaning 'to renew life':[31] we renew life by telling our dreams. 'Uhem ankh' refers both to the renewal of life in the broader sense of the word and to the Dream as a vehicle for the process of reincarnation.

The suggestion in Anna's dream that we could imbibe – assimilate into our moral system – knowledge from ancient Egypt had now, through our instruction in the Law of Maat, been explicitly borne out. We had learnt that avision is the means to have a real understanding of life; that is, to have knowledge – literally, a ledge of knowing – that one can stand upon. We were being shown that the guidance we are given through our dreams is not simply to be comprehended, it has to be lived. This led us to think again about the instruction that what we were seeking could only be found in silence. Consequently, we determined to dispose of our stereo, radio and television in order to experience ourselves and our surroundings without intrusion. Our life became a seamless world of silence embroidered with our thoughts and dreams and our sharing of them. Silence is not absence; it is the purest presence. Through silence we were confronted with the thusness of life.

In the *Great Treatise on the I Ching*, it is said "Heaven is high, the earth is low; thus the Creative and the Receptive are determined."[32] That is, the function and nature of the Earth is to receive the creative impulse from Heaven; and, being a creature of the Earth, Man partakes of its nature, so his primary nature is to be receptive. Thus, Lao Tzu explains "Man models himself on earth, Earth on heaven, Heaven on the way, and the way on that which is naturally so."[33] The *Great Treatise* goes on to describe what we have been surprised to find is the characteristic quality of avision "The Creative knows through the easy. The Receptive can do things through the simple. What is easy, is easy to know; what is simple, is easy to follow... By means of the easy and the simple we grasp the laws of the whole world."[34]

Our understanding of the significance of the Dream was taken a stage further when, in July of 1995, two months after our instruction in the Law of Maat, I had a dream which consisted in my being told:

"Dreams are the Law of Nature."

The 'Law of Nature' was originally described as "implanted by nature in the human mind" – a definition which points to the practical identification of the Law of Nature with avision. Yet, by the mid nineteenth century, the term had come to mean "The order and regularity in Nature of which laws are the expression."[35] These definitions exemplify the shift from the primacy of receptivity to that of rationalism which has created such a gulf between contemporary society and the high civilizations of ancient times. "There is no doubt, it seems to me," said Laing, "that there have been profound changes in the experience of man in the last thousand years. In some ways this is more evident than changes in the patterns of his behaviour. There is everything to suggest that man experienced God."[36] He went on to make the striking statement, which has not received the attention it deserves, "True sanity entails... being the servant of the divine."[37]

It was evident that the instruction in the Law of Maat, to consider the relation between 'thought' and 'ought', was intended to be taken in conjunction with the statement that dreams are the Law of Nature in order that we would arrive at the conclusion that Maat is the Dream.

The *British Museum Dictionary of Ancient Egypt* defines 'Maat' as the "Goddess personifying truth, justice and the essential harmony of the universe... On a cosmic scale, Maat also represented the divine order of the universe as originally brought into being at the moment of creation. It was the power of Maat that was believed to regulate the seasons, the movement of the stars and the relations between men and gods. The concept was therefore central both to the Egyptians' ideas about the universe and to their code of ethics."[38] Maat regulates the relations between men and gods through the Dream. Maat is the Dream – not simply natural law, but also the means by which one is advised as to how to live in accordance with that law. This is the aspect of the Law of Maat which I had not understood.

"There is", wrote the Egyptologist Erik Hornung, "scarcely an Egyptian temple that does not include among its representations of cult scenes the 'offering of *maat*'. The king, who when in the presence of the gods is the representative of the entire world of humanity, holds up and presents a figure of *maat*... The gods do not need any material gifts, but they do need human response to their existence; they want to be experienced in the hearts of men... *Maat*, which came from the gods at creation, returns to them from the hands of men; it symbolizes the partnership of god and man which is brought to fruition in Egyptian religion. This partnership, this action and response, is the key to the otherwise inexplicable mixture we find of free will and pre-destination."[39] At its height, the whole Egyptian system was devoted to ensuring that everyone did what was required of them by the gods, with the pharaoh as the exemplar of that endeavour. It is for this reason that Schwaller de Lubicz could say "ancient Egypt did not have a 'religion' as such; *it was religion in its entirety*, in the broadest and purest acceptation of that term."[40]

CHAPTER THREE

God and the Dream

In December of 1995, the Nepalese friend who had invited Anna and myself to meet Lama Thupten died. On the night that we visited his body I dreamt:

> I am one of a small group of people gathered together on the bank of a mighty river in India. A sacred silence permeates the scene as we solemnly focus our attention upon the dark flowing water. Then, one of the group reads aloud from a massive ancient book "He has recognised God when he has recognised his dreams, for God and his dreams are one". It is understood by everyone present that God is a separate entity from Man whose presence is experienced by Mankind in dreams.

I was so shaken by the import of this dream that I woke with a start and immediately rushed to write it down to ensure that I retained the correct wording.

At the time of our first meeting, I said to Laurens van der Post that I thought that the primitive shaman was in some ways closer to the truth than the modern-day psychotherapist. Laurens replied that

Jung had said to him "What people don't understand is that I am just an old African witch-doctor who finds his God in his dreams." Elsewhere, I remember Laurens phrasing this as "I am just an old African witch-doctor for whom his God is the Dream", which is closer still to the wording of my dream. Laurens made it clear that this was Jung's definitive statement about himself and he said that he deeply regretted that it was the least understood by contemporary Jungians. Recounting this was Laurens' way of saying that, in his view, I was on the right track.

Crucially, Jung used the term 'God-image' in his writings when referring to God. I came across this when I acquired a copy of his autobiography, *Memories, Dreams, Reflections*, after seeing Laurens' television trilogy on him. In the glossary of that book, 'God-image' is defined as "A term derived from the Church Fathers, according to whom the *'imago Dei'* is imprinted on the human soul. When such an image is spontaneously produced in dreams, fantasies, visions, etc. it is from the psychological point of view, a symbol of the self, of psychic wholeness."[1] Then, in the text of *Memories, Dreams, Reflections*, Jung stated "I prefer the term 'the unconscious', knowing that I might equally well speak of 'God'."[2] and "It is only through the psyche that we can establish that God acts upon us, but we are unable to distinguish whether God and the unconscious are two different entities."[3] In my dream, it was known by those gathered together in India contemplating the dark flowing water that God is located outside of Man's unconscious mental processes – that "God and the unconscious are two different entities." It was this certainty, as well as the wording of the message of my dream, that so shook me. I had been given the answer to a question which had previously seemed to be unanswerable. At that moment my life was changed.

Parmenides, the father of Western logic, described himself as 'one who knows'. In ancient Greece, this was understood to mean that he was an initiate;[4] initiation being a process by which is revealed one's relationship to the divine.[5] By being told in a dream that we are linked to the divine through the Dream, Anna and I were returned to the understanding that had existed in antiquity.

Bulkeley argues that "The ultimate difference between 'ancient religious' and 'modern psychological' views of dreams is *not* that the one is naively superstitious while the other is hard-headedly scientific. Rather, the real difference is that ancient religious traditions have acknowledged that there is an irreducible mystery about where dreams come from and what they mean for human life. Many modern psychologists, by contrast, ignore that mystery, resist it, or try to explain it away."[6] Bulkeley's criticism of many modern psychologists is valid. However, as will become abundantly clear in the following chapters, the ancient religious view was itself originally the product of a high science which the science of modern times has not been able to match. It is, for example, impossible to comprehend the original religion of ancient Egypt unless one is aware that, as John Anthony West states, "Egyptian civilization was based upon a complete and precise understanding of universal laws."[7] In the ancient religious tradition it was known exactly where dreams come from and what they mean for human life. This tradition has informed the Indian civilization to the present day, leading O'Flaherty to speak of "the nondenominational pan-Indian science of the interpretation of dreams."[8] It has also had a determining influence on Indian mythology: "The Indian myths... describe moments when adults, suddenly confronted with dreams that behave in ways they had not thought possible, are, like children, converted to an entirely new perception of reality."[9]

In using the phrase 'like children', O'Flaherty is making reference to the fact that "In the rather primitive perception of many early anthropologists, it was assumed that children, savages, and madmen were alike in their inability to distinguish internal perceptions from external perceptions; all of them took their dreams to be real. In recent years, although both anthropologists and psychologists have come to modify their views somewhat, there is still a general underlying assumption that normal people must move from understanding dreams as real and external to understanding them as unreal and internal. In this view, our Indian mystics, together with children, savages and madmen, have not yet seen the light."[10] "The Indian myths of dreaming dissolve the line between waking and dreaming reality... The philosophical goal of many of these myths is to dissolve the line, but the secret agenda of many of them is to understand the reality of life through the insights that come from dreams."[11] My dream of the great book is a case in point.

Some twelve years were to elapse before I learned that, in the Vedic literature, the word 'svapna', meaning 'sleep', also came to mean 'to dream' and, later, denoted 'the deity'.[12] Thus, in Sanskrit, God and the Dream are one. In the Upaniṣads "dreaming sleep gives us a glimpse of the god (Viṣṇu or Rudra) who creates us by dreaming us into existence."[13]

O'Flaherty recounts "It struck a Western observer as strange that 'The Indian patient says "The god told me" without needing to add "...in a dream" to prove his sanity; the dream's psychological reality is taken for granted'."[14] She notes that "both the dream and the god partake of an inner reality that is 'taken for granted' in India; each substantiates the reality of the other."[15]

Ironically, the Indian patient's attitude, which the Western observer found so strange, was actually intrinsic to the ancient tradition in the West, amongst both the intellectual elite and the general populace. For instance, as Cox Miller wrote, the early fifth century thinker Synesius emphasised that "whereas daytime knowledge comes from teachers, the knowledge in dreams comes from god. Neither sense-perceptive nor intellective – that is neither sheerly empirical nor sheerly metaphysical – dream knowledge provides the path for ascent to what is most hidden in things."[16] Indeed, it was the case that "Most of the late-antique theorists of dreams agreed that dream-speech was divine speech."[17] And Tertullian stated that "the majority of people get their knowledge of God from dreams."[18]

Bulkeley rightly observed "Most contemporary scholarship on dreams, even if it is friendly to religious issues and concerns, relies on conceptual models of religion that are narrow at best and erroneous at worst."[19] What is most heartening to observe is that, as modern science advances, it is developing an understanding which accords with that of the ancient civilizations; for, in the words of Dr. Manjir Samanta-Laughton, "The frontiers of science are revealing that the universe behaves as the mystics have told us all along... We are finding that soul or consciousness is not only a part of science, it is fundamental to the universe."[20] "From this new perspective, consciousness is not just an emergent phenomenon of the human brain, but is inherent in everything."[21] This supports the conclusion of Schwaller de Lubicz that "The Universe is nothing but Consciousness, and in all its appearances reveals nothing but an evolution of Consciousness, from its origin to its end, which is a return to its cause. It is the goal of every 'initiatory' religion to teach the way to this ultimate union."[22] Schwaller de Lubicz said this with full knowledge that in the highest of those religions it is Consciousness which invites or requires the individual to unite with It (as is demonstrated in the sequence of dreams I am presenting). And that the officials in those traditions act as mentors to the initiates; their qualification for this function being that they themselves have been initiated by Consciousness. The initiations into the Mysteries of Isis by the Goddess, through the Dream, are an illustration of this.

The physicist Peter Russell cites the mathematician and philosopher Alfred North Whitehead's judgement that *"More than anything else, the future of civilization depends on the way the two most powerful forces of history, science and religion, settle into relationship with each other."*[23] I would argue that the rapprochement between science and religion will ultimately arise when the primacy of the Dream has been re-acknowledged by both those institutions. With regard to science, this may come more easily than might be imagined; for, as Musès states, "Science is verifiable knowledge integrated by key concepts that render the data intelligible. The beginnings of such knowledge come from normally inaccessible levels of human awareness."[24] Musès cites F.A. Kekulé's "discovery of the idea of the benzene ring, which began modern organic chemistry." This discovery came to him through a dream of an ouroboros, a serpent that is swallowing its own tail. Kekulé "published an account of his *ouroboros*-type revelation in the 1890 proceedings of the German Chemical Society, ending with the memorable sentences:

'As though from a flash of lightning I awoke [and] occupied the rest of the night in working out the consequences of the hypothesis... Let us learn to dream, gentlemen'."[25] Similarly, as a teenager, Einstein had a dream in which he was shown the behaviour of the speed of light; "The contents of his dream went on to become one of the mainstays of modern physics."[26] Further examples include Neils Bohr, who, it is said, "saw the structure of the atom in a dream,"[27] and the physiologist Otto Loewi, who was awarded the Nobel Prize for Medicine after dreaming how to prove his theory concerning the chemical transmission of nerve impulses.[28] As the physicist Lee Smolen said, "In the end, perhaps the history of the universe is nothing but the flow of information."[29]

It may well be that when Jung wrote that he was unable to distinguish whether or not God and the unconscious are two different entities, what he felt able to assert as a scientist differed from his privately-held view. This was certainly the case in his public statements regarding the subject of reincarnation. In his autobiography, Jung wrote "Have I lived before in the past as a specific personality, and did I progress so far in that life that I am now able to seek a solution? I do not know."[30] However, by chance Anna and I came upon a book on the life of the Egyptologist known as Omm Sety in which the author, Jonathan Cott, records a conversation he had with the Jungian analyst Erlo van Waveren. Cott recounts "According to Erlo van Waveren, Jung *did* in fact believe in reincarnation. 'I once spoke to Professor Jung about this subject, and later his wife came to me and said "Don't talk to anyone about this, the time isn't right for it." That was in 1950, and I also had a warning dream that told me not to speak openly about this... So I kept quiet, because the world to which Professor Jung wanted to prove that there *was* such a thing as a psyche wouldn't have gone along with the notion of reincarnation... Now that I *myself* am in my eighties, I can tell you that Professor Jung informed me that he had come back every hundred years since the thirteenth century... [Jung added that, prior to this, he had rested for a thousand years.] Jung recounted several of his dreams – I wrote them down – that revealed to me a number of his incarnations."[31] In *Memories Dreams, Reflections*, Jung describes a journey he made to Kenya in 1925 and of his seeing from the train in which he was travelling that "On a jagged rock above us a slim, brownish-black figure stood motionless, leaning on a long spear, looking down at the train. Beside him towered a gigantic candelabrum cactus. I was enchanted by this sight – it was a picture of something utterly alien and outside my experience, but on the other hand a most intense *sentiment du déjà vu*. I had the feeling that I had already experienced this moment and had always known this world which was separated from me only by distance in time. It was as if I were this moment returning to the land of my youth, and as if I knew that dark-skinned man who had been waiting for me for five thousand years."[32] There can be no doubt that when Jung said "What people don't understand is that I am just an old African witch-doctor" he meant exactly that.

This brings me back to the wording of my dream, which is beautifully considered, since an essential element of the meaning of 'to recognise' is 'to know again'. The gentle reminder that the Dream has been known before and that, when you know the Dream in the way you knew it before, you will know God again as you knew God before is breath-taking in its implications and deeply reassuring. It is, as we were to learn, consistent with the meaning of the Latin 'religio' being 'reunion'. Furthermore, what is being suggested in the wording is shown by the message being read from an ancient book. We progress by knowing what we have known before.

In December of 1997, I had this fateful dream:

> I am taken by an acolyte to the water's edge where I will find, at last, my teacher. I see my teacher, who is dressed in a white robe. It is Laurens, though somehow he is changed – he is very present, yet his features are less distinguishable. He begins by presenting me with the great book from my earlier dream. Even though I have been told he is my teacher, I don't take the meeting that seriously and I wait to see what exactly he has to teach me. We sit in silence by the water for a long time. Then, suddenly, he stands up and announces that he is leaving – that he is actually going away for good and that he has taught me all he can. At that moment, I realize he really is my

teacher, because I can see that, through silence, he has taught me a great lesson. I cannot bear to be losing my teacher as soon as I have found him and urge him to stay. But he replies "I am going away. I have taught you all that you need to know. You don't need me. You have to take my place."

A few days later, Laurens died. I had understood from the dream that he was about to die, but our meeting as he was moving into the region between life and death, and the nature of what was said there, made the news of his death an extraordinary experience.

Achilles Tatius wrote of dreams "It is a favourite device of the powers above to whisper at night what the future holds – not that we may contrive a defence to forestall it (for no one can rise above fate) but that we may bear it more lightly when it comes. The swift descent of unforeseen events, coming on us all at once and suddenly, startles the soul and overwhelms it, but when the disaster is expected, that very anticipation, by small increments of concern, dulls the sharp edge of suffering."[33]

After Laurens died, we learnt that an early meaning of 'teacher' was 'a person who entrusts something to someone'. This is enacted in my dream by Laurens presenting me with the great book from which was read "He has recognised God when he has recognised his dreams, for God and his dreams are one." That this gesture was made by a man who was about to die, emphasises the singular importance of the statement.

Jung had not been the first person to present Laurens with this relationship between God and the Dream. Laurens recounted "Dreams to my black and coloured countrymen were real, vital and decisive facts, rivalling the reality of any in the objective physical world around them. As a child already they made manifest to me, as Lévy-Bruhl was to proclaim later, the dream was the real god of primitive people."[34] In a similar vein, after providing an account of the Biblical dream of Jacob's Ladder, Laurens went on to expound in characteristically soaring, thoughtful prose "The ancient Chinese have defined meaning as 'that which has always existed through itself'. This dream for me was an intimation that the dreaming process must always have existed through itself, and that when the last secret of nature has been unveiled and the final problem of creation resolved, however opaque the heart of all matter, and swiftly changing as may be the many-faceted and elusive spirit, we shall still find, like stars in the night, images of the dream that always existed through itself. Many years later, I was greatly moved when one of the first men of Africa, a Stone-Age hunter in a wasteland greater I believe than even the wasteland in which Jacob dreamt his dream, informed me, 'You know, there is a dream dreaming us'. To this day I do not know anything to equal this feeling for what the dreaming process is to life or the implication that it is enough for creation to appear to us as the dreaming of a great dream and the unravelling and living of its meaning."[35] Elsewhere, Laurens wrote "In the beginning, St. John says, was the Word. I believe that is a way of saying that in the beginning there was meaning... I thought I should enlarge St. John's theme to include the idea that in the beginning there was a dream. This dream was with God and indeed was God. Somehow this dream demanded that it should be lived."[36] In these last two statements Laurens went further than Jung was prepared to go publicly.

When Laurens told me that I had to take his place (which was said within the context of my having been in retreat for several years), he meant that I would have to back the Dream publicly, as he had done, because he "knew that somehow the world had to be set dreaming again."[37] This book arose directly out of that instruction. Confirmation that my understanding was correct came when I started to write the first draft. At that time, Anna dreamt:

> Anthony and I are discussing our dreams and my poems with regard to his writing *Avision*. Laurens comes into the room. He puts a piece of paper into the typewriter on which I type the manuscript and types the following message: "It is in the writing of it that my life's meaning is fulfilled."

His life's meaning was fulfilled because he had been able to pass on the torch – the message, which is in fact about life's meaning – to a younger generation. I am reminded here that in the *Great Treatise on the I Ching* it is said "Heaven and earth determine the places. The holy sages fulfil the possibilities of the places. Through the thoughts of men and the thoughts of spirits, the people are enabled to participate in these possibilities."[38]

Laurens fully embraced and disseminated the ancient understanding that God is the Dream – a tradition so deeply rooted in the indigenous African culture for which he was such an eloquent spokesperson. By presenting me with the great book, he passed on to me the responsibility of conveying its message to others. We then focused on the water, as I had done in my earlier dream. There, my friend having died, I was silently contemplating the water with others and, then, the book was produced. Here, the book was produced, we silently contemplated the water and, then, Laurens died.

A wonderful symmetry can also be seen to have been woven into the emerging tapestry of Anna's dreams in combination with mine. We both dreamt of a wise old man who instructed us in silence. In Anna's dream, she was told "What you are seeking can only be found in silence"; in my dream, I realized that I had at last found my teacher because of the lesson in silence that he had taught me. Later, we were to learn that this common theme was intrinsic to the ancient practice of incubation, through which mystics silently journeyed into the great silence of the higher realms[39] of consciousness. Then, Anna was told "There is no need to play music"; whilst my teacher said "You don't need me"; at which point it became apparent that 'my teacher' referred ultimately, not to Laurens, but to the Dream – for, since God and the Dream are one, the Dream is our ultimate teacher. This point is being made by Laurens in the dream: when he says that he has already taught me all I need to know, he is referring to his statement that "the key to the door of what we need is the Dream." It is in the nature of this transcendent experience that I was taught the lesson through the Dream itself. The correspondences between Anna's dreams and mine exerted a subtle, though profound, harmonizing influence, drawing us closer together; while, though we did not know it at the time, their content drew us deeper into the incubatory traditions which had played such an important role in the ancient world.

So many of our most significant dreams have occurred in association with death that I can well understand why in Homer's *Odyssey* the world of dreams is located "in close proximity to the dwelling place of the dead."[40] Epimenides, too, learnt of the world of the dead in his dreams; and was taught by the gods, by Justice and Truth [Maat], through avision.[41]

The Dream is the means by which God guides, guards and inspires. It lies at the heart of the covenant between God and Man and is the foundation upon which all else rests. Anna's instruction that Love is the original religion, in which she was given the lines "Our altar One another", and the message read to me from the ancient book, combined with the knowledge that God is a separate entity from Man, became our primary co-ordinates with regard to the question of religion. Through them, we know what Jung meant when he said "Religious experience is absolute; it cannot be disputed... No matter what the world thinks about religious experience, the one who has it possesses a great treasure, a thing that has become for him a source of life, meaning, and beauty, and that has given a new splendour to the world and to mankind. He has *pistis* [faith] and peace."[42]

❦

CHAPTER FOUR

The Requirement

❦

In the summer of 1996, we made the decision that we would visit Egypt the following year. For me, this initiated, in September, a new cycle of several hundred dreams, many of which were instructional, beginning with a pair involving Ganesh and his consort Ganesha which perfectly demonstrated a shift that had to take place in our way of thinking about life. In the first dream:

> Anna and I are walking through a wood that lies behind the garden of my childhood home. As we do so, we see that one of our children is preoccupied with a statue of Ganesh which has been placed near the entrance to a school. He later comes to us with a message that Ganesh wants to speak to us and we leave at once to fulfil what is as much an instruction as a request.

In the second dream, three days later:

> It is explained to me that a particularly dangerous moment has arisen and that an elephant is going to lift me out of danger. I am warned that the elephant is huge and will have to raise me to a great

height and then place me on its head before it can lower me to the ground. The elephant suddenly appears and takes me in her trunk. Unbelievably massive, and yet exceptionally tender, she very slowly draws me up until I am next to her mouth. The most divine perfume exudes from her breath. She is exquisitely loving and caring, even to the extent of holding her breath while lifting me to ensure that I am not overwhelmed. As I have been forewarned, the ancient elephant lifts me to a great height, so that for a moment I am above her head, and then lowers me until my head touches hers at the point of the third eye, before carefully and deliberately placing me on the very spot where, in the previous dream, Anna and I had seen our child talking to Ganesh. As I gain my bearings, the elephant disappears. I then enter the school.

Though the message that Ganesh wanted to see us in the wood was as much an instruction as a request, and I had had the dream in which I was told to consider the relation between 'thought' and 'ought', it didn't enter our minds that we were actually required to go there. We failed to act in a 'religious' manner: "Action or conduct indicating a belief in, reverence for and desire to please a higher power."[1] And so, after a few days, the point was made in the kindest possible way, so lovingly that there was no chance I could ever forget it, by my being placed in precisely the spot that we had been told to journey to. It is interesting to observe that the advice as to how to act was illustrated rather than spoken. This is a primitive mode of communication which, for that reason, has a very deep impact. I was gently but firmly shown what was required of me.

After we were told "There is no need to play music. What you are seeking can only be found in silence." it was possible, over time, to consider the dream thought and arrive at the conclusion that there was good reason to act in accordance with the advice given. In doing this, we later learnt, we were acting in accordance with the fundamental dictum upon which the ancient Egyptian civilization had been founded: that it is the responsibility of all to 'order their footsteps by Maat'. This is the instruction in the Law of Maat that Ganesh was imparting to me when he told me to consider the relation between 'thought' and 'ought'. In ancient Egyptian, 'ap' meant 'steps';[2] and 'Apep' was the spirit of the Dream – thus, the order of one's footsteps is to be determined by one's dreams.

Walking, it will be remembered, was a central feature of the dream in which we were told that Ganesh wished to speak to us. Initially, we were walking through the wood and, at the end of the dream, we left at once to fulfil what was as much an instruction as a request. This part of the dream demonstrated how we were supposed to respond to the message. In the second dream, it was made clear that we were to order our footsteps by Maat, not only metaphorically, but also literally. At this point, we were made aware that our world view had to change; and the nature of that change was very specific: when we receive an instruction in a dream, we have to act in accordance with it, irrespective of whether or not we understand why.

Having been told that Ganesh wished to see us, it was consistent with all of my training as a psychotherapist that I thought that our going to see him within the dream was sufficient. Rationally, we had no reason to think that Ganesh was actually waiting for us in the wood. But, in placing me on the very spot that we had been told to go to, Ganesha demonstrated that these parameters do not apply. Through this, we were being given a central teaching of the Egyptian temple. In order to be able to embrace the teaching, we had to work through and discard acquired patterns of thought to do with 'egotism' and the notion of being self-determined. As Schwaller de Lubicz said, "There is no more perfect divorce from the mentality of natural wisdom which prevailed in ancient Egypt than the one imposed in recent times by western mentality. The latter is purely cerebral. They are two epochs, two humanities that cannot understand one another."[3] "When the temple, endowed with the wealth of its sacred science and its power of truth, is no longer in existence and can no longer orient and order, men have no choice but to negate, for no rationalization can replace revelation."[4]

The ancient Egyptians had a sophisticated understanding of the anatomy of the brain. This is revealed in the *Edwin Smith Papyrus* which deals with traumatic injuries to the head and upper part of the body including the spinal column. Schwaller de Lubicz commented "Among other things, this surgical treatise proves that the Ancients had sure knowledge of the organs of the head and their actions and reactions on parts of the head not directly affected by the injury; the circulation of the blood and the internal nerves of the brain; and the effects of head injuries that are transmitted by the nervous system to particular parts of the body."[5] This indicates that we are dealing with a culture whose medical science has to be taken very seriously. In fact, at the time that the papyrus was translated, in 1930, some of the knowledge it contained went beyond the existing understanding of western medicine. In addition, it is necessary to be aware that, as John Anthony West put it, "every aspect of Egyptian knowledge seems to have been complete at the very beginning. The sciences, artistic and architectural techniques and the hieroglyphic system show virtually no sign of a period of 'development'; indeed, many of the achievements of the earliest dynasties were never surpassed, or even equalled later on. This astonishing fact is readily admitted by orthodox Egyptologists, but the magnitude of the mystery it poses is skilfully understated, while its many implications go unmentioned."[6] When writing of the ancient Egyptian religion, I am, unless otherwise stated, referring to the religion of that earlier, higher civilization, which was passed on in increasingly corrupted form until the year 535. Glimpses of the authentic teachings have appeared throughout ancient Egyptian history, indicating that knowledge of the original religion was either preserved by elements of the priesthood or renewed through avision.

After eight years of uninterrupted surveying of Luxor Temple, during which every detail of the temple was measured in every aspect, Schwaller de Lubicz published his preliminary findings in a short volume entitled *The Temple in Man*. Here, he revealed "It is necessary to note that Egyptian figurations carefully mark – with a headband, crown, diadem, or joint – a dividing line for the top of the skull thus separating the crown of the skull. In Egypt the height of the body was measured exclusive of the crown."[7] "In their temples the ancient Egyptians speak only of the Principles of the World and of the Cosmic Man within terrestrial man (Microcosm). Thus, in detaching the crown when the intention so requires, they separate the organ, which is the symbol of the fall from divine, direct Intelligence into transitory nature."[8] "the removal of this part of the brain leaves man alive, but without discernment, hence with no *personal* judgement. Thus, this part of the organs of the encephalon plays a very important role in the evolution of consciousness. The two hemispherical lobes of the brain are the instrument of memory and decision, hence choice. Thus, 'Divine' man (without this part of the brain) represents the Principle or Neter, capable of living and acting, but only as the executant of an impulse that he receives; hence, he plays the role of an intermediary between the abstract impulse, outside of Nature, and its execution in Nature, without actual choice."[9] This is what is being referred to in Hexagram 43 of the *I Ching* – Breakthrough – when it is written "If a man were to let himself be led like a sheep, Remorse would disappear. But if these words are heard They will not be believed."[10] The key phrase is "hence, he plays the role of an intermediary between the abstract impulse [God], outside of Nature, and its execution in Nature, without actual choice." This precisely corresponds to what was being conveyed by Ganesha in my dream; which was, I realized, that, in order to understand our place within the universe, we have to discard notions of selfhood and, instead, think of our life in terms of function. In so doing, the central question is no longer "What do I want to do?" but "What does Life require of me?" This is what is being shown by the iconography in the Egyptian Temple. And it is why Lao Tzu said "I do my utmost to attain emptiness;"[11] and why, in the Christian myth, Jesus, at the climactic moment of his life when faced with the prospect of crucifixion, arrived at the point at which he could say "not as I will, but as Thou wilt" and, from then on, was able to meet his fate with equanimity. Plato, too, made it clear at the end of his life that those in charge of the laws should simply follow the instructions that the gods provide when they impart laws through avision.[12] Indeed, he insisted that no detail imparted through avision be altered.[13]

CHAPTER FIVE

Reconnection

❧

In September of 1996, I dreamt:

> I am lying on my side in bed. Suddenly, the most shocking sound
> of the beating of wings, accompanied by draughts of air, comes from
> above and behind me. I turn and am horrified to see a large, devil-like
> creature, something akin to a vulture, swooping down and landing
> on my thigh. I cry out "Oh, no!" as I feel the weight of its body on
> mine and the grasp of its talons around my side.

When I described the face of the creature to Anna, she identified it as
that of the Egyptian god Set, a picture of whom she had come across in
an encyclopaedia a year earlier while researching a dream of her own.
I later found illustrations of Set which confirmed that she was right.
However, I also found that in every book I turned to Set was described
as the god of evil, an ascription that, despite his appearance, was at odds
with my experience (and with Anna's, which I shall recount later). It
is true that his sudden and totally unexpected manifestation had been
terrifying – and, indeed, Terrifier was one of the titles of Set – but, once
I had recovered from the shock of my dream, I realized that he had

shown no sign of malevolence and I certainly hadn't been injured. On the contrary, this extraordinary creature – the most awesome elemental force I have encountered in my life – had been as careful to ensure that I was unharmed when its talons gripped my side as Ganesha had been, four days earlier, when she lifted me into the air. Subsequently, I learnt that the 'Nesh' of 'Ganesh' was an ancient Egyptian name of Set. Something was healed in me when I discovered this. Eventually, I found confirmation of my judgement: "The gods of Egypt", said Hornung, "can be terrifying, dangerous and unpredictable, but they cannot be evil. Originally this was true even of Seth."[1]

I was in no doubt that I had actually encountered Set in my dream. As Hornung relates, "in the Egyptian view the sleeper dwells in the world of the gods."[2] Similarly, Kingsley informs us that "in antiquity the best way of actually making contact with divinities of the underworld was through the practice of 'incubation' – of awaiting a dream or vision."[3] We were increasingly to find that our understanding of our experience of a vision was that held in antiquity. At the same time, our experience of a vision itself confirmed the wisdom of that ancient philosophy and science. With regard to the meaning of my dream, I could see that a visual metaphor was being used to convey that Set had come down on my side.

Some years afterwards, I came across the Egyptologist E.A. Wallis Budge writing of Set that "in primitive times the attributes of the god were very different from those which are usually ascribed to him in the late dynastic period."[4] He went on to say that in the Pyramid Texts Set is always "a god who is a friend and helper of the dead."[5] And added that the hieroglyphs of his name indicate that Set was the personification of "the regions of death".[6] There is a suggestion of this association with death in the vulture-like features of Set in my dream.

Two weeks after the appearance of Set, I had another dream which filled me with fear:

> I am sitting at a table next to a tunnel that is connected to the ancient Egyptians. A wasp, which is the guardian of the tunnel,

hovers over me and carefully brings its head into contact with my hairline at three points. I am transfixed by the uncanny significance of what is taking place. I feel frightened, but to my amazement I realize that I have not been stung.

This dream was pivotal, depicting a rite that still resonates at a very deep level of my being – it was a rite of passage. In this, as in the previous dream, I was approached by a winged being. There is a parallel, too, in the wasp bringing its head into contact with mine as Ganesha had. Later, we learnt that 'Nesh', as well as being a name of Set and the principle component of the names 'Ganesh' and 'Ganesha', meant 'to hover over' in the ancient Egyptian language. What is more, we found that in English 'nesh' means 'tender, gentle and kind',[7] precisely the qualities that Ganesha, Set and the wasp all manifested. This verbal linkage provides a profound insight into understanding the mechanisms of transition in dreams from one culture and time into another, as well as raising questions about the nature of language itself.

I then moved from being seated next to a tunnel connected to the ancient Egyptians to being told in a dream on the following day that:

> Anna and I are as connected with the Sphinx now as we were in our Egyptian lifetime, so we can just move on from here.

It became apparent that the ancient Egyptians in question were ourselves; and it is fascinating to observe how the word 'connected' is used in both dreams in such a way that our being connected to the ancient Egyptians and our being connected to the Sphinx merge into one continuum. At that very moment, with the word 'now' and the phrase 'so we can just move on from here', we were brought back into the present. In the context of reincarnation, this phenomenon is symbolized by the ouroboros – the serpent that swallows its own tail/ tale. But to say we were brought back into the present is to simplify what was being conveyed, since the rather casual phrase 'so we can just move on from here' was understood in the dream to imply that we can now carry on from where we left off in our Egyptian life. So, when I say we were brought back into the present, I am actually meaning, not only that Anna and I were brought back into the present, but that the Dream had arranged for something essential of the understanding that we had in ancient Egypt to be brought back as well; and that our existence then and our existence now were merged. That this happened so easily is because the ground of our being is the same in each life; it is largely our experience that is different. Thus, I could have a dream two days after Set landed on me in which:

> Anna and I are in Egypt and I say to her that we do not need to perform any rituals – that the benefit from being there accrues automatically, the ritual issues having been worked through in the earlier lifetime.

Here, I am reminded of another dream from later that year in which:

> I am told of the difficulty in deciding from exactly where to measure the emergence of a past life and its issues because they link into the mainstream of one's present life at many points.

The process of return was also operating within the dream sequence itself, in that the message of the dream in which the statement was read from the great book was strikingly similar to the message of the dream concerning our relationship with the Sphinx. In the former, the word 'recognise' in the phrase "He has recognised God when he has recognised his dreams" means 'to know again'; and this was concordant with my being told that Anna and I are as connected with the Sphinx now as we were in our Egyptian lifetime.

The effect of that dream was revealed in another at the beginning of October 1996:

> I cry out with a shout as I emerge after having been submerged in extremely dark water.

I was aware that, in ancient Egyptian mythology, Atum – the self-created one – "emerged from Nun, the primordial waters, before sky and earth were born"[8] and I thought of this as soon as I awoke. It is important to understand why this image appeared in my dream life at that time. Looking back, I can see a progression. Originally, my personal psychotherapy focused upon a thorough exploration of my childhood. Then, it became clear that intrauterine experiences were dominating my dreams and emotional state. It was in order to understand those experiences that I went into therapy and trained with R.D. Laing. Subsequently, the movement continued from the womb, back through death, into my existence before this life – a process which implicitly created the requirement to recall my previous lives. It was at this point that conventional psychotherapy, which is founded upon the Judeo-Christian principle of one life, necessarily utterly failed to address the issues involved. For instance, a few years ago I had the following dream:

> I am shown that the deepest upset of my childhood is that Anna and I were not together.

This dream completely put my childhood in perspective – it was saying, which I immediately recognised as being true, that even more upsetting to me than the trauma that I underwent during my upbringing was our being apart. I mention this as an example of the different perspective that arises when reincarnation is taken into account. The focus changes from simply being directed towards understanding how the circumstances of one's upbringing have shaped one – in itself, an important and necessary endeavour – to recognising what one inherently is in each lifetime. Here, reference should again be made to Anna's dream of November 1994:

> Anthony is standing behind me. I twice turn my head back towards him and say the word 'recense'. This word has been coined to denote the relationship between one's present life and one's past life, especially during the early part of one's present life.

I came to realize that, remarkably, the structure of the word 'present' encapsulates the message of Anna's dream, since it contains within itself the pre-sent and the re-sent. This applies both to the present moment and to our present existence as, in terms of reincarnation, we are re-sent into this world.

The knowledge of our identity in our past lives has come to Anna and myself almost exclusively through our dreams; and it has been fascinating to observe how there are certain permanent attributes that are common to our nature in each lifetime. Leaving aside the cosmological significance of the myth about Atum as the self-created one, its esoteric significance relates precisely to this reality. I had been shown (as had Anna in a dream of her own) that I was not simply the product of my upbringing and the forces operating in the world about me, but that Anna and I had returned to this world to carry on from where we left off. At the moment of understanding this, I emerged from the darkness. In order for us to be able to carry on from where we left off, the Dream had to re-present us with certain key pieces of information so that we could understand life now as we understood it then. Thus, one of my dreams of the past year consisted of the phrase:

"To see a dream crossing him for centuries."

Recently, I came upon the following Egyptian text that corresponds with our experience: "I was born from the creative power, born of herself. She conceived me in her heart, She created me with her magical power. I was not born of a human childbirth."[9]

Also in October of 1996, four days after emerging from the dark water, I dreamt immediately upon falling asleep:

I enthusiastically say to myself "Off into the Tuat."

Again, I awoke with a start at the significance of this statement. The Tuat – the Otherworld or Underworld – is usually understood to be the land of the dead. Knowing that death is the state into which we pass at the end of a life and from which we emerge into the next life, the ancient Egyptians described the Tuat as "the place of transformations."[10] It will be recalled that Lamy commented "Many are the [ancient Egyptian] texts alluding to reincarnation, either overtly or implicitly through such locutions as 'renewal of life' or 'repetition of births'." Her assertion that the phrase 'to renew life' referred to reincarnation links with our experience that the Dream is intrinsic to that process. Hence, the ancient Egyptian word 'uhem' meaning 'to tell a dream' and 'uhem ankh' meaning 'to renew life'. We were now being shown that the Dream itself is the Tuat, the place of transformation – the means by which our past lives link into the mainstream of our present life. Also in accordance with the message that the Dream is the Tuat, is the fact that, in the highest practices of Tibetan Buddhism, the initiate is taught that to die is to enter a dream state; and they prepare themselves for death by learning to enter the world of dreams at will.

In the dream I had just before Laurens died, we sat in silence by the water for a long time. The lesson in silence that Laurens taught me was that the most solemn purpose of my existence is to contemplate the endless flow of the Dream within which the movement from life into death and back again is initiated, reflected and ministered to.

In the middle of October 1996, a few weeks after having dreamt that I emerged from the dark water, I had the following dream:

> Anna and I find that we have completed an ancient Egyptian activity involving a waterway. There are five words associated with it. When we look them up, we find that we have already understood and fulfilled their meaning.

On the same night that I dreamt I emerged from the water, Anna also had a dream featuring both water and my reappearance – one which profoundly affected us. It is interesting that this dream begins, like Anna's dream of the school, with our arriving at a mansion. In that dream, food is served to us; whilst, here, Anna acquires food for our children. Statues of horses and unicorns make reference to our earlier encounter with Pegasus and the Unicorn.

> Anthony and I enter the front drive of a mansion. There is a circular lawn on which are about twenty standing stones or tombstones. I rearrange them so that they stand around the edge of the circle. We walk past the house and a series of out-buildings and, then, through the back garden, in which there are large statues of horses and unicorns. We reach a road, which we cross. For a time, we become separated. I find our children, acquire food for them and lead them down a tunnel at the end of which we board a ferry. Then, I see Anthony. He is the ferryman, dressed in black, standing on a platform toward the prow (with his back to the direction in which we are travelling), in charge of the many rowers in the galleys below. It is a difficult and dangerous journey. When we finally reach our destination and disembark, we are reunited. Anthony has kept my black bag containing valuable items safe for me. One of the children asks "Why did we have to make this journey?" Anthony answers "It is an initiation that some must go through." The child asks if we shall ever recover. Anthony answers "We shall not recover – we shall be changed for ever."

CHAPTER SIX

The Sphinx

☘

Our being made aware that we are as connected with the Sphinx now as we were in our Egyptian life filled us with excitement and anticipation about what our experience would be in Egypt the following year. So, it came as a disappointment when we actually visited the Sphinx to find that we could only look at it from a distance on a viewing platform which was constantly crowded with tourists. This was definitely not the connection that we had with the Sphinx in our Egyptian life. We had, however, been prepared through two dreams of mine to meet such disappointments with equanimity. The first dream, which occurred in June of 1995, a few days after Ganesh had instructed me in the Law of Maat, provided the guidance we needed to find a position of balance in the face of adversity and, so, constituted an essential continuation of the instruction in the Law of Maat which Ganesh had initiated. At that time, we still had a television. The news about the state of the world had been particularly distressing during the day preceding my dream and we had gone to bed feeling despondent. Then, in the dream I was told:

"Your upset is misplaced. Things are always as they have to be.
There has never been a time on Earth when things were other than

exactly as they had to be. If you are upset by the way things are, then that simply points to a lack of understanding on your part."

This revelation changed our view of life. When we considered the message of the dream, we could see that all experiences, including the most heart-rending events in our lives, have a purpose. We were being told that there is a design to life that is not of our making – an awesome purposiveness which informs and gives meaning to every event in every moment of existence, an organizing principle in which we must have complete confidence. It is a view of life that is inspired by the knowledge that evil can never usurp the divine order. This, as we later learnt, led the ancient Egyptians to hold that evil, being contrary to the Law of Maat, will inevitably run its course and destroy itself. Which brings me back to my being told that "we can just move on from here." For, what we are prevented from doing in one life, we can, if it is essential, continue to do in another – hundreds or thousands of years later if necessary, when circumstances again allow for it or are right for it to happen. As Anna was told, in a dream of 2002:

"Continual reincarnation satisfies all."

It wouldn't be true to say that we never get upset about how events unfold, but, when this does happen, instead of thinking that things are going wrong, we ask why we ourselves got it wrong. Why did we think that life should or would go in a certain direction when the actuality is different? We have learnt a great deal by observing the disparity between our expectations and the actuality.

Then, in a dream of December of 1996, the instruction that "things are always as they have to be" was specifically applied to our forthcoming visit to Egypt:

I am asking one of our children how he feels as it gets closer to our going to Egypt. On the basis of his reply, I say: "Some people have a feeling of completeness about going to Egypt, but they are disappointed when they are there because they had expected to find that feeling reflected in the ancient buildings, which are actually in a deteriorating state – and, so, they lose the feeling of being complete. You have to see that the buildings are in exactly the state that they have to be in and you have to be able to keep the feeling of completeness in the light of that understanding."

Because of this perspective, our time in Egypt was, as we had intended it to be, for ourselves and our children, the holiday of a lifetime; and we had by the end of it exhausted our financial resources.

Returning home on 2nd June, laden with experiences it would take many months for us to integrate, we could never have anticipated that just over a week later, on 11th June, Anna would dream:

> The Sphinx is calling us – "Come to me. Come to me." – so forcefully that I am woken up. As it does so, it moves physically into our bedroom with a strange, loud, echoing, grinding sound of stone sliding over stone, filling the room with its presence. [When I fall asleep again] I am told that when we go to the Sphinx we will be shown what to do: we are to walk certain prescribed routes.

I do not have the means to convey the impact that this dream had upon us. The insistent tone of the Sphinx seemed to echo around the house throughout the day and into the next night.

Then, three days later, I dreamt:

> The Sphinx appears, saying: "And now you have to express your appreciation for the Sphinx." I am shown a haunting image of Anna and myself gazing at a particular portion of the Sphinx's body – though not at all an area that one would expect one's attention to be drawn towards – while being given precise instructions as to what we are to do at this point. I am then told that I have to earn a lot more money to pay for the trip.

The Sphinx

As a result of the instruction to consider the relation between 'thought' and 'ought' and the pair of dreams in which I was told that Ganesh wanted to see us and then, having failed to go there in material reality, was placed by Ganesha on the very spot we had been told to journey to, Anna and I were in no doubt that we had to return to the Sphinx. The preceding dreams had presaged the summons from the Sphinx in a way that had removed any obstacle to our acting upon it.

Our experience of being guided continued when, two days after my dream about the Sphinx, I dreamt:

> I am told that going to the Sphinx does not require any preliminary activity on our part; the only requirement being that we go there.

This came as an enormous relief. The simplicity that is the hallmark of how Heaven and Earth proceed is particularly evident here; and it added to the heady effect of the mystical union of the mythological and the mundane. Here, I am not referring to the notion of myth as "A purely fictitious narrative."[1] Anna and I consider this to be a reversal of the true nature of myth and concur with the *Encyclopedia of World Mythology* which states: "The scientific study of archaic societies – those societies in which mythology is, or was until recently, 'living' – has revealed that myth, for the 'primitive' man, means a true story and, beyond that, a story that is a most precious treasure because it is sacred, exemplary and significant."[2] Laurens was right when he wrote of dreams: "I had an inkling that they... were the true sources of mythology, religion, legend and art, seeking and re-seeking recognition and expression."[3] Our experience was confirming this; and it supported, too, Jung's statement that "it is not that 'God' is a myth, but that myth is the revelation of a divine life in man. It is not we who invent myth, rather it speaks to us as a Word of God... There is nothing about this Word that could not be considered known and human, except for the manner in which it confronts us spontaneously and places obligations upon us."[4] The obligation that the Sphinx had placed upon us through the Dream was that we should respond to its call and that I should show my appreciation for it. Significantly, 'Hu' was an ancient Egyptian name both of the Sphinx and for the 'Word of God'. We were being instructed that, as Hornung said, "The Egyptian gods desire that mankind should respond to their presence and their actions. They do not require to receive a cult and do not have to have material offerings, but they rejoice over the echoes that their creative word produces."[5] Through the instruction that God and the Dream are one, Anna and I were shown that avision – the advice that is received through a dream or vision – is that Divine Word. Cox Miller says that in Philo's dream theory one cannot distinguish between his use of the word 'dream' and the phrase 'Divine Word'.[6] It is in keeping with this ancient nomenclature that Hu – the Sphinx – communicated with us through dreams. Five days after being told that going to the Sphinx did not require any preliminary activity on our part, I had the following dream:

> I am journeying to the centre of somewhere which is Anthony.

With this dream, another dimension was added to our journey. In journeying to the Sphinx, we were journeying to the centre of our being. And that is how it felt. In simply following our dream instructions, we had never been more truly ourselves. This is because, to be truly Human, Hu – the Word of God – must come first.

Amazingly, the money we needed for our journey started to come immediately in ways that we could not have predicted, so we returned to Egypt at the earliest opportunity, which was at the end of August. Full of emotion, we made our way to the Sphinx, went to the spot on the viewing platform indicated in my dream and acted precisely as instructed. Within seconds, the most unexpected series of events began to occur so that, by the next morning, without our having asked, we had been given official permission by the Antiquities Department to stand between the paws of the Sphinx.

Our standing between the paws of the Sphinx was the most profound moment of our lives – utterly sacred. The rest of the world no longer existed. We stood in communion with the serene presence of the Sphinx, as we had thousands of years before. The sense of return was overwhelming. Time was something other. Towering over us was the embodiment of Fate, the awesome power which was constantly revealed during our visit to Giza, as key events turned out to be exact enactments of dreams we had been given during the previous year. These were the 'prescribed routes' of Anna's dream. For we were, at each step, provided with the demonstration of a truth that a dream of mine had imparted two weeks earlier; a dream which had been repeated to ensure that I had grasped its message:

> I am shown how a series of events in material reality unfolds along a pre-existing sequence of dreams; and how, in the area where mind and matter meet, each dream provides a firm link that holds its enactment fast.

This instruction is a development of the message read from the great book that God and the Dream are one, as it is now stated categorically that the Dream has a determinative, as well as a predictive function. Since God is the Dream, then it naturally follows that the Dream can have a creative purpose. Rosalie David says the ancient Egyptians believed that "Essentially the spiritual and material were... woven from the same substance."[7] As Samanta-Laughton explains, "some quantum theorists are suggesting that consciousness is fundamental to the universe, and that matter comes from consciousness, not the other way round."[8] With regard to the sacred science of Egypt, Schwaller de Lubicz emphasised: *"The science of Thoth* [god of wisdom and Lord of the Divine Word] *is the sacerdotal science of all times...* what is involved is... *a generation of the matter of the world in the image of creation.* Thus we are concerned here with *revealed* knowledge."[9] For Anna and myself, watching events in Giza unfolding along a pre-existing sequence of dreams altered forever our way of perceiving life. We were, in part, called to the Sphinx in order that this would happen.

I was interested to learn that the view we had arrived at on the basis of our experience was that held by the Stoics in late antiquity. Cox Miller recounts: "The Stoic idea was that, in dreams, the individual human soul could make contact with, and learn from, a pervasive governing principle within whose purview all life unfolds. One of the names by which the cosmic principle was discussed among the Stoics was fate. In their understanding of this term, fate did not designate a hostile structure that imprisoned human lives in a relentlessly deterministic world; it was used instead to give assurance that life has meaning, that it is not simply a collection of random, accidental events."[10]

Between the paws of the Sphinx stands a beautiful stele that was erected by Tutmose IV to record for posterity the remarkable event which led to his becoming pharaoh. It tells how "a great magical power had existed in this place from the beginning of all time and it extended over all the region... And at this time, the Sphinx-form of the most mighty god Khepera came to this place and the greatest of Souls, the holiest of the holy ones, rested therein."[11] Tutmose who, though a prince, was not in line for the throne, decided, when in the vicinity of the Sphinx, that he wished to worship this god. Later, in the heat of the day, as he slept in the shade that the Sphinx provided, it spoke to him in a dream, telling how it was suffocating beneath the weight of sand that had collected around its body. The Sphinx promised Tutmose that he would become pharaoh if he cleared away the sand. This Tutmose did and, in due course, he ascended the throne.

Academia is cynical with regard to Tutmose's account. In the *British Museum Dictionary of Ancient Egypt*, it is argued that "In royal propaganda, stelae sometimes recount the pseudo-prophetic dreams of pharaohs as a means of justifying their succession to the throne. The classic example of the royal dream stele was erected by Thutmose IV."[12] This is a pointed instance of Schwaller de Lubicz's observation that "When the temple, endowed with the wealth of its sacred science and its power of truth, is no longer in existence and can no longer orient and order, men have no choice but to negate, for no rationalization can replace revelation." On the basis of our experience, I have no doubt that Tutmose was accurately describing the actuality. I feel there is sincerity in the way that he expresses himself. Rather than self-justification, I see the dream stele as a reverential account of the decisive moment of his life for future generations to ponder. Decisive, not merely because it led to his becoming pharaoh, but because the living truth of the religion that was Egypt had been revealed to him. All he claims for himself is that he followed the Sphinx's instruction.

What is so striking, if Tutmose's account is taken at face value, is his encounter with destiny and the unexpected part that the Sphinx played in that. If we are to deepen our understanding of life, we have to be able to think about these experiences in their own terms because, as Hornung emphasised, "In order to understand the forces that circumscribe the very closed and homogeneous world of the Egyptians, we must inquire after their gods and employ all our conceptual armory in order to seek out the reality of these gods – a reality that was not invented by human beings but *experienced* by them."[13] It will be remembered also that I quoted Hornung as saying: "in the Egyptian view the sleeper dwells in the world of the gods." What is fascinating is that the Sphinx we encountered in our dreams required us to go to Giza to be in the presence of its material form, confirming Tutmose's statement that divinity resides in that place. The Sphinx presents itself as straddling the divide between the world of the Dream and the world of material form, exerting, as it does so, a powerful influence upon material reality. How this can be was soon to be made clear to us.

Part of what made our experience so affecting (and I am sure that the same held true for Tutmose) was the personal nature of the encounter and the element of reciprocity. Though we had satisfied the criteria of the call of the Sphinx simply by going to Giza, I was left concerned about the question of whether I had shown my appreciation in the way that was required. That night, I dreamt:

> We are again beside the Sphinx, whom I ask "Have I done it?"
> "Yes." is the reply.

I awoke from this dream with a wonderful sense of completion and gratitude that I had received the confirmation I needed, as well as with greatly increased confidence that we had understood what the Dream had been teaching us and requiring of us. My confidence increased further still when Anna had a corresponding dream a week later:

> Anthony and I are between the paws of the Sphinx. The Sphinx confirms that we are doing everything right.

CHAPTER SEVEN

The Otherworld

When I ponder the alternating pattern of our being with the Sphinx in our dreams and our being in the presence of its material form, I am reminded of the way in which sunlight passing through the leaves of a tree on a summer's day can be seen mirrored in a river whilst the reflection of the water's movement is itself dappling those leaves and reflected by them. This pattern originated with a remarkable sequence of dreams that Anna had in late August and early September of 1996 covering the exact period, a year later, during which we were in Egypt to fulfil the summons to the Sphinx. On the first night, she dreamt:

> Twin lion beings with human heads, which seem to be joined from the waist down, are in the presence and shadow of a goddess who is sitting upright in the shape of a huge pyramidal mound.

On the second and third nights, the same dream was repeated:

> I am shown a series of pairs of things, with the Sphinx nodding confirmation of each pair in turn.

On the fourth night, she dreamt:

> I am shown that all places can be reduced to one word. This is confirmed by the Sphinx.

Finally, on the fifth night, she had the following dream:

> I am inside a pyramid in which there are steps leading up and then down again.

Nearly two years later, having twice visited Egypt and feeling a need to learn more about the sites we had seen and the culture that had given rise to them, we began to research the literature and discovered that the images in the first dream correspond with what is depicted as existing in the Fifth Division of the Tuat in the papyrus entitled *Book of What Is in the Tuat*: two human-headed lion sphinxes are set tail to tail on either side of a pyramid so that only their heads and fore-quarters appear; the pyramid has the head of a goddess at its apex. Alexandre Piankoff describes the Fifth Division as it is depicted in the tomb of Ramses VI: "It has three registers... At top (register 1) is a mound with a bird on either side, symbolizing the night. From the under part a beetle [Khepera] emerges. Below (register 2) is a pyramidal mound surmounted by the head of a woman."[1] At the base of the pyramid are the Aker: the two human-headed lion sphinxes.

It was in October of 1996, the month after Anna had this series of dreams, that we were shown that the Dream itself is the Tuat.

In *Keeper of Genesis*, Robert Bauval and Graham Hancock quote the Egyptologist Selim Hassan as saying of the Fifth Division that it "had its geographical counterpart in the Giza necropolis."[2] Hassan notes that "the Fifth Division was originally a [complete] version of the *Duat*."[3] This statement provides an answer to the riddle in Anna's dream that 'all places can be reduced to one word' — since the twelve divisions of the Tuat can be reduced to one, the fifth, the name of which is Ament. As a universal, the answer to the riddle is 'Here' (because all places can be described as 'Here'), a word very similar to 'Heru', another ancient Egyptian name of the Sphinx.

The ancient Egyptian name for Giza was Rostau. Bauval collected evidence that Rostau was "considered the gateway to the Duat region."[4] So, when we were summoned to the Sphinx, we were being summoned to the geographical counterpart of the gateway to the Tuat; that is, the gateway to the world of the Dream.

What is as extraordinary as the correspondences to the Fifth Division I have mentioned is that the words spoken by the Sphinx in Anna's later dream, "Come to me. Come to me.", are a more intimate expression of the text of the Fifth Division: "Come to Kheperà, O Rā! Come to Kheperà!"[5] (Khepera, it will be remembered, is the god that Tutmose names on the Dream Stele as being resident within the Sphinx.) This detail is significant, since it suggests that the summons in the text is rooted in experience. It is both an echo of the statement 'we are as connected with the Sphinx now as we were in our Egyptian lifetime' and a verification of it.

Through our experience of the summons to the Sphinx and its fulfilment, we came to realize that, as the Stoics had expounded millennia before, "dreams allow the soul to stand outside of its immersion in the everyday and to reflect on its course in a broader context, conceived theologically as a cosmic structure undergirded by the gods."[6]

The *Book of What Is in the Tuat* is, as the name suggests, a guide to the Otherworld. The book is divided into twelve divisions or hours, corresponding to the twelve hours of the night, and is said to depict the journey of the sun through those hours. Hornung adduces that "The nightly journey of the sun is the focus of all the Books of the Netherworld, and consistent with this, it also furnishes the ordering and creative principle for the spaces in the hereafter. This nocturnal regeneration of the sun demonstrates, by way of [metaphorical] example, what powers of renewal are at work on the far side of death. At the same time, the journey occurs in the spaces of the human soul, in which a renewal

occurs in the spaces of the human soul, in which a renewal

from the depths becomes possible. That it is an odyssey of the soul is emphasized by the Egyptians through the indication that the sun god descends into the depths as a *ba*-soul (and thus is ram-headed, since *ba* is also the word for ram); herein lie significant antecedents of modern psychotherapy."[7]

Anna and I were very glad that, through the Dream, we had undergone our experience of the Fifth Division prior to reading about it. I say this because we were, thereby, able to know that, to use Hornung's evocative phrase, the ancient Egyptians had not invented the Fifth Division of the Tuat, but had recorded their dream experience of it.

Hornung's account was of particular interest to us because of his indicating that the *Book of What Is in the Tuat* presents "significant antecedents of modern psychotherapy;" and also because it pointed to the same patterns operating within Man as within other parts of material and immaterial existence. However, our journey into the Fifth Division, which 'occurred within the spaces of our human souls', was first undertaken in the world of the Dream and, subsequently, conditional upon our being present in Giza, the geographical location of the Fifth Division – the reason being that "the powers of renewal" in the world are at their most intense in the vicinity of the Sphinx.

Hornung states that the "god descends into the depths as a *ba*-soul." Lamy distinguishes between the 'ba' that is the human soul, symbolized by a human-headed bird, which, as "the determining individualizing force,"[8] "incarnates itself... [and] defines the character and affinities of the individual, 'each according to its nature';"[9] and the divine 'ba', "symbolized by the ram with horizontal horns... [which] is the soul animating all those beings who... are subject to cyclic rebirth."[10] She explains that "According to the funerary texts... The mortal body *kha* is animated during its existence by the [individual] *ba*."[11] When a person dies, the kha, being mortal, perishes; while the ba, which is immortal, may incarnate in a new kha.

That the *Book of What Is in the Tuat* is concerned with the process of reincarnation is quite clear from Hornung's analysis of the Twelfth (and last) Division: "The backward direction, from tail to mouth, indicates the necessary reversal of time: according to the caption, all these beings enter the serpent's tail old and frail, weakened by age, and emerge from its mouth as newborn babes."[12] Schwaller de Lubicz draws attention to the link between this division and the iconography of the Cave Temple of Ramses II in Abu Simbel, making the same observation as Hornung: "It is precisely the characteristic of reversal, moreover, that underlies the deeper meaning of this rock-hewn temple."[13]

However, the *Book of What Is in the Tuat* cannot simply be concerned with the process of reincarnation as it unfolds in the world of the dead because, in that process, the ba is that of the human-headed bird. From our experience in the Fifth Division at Giza, Anna and I realized that the *Book of What Is in the Tuat* was originally concerned with a process which unfolds as much in the world of the living as it does in the world of the dead. Hence, Schwaller de Lubicz went on to say of the Cave Temple of Ramses II: "The Pharaonic name for this temple is *Per-mes-s*, that is, '*the house* (or temple) *that generated him* (or put him into the world)'."[14] This process involves the divine Ba soul "animating all those beings who... are subject to cyclic rebirth." Thus, in the *Book of What Is in the Tuat*, a force far greater than our individual souls is depicted as making the journey to Giza.

The journey into the Otherworld is a fundamental shamanic experience. As Musès, in his address to the Fourth International Conference on the Study of Shamanism, stated, "One of the most elaborated (indeed, the most anciently documented shamanic religion) is that of ancient Egypt."[15] Our being summoned to the Fifth Division and our experiences therein were profoundly shamanic; and one cannot understand what the ancient Egyptians were depicting within the *Book of What Is in the Tuat* unless one takes the shamanic basis of their religion into account.

In his address, Musès explained: "Whatever else one can say about it, we can say that shamanism seeks to communicate with suprahuman powers – those that hold the reins of life and death and govern the forces of nature. These are invariably taught to be intelligent entities. Thus, the shamanic way in any culture is the way of theurgy: working with a hierarchy of suprahuman intelligence and enabling."[16] In Mongolian, the word 'shaman' translates as 'one who knows'.

At the beginning of September 1997, on the night of our return from the Sphinx, Anna had a dream that added another dimension to our understanding of what we had experienced:

> Anthony and I are between the paws of the Sphinx. We are shown an umbilical cord hanging from the heavens through which we receive knowledge.

We were to discover that this image is connected with the symbol of the mound with the bird on either side (in the upper register of the Fifth Division). Robert Temple cites Livio Stecchini demonstrating that this mound is an omphalos, or navel stone ('umbilicus' being the Latin for Greek 'omphalos'), indicating that the Fifth Division is the site of an ancient oracle centre.[17] Piankoff's description of the mound as representing night identifies the oracle at Giza as being a dream oracle; for, Plutarch stated that the 'krater' through which Orpheus entered the Underworld was "an oracle shared by Night and the Moon" to be found "in dreams and visions."[18] Here, Plutarch was describing the Orphic version of the journey into the Tuat, since Orphics regarded the moon as the land of the dead. Kingsley goes to some lengths to prove that the krater is not only to be found in the realm of dreams and visions, but was "also a geological crater... [located in] southern Italy or Sicily."[19] He describes it as "a specific physical phenomenon... a point of descent and entry into the underworld... associated with oracles and dreams."[20] In ancient times, it was known that certain geo-physical locations and environments were particularly suited to facilitating the experience of avision. The underground cave system spanning southern Italy and Sicily is one such place. We know from Anna's dream of the umbilical connection that Giza is another. Thus, it was because of the dream oracle that Giza was "considered the gateway to the Duat region."

Anna's dream of the umbilical cord hanging from the heavens was a development of the instruction to "Believe in the stars and that they directly affect everything that happens to us", in that we were being shown that the source of the energy located at the Sphinx has a heavenly origin. I had been given an intimation of this in a dream, in June of 1997, two weeks after the summons to the Sphinx:

> Anna and I are in Egypt, in the vicinity of the Sphinx. We are waiting for something when, suddenly, a large face which is to be our guide appears in the sky. It seems that it may be the face of the Sphinx.

This image was clarified in a dream of Anna's, in September of 1997, shortly after our return from the Sphinx:

> The Sphinx is gazing at another Sphinx slightly to its right in the distant heavens.

Through these dreams, it was being suggested that the Sphinx on Earth is a representation of a celestial Sphinx with which it is in contact and which is actually the source of our experience of avision.

The Dream is eminently suited to be the focus of an oracle centre; for, as was stated to Anna in a dream of 1998:

> "Each person's dreams tell of their destiny."

Our experience of being summoned to Giza in a dream, and of our time there being underpinned by avision, demonstrated to Anna and myself that the dream centre at Giza is as operative now as it was in antiquity.

In its earliest usage, the word 'shaman' meant 'a diviner-priest'.[21] Divining would, of course, have been a function of the priests who officiated at the oracle centre in Giza. Musès notes that "the reason the ancient cultures could leave so great a spiritual heritage is precisely that their psychiatries were embedded within their religions and grew from them."[22] The ultimate concern of the diviner-priests was "facilitating a higher level of the evolution of human insight, in turn resulting in enhanced capabilities in consciousness and its implementation."[23] Intrinsic to this theurgic goal was the diviner-priest's role as "an ecological transformer, working with natural powers in reverence and even awe at their fantastic potential. The entire Weltanschauung [world view] of shamanism is singularly free from the hubris of 'conquering', 'exploiting', or any other *de facto* rape and abuse of the natural environment and its fauna or flora... So, far from being 'archaic', this deeper aspect of shamanism is more modern than the future, and it is well that we examine it in the light of the beneficial changes in both our physical and psychological ambiance that such examination can make, inner and outer. Not unconnected with such a project of holistic environmental renewal, and in fact an ultimate *sine qua non* for it, was a penetration into the very meaning of our natural environment and biological constitution."[24] Musès goes on to say: "To this end, perhaps the highest shamanic experience" is brought about by "bodily death... but made before the actual disfunctioning and subsequent molecular dissolution of the physical body. The charting of the topography of that eschatological realm is one of the major contributions to its culture that the shamanic way can make possible."[25]

The Aker were the guardians of the entrance and exit to the Otherworld. In terms of our experience, this means that they guard the juncture between the world of the Dream and the world of material reality, which merge, as the bodies of the Aker merge. From the point of view of reincarnation, the Aker guard the juncture of one's past and present lives, which also merge. This corresponds to my being told that 'we are as connected with the Sphinx now as we were in our Egyptian lifetime, so we can just move on from here'.

In May of 1997, on the night before we first went to Egypt, I had a dream which I didn't completely understand at the time:

> I set off with Anna and our children in a large boat. I am steering, but cannot see where we are going as Anna is positioned directly in front of me. We are travelling at great speed.

76

This was followed by another dream in early June, four days before Anna's dream of the summons to the Sphinx:

> Anna and I are travelling in a ferryboat through shallow water and over land. I am the pilot. We arrive at our destination, which is the Sphinx. As we do so, the boat and the Sphinx become one.

In the *Book of What Is in the Tuat*, which one could translate as '*Book of What Is in the Dream*', the divine Ba soul proceeds on its journey by means of a boat. Our dreams used the same imagery for our own journeys into the Tuat. Mine developed the theme of Anna's earlier dream in which I was the ferryman. In that dream, I was instructing the crew with my back to the direction in which we were travelling; here, I was steering without having a view of our direction. This is because the course we were following was being determined by the Dream. In my first dream, my being unable to see the way ahead represented our not consciously knowing that we were destined to stand between the paws of the Sphinx. In my subsequent dream, the Sphinx was both our destination and, as Hu, the Divine Word, the means by which we got there. This accords perfectly with our experience regarding Giza. Lamy writes: "At the front of the boat is the 'Opener of the Ways', followed by Sia, 'Knowledge', and the 'Mistress of the Barque' [the divine Ba being in the centre]... in the back of the boat we should take note of Hw, 'The Word', standing just in front of the pilot."[26] When in Giza, we witnessed the influence of the Opener of the Ways removing seemingly insuperable obstacles to our standing between the paws of the Sphinx. This happened without any effort on our part other than our acting upon Sia, the Knowledge, or, as Hornung defined it, the Percipience, imparted to us by Hu, the Divine Word. This symbolism encapsulates both the means by which we proceeded on our journey to the Sphinx and the nature of that venture.

Lamy states that, in the *Book of What Is in the Tuat*, the divine Ba soul symbolized by the ram with horizontal horns [which Lamy calls the ba, but Anna and I call the Ba in order to differentiate it from the individual ba soul symbolized by the bird] is named 'Iwf', meaning

'Flesh'.[27] In one of the hours, Iwf states: "I have come here to see my body in order to inspect my image which is in the Dwat."[28] to which the entities in the Tuat answer: "Come then to us, thou whose flesh sails, who is led towards his own body... The sky is for thy soul, the earth for thy body... Illumine the primordial darkness so that the 'flesh' may live and renew itself... [Thou art] He who becomes, He who metamorphoses himself."[29] Lamy comments: "There is no doubt that we are dealing here with the incarnation – the becoming flesh – of the divine principle of light... The Dwat is then the world of metamorphoses, of which the scarab Khepri is the pre-eminent symbol."[30]

Anna and I agree with Lamy's interpretation in so far as it goes, but her explanation does not touch upon our experience that our journey into the Fifth Division was made while we were alive. That the Ba soul is named 'Flesh', is a forthright statement that the process depicted in the text is one which is undergone by a being who is flesh; which is to say, by one in whom the individual ba soul has already incarnated. This concurs with Musès' understanding of the ancient Egyptian *Book of the Dead*: that "the oldest meaning of the process their texts recorded refers to life, not death" and, hence, the correct translation of the title is *Book of The Coming Forth Into Day*. Lamy was quite right in her assessment that the text depicts "the becoming flesh of the divine principle of light." Since God is the Dream, the process of incarnating the divine Ba soul is undergone within the world of the Dream. Precisely what it means to incarnate the light of Ba was gradually revealed to us in the months and years ahead.

In October of 1997, six weeks after our return from Egypt, there was an unexpected sequel to our being summoned to the Sphinx. I dreamt:

> I am asked "But what image does the Dreaming Mind itself most want to focus on?" I am aware that the image is from a dream that Anna or I have already had. I look through the upper portion of the images from a number of dreams as if I am going through photographs. Then, I find it. The image, which comes alive, is of Anna and myself, in this lifetime, walking happily and determinedly up a slight incline

in Giza. The scene, which is bathed in the most beautiful white light, is set close to the Great Pyramid, but our focus is upon each other and the joy of walking hand in hand in that place. I am aware through my peripheral vision that there are pillars in the vicinity which are intact (as they no longer are). We are walking towards the Temple of Isis, which is also intact, and beyond to the Sphinx.

In acting upon the summons to the Sphinx, Anna and I were ordering our footsteps by Maat. The Dream catches an intimate moment in which our delight in being together in the present, which is an expression of the bond of love between us, is felt whilst we are engaged in an activity that is intensely future-directed. Our goal is the Sphinx and it is equally in our minds that we are as connected with the Sphinx now as we were in our Egyptian lifetime. This link with the past is powerfully conveyed by the pillars in the Temple of Isis being depicted in the pristine condition that was theirs in antiquity, rather than in the ruined state that they are to be found in today.

Acting upon the Word of God in the present (which is the gateway to the future) whilst being deeply concerned with the links to the ancient past was a hallmark of the pharaonic civilization. This was what the Dreaming Mind most wanted to focus on at that time.

The scene presented a distillation of all the dream instructions (and their realization in material reality) that we had hitherto been provided with, whilst, at the same time, energetically directing us towards our next task.

Two of Anna's dreams, from November 2000 and February 1999, expand upon the requirement for the individual to make links with their past:

> I am undergoing a process whereby several of my lives become integrated. I realize that in one of them I lived in the place that is now called Istanbul. I am shown that this process of integration involves returning to the places where I lived previously.

I am told that certain of my and Anthony's experiences of this lifetime precisely overlay those of a past lifetime. The example I am shown is how, when we were in Karnak, we were unconsciously driven to repeat specific acts that we had performed there in a previous life.

The fact that the text of the Fifth Division of the Tuat existed and that we could see we had dreamt of it gave us the confidence to judge that we were going through the same process of initiation we had undergone in our Egyptian lifetime.

CHAPTER EIGHT

Restoration

In September of 1997, a week after we returned from the Sphinx, I had the following dream:

> I am at what seems to be the Saqqara necropolis in Egypt; but then the scene changes and it could be anywhere in the world. I am shown a mechanical crane collapsing. There are a number of people trapped inside it because the crane also functions as a vehicle. I am told that I have to restore the crane.

Almost a year to the day before, I had had the dream in which Ganesha lifted me to a great height and then placed me on the spot that I had been instructed to journey to. As a result of her assistance, I was moved from my mistaken attitude regarding my dream instructions to the appropriate one, in order that I should be aligned with the unfolding pattern of events and play my part accordingly. In the modern world, the mechanical crane performs the same function that elephants have traditionally been used for: lifting things to a height and then moving them to where they are required to be. By the superimposition in time of the dream of the crane upon that of Ganesha, I was being shown that the crane symbolizes that function of the Dream which corrects a person's understanding, moving them from a mistaken attitude to the appropriate one in order that they are aligned with the unfolding pattern of events and play their part accordingly. It is this function of the Dream which has collapsed and which I was told I have to restore.

The opening sequence of my dream suggests that the Saqqara necropolis (which at that time we had not yet visited) was associated with the realigning aspect of avision. We later learnt that there had in ancient times been a dream sanctuary at Saqqara. As this is no longer the case, it is true that the crane has collapsed there – as it has throughout so much of the world.

The association of the mechanical crane with the bird of the same name is relevant. Wallis Budge suggests that the ancient Egyptian word 'tchaau' denoted the 'crane'.[1] I am sure that he is right, since the closely related 'tchaas' meant 'knowledge, foreknowledge and the wisdom of ancient times'[2] which, as I have shown, were known in antiquity to be bestowed through avision. (At the time of my dream, I was not clear about the significance of the people trapped within the crane, so I shall return to this feature in a later chapter.) Confirmation that I had sufficiently understood what was required of me was given to me in another dream a week later:

> Anna and I are camped near the resting place of a pride of lions. They possess a powerful, though non-aggressive, presence. Eventually, the pride leaves, except for a lioness who remains watching to be sure that we are safely where we ought to be. Only when certain of this, does she turn and gracefully walk off into the night.

The tender concern of the lioness was deeply reassuring. As was the message that we were safely where we ought to be.

The following night, two weeks after our return from the Sphinx,
I dreamt:

> I am on a journey. It starts from the bedroom of my
> childhood home – the room in which I first began to record my
> dreams. I am told that the Dream is central to the journey and that it
> has been deliberately undermined because it can be a source of great
> power; this undermining having been effected by the Dream being
> categorized as being both outside of and less than material reality.

After my having understood that the crane represents an aspect of
avision, I was now provided with the information as to why and how the
Dream had been undermined. Since the Dream is central to the journey
of my life, it had begun to provide the information and experience
required to correct the effects of that undermining. This capacity of
the Dream is a reason why those who seek to control the minds of
the populace must necessarily be opposed to avision. Furthermore, it is
important to remember here the message read from the ancient book
that 'God and the Dream are one', since this makes it clear that, with
the undermining of the Dream, there has been an undermining of the
dreamer's personal experience of God.

It is because the Dream was so revered as a source of guidance
in antiquity that Christian polemicists sought to counter and usurp
the philosophical and spiritual systems which were supportive of
the practice of incubation as the evolving Church moved to assume
authority over the Western world. With regard to the Platonists, for
instance, this attack took the paradoxical form of the demonizing of
demons. Ananda Coomaraswamy states that, in its original meaning,
'daimon' was synonymous with 'God';[3] hence, a demon denoted that
aspect of the Mind of God which communicates with Mankind through
avision. In ancient Greece a 'demon' was "a supernatural being of a
nature intermediate between gods and men."[4] Cox Miller informs us that
"The view that dreams could shape human subjectivity by enlarging its
sphere of reference was shared by Platonic theorists, although for them
the sphere was populated not by gods but by daemons."[5] However, for

the Christians, a 'demon' became an "evil spirit" "with the term being applied to the idols and gods of the heathens."[6]

In *Timaeus*, Plato stated: "No man achieves true and inspired divination when in his rational mind, but only when the power of his intelligence is fettered in sleep or when it is distraught by disease or by reason of some divine inspiration. But it belongs to a man when in his right mind to recollect and ponder both the things spoken in dream or waking vision by the divining and inspired nature, and all the visionary forms that were seen, and by means of reasoning to discern about them all wherein they are significant."[7] "The major spokesmen for a daemonic provenance for dreams were the Middle Platonists Plutarch and Apuleius, whose placement of dreams in a daemonic context served to underscore their mediatorial and transformative function."[8] As Shakespeare wrote, "We are such stuff As dreams are made on."[9] "In Middle Platonist theorizing about daemons, the boundary that separates human life from the region of the gods is recognized, but its importance lies, at least in part, in its 'brokenness', in its permeability by the daemons whose function it is to relate the human with the divine."[10] For Plutarch, "the daemon-as-hermeneut [demon-as-interpreter] saves human beings from the 'shipwreck' of the unreflected life."[11] "for Apuleius as for Plutarch, the placement of oneiric phenomena in a daemonic context was not a demotion of dreams to irrationality. Instead, his daemonizing of dreams was based on his view of such 'sign languages' as an important psychic apparatus with distinctive ethical overtones, 'promoting the good', as Apuleius says, by encouraging an interpretive, selective, meditative style of perception... As a daemonic language – that is, as a medium of exchange between an ideal world (of the gods) and a flawed world (of human beings) – the dream can provide a discourse for articulating the need for finer tuning of the sensibilities... Thus when dreams were seen as a daemonic production, they took on an epistemological function as sources of self-awareness and ethical reflection."[12]

Cox Miller continues: "Among the apologists of the second century whose aim was to prove to the Roman world that Christianity was a rational religion worthy of legitimate status, the attack on dreams took the form of an attempt to show that Christians have no truck with demons. Thus Justin Martyr warned the readers of his first apology that they should be on their guard against demons who would try to cloud their apprehension of the truth of Christianity through appearances in dreams and in magic. Similarly, Athenagoras in his plea on behalf of Christianity warned that a 'tender and susceptible soul which is ignorant of sound teaching' is prey to the irrational fantasies of demons who bedevil the soul in dreams. In the third century, Clement of Alexandria took another line of attack: for him, proving the superior qualities of the Christian religion entailed a demonstration of the fantastic foolishness of the polytheist traditions. Among those ruled by the 'tyranny of demons' are practitioners of divination, including specifically those who interpret dreams. Such structures of religious knowledge are impious sophistry, 'gambling games of pure illusion'."[13]

This outbreak of polemical oneirophobia reached its zenith among the zealot Coptic Christian ascetics of Egypt. MacDermot explains: "To the Egyptian ascetic... sleep represented a time when his soul was subject to his body and to those influences which derived from his old religion. He endeavoured to regulate his sleep in such a way as to lessen its dangers for himself; his ideal was to sleep for as short a time as possible... In dreams, he felt himself subject to the ancestral forces and nature powers with which... he had in the past been identified."[14]

Yet, in turning against the Dream, Christianity began to depart from Biblical tradition. It was, after all, by means of a dream – Jacob's dream of the ladder – that the Jewish God formed a covenant with his people. Thereafter, in the book of *Job*, it was declared: "For God speaketh once, yea twice, yet man perceiveth it not. In a dream, in a vision of the night, when deep sleep falleth upon men, in slumbering upon the bed; Then he openeth the ears of men, and sealeth their instruction."(Job 33: 14-16) Additionally, in *The Septuagint Bible* (the oldest text of The Old Testament), it is written: "For thou shouldst not say, There shall be no visitation of man. He shall indeed have a visitation from the Lord. Therefore harken to me, ye who are wise in heart."(Job 34: 9-10)[15] Such visitations were the provenance of the prophets, for it was said: "If there be a prophet among you, I the Lord, will make myself known unto him in a vision, and will speak to him in a dream."(Numbers 12: 6) However, in Jewish law, there was an ambivalence towards the Dream insofar as the message that a prophet imparted was required to conform to the established religion; in other words, the Dream was used to support the system rather than the system supporting the Dream. Thus, as Paul Carus noted, "Deuteronomy commands that prophets and dreamers of dreams, who by signs and wonders that come to pass would persuade Israelites to obey other gods, 'shall be put to death' (xiii.5-11)."[16]

Subsequently, "in New Testament times, divine revelation is presumed to occur in visions and dreams, and such inner experience is treated as a normal way of God's revelation."[17] So, it is not surprising to learn that "In the early Church, many Christians followed their dreams to find God's will and to understand how God was working in their lives."[18] "According to Luke in the Book of Acts, dreams and visions occurred frequently and at important moments in the life of the early Christian community."[19] "Dreams and visionary material were treated seriously and given much authority in the nascent Church."[20]

There was, as I have already indicated, a precedent for this in the gospels with regard to the survival of the infant Jesus. Although there are no records of Jesus' own dreams, there is evidence that he was influenced by the Essenes[21] who were renowned oneirologists. There are also references in the *Gospel of St. John* to the Judaic oneiromantic tradition.

As can be seen from the quotations provided by Cox Miller, the main concern of those who were opposed to avision was that the guidance received through dreams would be contrary to the emerging Christian religion. The Dream had, therefore, to be undermined; with the consequence that the "reverential attitude towards the dream fell into disrepute. Dreamwork as a Christian tradition was practically lost for many centuries."[22]

In contrast to Christianity, one can speak of "The ubiquity of the dream in Muslim civilization."[23] In his introductory paper to the first international Colloquium on the Dream, G.E. von Grunebaum stated: "It cannot be emphasized enough that to the Medieval Muslim, scholar or lay, the cognitive power of the dream does not present an epistemological problem. Not a single time does the latest authority on *oneirokritika*, the theologian 'Abdalghanī an-Nābulusī (1641-1731), the compiler of an encyclopedic guide to dream interpretation... in the six hundred pages of his *Ta'ṭīr al-anām fī ta'bīr al-manām*, question the objective validity of oneiric data. The cognitive significance of the dream is sufficiently established and explained by the observation that 'the prophets were wont to consider dreams as revelation to them of the sacred laws'."[24] This applied to The Prophet himself.

Von Grunebaum, however, concluded his paper by arguing that "In a sense, we have less need of our dreams than had the Muslims and our forefathers. For one thing, we are no longer so deeply concerned with the Hereafter and the supernatural; better put, the borders of the 'natural' have been pushed out, and with this expansion of the rationally, even experimentally, accessible, the importance of the dream, the vision, the revelatory communication has shrunk within our daily lives and our intellectual life as well. Better knowledge and wider control of our universe have relieved us of anxieties and fears... As a result of our scientific advancement we have become able to afford a renunciation long overdue; we have been able to yield the idea that the dream is symptomatic of a reality divorced from the psychological reality of the dreamer and his society."[25] It is ironic that the first international Colloquium on the Dream should commence with an espousal of the very attitude that, as the Dream informed me, has been used to undermine it.

Earlier, von Grunebaum cited Nābulusī commenting on the statement in the *Koran*: "Thus your Lord will prefer you and teach you the interpretation of events" as "meaning the science of dreams, the prime science since the beginning of the world, which the prophets and messengers did not cease to study and act upon."[26] It is hubris to argue that modern Man no longer needs this sacred science because he has advanced beyond it. It is worth bearing in mind that, as Aldous Huxley observed, "The Greeks... knew very well that hubris against the essentially divine order of Nature would be followed by its appropriate nemesis."[27]

The belief that modern Man has advanced beyond the need for avision has led to a misunderstanding, if not a denigration, of the minds of people in those societies that do not share this view. This issue was addressed by Roger Caillois in his presentation to the 1962 Colloquium: "It has been frequently maintained that the so-called primitive peoples do not distinguish the dream from the waking state. I think that this idea has to be modified somewhat. They know perfectly well what a dream is and what it is to be awake, but they attribute no lesser degree of reality to the dream than to the waking experience. Sometimes, rather more impressed by dreams, they accord them greater weight than they do a simple, banal perception, and they are convinced that the dreams bear witness to a superior reality. In other words, the distinction is made, but it does not follow, that the dream seems illusory or the waking world incontestable."[28]

What Caillois has described with regard to 'primitive' peoples was, of course, the attitude held by individuals of the intellectual calibre of Pythagoras and Parmenides, who "dealt out all the ideas that Western thought has played with ever since." That academia in general has refashioned the truth about the pre-Socratics to make it consistent with the contemporary world view, thereby concealing the fact that the seeds the pre-Socratics sowed had been received by them through avision, is another example of the way in which the Dream has been undermined. Whenever a hierarchical order wishes to attain social control, the autonomy that the Dream confers will be seen as antithetical to their interests and recognition of avision as the guiding influence will be withheld.

In the year 405-6, the Neo-Platonist Synesius wrote his essay *On Dreams*. Synesius had been a student of Hypatia, the brilliant professor of philosophy at Alexandria. Hypatia was the last of the scholars who had had access to the great Alexandrian Library before it was destroyed by a Christian mob headed by Bishop Theophilus in the year 391. She was later murdered in the most horrendous manner by a similar mob in the year 415. Synesius advised that "one should consult one's bed as one would the Delphic Pythia's tripod"[29] because "The god comes to one's side when one is asleep – this is the whole system of initiation."[30] "This accessibility to all makes divination [by dreams] very humane for its simple and artless character is worthy of a philosopher and its freedom from violence gives it sanctity."[31] In the midst of those terrible times, Synesius observed: "No tyrant is able to carry out an edict against dreams" and that any attempt to do so is "in opposition to the desires of nature and God."[32]

CHAPTER NINE

Resonance

As a consequence of reading about ancient Egypt and its language, Anna and I were able to develop our understanding of the guidance that we had been provided with through some of our more enigmatic dreams. Why we were not provided by the Dream with all the information we needed is a question which was to be answered by a later dream of Anna's (that I shall discuss in the concluding chapter). As we read about the pharaonic civilization, we became aware of the veneration in which the star Sirius had been held by the ancient Egyptians.

In his introduction to *The Sirius Mystery*, Robert Temple quotes a paragraph from the work of the anthropologists Marcel Griaule and Germaine Dieterlen which initiated his interest in the secret teaching of the Dogon people of Africa: "The starting-point of creation is the star which revolves round Sirius and is actually named the 'Digitaria star'; it is regarded by the Dogon as the smallest and heaviest of all stars; it contains the germs of all things. Its movement on its own axis and around Sirius upholds all creation in space."[1] Temple comments that the "smallest and heaviest of all stars" the Dogon were referring to is the dwarf star Sirius B which does, in fact, orbit around the visible star Sirius; though this was only 'discovered' at the end of the nineteenth century with the aid of a telescope. At the time that Griaule and Dieterlen were writing, this otherwise invisible star was the smallest and heaviest of all stars that modern astronomers had identified.[2] Not only did the Dogon know of the existence of Sirius B, they knew that it has a fifty year orbital cycle around Sirius A and were able to accurately plot the movement of the two stars in relation to each other. Temple demonstrates that this information was known in pre-dynastic Egypt over five thousand years ago (and provides evidence for Dogon cultural heritage being partially derived from that of ancient Egypt).[3] Here, too, is evidence of the remarkable level of knowledge possessed by ancient Egyptian science. The ancient Egyptians identified the visible star, Sirius A, with the goddess Isis and the invisible star, Sirius B, with the god Amun – the Hidden One. This astronomically accurate appellation would seem to be the origin of the Dogon name for Sirius B, Amma.

Mention of Sirius B containing "the germs of all things" brings us into the domain of the instruction in Anna's dream of April 1992: "Believe in the stars and that they directly affect everything that happens to us." That instruction, which we came to see was one of the foundation-stones upon which the great ancient civilizations were built, sowed the seed for our comprehending the nature of human existence. As Giorgio Piccardi said, "Only by understanding the mechanism which connects him to the earth and the sky will man be able to understand his physical and psychic position in the universe today. In the context of the universe as it is, man will find his natural role."[4]

Man is made of the stuff of the universe. Professor George Wald, Nobel Laureate, explains: "We living things are a late outgrowth of the metabolism of our Galaxy. The carbon that enters so importantly into our composition was cooked in the remote past in a dying star. From it at lower temperatures nitrogen and oxygen were formed. These, our indispensable elements, were spewed out into space in the exhalations of red giants and such stellar catastrophes as supernovae, there to be mixed with hydrogen, to form eventually the substance of the sun and the planets, and ourselves. The waters of the ancient seas set the pattern of ions in our blood. The ancient atmosphere moulded our metabolism."[5] Thus, as the philosopher Oliver Reiser emphasised, "our bodies and our brains came ultimately from the super-novae that exploded far out in space many billions of years ago."[6]

In quantum theory, as David Bohm states, "One is led to a new notion of unbroken wholeness which denies the classical idea of analyzability of the world into separately and independently existing parts... We have reversed the usual classical notion that the independent 'elementary parts' of the world are the fundamental reality, and that the various systems are merely particular contingent forms and arrangements of these parts. Rather, we say that inseparable quantum interconnectedness of the whole universe is the fundamental reality, and that relatively independently behaving parts are merely particular and contingent forms within this whole."[7] And so, as the astrophysicist Fred Hoyle recounts: "Present-day developments in cosmology are coming to suggest rather insistently that everyday conditions could not persist but for the distant parts of the Universe, that all our ideas of space and geometry would become entirely invalid if the distant parts of the Universe were taken away. Our everyday experience even down to the smallest details seems to be so closely integrated to the grand-scale features of the Universe that it is well-nigh impossible to contemplate the two being separated."[8] Hence, our being instructed by the Dream to "Believe in the stars and that they directly affect everything that happens to us." This gives a very different perspective on the forces which determine Man's behaviour than that proposed by contemporary psychology and psychotherapy.

The ancient Egyptians were fully aware of and engaged with the multilateral determination of events on Earth. Lamy states that a "characteristic of the Pharaonic mentality is an appreciation of simultaneity. This is expressed in various ritual representations – encountered chiefly in the temples – by the superimposition in a single image of several points of view and moments of time."[9] As an example, Lamy cites the calendrical system of the ancient Egyptians: "This system is comparable to no other, for it is neither exclusively stellar nor solar nor lunar nor seasonal, but incorporates all these cycles in a simultaneity which seems inconceivable to us."[10]

However, Western science has made steps towards observing and understanding the phenomena that the pharaonic world knew to be intrinsic to Man's existence. For instance, in 1940, Edward Dewey, who had been Chief Economic Analyst of the United States Department of Commerce, organized the Foundation for the Study of Cycles; the board members of which included such eminent figures as Julian Huxley. Dewey writes: "evidence is mounting that we are surrounded by cyclic forces, of which, as yet, we know almost nothing... [man] and his universe vibrate in rhythms that are regular and at least partially predictable and are caused by a force or forces still unknown and possibly uncontrollable by him."[11] The Foundation for the Study of Cycles has accumulated a wide-ranging body of evidence that demonstrates the considerable extent to which human behaviour is determined by such cycles. From this, one can understand why Reiser concluded that Mind is *"a resonance process."*[12]

By far the most significant figure in this area was Musès, who "was the first mathematician to discover and develop the higher arithmetics of hypernumbers beyond the square root of minus one", and has been described as "one of the pioneers of new thinking in science in the twentieth century."[13] A world authority on human consciousness, Musès developed the science of 'Chronotopology', the study of the interactive connectedness of time. Musès stresses that "contrary to scientific views prevailing from the seventeenth through at least the early twentieth centuries, it appears that the concept of mechanical, billiard-ball, or impact causation is not the way causation actually proceeds in nature. Gross appearances to the contrary, all causation is finally resonant, although sudden resonant perturbations can generate as much gross impact as ever is needed. But the point is that, in principle, causality is a phenomenon of resonances or anti-resonances."[14] He explains: "Nineteenth century materialism, still hanging on in the twentieth, is seen to be inadequate... the naively mechanistic billiard-ball materialism that anachronistically still tyrannizes over great portions of school-taught biology, psychology, and sociology – simply becomes discredited scientifically and can no longer be reiterated with impunity in scientific treatises worthy of the name... Such regurgitations are now not merely *démodé* but wrong... The greatest fallacies of all for humanity are, of course, its psychological and emotional ones."[15]

Musès states there is "an all-embracing super-system of resonances guiding the cosmos"; and adds that "the theoretical breakthroughs and experimental confirmations of quantum physics put the concept of a *resonant universe* on a new, firm, and ubiquitous basis."[16]

Musès cites the old Samkhya doctrine of India, "whose roots very probably go back to ancient traditions in the Near East", that "posited a universal vibratory... substance termed *akasha*, which was conceived as a collection of innumerable nodes of vibration, thus quantizing space in at least three-dimensional lattice of micro-stationary states."[17] The Indian sage Patanjali "carried the idea one step further into a theory of qualitative time."[18] Musès explains: "The ordinary use of the time variable t is nothing but a linearly degenerate notion of time. We must do better than that to have a science adequate to the richness of experience. We must begin to think in terms of qualitative time, a time with inherent and shifting possibilities of change within its extension of duration, irrespective of the use or non-use we make of those possibilities. This view opens up a systemic approach to problems otherwise insoluble with a contentless and merely quantitive 't'."[19]

Manifestation of any particular aspect of a chronosystem (time system) occurs when "situations are in either the same phase or in harmonically related phases that permit resonance" with the "chronotopological modalities (time waves)."[20] "to regard individual phenomena thus: not as isolated but as all deeply interrelated was also the point of view that reigned supreme in the scientific thought of Alexandria at the time when it was the center of the profound transcultural synthesis epitomized in the Great Library there... The crown jewel of Alexandrian thought was the doctrine of the *ordered interrelatedness* of all things by the power of what was then termed *sympátheia* for want of a more technical terminology. To render this far-reaching thought into our analytic, scientific terms requires the sophisticated concept of holistic systems governed principally by the affinities (or antipathies) generated by resonances (or anti-resonances) in waves of some sort, i.e. in time periodicities, together with their cognate space periodicities."[21] Savary, Berne and Williams note that "According to Synesius [who, as a student of Hypatia, was steeped in Alexandrian thought]... the entire universe is a unity, and dreams express the meaning of the universe, including our relationship to it and to each other."[22]

So, the Dream, which, as Synesius said, is the means by which Mankind can maintain its relationship with the cosmos, is a cosmopsychophysiological process (or, to use Musès term, a chronopsychophysiological process). It is for this reason that "Synesius... believe[d] – as did almost everybody in late antiquity – in the efficacy of dream interpretation as a sound method of reading the future."[23] By means of the Dream, the human organism receives messages from the cosmos which convey the changing pattern of forces at any particular time. In the natural state, the organism then makes adjustments within itself and/or in its relationship to others and its environment in order to be aligned with the changes that are, and that will be, occurring. Hence, the importance of considering the relation between 'thought' and 'ought' – an instruction which is not only a moral injunction but, when acted upon, the means of survival.

In view of the foregoing, one can understand why the instruction to consider the relation between 'thought' and 'ought' was followed two months later, in July of 1995, by a dream which consisted of my being told:

"Wear the Tao."

The word 'Tao' is usually translated as meaning the 'Way'; and, as Thomas Cleary says, may also "mean the matrix, structure, and reality of the universe itself."[24] Hence, D.C. Lau writes that "'the One' is, in fact, very often used as another name for the '*tao*'."[25] Fung Yu-Lan, who speaks of the 'Tao' as the 'Great Way', observes that "Taoism as a philosophy teaches the doctrine of following nature."[26] "It is at once", says Wing-Tsit Chan, "the beginning of all things and the way in which all things pursue their course. When this Tao is possessed by individual things, it becomes [their] character or virtue. The ideal life for the individual, the ideal order for society, and the ideal type of government are all based on it and guided by it."[27] As Reiser (who originally named his approach to philosophy 'Scientific Humanism', but subsequently renamed it 'Cosmic Humanism') said, "'man is not alone'; that is to say, there is something in the vast cosmos that answers to, or resonates with, the fundamental tones of man's inner nature. Man's privilege, therefore, is to cooperate with cosmic guiding fields of force to stimulate his own self-evolution toward higher forms of consciousness."[28] That, of course, is the lesson Anna and I were being taught through avision. In this dream, the word 'wear' is used figuratively in the sense of "To carry about with one in one's heart, mind, or memory; to have as a quality or attribute."[29]

The underlying unity of the Eastern and Western traditions was presented to us in a dream of mine in February of 1997:

> It is explained to me that the Dream is the Tao.

Since the Dream is the Tao, one can rephrase the statement of Wing-Tsit Chan to read: 'The Dream is at once the beginning of all things and the way in which all things pursue their course. When the Dream is realized by individual beings, it becomes their character and virtue. The ideal life of the individual, the ideal order for society and the ideal type of government are all based on it and guided by it.' This is the principal upon which Pythagoras, Parmenides and Epimenides based their lives. It is in keeping with this principal that, as White stated, "Assyrians, Egyptians, Hebrews, Greeks and Romans (to mention only the Mediterranean world) were all profoundly convinced of the significance of men's dreams. Indeed, the gravest personal, political and economic decisions often rested upon their interpretation." It is also why Plato held that those in charge of the making of laws should follow the guidance given through dreams and insisted that no detail imparted through avision be altered.

One can see, then, that the instruction that "the Dream is the Tao" is another formulation of the instruction that "Dreams are the Law of Nature"; and this is consonant with Joseph Needham's summation that Taoists define the Tao as the Order of Nature.[30] This definition combines both dream statements; for, since the Dream is the Tao and the Dream is the Law of Nature, it follows that the Tao is the Law of Nature. Again, one cannot but marvel at the formal elegance of the process of instruction through avision – at the way in which profound issues are deftly presented by means of the simple and the easy.

Here, too, the Dream was both teaching us about itself and, as we were to learn when I read *The Shambhala Guide to Taoism* by Eva Wong, providing us with the foundation of the Taoist experience. Wong recounts how "By the twelfth century BCE, in the early part of the Chou dynasty, kings and nobles employed shamans as advisers, diviners, and healers."[31] The "shamans of ancient China laid down the foundations of Taoism."[32] A central function of the shaman was the interpretation of dreams: "Dreams are considered to be carriers of omens, and one of the shaman's tasks is to interpret these messages from the spirits. In ancient China, the dream was also linked to the shaman's journey to the other realms. The ceremony of summoning the souls of the dead was conducted by a shaman called 'the dream master'."[33] From these origins emerged Divinational Taoism: "Divinational Taoism believes that seeing and understanding the patterns of the universe will help us live in harmony with change, and to live in harmony with change is to live according to the principles of the Tao."[34] After describing how certain Taoist practices arose out of the shamanic journey, Wong continues: "An even greater influence on Taoism came through shamanism's impact on the philosophy of Lao-tzu and Chuang-tzu. This influence is often unrecognized."[35] "Lao-tzu, the founder of the philosophy of Taoism, lived in a society that had a strong shamanic culture."[36] It is simply not possible to completely grasp the nature of that philosophy unless one appreciates the significance that the Dream had in the life of Lao Tzu.

Musès demonstrates that "The Chinese doctrine... reflects Egypt."[37] In his exposition of ancient Chinese shamanic theurgy, he points out that, as in ancient Egypt, "Much of this process had to do with perceiving higher light associated with certain stars, in particular with the seven stars of the Northern Dipper [the Great Bear], named similarly in Chinese, and their two hidden celestial control centers."[38] These, Musès identifies as Sirius A and B. He emphasises that, in both cultures, "the ultimate basis for the method is based on the feminine aspect of divinity;"[39] that is, upon the star of Isis – the Goddess of avision.

The practice of incubation, of sleeping in a cave in order to have a dream, constituted one of the decisive moments of initiation in the secret tradition of Taoism before the monasteries were destroyed during the Cultural Revolution. Deng Ming-Dao described this initiatory event in the training of his Taoist Master Kwan Saihung. At the famous monastery on Huashan Mountain, Saihung was taken by the Grand Master – by whom he was to be told that he could consult the gods in his dream state[40] – deep into a cave which they journeyed through on a raft along an underground river. "They disembarked at a grotto. Walking to its end, about fifty paces from the water's edge, they came to a large stone couch. The sides were carved with strange anthropomorphic figures and an indecipherable cursive script... The Grand Master directed him into the proper position for dreaming... The Grand Master left. He would return the next morning to bring Saihung back and interpret the vision. Until then Saihung was to sleep, and dream. Everyone who had lain on that couch had had a vision; it was a certainty. The visions revealed different things. Some dreamers learned that they should go no further in ascetic training but should return to society. Others were shown a horrible future crisis they had to face. Some were given a special task. But no matter what came, both the acolyte and his master were bound to accept the omen. In most cases, the personal vision became the lodestone of the adept's life. It was a treasure, a jewel that shone only for him and guided him through the darkness of life."[41]

After the Cultural Revolution, the survival of the Taoist tradition lay in the hands of individual masters such as Wang Liping – the eighteenth generation Transmitter of Dragon Gate Taoism. *Opening the Dragon Gate* is a biographical account of the way in which Wang Liping was prepared from childhood for the duty of maintaining the purity of the teaching of this revered Taoist sect. The Dragon Gate branch continues to be nourished by Taoism's shamanic roots. Thus, "Master Wang Liping considers Taoist theory and practice dealing with dreaming to present the basic nature of the existence of the universe on a higher level."[42] With regard to his everyday life, "Master Wang Liping says that the capacity he normally uses most is thinking in dreaming."[43] When faced with a problem such as "a puzzling ailment that he doesn't know how to treat, or... a question about something he has never studied or encountered... he goes to bed, sets up the topic in his brain, and then dozes off... When he wakes up, he notes the thoughts that occurred in dreaming; this is the answer to the question."[44]

For Taoists, dreams "represent the relationship between humanity and the universe."[45] This was, of course, the same view voiced by Synesius, which the Catholic Church extirpated from Western consciousness. Yet, despite being subject to persecution from many sides over the millennia, the Taoist tradition has been able to retain the knowledge that the Dream is the means by which Mankind is aligned with the "cosmic guiding fields of force."

Reiser held that "The first goal of man should be to develop the syntropic relations between man and the earth, and the earth and the sun, in a manner that will perfect the configurations of man's mind and brain for resonance with the solar system dynamics. *What I am saying is that the development of human consciousness... is toward the evocation of a complete (cosmic) consciousness.*"[46] ('Syntropic' is an anatomical term denoting the arrangement of a number of parts of a body that are pointing in the same direction.)

For Reiser "cosmic consciousness is sun consciousness."[47] However, as Schwaller de Lubicz stated with regard to ancient Egypt, "In the spirit of the temple, Sirius plays the role of the great central fire for our sun."[48] This concurs with Musès' description of Sirius A and B as the "celestial control centers." Rodney Collin explains: "The diameter of the Earth... is one-millionth that of the Solar System; but the diameter of the Solar System is only perhaps one forty-millionth that of the Milky Way. When in our own system we find such relationships, it is not between sun and planets, but between sun and *satellites* of planets. That is to say, by analogy of scale and mass, we should expect the Solar System to be revolving about some greater entity, which in its turn was revolving about the centre of the Milky Way; just as the Moon revolves about the Earth, which in turn revolves about the Sun. What and where is this 'sun' of our Sun?... the most brilliant object in the heavens, after those within the Solar System itself, is of course the double star Sirius. This consists of an immense radiant sun, 26 times more brilliant than our own, which circles in a fifty year period with a white dwarf as big as Jupiter and 5,000 times denser than lead. The mass of the light star being two and a half times that of our Sun, and that of the dark one equivalent to it, the influence upon the Solar System of this starry pair, which lie at less than nine light-years remove, must certainly far exceed that of any other extra-solar body that we can think of. By physical distance as by radiance and mass a Sirian system would seem in some way to fill the excessive gap between the cosmoses of the Solar System and the Milky Way. Indeed, the distance from the Sun to Sirius – one million times the distance from the Earth to the Sun – falls naturally into the scale of cosmic relationships mentioned, and provided nineteenth century astronomy with an excellent unit of celestial measurement, the siriometer, now unfortunately abandoned. No astronomical data contradict the possibility that the Solar System circles about Sirius, in the course of the latter's circuit of the Milky Way, as Kant believed... As the ancient Egyptians observed, the apparent motion of Sirius – measured by its rising with the sun – is a little less than that of the apparent motion of all the other stars, which is recognised in the precession of the equinoxes. Whereas the general star mass rises twenty minutes later on a given day each year, Sirius rises only eleven minutes later. This corresponds to the difference in apparent motion between points outside a circle and the centre of the circle itself, when observed from a moving point on its circumference – just as, in a landscape seen from a moving car, far and near objects seem to run past each other. From such an observation we have good reason to believe that our Sun does circle about Sirius."[49] Thus, for the ancient Egyptians, Sirius was the "Queen of Heaven" – "the Star-Form of the Goddess."[50]

Anna and I came to realize that the requirement for us to acknowledge the Sirius system as the central sun of our lives has, from the outset, been one of the principal themes of our experience of avision; though our early dreams concerning Sirius were conveyed in a symbolic language that has, in individual instances, taken us as many as fifteen years to comprehend. The most important of these early dreams was one of Anna's in June of 1992. Such was the significance of the message given to us in this dream that (uniquely in our experience) it was presaged, on the night before, by another dream emphasising its status. The first dream of this pair was as follows:

> Anthony and I are in the countryside. The sun is shining. Suddenly, we come across a strange path and are drawn into another dimension where there is heavy mist. Holding hands, we are propelled by an invisible force along the path, across a long, narrow ridge and, finally, over the edge of a cliff. We land unhurt on damp earth and rotting leaves. Here, there is no mist. Before us, is a grassy plain upon which stands an ancient, stone ziggurat. We are to wait at the bottom for something of great value and import to be sent down to us, as down a helter-skelter.

A ziggurat was a Babylonian or Assyrian seven-staged, pyramidal tower in which the stages, arranged in a step-like sequence, represented the seven planetary spheres. There are several correspondences between this dream and Anna's dream of the ivory tower, the most obvious being the spiral pattern of movement. In the earlier dream, we ascend the spiral staircase in order to arrive at the top, where we encounter Pegasus and the Unicorn; in this dream, we are to wait at the bottom of the ziggurat for something of great value and import to make its spiral descent. As I have mentioned, the 'something of great value and import' was Anna's dream of the next night:

> Anthony and I perform an Indian dance upon a stage before an audience. Anthony is behind me. It is a ritual dance which culminates in our merging so as to look as though we are one person.

Though aware at the time that we were depicted as performing the Dance of Siva – the Lord of the Dance – that is performed at the heart of the universe and within the heart of Man, it was only when we read Temple's book that we understood what that Dance signifies; for, the Dogon say that Sirius B, whom they call Amma, created the cosmos by means of a spinning dance.[51] Confirmation of this identification came further on in Temple's book when we learnt that the Hindu equivalent of Isis (Sirius A) is Isi, whose partner is Isvara (Sirius B).[52] Isvara is the name of Siva as the Supreme Being, the God of Love ('Is' meaning 'Supreme Spirit').[53] Though, as a result of patriarchal convention, Siva is referred to as male, Stella Kramrisch explains that "Śiva is one who divides himself into god and goddess, Śiva and Śivā."[54] Thus, Siva is both Isi and Isvara. As Nataraja, Siva "dances the cosmos into existence, upholds its existence, and dances it out of existence."[55] "the Ānanda Tāṇḍva, Śiva's 'dance of bliss in the hall of consciousness', is Śiva's dance within the heart of man."[56] In truth, the Dance of Siva at the heart of the cosmos and the Dance of Siva within the heart of Man are one and the same. Full realization of this leads to "the union of the *ātman* [the soul] and Īśvara."[57] Anna's dream is of 'great value and import' because it portrays the pattern of our relationship as being inextricably linked to, and a manifestation of, the relationship between Sirius A and B – of the male and female aspects of Siva, the God of Love. It is this link which was further propounded in the beautiful poem that was given to Anna in her dream of August 1993, which I recounted in chapter one:

> Harnessed to one another,
> As Earth and Moon,
> Through measureless depths

And countless unfoldings we move
In undulating dance
While songs of love
Flow from our hearts.

This dream, in which 'we move in undulating dance', 'through measureless depths and countless unfoldings', develops the imagery of both Anna's dream of August 1990, with its phrase "The more intimate, The more infinite", and her dream of June 1992, in which we perform the Indian dance. The image of our being 'harnessed to one another, as Earth and Moon' corresponds to that of Sirius A and B as they move together through the cosmos; and the dream emphasises the influence of their dynamic relationship upon us.

In her dream of the Dance of Siva, Anna takes the part of Sirius A, while I take that of Sirius B – the Hidden One. This facilitated our correlating the Dance with the Sothic pattern. The identification of ourselves with the respective stars is not gender related but, as I will demonstrate in a later chapter, is indicative of a specific interplay of Yin and Yang. As 'we merge so as to look as though we are one person', we represent Ardhanarisvara, Siva who is half man and half woman, both god and goddess "in self-contained fulfillment of deity."[58] Here, the statement "The more intimate, The more infinite" is revealed as the ultimate transcendent possibility eternally realized within the God of Love. From this, it naturally follows that Love is the original religion. It is notable that the phrase "Our altar One another", which follows this guidance, appears in the *Liṅga Purāna* in the statement that the goddess, who is the mother of the universe, is the "altar of the god."[59] However, I would venture that the Dream, with its emphasis upon mutuality, re-presents the teaching of the *Liṅga Purāna* in its original form.

Fourteen years after her dream of the ziggurat, we obtained a copy of Musès' *The Lion Path* and were, at last, able to understand the symbolic meaning of that ancient edifice. Musès writes of "the old Chaldean priests evidently knowing in addition to the usual seven bodies, an eighth planet (Uranus) symbolized by an eighth and underground chamber of their seven-storied ziggurat-temples – where priest and priestess re-enacted the sacred marriage (hierogamy) of God and Goddess."[60] By 'the sacred marriage', he means the time when Sirius A and B "celebrate their fifty year *hieros gamos* or holy union."[61] This moment was enacted by Anna and myself in her dream when, at the culmination of the Dance of Siva, we merged so as to look as though we were one. The spiral movement referred to in Anna's dream of the ziggurat is, therefore, representational of the energy arising from the union of Sirius A and B as it moves around the planetary spheres before it is experienced by ourselves through avision.

It is often the case that the most meaningful words in the English language contain within themselves hidden treasures that lie like jewels waiting to be discovered. They seem to have been shaped in a time of sparkling intellects when words were appreciated for the skill with which manifold meanings were contained within their structure. Such a word is 'avis', meaning 'advice', which forms the root of 'avision', 'advice received through a dream', and is comprised of the letters of 'Siva' in reverse. In this way, the four letters function as a rebus which conveys that avis emanates from Siva. Since dreams arise during sleep, the Sanskrit root of 'Siva' means 'sleep'. As I mentioned earlier, in the Vedic literature the same word, 'svapna', meant 'sleep', 'to dream' and denoted the deity. The direct connection between Siva, the Lord of Sleep, and avision is inherent in the god's name: in Sanskrit, 'Siva' means the 'Auspicious One'.[62] 'Auspicious' means 'ominous';[63] that is, "of the nature of an omen, serving to foretell the future, presaging events to come."[64] Similarly, an early meaning of 'advice' was 'forethought':[65] "an anticipation or forecast."[66] Yet another of the worlds within worlds of meanings unfolds when it is known that much of the foregoing is contained in the Old English 'si' which meant 'to have seen'.[67] The 'vis' of 'avis' means 'strength',[68] directly related to 'wis' meaning 'certainty', 'to instruct, to teach, to guide and to show (the way)'[69] – hence, 'wisdom'. As one turns 'avis' around in one's mind different facets of meaning appear and merge and, ultimately, re-emerge reflecting Man's role within creation as they do so.

An earlier form of Siva was Rudra. Kramrisch writes "Rudra is *śiva*"[70] and speaks of "Rudra-Śiva".[71] She expands upon the subject saying that, like Siva, Rudra is both male and female; the dual aspect of Rudra's nature being represented by the epithet 'the bull who is also a cow'.[72] "Rudra in the sky is Sirius, star of stars, most exalted among them... In his most ancient figure he was the Dog Star," "watchdog of the sky"[73] and "guardian of the... cosmos."[74] Rudra is the equivalent of the ancient Egyptian Maat, the divine order; the affinity between the two civilizations being demonstrated by the fact that in Hindu the "Great principle... the ordering intelligence of the cosmos" is known as 'mahat',[75] Mahat being a name of Rudra.[76] Monier-Williams adds that 'mahat' means sacred knowledge,[77] of which my dream instruction from Ganesh regarding the Law of Maat is an example.

The equivalence of Mahat and Maat explains why an Indian god – Ganesh – instructed me in the ancient Egyptian Law of Maat. Through the Dream, Anna and I were being shown that there had once been a time when Mankind existed as an undivided whole, with all cultures united by a common understanding of Man's place within the cosmos. So, the destruction of the ancient Egyptian religion (which culminated in the Catholic Church closing the Temple of Isis at Philae and murdering the incumbent priesthood in the year 535) did not eliminate knowledge of the Law of Maat, for it continued to be preserved in the Indian culture.

It will be remembered that, in a later dream, one of our children was talking with a statue of Ganesh. This statue was of the size one would expect to find in an Indian household. Then, three days later, Ganesha appeared as a massive elephant. As a result of the information we had now acquired about the relative sizes of Sirius A and B, we realized that in these dreams Ganesh was the personification of Sirius B and Ganesha of the much larger Sirius A.

The identification of Ganesh/a with Sothis is confirmed by Musès who, writing under the pseudonym of Kenneth Demarest, provides an illustration from his own library in which the trunk of the elephant deity is depicted inside a yogi, representing an "integral part of the fiery Winged Power he is evoking."[78] He makes reference to the fact that 'Ganesh/a' literally means "Leader of the Host," an epithet which refers to the leader "of the stars and all manifest things"[79] – precisely the role which the ancient Indians, Egyptians and Chinese identified with Sirius. Musès, as I shall discuss in a later chapter, proves that the symbol of winged power represented power received from Sirius. Thus, bearing in mind that Mahat was a name of Rudra and that Rudra was Sirius, it follows that Ganesh, when instructing me in the Law of Maat, was actually instructing me about himself.

I should add that something about the function of Sirius A can be inferred by observing that it was Ganesha who moved me to the spot that Ganesh had instructed us to journey to.

In the dream, Ganesha brought my third eye into contact with her own before demonstrating that I have to act upon the instructions received through avision. The third eye is the mark of Siva;[80] that is, of Sirius, the Monitor of the Universe. The Bozo people of Mali, cousins of the Dogon, refer to Sirius B as the Eye Star. Temple rightly suggests that the Egyptian hieroglyph of an eye represented Sirius B. In addition, the Bozo describe Sirius A as 'seated'; the hieroglyph of a throne, which was the emblem of Isis, represented Sirius A.[81]

A process corresponding to the gesture made by Ganesha in my dream was identified by Musès as being represented in the second shrine of the tomb of Tutankhamun. There, "Star-Power Energy" is shown entering through the forehead of a mummiform figure. Musès points out that the ancient Egyptian word 'sba' meant both 'star' and 'door'; and, with the determinative for 'walking' (which also appears in the text), denotes "passing through a star-door (or time door)." He explains that, in the text, "the *ba* or winged soul shown under this glyph... indicates that it was the soul's passage through these doors that effected the... transformation or metamorphosis."[82] Musès argued that one should understand "the external mummifying process as symbol and, later, a corruption of an inner regenerative process;"[83] thus, the process illustrated in the text originally involved a living human being rather than a dead one.

The passing through a star door was depicted in my dream by Ganesha placing me at the entrance to a school, the door of which I then passed through. I say this because 'Sba' was also a name of Sirius B, the feminine 'Sba-t' being that of Sirius A; and both 'sba' and 'sba-t' meant 'teaching, training, learning, instruction, education and wisdom'. The school represents the education that is provided by Sirius A and B. Thus, the Bambara people, who are also cousins of the Dogon, call Sirius A and B 'the two stars of knowledge'.[84]

The identification of Sirius with knowledge is also to be found in the Hindu tradition where "Śiva... is the master of gnosis"[85] who "frees... the 'social animal', from the fetters of conventions;"[86] the "eternal lord of redeeming knowledge"[87] who "liberates... from ignorance."[88]

Such was the identification of Sirius with the Dream that, in ancient Egyptian, the same word 'upsh' meant both 'star' and 'dream'.[89] 'Up' meant 'leader or chief';[90] so, astronomically, 'upsh' denoted Sirius as the 'Leader of the Stars'.

In my dream of December 1995, the statement "He has recognised God when he has recognised his dreams, for God and his dreams are one." was read to a small group of people who were aware that God is a separate entity from Man whose presence is experienced by Mankind in dreams. Once one knows of the relationship between Sirius and the Dream, the situation presented by the above dream becomes entirely comprehensible. At the same time, this dream, particularly when combined with that of the Dance of Siva, presents a radical reformulation of the concept of Mind, because the Dream is conveying that the central location of Mind is outside the human body in the Sirius system.

Reiser, who describes his position as pantheistic, states: "In Pantheism, 'God' is man's name for the Guiding Field or Cosmic Imagination by means of which undifferentiated energy is focused in nodal points in space-time, subsequently to evolve under the influence of guiding fields on higher levels."[91] In order to avoid misunderstanding, Reiser chose to employ the term 'Cosmic Lens' rather than 'God'. Having explained that, according to Enrico Fermi and Bruno Rossi, the galactic spiral is a large cyclotron (an apparatus for accelerating charged atomic particles), Reiser goes on to say that "In the Cyclic-Creative cosmology the spiral galaxy has an Eye or Lens through which the Cosmic Imagination visualizes matter (atomic hydrogen) into existence... [It is] the focusing agent for concentrating cosmic field energy into particles."[92] "Life, mind and consciousness are manifestations of the force-fields."[93] "Thus the Cosmic Imagination... forms molecules, crystals, cells, many-celled organisms, up to man himself."[94] *"The Cosmic Lens is the Eye of God."*[95] This corresponds to the Dogon saying that Sothis B, the Eye Star, creates the cosmos by means of a spinning dance.

Significantly, Reiser, who was held in high regard by Einstein, arrived at a theory of the nature of human consciousness quite different from the prevailing view, that consciousness is a function of the brain only, concluding that "consciousness reflects a bipolar relationship."[96] Reiser suggests that "there is a relation between the galactic [hydrogen] plasma field, the ionosphere... and the so-called alpha, beta, theta, and delta waves in the human body."[97] Support for this is provided by the work of Dr. Harold Burr, emeritus Professor of Anatomy at Yale Medical School, who stated that the pattern of the human brain is determined at birth by just such a complex magnetic field and that the dynamics of that field continue to govern one's brain throughout life. Burr declared that the human central nervous system is the most refined receptor of electro-magnetic energies to be found in Nature.[98]

Reiser's earlier-cited, suggestion that "The first goal of man should be to develop the syntropic relation between man and the earth, and the earth and the sun, in a manner that will perfect the configuration of man's mind and brain for resonance with the solar system dynamics", if extended to include the configuration between the sun and the Sirius system, succinctly encompasses the challenge ahead for Mankind in the twenty-first century. In order for this to be effected, it has to be accepted that Man's nature is primarily receptive and that the primary purpose of Mankind is to act in accordance with the guidance received through dreams. Conventional psychotherapy necessarily fails in this regard, since it conceives of the dreaming mind as a discrete entity which exists outside of its cosmic context. Reiser's definition of God as "man's name for the Guiding Field" concurs with my dream instruction that God and the Dream are one. Thus, one can think of the Dream as that part of the Guiding Field of the Cosmos of which one can become conscious during sleep.

Since the Dream is a manifestation of the Guiding Field, it follows that, as my dream instructed me, life unfolds along a pre-existing sequence of dreams and that, in the area where mind and matter meet, each dream acts as a firm link that holds its enactment fast. The instruction that "The Dream is the Tao" provides a formulation of the actuality, which teaches that all dreams are to be considered a manifestation of the Tao. Support for the ancient identification of the Dream with the Tao is given by Musès, who writes: "To the ancient China of Lao-tse's inspiration, *tao* as a verb (as in the second use of the character in the first sentence of the *Tao Te Ching*) meant 'to define by following a sequence, path or road of meaningful symbols'."[99]

One can substitute Musès concept of time waves for the Tao and say that some dreams are a direct revelation of the qualitative content of time waves emanating from Sirius whilst others depict the response of the dreamer's psychobiological system to the influence of those forces.

That the ancient Egyptians thought in terms of time waves is attested. Musès states: "On a wall in the tomb of Seti I (19 Dynasty, Thebes, *ca.* 1300 B.C.E.) is shown the symbol of the power of all change and transformation (Khepera) being carried along by... a future-interacting wave... stylized by the old cosmologist-priests in serpentine form. This highly nonlinear wave form reappears constantly in ancient Egyptian symbolizations of the wave-like, serpentine time-process."[100] Support for the view that the ancient Egyptians conceived of time waves as the medium by which avision is transmitted is provided by the fact that their god Thoth, Lord of the Divine Word, was both "the master of chronology"[101] who "knew the future as well as the past"[102] and "the lord of all knowledge and understanding"[103] who was "the reason and the mental powers of the god, and... the means by which [the god's] will was translated into speech... [and] carried into effect."[104]

In antiquity, nothing was more important than putting into effect the will of the gods. In practice, this meant ensuring that the actions of Mankind were in alignment with the forces that were operating within the galaxy. So long as the Dream continues to be regarded as entirely the product of processes operating within the individual, it will be impossible for the full alignment of Mankind with the galactic forces to be restored.

In the ancient world, the fact that ideas are released from Sirius was graphically depicted in symbolic form. An example of this is to be found in the Inner Sanctum of Luxor Temple. There, the iconography is dominated by representations of the god Amun, in the form of Min, with an erect phallus. Wilhelm's definition of the 'Tao' as that "which releases the seed of ideas into existence"[105] corresponds to ancient Egyptian texts which refer to "holy emanations proceeding from Sirius... which 'vivify... gods and men', and are a pouring out of the seed of the soul,"[106] revealing the profundity of what was represented by the phallus.

Wilhelm explains that the word 'Dao' ('Tao') "is written as a combination of the symbols for 'head' and 'to go'... It means 'the way that leads to a set goal', 'the direction', 'the prescribed way'. It also means 'to talk' and 'to lead'. It seems that the symbol was first used to indicate the astronomic course of the stars."[107] It is interesting to note the correlation between Tao being that "which releases the seed of ideas into existence" as well as meaning 'to talk' and the ancient Egyptians stating that 'to tell one's dreams' is 'to renew life'. Telling one's dreams is another stage in the fructifying process following upon the release of the seed. O'Flaherty provides the valuable information that, in India, "the same verb (*srj*)... encompasses the concepts of seminal emission (making people), creation (making worlds), speaking (making words), imagining (making ideas), and dreaming (making images)."[108]

I shall, in the next chapter, have more to say about the symbolism of that which releases the seed of ideas, since it is a key to the ancient Mysteries. It remains for me, in this chapter, to demonstrate the considerable benefits that are to be gained from applying a chronotopological analysis to one's experience of avision.

In the opening chapter of *The Lion Path* ('The Lion Path' being Musès' reconstruction of an ancient Egyptian process of regeneration and transformation), Musès, having observed that "The standard religions, Western and Eastern, seem more and more worn or bankrupt and have no useable answers for the world's situation", goes on to suggest "perhaps there is a ray of hope in the most ancient teachings recorded by mankind and also in the stars."[109] He then proceeds to a discussion of the significance of the god Pluto, followed by an account of the orbit of the planet of that name. In 1978, Pluto "crossed *within* the path of Neptune, something no other planet can ever do – cross within the orbit of the next nearer planet to the Sun. But Pluto so crosses, and then is nearer to the Sun (and hence the Earth) than is Neptune, between 1979 and 1999. During this time, Pluto makes its closest approach to Sun and Earth in 2½ centuries; and from 1984 to 1994 is in its own zodiacal sector or sign of Scorpio – the sector classically allocated to Death and Transfiguration... Pluto conjoined the Sun for the first time in Scorpio in late October 1984, so that the years from then to perihelion would be filled with increasing Plutonian power as the crescendo builds up. A time for some ultimate initiation, one could surmise... It is during these years that certain resonant energies are flowing in time and Pluto is simply the space indicator of them – the needle on the ammeter, so to speak, that indicates the flow of an otherwise invisible current of power."[110] This greatly interested us because, from 1984 onwards, both Anna and I began to have an increasing number of experiences, both in dreams and in waking reality, which concerned people who were either about to die or already dead. I made reference to some of mine in my first book but, until reading Musès' account, we had no means of explaining why this course of events unfolded at the time that it did. Musès goes on to say "What is rare and hence striking here is that not only does Pluto then most closely approach Earth and Sun, but also passes through the Scorpio sector of the earth's orbit and not only that, but achieves a rare and precise synchrony with the periastron of Sirius B, the Dark Companion – the time (April 1994) when Sôthis [Sirius A] and... Sopdu [Sirius B] celebrate their fifty-year *hieros gamos* or holy union. Such close timing between the solar system (Sun, Earth, Pluto and Neptune) and the Sirius or sothic star system occurs but once in some ninety thousand years, giving some inkling of the stunning rarity of the evolutionary opportunity for humanity during the last two decades of the twentieth century."[111]

Musès provided the dates of a series of cycles of opportunity during which one could meditate so as to be aligned with these energies, thereby facilitating their having a transforming effect – the last such 'window' occurring in March of 1989. I mention this because it was in March of 1989 that Anna had her dream of the ivory tower with which this book begins. In that dream, our ascending the spiral staircase depicted our forthcoming alignment, through avision, with the spiralling stars of Sirius. Anna, being dressed in white, represented alignment with the visible Sirius A, the brightest star in the heavens; whilst I, being dressed in black, represented alignment with the invisible Sirius B. This pattern reappeared in the dream of the Dance of Siva in which Anna, by dancing in front, represented Sirius A; whilst I, being hidden behind her, represented Sirius B. The Unicorn, as a "phallic horse deity,"[112] was a personification of 'that which releases the seed' – Sirius B. Pegasus, who represented divine inspiration through dreams, is generally identified as a male horse. However, in her dream, Anna had believed Pegasus to be the female consort of the male Unicorn. We later learnt that "Pegasus had archaic, matriarchal origins" and, in early Greece, appeared in female form.[113] Pegasus was said to have sprung from the "wise blood of the Moon-goddess Medusa, who embodied the principle of *medha*, the Indo-European root word for female wisdom."[114] Thus, in the dream, Pegasus was the equine personification of Sirius A.

The mythological statement that Pegasus sprang from the 'wise blood' of the moon is a reference to the transformational Sirian energy which Musès brilliantly identified as being associated with the moon cycle and as being most accessible in the period after the full moon. (I shall expand on the subjects of 'wise blood' and 'the association of the moon with Sirius' in later chapters.) The full moon is an important feature in Anna's dream and the transformational effect of the Sirian energy which is manifest as the moon wanes is enacted by Pegasus and the Unicorn being transformed into dolphins. Musès specifically makes reference to dolphins as being an ancient symbol of the process of Sirian regeneration.[115] Thus, the transformational process that Anna and I were undergoing was laid out for us by means of a wonderfully economic use of Sirian symbolism.

It was also in March of 1989 that Sirian symbols first appeared in my dreams:

> I am retrieving a book that I had previously placed underwater for safe-keeping. As I do so, a number of images and objects start to appear. I am told that I am being provided with what is needed for the task ahead.

When I awoke, the only image I could remember was △. Knowing nothing about hieroglyphs or the significance of Sirius, I assumed that this symbol was a tepee and that my dream must relate to the Native Americans. I realized I had been mistaken when, on our first visit to Egypt in May of 1997, we came across the symbol in the form of a hieroglyph inscribed in a temple. Then, when I obtained a copy of *The Lion Path* in 2006, I learned that the ancient Egyptian hieroglyph for initiation into the Mysteries was △, meaning 'to be prepared' or 'equipped with appropriate means';[116] which precisely equates to the guidance in my dream that I am being provided with what is needed for the task ahead. Musès writes: "Interestingly, the same glyph was the symbol of the star Sirius and of its presiding divine power, nothing less than that of Goddess spelt with a capital G, She of the Myriad Names... the Dispenser of the Unexpected."[117] Here, Musès is referring to the goddess Isis who dispenses the unexpected through dreams. It will be remembered that "the initiations of Isis [the initiations into the Sirian Mysteries] were given to those priests or laity selected by the goddess through having had significant dreams. Sometimes the dream itself might be the initiation." Walter Burkert provides the information that the initiations of Apuleius (a Roman writer of the second century) into the Mysteries of Isis were "not linked to a fixed festival date but determined by divine command through dreams."[118] In this, one sees the Dream being revered as the supreme "Cosmic Guiding Field of Force" with "the ideal life of the individual and the ideal order of society being based upon it and guided by it."

The Dream presented me with the information that what I needed for the task ahead was to be provided by Sirius. Yet, although it was through this dream that I began to be initiated into the Mysteries of Isis, by presenting that information to me in the form of a hieroglyph which I could not even identify as such, let alone comprehend, the Dream ensured that I underwent the experience of being affected by the Sirian energies unselfconsciously. It was only with hindsight that I understood the nature of the experience I had undergone. The same held true for Anna's dream of the Dance of Siva (in June of 1992), in which 'our merging to look as though we are one person' anticipated the culmination of the 'holy union' of Sirius A and B (in April of 1994). The Dance correlated precisely with the astronomical event with which we had to be aligned. It is consistent with the Dream statement of November 1994, "Our altar One another", that the emphasis of Anna's dreams over that time was upon the way in which the forces involved informed our relationship.

How, then, did the alignment take place? Reiser mentions that the NASA scientist Ottman Stehle accepts the proposition of a connection between the galactic field, the ionosphere and the human brain. Reiser goes on to say of Stehle that "His own further advances inform us that he thinks of 'symbols' as antenna... and he conjectures that they can represent polarized fields exhibiting similarities of energy patterns... on various levels – physical, biological and mental."[119] Musès cites just such a view being held in antiquity by Proclus, who wrote that symbols (such as the Sirian double-triangle or the Dance of Siva) "effect a theurgic unification" (that is, a unification with the divine power). Continuing his exposition of Proclus, Musès explains: "the outcome is not brought about through our limited thought or reasoning. Rather such divine symbols which focus in themselves so many powerful meanings... will be able, far better than any conscious thought of ours, to effect a theurgic unification, because the hidden divine powers on which such symbols draw resonate and are attracted to their appropriate symbolic depictions."[120] Proclus' statement can be applied to both theurgic ritual and dreams. The aim of theurgic ritual was "the incarnation of a divine force either in a material object, such as a statue, or in a human being, the result being a state of prophetic trance."[121] Proclus "believed himself to have been called to philosophy by Athena in a dream."[122] Athena, who was sometimes called Isis Athene by the Egyptians, was the consort of Pan[123] – the dance-master, Sirius B.

However, Musès emphasises that there is a proviso; one which totally accords with the guidance we received through avision: "only when love has become the central priority in one's life, not as mere sentiment but as a universal call and mandate, is one actually ready to begin the path of regenerative metamorphosis."[124] Musès defines the 'cosmic power of Love' as 'universal connectedness';[125] and adds that free choice "is the hallmark of love, by which love in turn is guaranteed since non-voluntary love is a contradiction in terms."[126] He explains that "Love in action (rather than only words) is the sunlight and water which thus enables our higher destinies to grow, plant-like, and blossom in Time, transforming a predatory into a symbiotic ecology and psychology."[127] Elsewhere, Musès recounts: "That entire host of beings who chose *not* to love as their 'freedom' (thus perforce placing others in bondage and suffering) are called in ancient Egyptian tradition 'Children of the Rebellion'."[128] Free choice, therefore, is necessarily the hallmark of avision. This is exemplified by the instruction to "Wear the Tao", since various meanings of the word 'wear' are "To stand the test of experience, criticism etc.", "To bring (a person) gradually into (a habit or disposition)" and "to instil (a view or opinion) gradually into the mind."[129] Thus, we were being told by the Dream to test for ourselves the benefit of acting upon the instruction received through avision. The decision to replace conscious choice by the guidance received through dreams has to be one that is arrived at gradually over a period of time on the basis of all such advice being tested and criticized by oneself until one is clear that "that which dreams through us" is infinitely wiser than we.

Amongst the most abiding memories of "Love in action" I have experienced through avision is the tender concern of the lioness and her powerful, non-aggressive, presence as she waited to ensure that Anna and I were safely where we ought to be after our return from the Sphinx. The identity of that graceful, loving protectress was revealed to us by Musès when he cited a translation from an ancient Egyptian coffin text which reads: *"Mistress of those who truly see, the Lioness, my mother Sôthis prepares my path."*[130] ('Sothis' was the Greek name for the Latin 'Sirius'.) Through my dream, we knew that Musès was right to say that the system he rediscovered was called 'The Lion Path'.

As we became aware of the significance of Sirius, we began to ponder the question as to which of the different Egyptian or other names of the star was the right one for us to be using in this lifetime. I was given the answer, in May of 1998, in a dream:

"The word that you are looking for is 'Sothis'."

CHAPTER TEN

The Earth Womb

I n February of 1997, I dreamt:

> I am horrified as one of my teeth moves in front of another and
> is then positioned at an odd angle; after which the tooth behind
> becomes elongated, before assuming the shape of a phallus.

Some months later, we learnt from Temple that the ancient Egyptian
words for 'tooth' and 'Earth' shared the same hieroglyph, a tilted form
of the hieroglyph for Sirius.[1] It was then apparent that the tooth at
an angle in my dream represented the Earth. Temple illustrates the
hieroglyph for 'Earth' as ▽;[2] and states that the hieroglyphs denoting
'the Goddess Sirius' are 𓂝𓃾 which can, by pun, literally be read as
'serpent's tooth'.[3] I immediately recognised in this illustration the
elongated tooth of my dream, which thus represented Sothis A, before
it assumed the shape of that which releases the seed of ideas into
existence, Sothis B. The hieroglyphs as rendered by Wallis Budge in
his *An Egyptian Hieroglyphic Dictionary* are: ↘ for 'tooth'[4]/'Earth'[5] and
𓏭 for 'Sothis'.[6] In my dream, the tilted tooth (representing the Earth)
and the tooth behind it (representing both Sothis A and B) depicted

the process by which the Earth and Sothis were being aligned within me. By depicting this as taking place within my mouth, the Dream indicated that I was now in the position Musès cites from Utterance 149 of the ancient Egyptian *Book of The Coming Forth Into Day*: "*my language is that of the star Sirius*."[7]

The explanation as to why the hieroglyph that denoted Sothis was used in tilted form to denote the Earth is provided by the work of Hans Cousto, who demonstrated that, if the astronomic period of the precession of the equinox, which is created by the tilt of the Earth's axis, is transposed into a musical tone, then the tone produced is almost identical to that of Sothis A and B combined.[8] Thus, the visual symbol depicts the affinity through resonance between Sothis and the Earth.

The ancient Egyptians understood that, if the life of Man is to be harmonious, it has to be lived in accordance with the Sothic cycle. To this end, they used a Sothic calendar of 1460 years in addition to solar and lunar calendars. As West says, the Sothic year has "its phases and seasons; and an understanding of their implications would allow a civilisation to take measures to promote and enhance those aspects favourable to its own ends... We do not understand those implications, but it seems Egypt did."[9] Any comprehensive science of Man must necessarily take account of the influence of Sothis. The parochial focus of psychology has to expand to encompass the dynamics of Man's cosmic context. This much is clear from the preceding chapter.

The symbolism of the dream of my teeth brought to our attention that the Earth functions as another determinant of Man's mind. We learnt from Reiser: "[The NASA scientist] Stehle notes that we cannot ignore the gravitational waves, which, he surmises, may be in the same general range as the brain waves. Indeed, he even conjectures... perhaps there is some mutual interference of brain waves and gravitational waves; or a resonance between alpha waves and earth's electromagnetic field."[10] Commenting upon Stehle's proposal, Reiser exclaims: "The components of a prodigious and awesome synthesis are staring us in the face."[11]

Having understood, through Temple's book, the symbolism of the dream of my teeth, we realized that this provided a valuable clue as to the meaning of a dream of Anna's from 20th July 1990, which had featured triangular symbols:

> I am with Anthony on a beach. We are exploring the rocks and find an enormous cave, which we enter. Painted on the wall of the cave are three reddish-brown triangles ▽ ▽ △. We feel a sense of great excitement – something to do with the sea, with the tides.

It was evident that in this dream, too, the symbol ▷ represented the Earth.

One finds the symbol of the triangle being used from ancient times to the present day in India. There, ▽ is the Yoni Yantra (a 'Yantra' being a mystical diagram used for the purposes of meditation) which represents both the creativity of the Goddess and the female organs of generation. Its inverse △ is the Linga Yantra which represents both the creativity of the God and the male organ of generation. These two symbols are presented in Anna's dream on either side of the symbol for the Earth – depicting, by use of the same triangle in three different positions, the close relationship that exists between the Earth and Sothis A and B. This is an exact correlate of my dream, in which the tooth representing the Earth is aligned with the tooth that represents the Sothic stars. When combined, the Yoni Yantra and the Linga Yantra form the Great Yantra representing the 'divine procreative energy'[12] of Sothis and the cycles of time. Another link between the ancient Indian and Egyptian civilizations is revealed by a further meaning of 'Yoni' being 'seat'[13] – corresponding to a seat or throne forming the hieroglyph for Isis.

Kramrisch provides the information that "Śiva is the lord of caves,"[14] indicating that the Indian sages perceived that caves are resonant with Sothic energy. It is consistent with this that, in Anna's dream, the Yoni Yantra and Linga Yantra are to be found within a cave; since, together, they represent Siva as Ardhanarisvara, the androgynous deity, Sothis A and B combined. We were to learn from Temple that within this location lay another link between our two dreams, in that the ancient Egyptian word 'tep' meant 'mouth', whilst 'teph-t' meant 'cave'.[15]

Ajit Mookerjee explains that, in yogic art, a symbol "operates as the link between observation of the outer world and a very precise extraction of its essence."[16] By means of the exact symbols that were presented in Anna's dream – the Yoni Yantra and Linga Yantra – the yogi "approaches certain sets of physical-into-metaphysical correspondences which he intuits as explanations of being, both in the world surrounding him and in himself, the macrocosm and the microcosm."[17] "Many yogic symbols are also universal symbols; not so much calculated constructions of logic as a spontaneous record of mystic experience that discovers and exposes the subtle interpenetration of the part and the whole."[18] "The visual symbol or *yantra* is the power-diagram by which the physics and metaphysics of the world are made to coincide with the psyche of the meditator."[19]

The dream in which my teeth represent the relationship between myself, the Earth and Sothis A and B that exists within me can be seen as an exposition of Mookerjee's conclusion that "The yogi-artist's work culminates in a simultaneous diagram of himself and the world within which he is a world."[20]

In Anna's dream, whilst our attention is taken by the pattern of triangles, we experience a deep sense of excitement about the sea and the tides. We were, at that time, greatly drawn to the sea, especially at night. Later, we learnt from Giorgio de Santillana and Hertha von Dechend that Pliny wrote of Sothis: "the whole sea is conscious of the rise of that star."[21] Citing the Babylonian New Year ritual in which it was said that Sothis "measures the depth of the sea;"[22] the *Avestra*, in which, as Sothis rises over Lake Vurukasha, it causes the lake "to surge up, to flood asunder;"[23] and the fact that Isis-Sothis was "the guardian deity of navigators,"[24] Santillana and von Dechend conclude that Sothis is 'Stella Maris'[25] – the 'Star of the Sea'. In ancient Egypt, the rising of Sothis marked the beginning of the Inundation of the Nile and the start of Akkhet, the first season of the year. Akkhet commenced on

20th July – which is particularly relevant here, since this was the day on which Anna had her dream. The human body is composed of seventy-five percent water, with brain tissue being eighty-five percent water.[26] It is well established that our bodies respond to tidal forces caused by the gravitational pull of the moon; a similar physiological impact is experienced with the rise of Sothis.

Both my dream of the teeth and Anna's of the triangles depict the relationship between Heaven, Earth and Man. In my dream, I am experiencing that relationship as it unfolds within me. In Anna's dream, we are experiencing how we are affected as the relationship between Heaven and Earth unfolds in the world about us. These perspectives are complementary and equally essential. They correspond to Confucius' comments on the first and second hexagrams of the *I Ching* respectively. The first hexagram of the *I Ching*, Ch'ien, represents the creative power of Heaven. Confucius comments: "The way of the Creative works through change and transformation, so that each thing receives its true nature and destiny and comes into permanent accord with the Great Harmony: this is what furthers and what perseveres."[27] The process of coming into accord with the Great Harmony is graphically represented in my dream by the realignment of my teeth. The second hexagram, K'un, is the complement of the first as it represents the receptive nature of the Earth; which is, in Anna's dream, demonstrated by the responsiveness of the sea to Sothic energy and illustrated symbolically by the triangles within the cave. Of this hexagram, Confucius says: "Perfect indeed is the sublimity of the Receptive. All beings owe their birth to it, because it receives the heavenly with devotion."[28] Wilhelm explains: "The Receptive is dependent upon the Creative. While the Creative is the generating principle, to which all beings owe their beginning, because the soul comes from it, the Receptive is that which brings to birth, that which takes the seed of the heavenly into itself."[29] Applied to the world of human affairs, this means that one must take the heavenly seed inside oneself and then act on the basis of the guidance received. Thus, as Wilhelm says, "The superior man lets himself be guided."[30] This is echoed by Alfred Huang, who urges: "As a human being, one has to be submissive to Heaven and be responsive to Heaven's will."[31] And so, in the *I Ching*, it is stated that if a man in authority "tries to lead, He goes astray;"[32] that is, if such a person acts on their own initiative rather than following the will of Heaven, they will lose the Way. As the *Kūrma Purāna* states, "The wise men who know the Great God as the father who casts the seed are never bewildered."[33] It will be remembered that, for the Hindus, Sothis is Rudra/Siva, "the possessor of the seeds and their light... cause of causes and source of all creativity."[34] "He is God, and he is the seed of the universe... the cosmic substance of things to be."[35] In the Hindu scriptures, Siva took the form of a phallus – "The *linga* [which] is the object of the greatest sanctity."[36] Kramrisch writes that "The stone *linga* of Śiva has been set up in the center of the inner-most sanctuary of every Śiva temple over the last two thousand years."[37] In the *Linga Purāna*, it is stated that "the goddess is the mother of the universe. Her name is Bhagā (womb). She is the altar of the god who has the form of the *linga*... Together they created the universe... God and goddess, *linga* and *yoni*, are the cocreators of the universe."[38] In the *Śaunaka Saṁhitā*, an Indian sage proclaims that "Dream is the embryo of the wives of the gods."[39]

Kramrisch defines "the omphalos stone as a replica of the primordial *linga*."[40] The most famous omphalos stone in late antiquity was sited in Greece, at Delphi; the name 'Delphi' being derived from 'delphos' meaning 'womb'.

The significance that Sothis held in the ancient Greek civilization can be judged from the fact that "Leading religious and political sites in Greece, such as Olympia, Delphi, Athens and Epidauros, chose the month of the early rising of Sirius as the first month of the year."[41] In addition, one learns from Carl Kerényi that the Greek god Dionysus was called 'Iakchos', a title which was derived from 'Iaker', a name of Sothis; and that the god was represented as a torch-bearer because of this identification with the brightest star in the heavens.[42] "Dionysos brought this aspect with him from his Minoan origins, from the days of his connection with the flaming onset of the Sirius year. In Athens the procession in which a statue of the torch-bearing Iakchos was borne was held at the end of the *opora* [the season that began with the rising of Sothis]; it ushered in the great Mysteries of Eleusis, in which, at the time of the wine harvest, a Divine Child was born in the underworld. The loudly invoked Iakchos was the 'light-bringing star of the nocturnal mysteries."[43]

In Athens, Dionysus "did not possess a cult statue but only a cult symbol, in the form of an erect phallus," the significance of which was secret.[44] In this symbol, too, the common identity of Dionysus and Siva is displayed. According to Herodotus, it was the seer Melampous who first introduced the phalli to Greece and made them cult implements comprehendible through his interpretation.[45] It is not known what his interpretation was. However, Kerényi speaks of "Threads of the tie with Egypt, which Herodotus assumed to exist in connection with Melampous."[46] In view of the fact that, as Godwin states, Dionysus is a deity who is "creative through thought,"[47] one can safely conclude that the phallic symbol of Dionysus-Sothis represents the god as being that which releases the seed of ideas into existence. With regard to material creation, the phallus, as Kramrisch wrote of the linga of Siva, "consists of the conceptualized potentialities of *prakrti*[48] [the uncaused cause of phenomenal existence[49]]" – "the imperceptible essence of a thing even before the thing in its concrete shape has come to exist."[50] These two aspects are shown to be homogenous in my dream instruction that 'a series of events in material reality unfolds along a pre-existing sequence of dreams'.

Having mentioned that the Dionysian ritual cycle covered a two-year period, and that originally a two-year ritual calendar operated at Delphi where were celebrated "the most impressive form of festivals based on the... Dionysos myth,"[51] Kerényi observes: "The [Delphic] calendar as we know it is clearly not the same as that corresponding to the original myth of Delphi. Its conversion to a single year corresponding to the course of the sun and the seasons... was undoubtedly determined by the reign of Apollo, who more than any of the other great gods was identified with the sun."[52] He continues: "On the strength of the tradition and of archaeological findings, the existence of a pre-Apollonian earth oracle at Delphi may be taken for certain."[53] "In *Iphigenia in Tauris*, Euripides mentions the goddesses Gaia and Themis, mother and daughter, as possessors of the oracle before Apollo and tells of the killing of Python... Euripides had them defend their privilege. Earth, the 'nocturnal one', sent oracular dreams with which the child Apollo could not compete."[54] It is said that "prophetic dreams could be expected from mere contact with the earth."[55] Kerényi adds that "Themis evidently gave oracles without a tripod [which was later used for the boiling of hallucinogens, the steam of which was inhaled by the prophetess], that is, she sent dreams."[56] The dream oracle at Delphi, which issued from the alignment of the goddess Earth with Sothis, is a perfect example of the relationship between Heaven, Earth and Man as spoken of by Confucius.

Hypothesising about the relationship between the Earth and the cosmos, Reiser suggests, using a phrase strikingly similar to that presented in the poem of Anna's dream in which we are moving together, as Earth and Moon, through the cosmos (with its lines "While songs of love Flow from our hearts"), "What goes on looks like a Cosmic Communion Service... Or is it more like the singing of a 'heavenly' love song?"[57] And he asks "Could it be that GAEA, *Mother Earth*, and Uranus, *Father Sky*, are making love to each other? [Here, Reiser is referring to 'Uranus' as the Greek god whose name meant 'Heaven', not to the planet of the same name.] If so, the morphogenetic task of the two parents is to cybernate the spiral movement of the 'double helix' toward the planetarily polarized objective of all global history – the birth and the maturation of the 'celestial child'."[58] Reiser's hopes for the maturation of the 'celestial child' were, as Musès has demonstrated, realized by the ancient Egyptian priesthood, who specifically identified energies received from Sopdu (Sothis B) as the means of producing the "higher embryological development – our too rarely claimed birthright."[59]

During the Graeco-Egyptian Ptolemaic period (305-30 B.C.), 'incubation' or 'Bes' chambers were built at Saqqara for the purpose of receiving divinely inspired dreams.[60] Bes was a very ancient phallic dwarf god with a leonine mane and tail and a protruding tongue[61] – the traditional Sivan sign of greeting. He was "one of the most popular and widespread of Egyptian gods."[62]

Wilkinson describes Bes as a composite of a number of gods, including Amun (the Hidden One) and Sopdu (Sothis B). Thus, the dwarf god Bes is a personification of the dwarf star Sothis B. This is confirmed by Wallis Budge, who cites examples: "of the various forms under which Sept [Sothis] is depicted... On a shrine discovered at Saft Al-Henna by M. Naville he appears in the form of the god Bes."[63] Egyptologists rightfully emphasise the role of Bes as "patron and protector of pregnant women,"[64] without being cognizant of the ancient view that "Dream is the embryo of the wives of the gods" and, hence, that Bes, as 'that which releases the seed of ideas into existence' was the guardian of the place of incubation, where the conceptualized seed received from Sothis came into the world through the mind of Man before its realization in material reality.

Bes is often depicted carrying "the hieroglyphic *sa* sign signifying protection."[65] 'Sa' also meant 'to take care of' and 'to take heed';[66] both terms which are directly relevant to avision. Wallis Budge mentions a god named 'Sa' who was 'wisdom or knowledge deified'; and Walker defines 'Sa' as the "Egyptian word for the holy blood of Isis... said to contain the spirit of all intelligence."[67] Though 'Sa' as 'protection' and 'Sa' as 'intelligence' were represented by different hieroglyphs, their meanings are closely associated; since one meaning of 'intelligence' is 'knowledge', and knowledge affords protection. This was conveyed in the text known as the *Instruction of king Amenemhat I*, in which the deceased Amenemhat appears to his son to warn him of the threat of assassination and counsels that dreams are "a revelation of truth."[68]

In Anna's earlier-mentioned dream on the night of our return from the summons to the Sphinx:

> Anthony and I are between the paws of the Sphinx. We are shown an umbilical cord hanging from the heavens through which we receive knowledge.

I have already mentioned that the Bambara identified Sothis A and B as "the two stars of knowledge." When one takes into account that the Dogon refer to the same stars as the "double placenta in the sky,"[69] it follows that Sothis A and B are the placental source of the umbilical cord hanging from the heavens through which we receive knowledge; and, hence, that Sa, the Blood of Isis – the Spirit of All Intelligence – is conveyed to us by that means. It is consistent with this that Bes carried the associated 'sa' hieroglyph as he guarded the places of incubation.

From Anna's dream, we deduced that certain energy from Sothis is received into the human system through the umbilical chakra.

Musès cites the behaviour of the tides to demonstrate that macrocosmic dynamics induce microcosmic (local) dynamics on the Earth.[70] One can infer from this that, although the entire planet is affected by the energy from Sothis, not all places are equally resonant with Sothic energy. It is our understanding that Anna's dream of the umbilical connection with the heavens indicates that the Sphinx marks the point on the Earth that is most resonant with Sothic energy; and that this was known by the ancient civilization which carved that monument.

Musès also makes the fascinating point that, in some localities, "the maximal high or low tide... *precedes* the time of the external astronomical forces."[71] He then observes that "The systematic lags in tide-peaks indicate that such phenomena have to do with nonlinear feedback relationships; and that when [as in the above example, where the high tide precedes the astronomical forces which cause it] the lag involved is *negative* with future-feedback or the future's interaction with the present."[72]

That the Sphinx functions as a receptor for Sothic energy is revealed by its title 'Shep', a word meaning 'to receive seed';[73] 'shep-t' was 'a chamber'.[74] On the basis of this and our encounters with the Sphinx through avision, Anna and I are certain that the recently discovered chamber within the Sphinx was once used for the purpose of incubation; that is, both for the reception of the seeds of ideas and their gestation.

The Earth Womb

In April of 1997 (that is, in the month before we first visited Egypt), I had a dream in which:

> Anna and I are shopping for fabric. As I hold the fabric we are looking at, the face of the Sphinx becomes manifest as a raised image in the centre of the material. It then appears in the centre of every fabric we examine.

The same iconographic device is used in this dream as in Anna's dream of the heron. There, the raised image of the heron that she was drawn towards prefigured our encounter with the heron in material reality. Here, the raised image of the Sphinx prefigured our being summoned by it two months later; after which it became, as in my dream, the centre of our experience in material reality. According to Schwaller de Lubicz, a piece of woven material formed the hieroglyph 'Sia' denoting 'knowledge, science and comprehension'.[75] As I have explained, the Sphinx is the optimal point on Earth for contact with Sothis. Thus, my dream was showing us that Sothis lies at the heart of all knowledge, science and comprehension.

I started to write this chapter towards the end of October 2006. Within two days of my doing so, Anna had a dream which was of such significance that it was obviously intended to be included in the book at this point:

> Anthony and I are seated at a convention. There are, perhaps, fifty people present. As my contribution, I stand up and say that the name of the Sphinx contains within it the name of Siva, thus:

> S ph i n x
> S   v i

Since we had just obtained a copy of Monier-Williams' *A Sanskrit-English Dictionary*, Anna, who had not yet consulted the book, was able to check if there was in Sanskrit an acknowledged connection between 'Siva' and 'Svi'. There, she read that the 'Si' of 'Siva' means '"in whom all things lie', perhaps connected with 'Svi' [meaning] auspicious, propitious, gracious, favourable, benign, kind, benevolent, friendly, dear."[76] We were fascinated to observe how the Dream only presented us with this information when we possessed the means to affirm its validity. Anna's dream confirms the link between the Sphinx and Sothis; and, at the same time, that between the ancient Egyptian and Indian civilizations. It will be remembered, too, that, in the English language, the meanings of 'Nesh' (an ancient Egyptian name of Set) are "Tender, mild, gentle, kind," which correspond exactly with those of 'Svi', "benign, kind, benevolent, friendly." This provides a connection between Sothis, the Sphinx, Siva and Set.

The Dream instruction that the name of Siva is contained within the name of the Sphinx suddenly brought to Anna's mind two earlier dreams of hers. The first, from April 1998, was a dream within a dream:

> In a dream, I am shown two identical figures. When I wake, I describe them to Anthony. He says they are scarabs; and that the dream is very important and must be recorded.

The second dream, from July 2002, made reference to the first:

> I am reminded how, in one previous dream, I was shown the twin scarabs, Khepera and Kheperat, and, in another, I was depicted as joined with Anthony in the Dance of Siva. Now, these images are brought together: I see the twin scarabs, Khepera and Kheperat, joined together in the Dance of Siva. As I watch this moving scene, I am then shown an ancient Chinese text that describes it. The twin scarabs are gilded and gleaming, dancing in darkness that has great depth. Around the edges of the scene, like a frame, are sinuous serpents that are at the same time streamers of foliage.

Anna's dream of 2002 expands upon that of 1998 by providing the information that the twin scarabs are the divine pair Khepera and Kheperat. This, in itself, is significant because, in ancient Egyptian iconography, the scarab is always depicted singly. Barbara Watterson quotes Plutarch: "As for the scarab-beetle, it is held that there are

no females of this species; they are all males. They place their seed
in a round pellet of material which they roll up into a sphere and roll
along, pushing it with their hind legs, imitating by their action the
course of the sun from east to west."[77] One can see the influence of
patriarchy here; since, in reality, it is the female who lays her eggs in
a ball of mud or dung, pushing it along the ground after doing so.
Geraldine Pinch says: "The scarab beetle's habit of pushing a large ball
of dung was transformed into the image of a giant beetle pushing the
sun and other celestial bodies across the sky."[78] Note that Khepera is
depicted as pushing the sun, rather than as being the sun. Nonetheless,
Khepera, whose "name derives from the Ancient Egyptian word *kheper*
meaning 'to become' or 'to be transformed',"[79] has conventionally been
designated as "The dawn manifestation of the sun god."[80] However,
Wilkinson comments that "it is impossible to know whether the god
[Khepera] originally functioned in this carefully delineated role or
whether he was accorded the position when, at some point, he was
fused into the Heliopolitan cult of the sun."[81] Wallis Budge states that
the sun god "took upon himself the form of Khepera... the god who was
most intimately connected with the creation of things of every kind."[82]
Here, one is reminded of the Dogon teaching that the creator god is
Sothis B, who creates by means of his spinning dance around Sothis
A. The correspondence between this and the Dance of Siva has already
been demonstrated. In Anna's dream, the twin scarabs Khepera and
Kheperat are manifestations of Sothis A and B. Through their merging
so as to appear to be one, we were shown that the reason only one scarab
is depicted in the ancient Egyptian iconography is that Sothis B is
invisible to the naked eye.

It will be remembered that Thutmose IV had inscribed on the
Dream Stele that stands between the paws of the Sphinx: "Now a
great magical power had existed in this place from the beginning of
all time and it extended over all the region... And at this time, the
Sphinx-form of the most mighty god Khepera came to this place and
the greatest of Souls, the holiest of the holy ones, rested therein." The
magical power that resides in that place is the energy of Sothis. It was
the manifestation of this power that we experienced when we received,

and responded to, the summons from the Sphinx. That summons, it will be recalled, echoed the words of Khepera: "Come to Khepera, O Ra! Come to Khepera!" In the iconography of the Fifth Division of the Tuat, the image of Khepera emerging from an omphalos indicates that it is Sothis that is the source of the oracle at Giza; and, hence, that it is Sothis, through the medium of the Sphinx, that was calling "Come to me. Come to me."

CHAPTER ELEVEN

The Phallus

Musès' statement that "only when love has become the central priority in one's life, not as mere sentiment but as a universal call and mandate, is one actually ready to begin the path of regenerative metamorphosis" takes me back to the summer of 1971. Then, at the age of nineteen, I was in the garden of my childhood home on a hot Sunday afternoon when I became enchanted by the most wonderful sound of a girl's laughter issuing from a wood just a few yards away. It seemed to me that this was the sound of 'Woman' that I had always been in search of; but I felt so discomforted by her obviously not being alone that I hesitated to go into the wood to speak to her. Eventually, though, after a few weeks of hearing, each Sunday, the same lovely, lilting laughter, I overcame my inhibitions and went to look for the siren who had captured my heart; only to find that she had disappeared, never to return. Some ten years later, I dreamt:

I am walking through the wood behind my childhood home. There, I see a beautiful teenage girl surrounded by a number of young men who want to have a relationship with her. However, they are bewildered and unsure what to do. I continue to walk steadily towards the girl until I am able to touch her. As I do so, there is an extraordinary explosion of light.

When Anna and I met, our initial experience was one of familiarity. Subsequently, while we were discussing the wood, Anna mentioned to me how, in the summer when she was fifteen (and I was nineteen), she would go there each Sunday afternoon and climb into a high tree (while the person accompanying her preferred to remain on the ground). This immediately brought back to my mind the memory of my teenage experience and I realized that Anna had been the girl whose laughter I had been captivated by. When she showed me a photograph of herself at that age, I found myself looking at the girl from my dream.

Anna, too, had had precognitive experiences of me during her teens. She once saw an apparition of me in the garden of her childhood home (also verified by a photograph); and, later, she dreamt of my entering through her bedroom window. On the day we first met, Anna wrote in her journal: "In that first glance, a haunting sense of recognition."

Caillois states that "Ancient Indians knew the mystery of parallel dreams in which two persons, unaware of each other, have a common destiny announced to them."[1] In this way, the Dream functions as the means by which one can see the blue-print of one's destiny. The Dream can be seen to be integral to Anna's and my predestined union and to that union's purpose. Having met, our dreams initiated, and continue to initiate, different stages of our development in much the same way that biological instructions (which already inhere in the fertilized ovum) initiate the orderly unfolding of the various stages of development of the embryo – the pattern of these instructions being determined by immutable laws.

My dream was allegorical of the process of conception: Anna represented the ovum; and the young men, including myself, individual sperm. The explosion of light upon my touching Anna depicted the transformative moment of conception. The dream presented Anna exactly as she was when her laughter called me to her – a physiologically accurate metaphor, as the ovum does actually transmit messages to the sperm, drawing them toward it, and then does not necessarily accept the first to arrive. The dynamic between ovum and sperm was also used in my dream to convey that each partner needs the other equally for the fulfilment of their potential. This is achieved, as Ganesh instructed me, through the mutual exchange of the advice that has been received through dreams. Through this process, while both individuals retain their integrity as separate beings, they merge – as in the Dance of Siva – so as to become two parts of one whole.

My dream depicted the coming together of Anna and myself as the first stage in the metamorphic process that Musès spoke of: "The context for regeneration in the ancient Egyptian teaching is biological and psychophysiological; little known processes within the brain and body trigger, when activated, a supra-biological, transformational and higher embryological development."[2] Musès cites "The greatest book of secret instruction for using the Vedas, the Śatapatha Brāhmaṇa... preserving remote oral tradition," which specifically refers to a man and a woman who undertake the process of embryonic development "jointly and in love" and through which the one completes the regeneration of the other.[3] Thus, Anna's dreams concerning Love were a development of a sequence that began with my dream of our meeting (dreamt several years before we met). Significantly, whereas the Satapatha Brahmana provided instruction for the construction of an altar to facilitate the process of the couple's regeneration, in Anna's dream, we were told that our altar should be one another – a teaching that was entirely in accord with the paradigm of our coming together as ovum and sperm.

It will be remembered that, in ancient Egyptian, 'Tep Ra' both meant 'dream oracle' and denoted the two points at the base of a triangle. The apex of that triangle is Sothis. Though we were not yet aware of Sothis being the source of the Dream, my dreams of Ganesh and Ganesha in the wood demonstrated that we were required to act upon the guidance received through avision. This demonstration took place in the wood behind my childhood home from which I had heard Anna's laughter and in which my dream of the beautiful teenage girl had been set. Thus, when Ganesh sent word that he wanted to speak to Anna and myself, he was requiring us to return, this time together, to the location where it had been revealed that we were destined for one another.

The school which featured in my dreams had in material reality, throughout my childhood, been named 'The Grove'. Groves were the Druidic places of worship in Britain. Through this association, Anna and I were being shown that we were being instructed in the ancient Druidic tradition of avision. At the same time, through the appearance of Ganesh and Ganesha (the personifications of the stars of Sothis), the Dream was making us aware of a connection between Druidic groves and Sothis.

There is a weird ('weird' meaning "the principle, power or agency by which events are predetermined"[4]) link between Anna's and my relationship, the wood and the grove, since all are united by the name 'Lunt' which means "wood or sacred grove."[5]

Confirmation that we had understood what was required of us and that we were proceeding correctly came the following year through a dream of Anna's, in August of 1997, shortly before our return to the Sphinx:

> Anthony and I are at a grove in the countryside at night. The entrance to the grove is marked by two identical statues, like sentries, of the head of a renowned ancient poet on a short pillar. Looking towards the grove, I approach the statue on my right. When I am close to it, the head comes to life and imparts to me that we are doing everything right.

Whilst the message of the dream was clear, we could not determine from that communication the identity or significance of the statue head.

Juliette Wood recounts that, in Druidic Britain, "The image of the head appears everywhere – carved in the round, or as a decoration on pillars, coins, cauldrons and altars."[6] She adds that it is "a symbol of the divine and a reminder that life continues after death."[7]

Wood speaks of "the exalted position of poets and bards in the Celtic world. The bards are the keepers of tribal wisdom and by their craft they preserve the very identity of their people."[8] She explains: "The sight, or *in*sight, of Celtic poets works on three levels. It looks to the past wisdom of their world, it provides intuitive understanding of the present, and it allows them to foresee the future."[9]

Anna dreamt of the Druidic poet coming alive and confirming that we were doing everything right a week before our return to the Sphinx. Then, a week after that visit to Egypt, she dreamt that the Sphinx, too, confirmed that we were doing everything right. Through these dreams, a link was formed in our minds between ancient Druidic Britain and ancient Egypt. Both were presented as sources of wisdom that are as alive now as they were in the past. Spence describes Britain as "the Egypt of the Occident" and explains that "To the peoples of antiquity the isle of Britain was the very home and environment of mystery, a sacred territory, to enter which was to encroach upon a region of enchantment, the dwelling of gods, the shrine and habitation of a cult of peculiar sanctity and mystical power."[10] Many correspondences can be seen between the ancient Egyptian and Druidic traditions. For instance, Spence compares the mythic voyage that Arthur made by boat into the Underworld with the Ba-god's journey along "the dark waters of Amenti, the Egyptian Underworld [the Tuat]" and concludes that "The two myths are, indeed, one."[11] He notes that in Druidism, which "arose out of a Cult of the Dead,"[12] Annwn (the Underworld) is ruled by the god Gwyddno and the goddess Keridwen.[13] Thus, Gwyddno was the Druidic name for Sothis B, the governor of the Underworld. Gwyddno was also known as 'Celi', meaning 'Concealing',[14] corresponding to the Egyptian Amun being the Hidden One.

Gwyddno's surname, 'Garanhir', meant 'long, high crane'.[15] This corresponds to the Dogon creator god Amma (who, as I demonstrated, was the Egyptian Amun) being represented "by a dancer wearing 'a crane-beaked... mask'."[16]

It is not without significance that the dream in which I was instructed to restore the crane occurred on the same night that the Sphinx confirmed to Anna that we were doing everything right. In addition, there is here another link to Anna's dream of the poet's head, since the Greeks held that the crane was the bird sacred to Hermes.[17] These associations supported our intuition of a shared identity between the mechanical crane of my dream and the avian crane. We could then see that restoring the crane involved restoring a dream function that is derived from Sothis B.

In the Graeco-Roman world, short pillars bearing stone heads of Hermes, or images of his erect phallus, were placed at crossroads.[18] Later, when we understood the significance of 'that which releases the seed of ideas into existence', it was obvious to us that Hermes – the god of wisdom – was the personification of Sothis B; which is why it was said that "Hermes ascended to heaven in the form of Sirius, the Great Dog."[19] As the god of wisdom, writing and medicine, Hermes was identified with Thoth; and, as the Lord of Death and Conductor of Souls, with Anubis[20] (the Great Dog of Isis-Sothis[21]). Referring to Anubis, Plutarch noted: "In the more remote and ancient times, the dog had the highest honour paid to him in Egypt."[22] Walker points to the common identity of jackal-headed Anubis and Siva, whose name meant 'jackal'.[23]

In the Vedas, "Sirius, the hound of heaven, the star form of Rudra [Siva], the Wild God, is mythically the most eminent of all stars."[24] The unity of Sothis A and B, the Hindu Ardhanarisvara – the god who is half man and half woman – was known by the Graeco-Romans as Hermaphrodite – Hermes and Aphrodite (the Great Goddess) combined.

Walker notes that "Next to a cave, a grove was the most popular uterine symbol in ancient religions."[25] This points to the relationship between the grove and 'that which releases the seed'. In Rome, Hermes went under the name of Mercury. Walker mentions that, in the Tarot, Hermes was identified with the Magician; and that a Mantegna Tarot specifically showed the Magician as Mercury "stepping over a severed head – symbol of oracles."[26]

Walker states that "The phallic principle was covertly worshipped in sacred posts and pillars" throughout Europe at least until the thirteenth century, despite repeated edicts issued by the Catholic Church forbidding the veneration of the 'fascinum' – the Latin for 'an erect penis' – in the eighth, ninth, twelfth and thirteenth centuries.[27] Unexpected evidence of the widespread worship of 'that which releases the seed' was uncovered in 1946 when Professor Gregory Webb, who was then secretary of the Royal Commission on Historical Monuments, found that the bomb-damaged altar of a fourteenth century church in the south of England contained a stone phallus. Upon further investigation, he discovered that ninety percent of churches in that region that had been built before 1384 contained such images within their altars.[28] Thus, in England too, 'that which releases the seed of ideas' was – like the Egyptian Amun, who was sometimes represented by a phallus[29] – the Hidden One.

Neo-Platonists called Hermes the 'Logos'[30] – 'the Divine Word made manifest'.[31] Walker mentions that for pagans the "'Word made flesh' was usually Hermes, representing the *Logos spermatikos*" – the incarnation of the seed.[32] "Christian images of Jesus as the Logos were borrowed from the older deity [Hermes], whose hymns addressed him in terms similar to those used in the Gospels."[33] Thus, by placing the head of the poet on top of a pillar, the Dream was signifying that he was, at the very least, the embodiment and realization of the Divine Word, if not an incarnation of Sothis B.

Musès cites an ancient Egyptian stele which records how a Mesopotamian princess was cured by an Egyptian priest; and notes: "The priestly psychiatrist was considered a living incarnation very similar to a Tibetan 'living Buddha'."[34] The comparison is particularly apt, for "Hermes [who was identified wth Thoth] was a universal Indo-European god. An Enlightened One born of the virgin Maia, he was the same as the Enlightened One (Buddha) born of the same virgin Maya in India."[35] In support of this, Walker cites the *Mahanirvanatantra*, which states that "Buddha was the same as Mercury (Hermes), the son of the Moon (Maya)"[36] – a statement which esoterically refers to the incarnation of the Word being born of the energy received from Sothis via the moon.

Musès recounts that it was observed by the ancient civilizations that the waning lunar fortnight is "a time of the absorption by all animate creatures of a cosmic life power,"[37] which, if properly harnessed, can lead to "accelerating higher human development and awareness."[38] Musès emphasises of the waning moon: "It should be clearly understood that the lunar motion is used here in the context of a synchronous signal, and not as the origin of the power."[39] The origin of the power is Sothis. Although "Isis was long connected with the moon,"[40] that connection was understood to be by resonance. This was expressed in the iconography of the temples of Isis by the image of "a carved stone moon-boat containing her figure,"[41] demonstrating that the moon was identified as being a vehicle for Sothic energy. Thus, Musès speaks of "the undying flame of Isis... that is so intimately bound up with lunar affinities."[42]

The same message of a deep affinity between Sothis and the moon is conveyed by the designation and representation of Siva – the eternal lord of redeeming knowledge – as the "God with the Moon in His Hair."[43] Similarly, Thoth, the ancient Egyptian god of wisdom, was often depicted "with the lunar disk and crescent on his head,"[44] symbolizing the waning lunar fortnight that provides the opportunity for gnosis. Significantly, in Egyptian mythology, Thoth, in his aspect as a moon god, often functioned as a messenger between the other gods;[45] that is, he represented the link that the moon provides between Sothis and the Earth and, hence, between Sothis and Man. With regard to the receiving of these energies, "Plato undoubtedly was repeating a phrase he had heard in the Mysteries, in which he was admittedly initiated, when he said in the Timaeus (90A) that man is 'a holy plant with roots above'."[46]

Shortly before encountering Musès' understanding on these matters, I had a dream in which:

> I am looking up on a calendar the small-print detailing the phases of the moon.

The Dream was drawing our attention to the phases of the moon; and this led us to wonder how they correlate with our dream life. As a result, we found that there is a vital connection between the moon cycle and our experience of avision.

If the thesis I am presenting concerning the relationship between Sothis and the Dream is true, one would expect to find supporting evidence in the dream-life of others, in particular in that of Jung, as he was the first psychiatrist to recognise the moral and spiritual relevance that the Dream has for the life of modern man. Jung recounts that, when he was between three and four years old, he had the earliest dream he could remember, "a dream which was to preoccupy me all my life."[47] (For the purposes of this chapter, I quote all but the last episode of his dream.) At that age, Jung lived with his parents in the vicarage in Laufen, Switzerland: "The vicarage stood quite alone near Laufen castle, and there was a big meadow stretching back from the sexton's farm. In the dream I was in this meadow. Suddenly I discovered a dark, rectangular, stone-lined hole in the ground. I had never seen it before. I ran forward curiously and peered down into it. Then I saw a stone stairway leading down. Hesitantly and fearfully, I descended. At the bottom was a doorway with a round arch, closed off by a green curtain. It was a big, heavy curtain of worked stuff like brocade, and it looked very sumptuous. Curious to see what might be behind, I pushed it aside. I saw before me in the dim light a rectangular chamber about thirty feet long. The ceiling was arched and of hewn stone. The floor was laid with flagstones, and in the centre a red carpet ran from the entrance to a low platform. On this platform stood a wonderfully rich golden throne. I am not certain, but perhaps a red cushion lay on the seat. It was a magnificent throne, a real king's throne in a fairy tale. Something was standing on it which I thought at first was a tree trunk twelve to fifteen feet high and about one and a half to two feet thick. It was a huge thing, reaching almost to the ceiling. But it was of a curious composition: it was made of skin and naked flesh, and on top there was something like a rounded head with no face and no hair. On the very top of the head was a single eye, gazing motionlessly upwards. It was fairly light in the room, although there were no windows and no apparent source of light. Above the head, however, was an aura of brightness. The thing did not move, yet I had the feeling that it might at any moment crawl off the throne like a worm and creep towards me. I was paralysed with terror... This dream haunted me for years. Only much later did I realise that what I had seen was a phallus, and it was decades before I understood that it was a ritual phallus... The abstract significance of the phallus is shown by the fact that it was enthroned by itself, 'ithyphallically' ('upright'). The hole in the meadow probably represented a grave. The grave itself was an underground temple whose green curtain symbolised the *meadow*, in other words the mystery of Earth with her covering of green vegetation. The carpet was *blood-red*. What about the vault? Perhaps I had already been to Munôt, the citadel of Schaffhausen? This is not likely, since no one would take a three-year-old child up there. So it cannot be a memory-trace. Equally, I do not know where the anatomically correct phallus can have come from. The interpretation of the *orificium urethrae* as an eye, with the source of light apparently above it, points to the etymology of the word phallus (shining, bright). At all events, the phallus of this dream seems to be a subterranean God 'not to be named', and such it remained throughout my youth, reappearing whenever anyone spoke too emphatically about Lord Jesus."[48]

Although Jung did not know it, Sothic symbolism is central to his dream. The throne and the eye form the hieroglyphs for Sothis A and B. While still a child, as if sensing the dream's true meaning, Jung came to think of the throne, even though it was situated underground, as God's "golden throne far, far away in the blue sky."[49] Jung says that it was some time before he realized that what he had seen was a phallus and that, with hindsight, he still "did not know where the anatomically correct phallus can have come from." Being unaware of the association between Sothis and 'that which releases the seed of ideas into existence', he took it for a ritual phallus. However, he was closer to the truth when he described it as a "subterranean God"; for, Seker, the Lord of Death at the Saqqara necropolis, was a chthonic god who represented the phallus at the moment of sending forth seed[50] – Sothis B. Jung again approached the Sothic connection when he associated the eye with the etymological derivation of 'phallus' from the Greek meaning 'shining' and 'bright'.

Jung suggests that "The hole in the meadow probably represented a grave" – indicating, I believe, that the symbolism of his dream was something that he had been familiar with in a past life. He goes on to say that "The grave itself was an underground temple" – I shall say more about this shortly.

It is particularly interesting that the dream reappeared in Jung's mind "whenever anyone spoke too emphatically about Lord Jesus" – which would, one might imagine, have happened rather frequently, since Jung was brought up in a family of nine parsons. The timeless representations of the forces of cosmic truth asserted themselves against the platitudes of organized religion. Jung later reflected: "The dream of the ithyphallic god was my first great secret... it became increasingly impossible for me to adopt a positive attitude to Lord Jesus."[51] "Whenever I listened to them [the parsons] I had the feeling: Yes, yes, that is all very well. But what about the secret?... There must be someone who knows something about it; somewhere there must be the truth."[52] Though Jung admitted "I did not say anything about the phallus dream until I was sixty-five,"[53] he recognised, even as a teenager, that it was one of the crucial experiences of his life. Looking back over his life, Jung concluded: "my early dreams. They determined my course from the beginning."[54] "From the beginning I had a sense of destiny, as though my life was assigned to me by fate and had to be fulfilled. This gave me an inner security, and, though I could not ever prove it to myself, it proved itself to me. *I* did not have this certainty, *it* had me. Nobody could rob me of the conviction that it was enjoined upon me to do what God wanted and not what I wanted."[55]

The ancient Mystery rites were designed to exert the same influence upon the initiate that the dream of the phallus had upon Jung. "Mystery Festivals", says Burkert, "should be unforgettable events casting their shadows over the whole of one's future life, creating experiences that transform existence."[56] The intention of the Mysteries, as Dio of Prusa stated, was that the initiate would "come to surmise that there is [in the cosmos] some wiser insight and plan."[57] Burkert points to "the comparison [in antiquity] of the cosmos with a huge mystery hall"[58] – which was depicted in Jung's dream as an underground temple. He goes on to explain that "the texts insist that the true state of blessedness is... in the act of 'seeing' what is divine."[59] Burkert describes representations of the initiation to Dionysus, saying: "The most striking item in this imagery is a huge erect phallus in a winnowing basket, *liknon*, covered by a cloth, being unveiled... This evidently is 'showing a sacred object'."[60] He continues: "the *liknon* with phallus appears much earlier in Bacchic contexts [Bacchus being a title of Dionysus]... In a general way, phallus processions had always been present in the workings of Dionysus."[61] This is particularly relevant, since, as I have mentioned, a phallus was the emblem of Dionysus who was himself identified with Sothis.

The liknon, being a winnowing basket, was a basket for sieving the seed. Kerényi, making reference to a famous marble urn found in Rome on which are depicted several of the rites of the Eleusinian Mysteries, describes a scene in which the initiate is seated: "Over his head the priestess holds a plaited winnowing fan, an instrument with which the grain was ordinarily cleansed and in which the accessories of the Dionysian rites were kept and carried about: the phallus or the mask."[62] In holding the winnowing fan above the initiate, the priestess is symbolically separating the chaff from the cosmic seed – a process which one naturally undergoes through the experience of avision.

Hence, the close identification between 'Siva' and the English word 'sieve', an alternative spelling of which was 'sive'.[63]

There is good reason to think that the Mystery tradition was an institutionalization of what, in the natural state of affairs, is an entirely spontaneous experience. Jung's childhood dream, in which he was led into the presence of the Sothic Deity manifest in symbolic form, was such a spontaneous experience; and one can see how concordant it was with the priestly process of initiation into the Mysteries. The Dream came first, providing, to use a phrase of Synesius', "the mysteries without rites"[64] from which the Mystery tradition was developed.

CHAPTER TWELVE

The Imminent and the Manifest

∞

In order to relate how our subsequent sequence of dream instruction evolved, I return to Anna's dream of September 1994:

> Anthony and I go to visit a school in the countryside where we may send our children. The school is a mansion set in enormous grounds. Elephants and giraffes are roaming in the gardens. We are invited to stay for dinner. Soup is served to us in ancient Egyptian glazed bowls that have pillars on the inside painted with garlands of green leaves and blue flowers. It crosses my mind that food from ancient times is concealed behind the pillars and we shall imbibe it with our soup.

The imagery of the blue flowers in the ancient Egyptian bowls was developed in another dream of Anna's three months later, on 24th December 1994:

> I am in the desert. In the sky above, a bluish-white net of vast expanse is spread. An ethereal bluish-white goddess passes her left

breast through a gap in the net. This signifies the linking of the world of the gods with the material world.

The goddess is Isis, the personification of the bluish-white star Sothis A.

In Anna's dream sequence, the image of the two ancient Egyptian bowls containing food representing knowledge from ancient times that we will assimilate into our minds was followed by that of the Goddess with her 'seshti' – 'two breasts'[1] – which are themselves symbolic of the assimilation of knowledge; for, as Seshat, Isis-Sothis was the goddess of the recording of knowledge.[2] The 'menedj', the hieroglyph of 'a pendent breast', was particularly identified with Isis.[3]

The appearance of Isis heralded an essential instruction which came a few days later, on 1st January 1995, in a dream that initiated my own on-going experience of avision. This dream was comprised of the words:

"Osiris is a false position."

My knowledge of Osiris did not extend beyond what I had learnt of the Osirian myth when, at the age of twenty, I bought a copy of Jung's *Symbols of Transformation*. There, I had read that the god "Osiris was killed in a crafty manner by the god of the underworld, Set;"[4] "Osiris, although only a phantom, now makes the young sun (his son {by Isis} Horus) ready for battle with Set, the evil spirit of darkness;"[5] "Horus vanquished the wicked Set who had murdered his father Osiris, but Isis set him free again... Horus then vanquished Set for a second time."[6]

At the time of my dream, it was sufficient for Anna and myself to be put on our guard against the notion of Osiris. Our understanding of how 'Osiris is a false position' developed subsequently as our sequence of dream instructions unfolded.

In February of 1995, the month following my instruction regarding Osiris, Anna dreamt:

> I am shown the connective flow from my vision, at the age of five, of ass-headed Set standing in the Thames, through my finding Anthony, to our life together in the present.

The dream was referring to a vision which Anna had when she was five years old while travelling over Caversham Bridge (which is situated a hundred yards or so as the crow flies from where we now live). This vision was the determining experience of Anna's life:

> A huge, ass-headed creature, having an upright body like a human, a tail and cloven hooves, dressed in a loin-cloth and belts, was standing in the River Thames looking down at me benignly. He had a kind, intelligent face.

Although she was so young, Anna knew that she had witnessed something of great significance and that the experience had to be protected. Up until this point, I have been the sole person to have known of this vision.

It was only through her dream of February 1995 that Anna learnt the creature of her vision had been Set. Subsequently, she went to the local library and found, in an encyclopaedia, confirmation that the ass-headed creature was indeed one of the forms of Set. However, it became apparent that the kind, intelligent being of Anna's vision bore no relation to the evil force that Set was purported to be in the book she consulted. It was as a result of this research that Anna was later able, from my description, to identify Set as being the large, vulture-like creature which swooped down and landed on my thigh in my dream of September 1996. Had it not been for this chain of events – Anna's vision of the benign, ass-headed creature with his kind, intelligent face, followed by the dream instruction that the creature was Set, which then motivated her to seek confirmation and later enabled her to identify the vulture-like creature of my own dream as Set – I would, like almost everyone else, have been caught in the trap created millennia ago which leads one to experience the awesome might of Set as the personification of evil.

In October of 1996, the month after Set landed on my thigh, I dreamt:

> I am looking towards the top of a gently sloping hill, watching a sunset. As soon as the sun has set, another sun, slightly less bright, rises from the same place. I am told "Only when the sun has Set, is the sun the number one city of the horizon."

In this dream, which occurred in the year before we read Temple's book, my attention was directed towards a double star system in which one star was brighter than the other, and I was told that the god Set is intrinsic to the stellar system that is "the number one city of the horizon." At the time, I was at a loss to understand what this phrase meant. Some years later, when we had acquired a copy of Musès' *The Lion Path*, I found in the text an illustration of the hieroglyph of a rising sun, which Musès explains was first inscribed in the pyramid of Unas where it meant *Niw-t Nwtr* – "the 'City of God', the stable Center of the Universe, which existed even in 'The First Time'."[7] Musès cites Rundle Clark, who states: "'City' hardly gives the correct sense of 'niwt', which is charged with emotion in a way that is not paralleled by the word 'city'; 'niwt' here means the numinous centre of the universe, the seat of God."[8] Musès adds: "The concept persisted in later Egypt; for example, 'the Eternal City' mentioned on the Coffin of Pankhmeses."[9] So, though we did not know it at the time, my dream was pointing to Sothis as 'the seat of God' (hence, a throne forms the hieroglyph for Sothis A) and indicating that Set is an essential element of that stellar configuration.

A month later, in November of 1996, I had a second dream concerning Osiris:

> Anna and I consult an ancient Egyptian woman regarding the ancient Egyptian view of Osiris. She finds the contemporary

147

understanding of Osiris amusing and shows us how the Osirian priesthood interpolated Osiris into existing texts.

Ostensibly, as Wilkinson says, "Osiris was unquestionably one of the most important deities of ancient Egypt, figuring prominently in both monarchical ideology and popular religion as a god of death, resurrection and fertility."[10] However, as Rundle Clark states, "There is no definite evidence as yet that Osiris was worshipped in the prehistoric period. Even if he were, that would not imply that the primitive figure had much in common with the highly developed god we encounter in historical times. A symbol of Osiris has recently been found that dates from the beginning of the historical times, about 3000 B.C., otherwise there is no specific proof of his existence until he appears in the Pyramid Texts which were inscribed between 2400 and 2200 B.C. In these texts he is already fully developed, not only already provided with a complete mythology but a carefully thought-out theology as well. Moreover, the power and pretensions of the god increase as time goes on."[11] Wilkinson notes that "His birthplace was said to be Rosetau in the necropolis of the western desert near Memphis, but this is doubtless a mythical placement related to the god's funerary role... As time progressed and the cult of Osiris spread throughout Egypt, the god assimilated many other deities and rapidly took on their attributes and characteristics. It seems probable, for example, that the god took over the story of an earthly ruler who was resurrected after his death from the ancient god Andjety of Busiris whose insignia were also the same as those used by Osiris. Many of the epithets accorded Osiris may also be seen to have been taken over from other deities."[12] Through my above dream, we were shown that, despite Osiris being a false position, the texts into which he was introduced still retain their original value; and that the falsity of Osiris was obscured by his identification with texts which embody the truth.

In January of 1997, four months before our first visit to Egypt, I dreamt:

I am told that Set is associated with preparation and that as a result of the dream I am now having it will later be easier for me to perform a task.

This dream developed the theme of my earlier-mentioned dream of March 1989 in which a number of images and objects appeared before me and I was told that I was being provided with what I needed for the task ahead. As I have said, upon waking the only image I could remember was ⏶; which I later learnt was both the hieroglyph meaning 'to be prepared' or 'equipped with appropriate means' and a symbol of Sothis. Both of the above dreams are concerned with preparation for a future task; the task in question being that of restoring the crane, which was presented to me in my dream of 9th September 1997, a few days after our having fulfilled the summons to the Sphinx. It will be remembered that, in the ancient Egyptian language, 'Nesh' was a name of Set; 'nesher' denoted the avian 'crane'.[13] Since ⏶ meant 'to be prepared' and was also a symbol of Sothis, and Set is associated with preparation, we were again being shown by the Dream that Set is associated with Sothis.

Discussion of Set may seem alien to modern life, but a moment's reflection reveals how mention of the god is part of everyday experience in the English-speaking world. For instance, one finds the instruction that Set is associated with preparation in the phrases 'Set the table' and 'On your marks, get set, go'. Then, the process of alignment with which the crane is associated is implicit in the phrases 'Set your watch', 'Set a course', 'Use a set square' and 'Set someone straight'. People are 'set tasks', 'live in settlements' and 'settle their differences'. There can be no doubt that, once, Set had a place in English culture that has been expunged from the historical record. Since 'nesher', meaning 'crane', is derived from 'Nesh', the instruction to restore the crane constituted an instruction to restore an element of Man's relation to Set that has been undermined.

The advice received in my dream, that Set is associated with preparation, followed by my dream instruction to restore the crane, manifested a specific pattern of the Cosmic Guiding Fields of Force that was identified and recorded by those who created the ancient high-science of the *I Ching*. The same sequence appears in Hexagram 61,

Inner Truth, where the first line, corresponding to 'Set is associated with preparation', begins:

"Being prepared brings good fortune;"

whilst the second reads:

> "A crane calling in the shade.
> Its young answers it.
> 'I have a good goblet.
> I will share it with you'."[14]

This correspondence between the syntax of avision and the arrangement of the text attached to individual lines of the *I Ching* is a natural outcome of avision lying at the heart of the shamanic roots of Chinese culture.

The 'good goblet' which the crane offers to share appeared to me in a dream on 24th September 1997, two weeks after I had been instructed to restore the crane:

> The grail cup is floating within a doorway. Splendid and serene,
> it is absorbing energy into all of its parts.

Since the grail cup is emblematic of the ultimate goal of the spiritual path, through the image of the grail absorbing energy into all of its parts, we were being shown that the object of the quest is a state of total receptivity – as Confucius said, "Perfect indeed is the sublimity of the Receptive."[15] Elsewhere in his commentary on the *I Ching*, Confucius identifies the hidden crane (in the shade) offering a goblet to its young with the influence that a sage exerts upon the people.[16] In ancient Egypt, too, the crane was associated with both a wine cup and wisdom: for, 'tekhi', which meant 'crane', was also a title of Thoth; whilst 'tekh-t' meant 'wine cup' or 'wine bowl'. 'Tekh', which denoted 'a mixture of bread and wine',[17] was a precursor of the association of the wine cup with the Last Supper.

In the sacred iconography of ancient Crete and, later, of Greece, Dionysus was often identifiable by virtue of the fact that he was bearing a wine cup. It will be remembered that Dionysus was called 'Iakchos', a title derived from 'Iaker', a name of Sothis. The Ionian historian Hekataios Miletos related that it was said that Sothis, the Dog Star, in the form of a she-dog, gave birth to a stick which was then buried and from which emerged the first vine as a gift to Mankind from the celestial deity.[18] Thus, in the Dionysian sphere, wine exists "in material identity with the god."[19] The drinking of wine is, therefore, both a means of absorbing Sothic energy and symbolic of so doing. From the foregoing, it can be seen that, in my dream, the doorway in which the grail cup is floating is that of 'Sba', Sothis as the 'Great Door of Heaven'.[20]

Kerényi observes that "the Mediterranean wine culture was the common concrete background of two very divergent realities, the founding of Christianity on the one hand and everything that can be subsumed under the comprehensive term 'Dionysian religion' on the other."[21] "The existence of a massive non-Greek religion of Dionysos between the lake of Genesareth and the Phoenician coast was attested by the founder of Christianity, who journeyed through that region as far as Tyre."[22] In the Gospel, when, at the Last Supper, Jesus said of the wine "this is my blood" (Matthew 26:28), he was making a characteristically Dionysian gesture. Indeed, Walker describes Dionysus as "A prototype of Christ, with a cult center at Jerusalem as well as nearly every other city in the middle east."[23]

Arthur Waite recounts: "the Holy Graal, considered in its Christian aspects and apart from those of folk-lore, is represented invariably, excepting in one German version of the legend, as that vessel in which Christ celebrated the Last Supper or consecrated for the first time the elements of the Eucharist. It is, therefore, a sacramental vessel, and, according to the legend, its next use was to receive the blood from the wounds of Christ when His body was taken down from the Cross, or, alternatively, from the side which was pierced by the spear of

Longinus... this vessel, its contents included, was carried westward in safe guardianship – coming, in fine, to Britain."[24] However, Walker notes that, as I have outlined, "The real origins of the Holy Grail were not Christian but pagan,"[25] pointing out that "The Grail was first converted into the chalice of Christ's last supper in the *Joseph d'Arimathie* of the Burgundian poet Robert de Borron, between 1180 and 1199."[26]

In Greece, Dionysus was god of the Underworld. Kingsley recounts that "wherever in the ancient world... craters are mentioned as occurring they are almost always described as points of descent and entry into the underworld... through this special link with the other world they became 'places of power': sites of oracles, appropriate spots for the taking of oaths, places of ordeal where truth was revealed and untruth exposed, and locations associated with dreams and their interpretation."[27] He explains that 'krater', "a word which originally meant a mixing-bowl used for mixing water and wine... later acquired its by now more familiar sense through being applied metaphorically to hollows in the earth and volcanic 'craters'."[28] And he speaks of the "immense influence" the symbol of the krater "subsequently exerted on the legend of the Grail."[29]

Musès speaks specifically of "The living [Sothic] water of eternal life in the *Crater* or *Cup* (cf. the Grail) of the very ancient Trismegistic or Thoth tradition."[30] Here, he is referring to the chapter in the *Hermetica* where Hermes explains to his son that God sent down a large Cup or Bowl filled with Divine Mind in order "that thou shalt return to him that sent this Cup; thou that acknowledgest whereunto thou wert made"[31] Those who dipped or bathed in the Cup were "baptised or dowsed into the [Divine] Mind, these were made partakers of Knowledge, and became perfect men, receiving the [Divine] Mind... the Knowledge of the Mind, the beholding of Divine Things and the Understanding of God, the Cup itself being Divine."[32] The Grail cup is inextricably linked with the Dream; for, as Plutarch said, "the true nature of the *krater* which Orpheus arrived at 'has no boundary anywhere on earth and neither does it have a single set base, but it wanders everywhere throughout mankind in dreams and visions'."[33]

Spence relates that, for the Druids, "all good gifts emanated from the Underworld, and many are the stories told of men and women who penetrated the fairy-hill [the world of the dead – and of dreams] to gain either hidden lore or magical objects... In numerous instances these had first to lose their senses, to become unconscious or fall asleep before admittance to the fairy realm. The Grail legends are merely Christianized versions of this theme... They enshrine the remains of an ancient British code of initiation deflected to the uses of Christianity."[34] In short, the Catholic Church has used a ritual act performed by an officiant to replace personal communion with Sothis through the Dream.

Following the appearance of the Grail on 24th September, the process of restoring the crane began to unfold in my dreams. On 27th September 1997 there occurred the first of a pair of dreams which took us deeper into the world of the true religion of ancient Egypt:

> Anna and I are walking along a corridor. As we pass a room whose door is open, the voice of God calls out "Anthony" and, in so doing, bids us to enter. Upon entering the room, which is enormous, we find that it contains a huge table, somewhat akin to a bench in a science laboratory. An ancient Egyptian priest enters the room and places on the table the pieces of a stone which we once possessed and then discarded. I recognise it, even though it is broken. As we look at the pieces, they start to move and fit together like a jigsaw, assuming the shape of a right-angle in the position of the upper left-hand corner of a square. We see that contained within the stone is an image of the Universe and realize that, in forming a right-angle, it reveals itself to be a corner-stone of the Universe.

Here again we were summoned, as we had been to the Sphinx, and were required to do nothing other than enter the room and observe what took place.

The table that dominated the room made reference to the dream of mine of 25th September 1996, in which I was sitting at a table next to a tunnel connected with the ancient Egyptians. It had been the next day, on 26th September 1996, that I dreamt that 'Anna and I are as connected with the Sphinx now as we were in our Egyptian lifetime'. Now, on 27th September 1997, a year and a day after being reconnected with the Sphinx, we were reconnected with the stone. From the correspondence between the dates, the thematic content of these dreams and the presence of an Egyptian priest, we were able to deduce that the stone represented something we had possessed during our life in ancient Egypt.

Then, in the second dream two nights later:

> An ancient Egyptian priest approaches Anna and myself and says that, as we have undertaken such a difficult task, we have been allocated an assistant. Anna and I argue strongly that we are not in need of one. This the priest counters by offering an explanation of the issues that we are tackling. What he tells us is completely contrary to the conventional understanding that exists in the contemporary world, but we can see that reality conforms to the account he has given. As a result of this interaction, we accept that we are in need of assistance. We are then joined by a second priest who reads to us instructions as to what we are to do in our waking life. As he speaks, I can feel the presence of the pyramids at Giza.

These ancient Egyptian priests entered into our lives as a reassuring educative presence whose sense of gravitas was the natural corollary to their depth of knowledge.

We later discovered that the broken pieces of the stone had reformed themselves into the hieroglyph of 'a corner-stone'. Reference to corner-stones is made in an inscription at the Temple of Edfu in which the king proclaimed "my gaze has followed the course of the stars; my eye has turned toward the Great Bear; I have measured time and counted (the hour) with the clepsydra [water-clock], then I established the four corners that define the temple."[35] Here, the king is referring to the 'stretching of the cord' ceremony, one of the most sacred and essential acts that the pharaoh undertook. It was by means of this ceremony that the orientation of a new temple was determined. The creation and placement of a brick in the first corner was a critical part of this ritual. That is what occurred spontaneously in my dream.

As will be seen in the next chapter, my subsequent sequence of dreams revealed that what we were witnessing was, not simply the restoration of the stone, but a symbolic restoration of myself. (I shall discuss Anna's corresponding dreams in due course.) This is consistent with Schwaller de Lubicz's statement that "all initiatory temples are founded on the principle of Anthropocosmos, that is, man as Universe, the anthropomorphization of divine thought."[36] The Dream restored something which had been destroyed both within myself and within Mankind in general. New possibilities emerged as that restitution was effected.

The Edfu inscription relates that the correct orientation of the Temple within the cosmos was achieved through affecting an alignment with the constellation of the Great Bear, which the ancient Egyptians called 'Meskh-t', and which, as Wallis Budge notes, was regarded by them as the abode of the Soul of Set. 'Meskh-t' also meant 'thigh', the image of which was used to represent the Great Bear.[37] I mentioned earlier how Musès demonstrated that alignment with the Great Bear and the two "celestial control centres", Sothis A and B, was essential in both Taoist and ancient Egyptian astrotheurgy. However, it is in the nature of avision that such alignments take place spontaneously if the guidance in one's dreams is properly integrated. The association of Set with the thigh was, with hindsight, confirmed for us through avision by the fact that, in my dream of September 1996, Set had landed on my thigh. However, through my dream, we were shown that Set does not inhere within the thigh, but rather that his energy arrives there from elsewhere. In other words, that the stars of the constellation of the Thigh are particularly resonant with the energy of Set. Through the association of the corner-stone with my own development, it followed that, if we were to be properly orientated within the cosmos, we had to be aligned with Set.

At the time of my dream, Anna and I did not yet possess a hieroglyphic dictionary, so we simply related to the dream's imagery. All of the foregoing analysis was arrived at on the basis of my subsequent dreams. I have, however, presented that analysis here because it is key to understanding how, following on from my dream of the stone, my later sequence of dreams unfolded.

It was two weeks later that I had the, previously mentioned, dream in which I was asked: "But what image does the dreaming mind itself most want to focus on?" In this dream, too, the theme of being reconnected with ancient Egypt appeared: in the image of the Temple of Isis, which was intact, as it had been in our past life. The image of our walking towards the Sphinx led, a few days later on 18th October 1997, to a dream in which:

> I am told that Anna and I have completed one stage to do with the Sphinx and we have now to begin another.

This was then elaborated upon the next night:

> I am instructed that I have to shift my position with regard to the Dream in order that I can begin the next stage.

Finally, on the succeeding night, 20th October 1997, I had a dream which provided the guidance I needed to make the required shift:

> I am told to consider the Dream in terms of imminence and to ask myself what is imminent within a dream that will later materialize.

It was on 15th August of the same year that I had been shown how a series of events in material reality unfolds along a pre-existing sequence of dreams. At that stage, it was sufficient for me to be cognizant of this instruction and to observe how it was confirmed by our experience when we returned to the Sphinx. Now, we were being required, not simply to observe with hindsight how events in our lives had been prefigured in our dreams, but to determine from the content of our dreams what future events could be seen to be impending. (Though the *O.E.D.* states that 'imminent' is "almost always [used with reference to] evil or danger,"[38] in my dream the word was understood to refer to all future events.) It is this movement from observing with hindsight to identifying in advance the "signs of a reality into which the present [will] flow" that was the shift we had to make. In other words, Anna and I were required to return to the way of relating to the dream that existed in antiquity.

On the same night that I was told to consider the Dream in terms of imminence and to ask myself what is imminent within a dream that will later materialize, I had a second dream:

> Anna and I are shown a sequence from someone else's dreams and the effect of their dreaming. The dreams are stacked precariously like a completely unbalanced pile of books. We are told that this is because the dreamer has acted upon these dreams of their own volition, making them manifest, without having been instructed within the dreams to do so. In consequence, they have put things out of sequence and, hence, out of balance.

Through this dream, Anna and I were being warned that, although we were to ask ourselves what is imminent within a dream that will later materialize, it is not for us to decide when to make the imminent manifest. One should not assume that the representation of a situation in a dream constitutes an injunction to act upon that representation. Dreams have various functions; for example, many are a preparation for future events. This is why one must only act upon a dream when 'instructed within the dream to do so'. A dream of the Sphinx would not in itself indicate that one is required to journey to it; whereas the call of the Sphinx – "Come to me. Come to me." – was an unequivocal command.

Wilhelm spoke of "the concept expressed in the teachings of Lao-tse, as also in those of Confucius, that every event in the visible world is the effect of an 'image', that is, of an idea in the unseen world."[39] He continued: "Accordingly, everything that happens on earth is only a reproduction, as it were, of an event in a world beyond our sense perception; as regards its occurrence in time, it is later than the suprasensible event. The holy men and sages, who are in contact with those higher spheres, have access to these ideas through direct intuition [including avision] and are therefore able to intervene decisively in events in the world. Thus man is linked with heaven, the suprasensible world of ideas, and with earth, the material world of visible things, to form with these a trinity of the primal powers."[40]

What Wilhelm described corresponds with ancient Egyptian thinking: *"Sacred science"*, wrote Schwaller de Lubicz, *"starts from this mysterious but demonstrated reality which shows an energetic (spiritual) world preceding the material and quantitative world."*[41] He added: "The fact of an energetic, nonquantitative state immanent in the quantitative material aspect exists for our physics as well as for sacred science, and it is impossible to sunder these two states in order to consider one without the other."[42] Reiser discusses this issue in almost the same terms: "With each passing decade it is becoming increasingly clear that contemporary scientific knowledge provides support for the hypothesis of an immanent spiritual factor in the cosmos, and this is expressed in and through invisible fields of force, that is, non-material guiding influences with exemplifications on the physical, biological, psychic, and social levels."[43] These statements are consistent with the guidance that we have received through avision: that events in material reality unfold along pre-existing sequences of dreams. Further, we have been shown that Sothis is the outlet of these "non-material guiding influences."

Having had, along with his patients, many precognitive visions and dreams, Jung asserted that "The psyche at any given moment is on the one hand the result and culmination of all that has been and on the other a symbolic expression of all that is to be;"[44] and that, in view of this, "if we are not able to understand prospectively, then nothing is understood."[45] However, he then argued that the psyche "gives a picture of... the outlines of what is to come, in so far as the psyche creates its own future."[46] On this point, Anna and I have found that the guidance we have received through our dreams demonstrates that the psyche not only gives a picture of the future it creates but, beyond this, is witness to a future that will necessarily unfold. As Reiser stated, "Human consciousness in its awareness and in its time-spanning purposes is man's most immediate experience of the cosmic guiding field as it functions on the level of organisms."[47] Man's consciousness should, therefore, have the purpose of that Guiding Field as its focus. It will be remembered that the ancient Egyptian civilization was founded upon this principle – the Law of Maat.

On the afternoon of 20th October 1997, following my dreams about the imminent and the manifest, I dreamt of:

> Something evolving into a winged being – at first it is Set; then, the name Horus is mentioned.

The theme of something evolving immediately brought to my mind the previous instruction concerning the movement of the imminent into the manifest. I could see that the same pattern was being presented in both dreams and that I was thereby being shown that Set embodies the imminent and Horus the manifest.

Wilkinson explains that "Horus was one of the earliest of Egyptian deities"[48] and that "Horus also came to be worshipped as the son of Osiris and the goddess Isis, though either this god was originally a separate deity with whom the ancient... god was fused, or the... [ancient] deity was incorporated into the Osirian family in a very different form – as a divine infant."[49]

The notion of Set evolving into Horus counters the contemporary view of Set as "the implacable enemy of Horus."[50] It will be remembered that I had already been prepared for such a disparity through the explanation that Anna and I were given by the ancient Egyptian priests regarding the issues we were tackling: that the truth 'is completely contrary to the understanding that exists in the contemporary world'. Building upon this and other dream instruction, I was able to determine that the knowledge we possessed in our ancient Egyptian life was that

Set and Horus represent the imminent and the manifest. This analysis was confirmed four days later, on 24th October 1997, in an extended dream in which:

> I am captaining a ship on a sea journey. The scene is punctuated throughout the night by my thinking about a similar journey that I made in ancient Egypt. I am told that I have understood the relationship between the imminent and the manifest in such a way that I can now facilitate that process. Towards the end of the voyage, I see the moon one-eighth full in the shape of the grail cup. I am deeply moved and heartened by this sign of what I have accomplished.

The association of the Grail with the imminent and the manifest confirmed my judgement that the door of my earlier dream, in which the Grail cup first appeared, symbolized Sothis. At the same time, the fact that the moon appeared in the shape of the Grail cup indicates that the moon is particularly receptive to Sothic energy. We were, therefore, through these dreams, able to determine the relationship between Sothis and the moon some years before we encountered confirmation of it in the work of Musès.

In Hindu mythology, "This lovely ornament, the moon, with its cool rays, and holding in its cup Soma, the elixir of life, was all that Śiva took from the cosmic ocean."[51] Here, there is another link between Siva and Dionysus; for, the Soma held in the cup of the moon is "the elixir of immortality,"[52] whilst the wine held in the cup of Dionysus possesses the nature of "the god, who was but indestructible life."[53] The relevance this has for my dreams will reveal itself shortly.

As a result of the advice concerning the imminent and the manifest and Set evolving into Horus, we were able to understand why the Dream had stated that "Osiris is a false position." In terms of the paradigm of the imminent and the manifest, the most characteristic feature of Osiris, his mummiform appearance, represents the unnatural preservation of the existing order. From this point of view, Osiris was the emblem of those who were opposed to Set. In the myth, the mummified body of Osiris lacked a phallus, which meant that "an artificial penis had to be manufactured"[54] in order that Horus could be conceived to combat Set. This is a critical symbolic statement, since it indicates that Osiris did not embody the creative power of Sothis B – of 'that which releases the seed of ideas into existence'. It shows too that, rather than being a materialization of the efflux from Sothis, the Child Horus as the progeny of Osiris – the unfolding of events in Egyptian society – was artificially conceived in an attempt to prevent the realization of the imminent. (Here, I should add that an authentic interpretation of the Child Horus is possible: the imminent made manifest can be conceptualized as an infant born of, and nurtured by, his mother Isis-Sothis; and I shall discuss this issue later.)

Hornung says that "From an early period the Egyptians believed that mankind could act independently or even against the gods. But they were also convinced that only the will of the gods is finally realized and produces lasting achievements."[55] This raises the question of what the short-term interests of the Osirian priesthood were.

In contrast to Osiris, it is well established that Set was worshipped extensively in pre-dynastic times and he appeared, around 3150 B.C., on the mace-head of the proto-dynastic ruler King Scorpion. However, from around 2500 B.C., royal power declined as that of the Heliopolitan priesthood increased. At the same time, feudalism arose and the cult of Osiris began to spread.[56]

Rundle Clark comments that "The battle of Horus and Seth for the kingdom was a long and bitter business... Finally, at least in the common recension, Thoth, as the personification of order, persuaded the two to submit their quarrel to arbitration before the great council of the gods at Heliopolis [the scene of the conflict]."[57] It is by this means that the myth indicates that the undermining of Set occurred at the time of the increase in power of the Heliopolitan priesthood. Rundle Clark states that "The Great Quarrel is a clash between two systems of inheritance"[58] and that when "Horus is adjudged the rightful heir of his father, the patrilineal principle is assured."[59] The principle of inheritance of an office is itself an example of the unnatural preservation of the existing order; the natural – and appropriate – alternative to which is selection on the basis of whoever is best suited to that office. This would have been a matter of considerable importance in a culture which "believed that they were a divine nation, and that they were ruled by kings who were themselves gods incarnate; their earliest kings, they asserted, were actually gods, who did not disdain to live upon earth."[60] J.P. Seaton writes of a time in pre-dynastic China "when the emperors were True Sages, ruling solely by the emanations of their personal virtues and passing on rule not to their own kin but to the most virtuous subject they could discover."[61] Anna and I have both had dreams which state that such was once the case in ancient Egypt.

In opposition to those who served Sothis, Heliopolis became the headquarters of "the priests of the famous brotherhood of Rā, the Sun-god."[62] Rundle Clark describes how far more ancient beliefs and ceremonies "were transformed and reinterpreted to suit the requirements of new religious ideas. There is no doubt that the priests of Heliopolis and Memphis were the leaders in this practice and that the centralizing kings of the time gradually forced the ceremonies of Heliopolis on the rest of the country. The process can be seen at work in the texts on the pyramids of the Old Kingdom, where the temple hymns have been taken from their contexts to provide the services of the then new funerary cult. It can be seen, too, very clearly in the rite[s]... which have been revised to fit the doctrines of Osiris."[63] It wasn't Horus who was opposed to Set; it was the Heliopolitan priesthood. The names of the gods became counters in a game of power – a means to control the minds of the populace. The Heliopolitan conspiracy was taken even further by that of Herakleopolis: previously, "the decisions of the High God... were accepted without question. The sceptical spirit of the Herakleopolitan Age... queried the ultimate rightness of the fates determined by God himself."[64]

The *British Museum Dictionary of Ancient Egypt* describes how "From the late Third Intermediate Period (*c*.800 BC) onwards, there appears to have been a change in the way that Seth was viewed. Whereas previously he had been regarded simply as an ambivalent force, avoided for most purposes but invoked for others, he began instead to be seen as evil and undesirable."[65] As Carus observed, "Set, the great and strong god of prehistoric times, was converted into Satan with the rise of the worship of Osiris."[66] In the words of Schwaller de Lubicz, "Designating Set and Horus as being evil and good is reducing a universal principle to a personal opinion."[67] The Osirian priesthood, knowing they could not eliminate Set, endeavoured to alter people's perception of him in order to counter his influence. This was best achieved by persuading the populace that Set was evil and that the appearance of the god, or of images associated with him, in a dream were manifestations of a malevolent influence. Since "Dreams played an important role in Egyptian culture, principally because they were thought to serve as a means of communicating the will of the gods and serving as clues to future events,"[68] it was in this way that the Dream (symbolized by the crane) was undermined. This machination was so effective that, thousands of years later, when Set appeared in my dream, I immediately thought of him as a devil-like creature. To the end of his life, Jung wrote in the same terms: "The Antichrist is something infernal, the devil or the devil's son, and is therefore Typhon or Set [Typhon being the Greek form of Set]."[69] For Jung, Set was synonymous with evil.[70] It is to the credit of Musès that he moved from similarly writing of "the Egyptian god of evil, Set"[71] to identifying "the highest (regenerate) form of Set with the highest form of Horus, thus explaining the otherwise obscure depiction of Horus combined with Set as one deific figure, as can be seen in the momuments and texts."[72]

Through a vision, Anna and I were provided with the understanding of the true nature of Set which had existed prior to the rise of the Heliopolitan priesthood.

In my dreams, Set, after landing on my side, next manifested as the wasp, the guardian of the tunnel connected with the ancient Egyptians. Thus, he appeared both as the Lord of the Underworld and as the god of reincarnation. This is entirely consistent with Set being both the imminent and 'the personification of the regions of death', since death is the state of imminence from which the next life materializes. Nature always provides the individuals who are needed to meet the exigencies of the time. The Heliopolitan priesthood, a group which was intent upon retaining power within its own families, necessarily sought to prevent the reincarnation of those who were better suited to assume the seat of authority. In a bid to protect their interests, they instituted an order based upon patrilineal inheritance and made Osiris, their god of mummification, into the god of reincarnation, thereby usurping Set. Tompkins quotes Manly P. Hall, who states: "it is certain that, in the eyes of the Egyptians, mummification effectively prevented reincarnation."[73] Later, the Catholic Church, another patriarchal priesthood intent upon the pursuit of power, went a step further with its declaration, in the year 553, that "Whosoever shall support the mythical doctrine of the pre-existence of the soul and the consequent wonderful opinion of its return, let him be anathema." In the present day, psychotherapy generally maintains the undermining of the crane through its being founded upon the Judeo-Christian premise that we have only one life, with the inevitable consequence that dreams concerning reincarnation are misunderstood and misinterpreted.

Schwaller de Lubicz, who was well aware of the central position of reincarnation in ancient Egyptian thought, arrived at a view of Set and Horus which, in certain respects, is exactly that presented to Anna and myself by the Dream. This can be seen in his statement that the Uas sceptre – the Sceptre of Set – "pertains to an activity, the creative function, which is not yet the created [the imminent];" and he associated this activity with "the flux of the Word... [which] is not yet really manifested."[74] Equally commensurate with our dream instructions is his definition of "Horus as appearance [the manifest]."[75] Furthermore, his monumental book, *The Temple of Man*, concludes with a chapter on Set and Horus that focuses on one of the key scenes in the iconography of Luxor Temple to which Schwaller de Lubicz appended the caption "Horus Born of Set."[76]

However, despite this, instead of the continuum – the movement of the imminent into the manifest, of Set into Horus, which follows naturally from the above-quoted definitions – Schwaller de Lubicz, under the spell of the Heliopolitan paradigm, speaks of "the fundamental scission of what Lao-tse calls *Tao ko Tao*, 'what is and is not', being and nonbeing"[77] and uses this to explain why "Pharaonic myth shows Seth and Horus as enemies."[78] Yet, Lao Tzu says of being and non-being: "The two are the same, But after they are produced, they have different names."[79] This cannot possibly be interpreted to mean that being and non-being are "enemies". Whilst Schwaller de Lubicz was right to cite Lao Tzu with regard to Set and Horus, in so doing he demolished his own argument.

Recently, I found that the message of my dream of Set and Horus was encoded in the ancient Egyptian *Book of Hours*. In that text, as Wilkinson relates, "Each hour of the day was personified... by a deity."[80] Schwaller de Lubicz brilliantly recognised that the ideas presented in the *Book of Hours* correspond to the understanding in Chinese Medicine that the body proceeds through a daily cycle in which Qi is concentrated in each of its twelve meridians in turn for a two-hour period. Qi may be thought of as a natural force which is the "cause, process, and outcome of all activity in the cosmos."[81] It is that which links Man to his cosmic environment. As Tu Wei-ming wrote, "All modalities of being, from a rock to heaven, are integral parts of a continuum. Since nothing is outside of this continuum, the chain of being is never broken. A linkage will always be found between any given pair of things in the universe... The continuous presence of Qi in all modalities of being makes everything flow together as the unfolding of a single process."[82] Meridians "are the channels or pathways through which Qi flows among the Organs and various bodily parts, adjusting and harmonizing their activity."[83]

Schwaller de Lubicz explains that the 'hours of the day' (inscribed in the tomb of Ramses VI) provide "an eloquent teaching on the correspondence of the time of day with organic life in general. For Chinese acupuncture, noon is the hour of the heart, and 2 P.M. the hour of the small intestine. It is in this fashion that the texts and images are to be interpreted."[84] He provides the information that noon "begins the hour known as *expansion of the heart*, the hour which *rises for Horus*."[85] However, although Schwaller de Lubicz was right to say that noon is associated with the heart, according to Chinese Medicine, the time period relating to the heart actually begins at 11 a.m., ending at 1 p.m.; and, whilst the hour from noon to 1 p.m. was indeed identified by the ancient Egyptians with Horus, the preceding hour from 11 a.m. to noon was identified with Set.[86] As I was shown in my dream, Set and Horus represent two aspects of the same process: what begins with Set, culminates in Horus. Thus, the ancient Egyptians chose to identify Horus with the hour when the sun is at its zenith; which, in Chinese Medicine, is understood to be the time when Yang energy is at its peak. Though this would seem to be the most energetically powerful time of the day, in Taoist thought and practice, the hour between 11 a.m. and noon is regarded as the more vital.[87] This dynamic has been repeatedly emphasised to Anna and myself by our Qigong Master, Dr. Bisong Guo, without whose instruction we would not have later understood the importance of the hour of Set. In order to be able to appreciate the significance of that hour, one has to be familiar with the concept of Yin and Yang. Ted Kaptchuk explains: "Yin-Yang theory is based on the philosophical construct of two polar complements, called Yin and Yang... they are convenient labels used to describe how things function in relation to each other and to the universe... [and] the continuous process of natural change."[88] Kaptchuk continues: "All things have two facets: a Yin aspect and a Yang aspect."[89] Yin is associated with quiescence, receptivity, water, darkness, cold and femininity; whilst Yang is associated with activity, creativity, fire, light, heat and masculinity. Hence, "The character for Yin originally meant the shady side of a slope... Yang was the sunny side of a slope."[90] In Chinese thought, the twenty-four hour cycle is divided into a Yin half and a Yang half. 11 a.m. has a particular significance (as does 11 p.m. for the reverse reason) because, although it is the time when Yang energy moves towards its peak, it is also the moment when one can detect the first signs of the emergence of Yin. The hour of Set is, therefore, a perfect representation of the imminent.

It can be seen that the understanding of Set which Anna and I have been provided with through avision was never completely eradicated in ancient Egypt. Carus recounts that "Sety I [c.1294-1279 B.C.], the second king of the nineteenth dynasty, the shepherd kings, derives his name from the god Set – a sign of the high honour in which he was held among the shepherd kings; and indeed we are informed that they regarded Set, or Sutech, as the only true God."[91] Similarly, from the fact that the Ptolemaic Temple at Kom Ombo was dedicated to Set and Horus jointly, it can be seen that the two gods were not always regarded as adversaries. Schwaller de Lubicz describes how, in the much earlier Temple of Ptah at Memphis, "The bulrush and the papyrus [symbols of Set and Horus respectively] were placed at the double door to the temple of Ptah: this signifies the reconciled and unified Horus and Seth."[92] This is especially relevant to my dream instruction, since the god Ptah is the Mind of the Universe who "materializes the metaphysical principles"[93] – that is, makes the imminent manifest through the power of his thought.

Schwaller de Lubicz observes that "The end of the completed genesis, the ultimate realization, is the union in *friendship* rather than in enmity of Seth and Horus."[94] "[H.] Kees has shown that in several Egyptian nomes a pair of falcons was worshipped. This pair of falcons was the divine pair Horus and Seth, worshipped in the cult as a single deity."[95] "A late priest's title like *śḥtp nṯrwy* (who reconciles the two gods) leads us to think that in spite of alterations in the national theology, the reconciliation of Horus and Seth was celebrated in this nome [the 10th nome in Upper Egypt] until late times."[96] Te Velde goes on to say that "The pharaoh is the representative of Horus, but also the representative of Horus and Seth, who are united and reconciled."[97] The pharaoh Khasekhemui, whose name meant 'the two powers have appeared', sometimes had a supplement added to his name so that he was then known as 'the two lords who are in him are reconciled'.[98] It is interesting to see how closely the "ultimate realization" that Schwaller de Lubicz speaks of corresponds to the instruction I received through avision and how nothing essential was added to our understanding through research. This is why, later in October of 1998, I had a dream in which:

> The superiority of getting one's knowledge directly from Set, rather than from other sources such as books, is emphasised.

It was by means of this dream that we were shown that Set is the god of avision. As the ancient Egyptian sage Ptah-Hotep declared, "Those who the Gods guide cannot get lost."[99]

At the beginning of November 1997, two weeks after the moon appeared as the Grail cup, I dreamt:

> The Grail cup appears in front of my head and, then, moves into it, becoming one with it – the base being aligned with my shoulders and the stem with my adam's apple. There is a gentle, sublime feeling accompanying the experience.

Here, the Grail completed its journey from the Great Door of Heaven, via the moon, to its final destination within my own body and mind. Some years after my dream, I found that Musès provides the, earlier-mentioned, illustration from the text of the Second Shrine of Tutankhamun in which the source and destination of my Grail dreams are united. Noting that the word 'sba' meant both 'star' and 'door', he describes the illustration as depicting "Star Power Energy... entering through the forehead." Musès, an internationally recognised authority on human consciousness, states that "the future of human evolution lies not in the molecular body per se – which has reached its optimal development already – but in the brain, in which there is a huge redundancy of apparently unused neural tracts, just as there is a huge amount of evidently unused DNA in human cellular nuclei. That DNA contains the as yet unactivated genomes for the development of the brain's unused neurons. The bottom line is that we all have a vast reserve of untapped and enormous evolutionary potential."[100] He points to Sothis as the source of the energy that stimulates the unactivated genomes and the unused neural tracts. According to Musès, it is necessary "to open the rather 'rusty' neural valve in the brain (among nuclei in the vicinity of the hypothalamus) that controls the window or lens-opening for a higher light and life energy to pour through into us;"[101] and says that these are "largely unknown and in any event barely used neurosecretory cells."[102] I shall later cite a dream of Anna's which indicates that the Dream can open the valve at the appropriate stage of one's development. It is also noteworthy, with regard to the dream in which Anna was shown that Love is the original religion, that Musès adds: "In states of inspiration and great love the window opens slightly."[103]

The fourth in my sequence of Grail dreams occurred in early December of 1997:

> The different aspects of my being are contained within the Grail cup. As they start to coalesce, my understanding of them is unified.

On the same night, I also dreamt:

> I am trying to fit a screw into a plug, but I can't get it to fit. Suddenly, as I push the plug, it unexpectedly moves into a position I hadn't thought of. Then, I can see that I had put the screw in the wrong place. Now it is obvious where it has to go and everything easily fits together. The plug is of the sort that is used to link one electrical lead to another.

The dream in which the Grail cup appeared in the doorway occurred on 24th September 1997. Significantly, it had been on 25th September 1996 that I dreamt I was sitting next to a tunnel connected to the ancient Egyptians; and on the following day, 26th September 1996, that I had been told that Anna and I are a connected with the Sphinx now as we were in our Egyptian lifetime. A year later, on 27th September 1997, I had the dream in which an ancient priest placed upon a table the pieces of a stone Anna and I had once possessed that started to fit together like the pieces of a jigsaw. It will be seen that the process depicted in that dream corresponds to the experience presented in my dream of December 1997 in which the different aspects of my being started to cohere within the Grail cup. The two dreams of September 1996 provided the clue that the different aspects of my being relate to my different lives. Since knowledge of the significance of Sothis had been the foundation of our thinking in earlier lives, reacquaintance with that knowledge created the continuity which enabled the different aspects of my being to cohere. The dream in which I was trying to fit a screw into a plug accurately demonstrated the difficulty that I had previously experienced in trying to understand those different aspects of my being through the conventional notions of psychotherapy. When, as a result of our dream instructions, we realized that the different aspects are different lives, everything suddenly fell into place.

It will be remembered that 'Tekhi', which was a name of Thoth, also meant 'crane'; and that 'tekh-t' was a 'wine cup'. Wilkinson notes that "The legend preserved in the 'Contendings of Horus and Seth' asserts that Thoth was the son of Horus and that he emerged from the forehead of Seth who had [unknowingly, having been tricked,] eaten the semen of Horus on some lettuce plants. A later version of the same legend has the seed of Horus appear on the head of Seth as a shining disk which Thoth took and placed on his own head as his emblem."[104] Typically, in this Osirian text, the flow of the seed has been reversed so that it is Set who receives the seed from Horus. None-the-less, the reference to the reception of the seed and its association with the forehead depicts a process whereby wisdom appears from the acquisition of Sothic energy, which is both aligning and transformational, through the forehead. With regard to the Grail cup, the wisdom received and contained therein is, in the first instance, knowledge of Sothis and, in the second, knowledge of the true nature of one's existence as a receptor of Sothic energy – the ultimate realization of the injunction at the entrance to the Delphic Oracle to "Know thyself."

In the myth and rite, the infant Dionysus, having been torn to pieces by his guardians, descended into the Underworld, from which, after a period of one year, he returned. (Here, too, the pieces are reassembled.) Kerényi explains: "What occurred, not in conscious thought but in an unconscious process expressed in myth and rite, was an orientation toward a pure dialectic: life out of death and death out of life in an endless repetition encompassing the indestructibility of life, though it would be more correct to say that the indestructibility encompassed the repetition."[105]

Dionysus suffered a cruel death, but, as indestructible zoë,[106] he survived. "The significance of *zoë* is life in general, without further characterization. When the word *bios* is uttered, something else resounds: the contours, as it were, the characteristic traits of a specified life, the outlines that distinguish one living thing from another."[107] "What resounds surely and clearly in *zoë* is 'non death'. It is something that does not even let death approach it. For this reason the possibility of equating *psyche* with *zoë*, the 'soul' with 'life', and of saying *psyche* for *zoë*, as is done in Homer, was represented in Plato's *Phaedo* as a proof of the immortality of the soul."[108] "Plotinus called *zoë* the 'time of the soul', during which the soul, in the course of its rebirths, moves from one *bios* to another... If I may employ an image for the relationship between them, which was formulated by language and not by philosophy, *zoë* is the thread upon which every individual *bios* is strung like a bead, and which, in contrast to *bios*, can be conceived of only as *endless*."[109]

Depicted, too, in the myth of Dionysus/Sothis is the return and restitution of the Sothic Mysteries after they had been torn to pieces by the Egyptian priesthood which should have been guardian of those Mysteries.

For Musès, as for Anna and myself, the restitution of the Sothic Mysteries became a primary focus. There are numerous correspondences between Musès' understanding and the instruction we have received through avision. I should point out that of fundamental importance in Musès work is his conviction that the goal of The Lion Path is a process "by which the gestative regeneration of the immortal body could be begun even during life on earth."[110] (An aim of the ancient tradition of the generation of the immortal body is to transcend the process of reincarnation in gross material form.) It will be seen that aspects of the process Musès describes have appeared in our dreams. However, since we have received no instruction about the goal he speaks of and since, in May of 1998, I had a dream in which:

> I am told that I must not write beyond what I know.

I shall restrict my account to the process upon which we have received guidance.

The instruction that has been bestowed upon Anna and myself through avision has provided us with the experience of our previous deaths being transcended through the re-emergence of various past lives, with their associated memories, dreams and sensibilities, and their subsequent integration into this life. There is good reason to believe that Musès was aware of this process, for he states that "we must all literally re-member or re-form our true selves."[111] One's true self has Sothis as its centre.

The movement from a past life into this one can be existentially pervasive. For example, as I have demonstrated with regard to our ancient Egyptian life, the symbolism of certain of our dreams only made sense in the ancient Egyptian language. Similarly, with regard to past lives of which there is a historical record, we have found that experiences from those lives have exerted a determining influence upon our emotional state and our dreams on the corresponding day of the year in this life.

The instruction concerning the imminent and the manifest confirms how right the ancient dream interpreters were in their view that the Dream is future-directed. The selection of past lives to be integrated into this life is also future-directed. It is tailor-made by "that which dreams through us" to meet the challenges that we will be presented with as our life's purpose unfolds.

With the instruction, in December of 1997, that the different aspects of my being are contained within the Grail cup, my sequence of

Grail dreams came to an end. This sequence had been pre-figured ten years earlier, in May of 1987, when I dreamt:

> Although I know intellectually that it is not to be, I am forced to accept that the Holy Grail is a living reality in my family.

This dream captures the moment when my mind was jolted into accepting the first intimation of a later reality that was to be completely at odds with my existing conscious attitude. Ten years were to pass before this preparatory experience was realized – before the imminent became manifest and what had previously been impossible to understand became comprehensible. The obstacle to my understanding had its origin in the undermining of the Dream.

One can see, in the movement between my Grail dream of 1987 and dream sequence of 1997, how another, greater, force is at work – a force which is fully cognizant of how the future will unfold and is, as the ancient Egyptians recognised, the Architect of that unfolding. In order for this unfolding to take place, there has to be "a partnership between god and man." It makes no sense to live one's life on any other basis. Yet, as the Dream has shown, a concerted effort has been made to try to prevent that partnership from occurring. In my own case, the realization of this partnership came at the moment that the Grail cup moved into my head and became one with it.

CHAPTER THIRTEEN

The Green Jewel

Anna's equivalent dream sequence to mine of the Grail began in August of 1989 when she dreamt:

> An enormous and very powerful serpent emerges from my head, through my nose. There are people who fear it and want to kill it.

Alexander Wilder, writing in 1877, cited John Baldwin who remarked: "the 'serpent' will convey a very poor notion of its meaning to those who do not understand what it was. The serpent was regarded as a symbol of intelligence, of immortality, or protection against the power of evil spirits, and of a renewal of life or of the healing powers of nature."[1] In the same vein, James Fergusson wrote: "the Serpent is always the Agathodæmon, the bringer of health and good fortune. He is the teacher of wisdom, the oracle of future events... Any evil that ever was spoken of the serpent, came from those who were outside the pale, and were trying to depreciate what they considered as an accursed superstition."[2] Wilder himself said of the Serpent: "If he conducted to the tree of prohibited knowledge in the Garden of Eden, he was also an Æsculapius, the healer of men in the wilderness of Sinai, the good spirit of many a world-religion, the source of diviner inspiration, and the imparter of the highest, holiest, most essential life. Indeed, Serpent-lore is the literature of the earlier periods of human history."[3] "In every known country of the ancient world the serpent formed a prominent object of veneration, and made no inconsiderable figure in legendary and astronomical mythology. Its consecration as a religious emblem preceded the later forms of polytheism."[4] "Its antiquity must be accredited to a period far antedating all history."[5] The remains of Serpent-worship were even to be found in early Christianity: "Whole sects, we are assured by the early fathers, used to partake of the Eucharistical Supper after it had been consecrated by a living snake coming from a coffer and entwining its coils about the loaves of bread."[6]

Returning to Siva, Hyde Clark states, "Many of the Hindu gods are decorated with snakes, for such is the inheritance of serpent-worship, but Siva is more particularly so provided."[7] Clark (in a paper that first appeared in *The Journal of the Anthropological Institute of Great Britain and Ireland*) used a philological approach which demonstrated that "*We are justified in regarding Siva and* [his consort] *Kali as a pre-historic legend, which has survived in Hindu mythology and been dealt with by a later dominant race.*"[8] In other words, Siva "was no part of the religious system of the Aryan invaders of India, but was a great divinity of the older population."[9]

Wilder, in an introduction to Clark's paper, condensed a significant section of Clark's argument into the statement: "SIVA, the god-name of India, is far from being as exclusive as we had supposed. We find it in Asia Minor as *Saba* or Sabazius; in Greece as *Seba*; in Central America as *Sibu*; in Africa as *Eshowo*."[10] This was of particular interest to Anna and myself, since it confirmed the instruction provided by two dreams of mine; the first of which occurred at about the same time that Anna dreamt of the Serpent emerging through her nose:

I am told: "Siva is the god from which all other gods are derived."

And the second, on 8th September 1997, two days before I was instructed to restore the crane:

> I am shown the word 'Saba'.

Of particular importance is the identification that Clark highlights between Siva as Saba and the ancient Egyptian god Seb or Sobek, which were both names of Set.[11] Thus, Clark demonstrates that a comparative philological analysis reveals that Set is Siva – a conclusion which Anna and I had arrived at through avision.

C. Staniland Wake (in a paper also published in *The Journal of the Anthropological Institute of Great Britain and Ireland*) cited Fergusson, who wrote that Siva has the title "King of Serpents,"[12] and confirmed Clark's identification of Set with Siva: "It can be shown that the Hindu deity is a form of Kronos or Saturn, one of the Semitic names for whom was Set or Seth. It was the serpent-symbol of this God [Set] which was said to have been elevated in the wilderness for the healing of the people bitten by serpents, and... Rudra (Siva) was called not only the *bountiful*, the *strong*, but the *healer*... There is another point of contact, however, between Siva and the god Set or Typhon, who was known to the Egyptians also as the serpent Apôphis, or the giant. An ancient writer states that one of the names of El, or Kronos, was Typhon; and the serpent and pillar symbols of the Phœnician deity confirm the identification between Set, or Saturn, and the Siva of the Hindu pantheon."[13] Wake continued: "That the idea of health was intimately associated with the serpent is shown by the crown formed of the asp, or sacred *Thermuthis*, having been given particularly to Isis, a goddess of life and healing;" and added: "a Moslem saint of Upper Egypt is still thought to appear under the form of a serpent, and to cure the diseases which afflict the pilgrims to his shrine."[14] "The Arabic word 'hiya' indeed means both life and serpent. This connection is supported by the association... between the serpent and the gods of the life-giving wind, and by the fact that these also possess the pillar-symbol of life. This belongs as well to Siva the destroyer, the preserver and the creator, as to Set or Saturn, to Thoth-Hermes, and El or Kronos."[15] Interestingly, with regard to Anna's dream of the Serpent emerging from her nose, the ancient Egyptian word 'fent' meant both 'serpent' and 'nose'; while 'Fenti' was a name of the god of wisdom Thoth.[16]

Wake noted that "Theodoret did not distinguish between an Egyptian sect called *Sethians* and the Gnostic *Ophites* or serpent-worshippers."[17] This has relevance for Anna's dream because the serpent emerging from her nose represented a play on the word 'gnosis' – 'a knowledge of spiritual mysteries through divine revelation'; an interpretation supported by Wake who stated: "This personification of divine wisdom is undoubtedly represented on Gnostic gems under the form of the serpent."[18] Arthur Lillie observes that Hippolytus identified the Ophites with the Naasseni "who professed to have received their teaching from James, the brother of the Lord."[19] Andrew Welburn says of James that "The Jewish Christians, in the years following the death on the cross, took as their representative James, the brother of Jesus who became head of the Jerusalem community."[20] He also explains that "The Gnostics drew their sense of strength not from an inner 'I' or centre of identity, but from their vision of man in his cosmic nature."[21]

Jean Doresse notes: "The *Philosophumena* [a Gnostic text] ascribes to the Naassenes... Sethians and others a number of references to the Greek Mysteries;"[22] for example, among the Naassenes "Hermes is the Word who has expressed and fashioned the things that have been, that are and that will be."[23] Lillie recounts that "According to Hippolytus the Naasseni... called the Father 'the many named, thousand eyed'." Lillie astutely observes that 'thousand eyed' is a literal translation of one of the names of Siva. And he goes on to cite a hymn of the Naasseni in which it is proclaimed of God "Thou art Pan as thou art Bacchus, as thou art Shepherd of brilliant stars." Lillie again points out that "The Shepherd of the brilliant stars must be S'iva."[24] One cannot but be struck by the fact that a sect who professed to have received their teaching from Jesus' successor identified God with Sothis.

Why, then, was the Serpent of Anna's dream feared to such an extent that people wanted to kill it? Patrice Chaplin recounts a conversation with the guardian of the Grail mysteries associated with

Rennes-le-Château in which he explained: "The [Catholic] Church saw them [the Gnostics] as the enemy because they believed in direct contact with the divine through no intermediary... Gnosis means direct knowledge of God. Which, of course, the Church sees as heresy;"[25] not in order to maintain the purity of Jesus' teaching, but because the personal autonomy that gnosis confers is a threat to the 'authority' of the Church. Had maintaining the purity of Jesus' teaching been a priority, it would not be the case that "on the whole the later church suppressed [the teaching of James] in the interests of what it had made into 'orthodoxy'."[26] The anathematization of the Serpent of Set by the Catholic Church was a continuation of the policies of the Heliopolitan priesthood.

Three months after her dream of the Serpent, in November of 1989, Anna dreamt:

> I am in possession of a large, precious green jewel. I am being pursued by an evil gang who want to take it from me. At first, this seems like a game – but, then, it becomes deadly serious and I fear for my life. I am caught and taken to a mansion where I am locked in a room with people who wish to harm me, but I manage to escape as I find that the door opens when I push against it backwards. In this mansion, I meet a man and woman who say they will help me. Accompanied by the man, I get into a car (into the driving seat) and a car-chase ensues, which ends with my out-manoeuvring my pursuers. We abandon the car and continue on foot along roads and down a subway. Then, we discover a path through trees that leads into the grounds of a dilapidated old house, which I recognise as being my old school. The house has many windows, but every single pane has been shattered. We walk past the house, along a cloister lined with stone statues. As we pass by, I see that within is an open coffin containing the body of a girl who has long, dark hair with a fringe and is dressed in white – and I have the chilling realization that she is me. I know she has been dead for many years, yet, though lifeless, there are no signs of decomposition. I feel she died in her childhood or teens, although she is an adult. I wonder what will happen to her when the

house is demolished – which I sense is to be soon. She may be buried under the rubble; or, perhaps, her parents will move her (here, I am not thinking of my parents of this life). Then, I have a strange feeling that she might start to breathe again. It disturbs me that she will be too young – innocent and vulnerable – for her age due to the years she has missed through being dead.

When the man and I reach the front of the house, we find the gang awaiting us. As they haven't noticed us yet, I tell the man to crouch in the bushes, but he is too clumsy and gives us away. I wonder whether it really is clumsiness or whether he doesn't understand the seriousness of the situation – and, even, whether he has given us away intentionally. We have to fight off our pursuers and run. The man then takes me to a 'safe house' where the woman is expecting us. She says she will hide me, but by now I don't trust her or the man. Soon the gang arrives at the front door and I suspect I have been betrayed. This time I escape (through another door) on my own. I am clutching the green jewel as I wake.

At the time of her dream, Anna and I interpreted the dead girl who 'might start to breathe again' as being a part of herself that had died during her childhood and, so, understood the threatening situation in which she found herself to be representative of her familial environment. It was obvious that the precious green jewel represented something very specific, but the meaning of that symbol completely eluded us.

Some years later, in 1995, our conversation again led to the dream and I remembered that, in the *Tao Te Ching*, which Anna had not yet read, Lao Tzu made reference to a green gem: "Therefore the sage, while clad in homespun, conceals on his person a priceless piece of jade."[27] Although we were none the wiser as to what the green jewel signified, we were now aware that Lao Tzu had understood its significance, since there was plainly a correspondence between the precious green jewel of Anna's dream and the priceless piece of jade that the Taoist Master made reference to. Later still, we discovered that the green jewel was an apt symbol within the context of Anna's dream in which her body from a past life might start to breathe again; since, for the ancient Egyptians, the colour green, as well as being representative of life, was "a potent sign of resurrection."[28]

The ease with which one is able to integrate a past life is in part determined by the circumstances of one's exit from that life. A peaceful death smoothes the way to integration; whereas, a traumatic death, through illness, accident or violence, creates an obstacle which will usually not be overcome until that experience and its consequences have been addressed, in the same way that a present-life trauma has to be faced if one is to be freed of it. The memory of a traumatic death will heavily determine the reincarnated child's fantasies, play, dreams, nightmares, general interests and, in some individuals, even their physical constitution (a fascinating account of evidence regarding such physical correlates, 'Reincarnation Effects on Biological Form', has been provided by Michael Cremo[29]). For a person undergoing psychotherapy, the difficulties in integrating such a past life trauma are heavily compounded if their memories of it are misinterpreted as being symbolic of inner conflict or disturbing events in their present life. As I have mentioned, Anna and I were ourselves caught in that trap and it was only through the Dream reacquainting us with our past lives that our thinking was corrected. "Pythagoras taught that every soul travels 'the circle of necessity', entering into different bodies at different times. Understanding this law was, to him, fundamental to understanding the truth in all other matters."[30]

Following her dream of August 1989, in which there were people who wanted to kill the Serpent emerging from her head, and her subsequent dream of November 1989, in which she escaped clutching the green jewel, Anna then dreamt, in March of 1990:

> I am in a hot, desert landscape, standing against a white wall. Suddenly, I am hit over the head several times with a heavy object. My mind remains calm and lucid. After the third blow, I know that I shall die – my skull has been smashed.

Some years after her dream, Anna discovered that the location of her murder was revealed through the detail of the white wall, as 'White Walls' was an ancient Egyptian name for Memphis. The memory of having been murdered in ancient Egypt brought to Anna's mind a recurring nightmare which had haunted her between the ages of eight and ten years:

> I am walking by a wall along a road. The sun is shining. There is a strange, sweet smell in the air. I see an old factory where the doors are open, so I enter. Inside is a large machine which moves up and down with a stamping action. The movement of the machine seems predictable, so I am not aware that I am in danger as I stand watching it. Then, suddenly, it is coming down onto me – I know it will kill me.

It was only relatively recently that Anna realized that the 'old factory' associated with the smell in the air referred to the 'olfactory' bulb and, thus, was linked to the Serpent emerging from her nose. From this, we deduced that the first blow to Anna's head had damaged her olfactory bulb. The fact that she was not aware she was in danger, suggests that she was murdered by someone whom she trusted. This scenario relates to the couple in her dream of November 1989 who said they would help her and then betrayed her.

Schwaller de Lubicz, when describing how Luxor Temple is patterned on the human figure, states: "The formation of the organized being begins with the head. The head is the place of ideal determination of the body's organic functions, and thus one must look there to see the governing principles. Among the three vital centres to which the three secret sanctuaries of the temple of Luxor are devoted, two are consecrated to endocrine glands – the pituitary body and the pineal body;"[31] whilst the third "is devoted to the olfactory bulb, the olfactory brain."[32] The three sanctuaries are aligned in accordance with the relative positions on a sagittal plane of the three vital centres within the head.[33] Schwaller de Lubicz explains that the olfactory bulb is "the seat of vital *distribution* to the two endocrine glands of the vital source;"[34] that is, of the energies vital for life (in particular, the energy from Sothis B which 'vivifies gods and men'). The pituitary, "the primary radio-receiver"[35] – the sanctuary of which was known as the Sanctuary of Amun,[36] the Hidden One (Sothis B) – transmits Sothic energies to the pineal, the gland which "is impregnated by eternal ideas."[37] The eternal ideas are the Divine Word, referred to by Schwaller de Lubicz as "the Verb", "which is at the basis of all becoming" and to which the three sanctuaries are devoted.[38]

We also learnt from Schwaller de Lubicz that "Among terrestrial vertebrates the olfactory brain, which is the most primitive, has its animal form in the serpent, for which the naja (the cobra) of Egypt is the typical representative, the symbol;"[39] hence, the Serpent emerging through Anna's nose in her dream of August 1989.

Anna's next dream in the sequence did not occur until April of 1997, a month before our first visit to Egypt:

> I am wrapped in strips of cloth, lying on a bed. Although I am dead,
> I am conscious and am distressed that my wrappings are to be removed.

In this dream Anna moved from a memory of having been murdered in her ancient Egyptian life to feeling distress that her mummified body was to be disturbed. That the experience of having been mummified leads to disturbing dreams in a later life was well known to the ancient Egyptians, for whom 'sukhet' meant 'to embalm' and 'sukha' was an 'evil remembrance' or 'bad dream'.[40] Here, the ancient Egyptian language confirms one of the most shocking realizations we have been provided with through avision: some sort of consciousness remains in the mummified body despite the brain being removed and, further, the traumas which the mummified body is subjected to have far-reaching consequences in a subsequent life.

On 6th September 1997, four days after our return from the Sphinx, Anna dreamt:

> Anthony and I go out into our garden to find that the stone Pan
> shell at the back has been smashed and removed. In its place are three
> white obelisks, arranged to form a triangle. We are very upset, but
> we feel that a new Pan shell may grow from the ground.

The reappearance in Anna's dreams of white architectural features –
the white obelisks corresponding to the white wall – within a scene
of violence is indicative of a connection between her murder and the
destruction of the Pan shell. This dream, with its broken Pan shell,
came three weeks before my dream in which Anna and I were shown
the broken stone we had once possessed being restored into another
form. Thus, the knowledge which we had possessed in our past lifetime
and which was now being restored was that the fertility god whom
the Greeks knew as Pan is a cornerstone of the Universe. It will be
remembered that Pan is Sothis B, the leader of the planets; a fact that
will soon be seen to be of particular importance. The breaking of the
Pan shell (corresponding to the dismemberment of Dionysus, with
whom Pan was identified[41]) represented the destruction of that which
receives the seed from Sothis B. It was replaced by three obelisks. The
origin of the obelisk has been traced back to "the temple of the sun-god
at Heliopolis."[42] When analysing Anna's dream, we understood it to be
depicting the understanding associated with Sothis B being destroyed
and replaced by the Heliopolitan cult of the sun. The Dream indicated,
thereby, that the priesthood of Heliopolis was responsible for Anna's
death in Memphis and that she had been murdered on account of the
knowledge she was receiving from Sothis.

Significantly, the Dream did not present the Pan shell as a man-
made object, but rather as something natural which may grow again
from the ground – indicating that the Pan shell is a manifestation
of the Earth's receptive nature. In this, the Pan shell is like Anna's
skull which, though smashed in ancient Egypt, has grown again as a
receptacle for Sothic energy.

The need for restoration was then presented three days later in
the dream of mine in which I was instructed to restore the crane. Two
weeks after that, on 22nd September 1997, the process of the restoration
of the Pan shell in our garden began in a dream of Anna's:

> The spirit of Thoth settles at the back of our garden. The
> atmosphere is vibrant and there is a deep sense of peace.

There was a distinct, almost palpable, sublime energy in our garden following Anna having this dream, which increased further still on the following day when it was demonstrated to Anna that, with the spirit of Thoth having settled at the end of our garden, other developments were occurring:

> I am shown – over a long time – the interweaving of the gods Hathor, Thoth and Seb, through the light and colour of stars and flowers in our garden.

Musès states: "the power corresponding to Venus was in Ancient Egypt Hathor: a form of the Great Goddess... Thus Venus and Sôthis are connected for Sôthis is the Star-Form of the Goddess."[43] Venus/Hathor is the Goddess of Love into whose Mysteries we were initiated through Anna's dreams on that subject. Thoth, as I have mentioned, personifies Sothic energy conveyed through the moon's resonance. Seb was the ancient Egyptian name of Set in his planetary aspect as Mercury.

In January of 1999, Anna discovered that Seb, Ta (Thoth) and Isis (who was identified with Hathor) are all depicted as weaver gods in the Eighth Division of the Tuat,[44] corresponding to the interweaving of those gods in her dream. This indicates that, having fulfilled the summons to the Fifth Division, we were then led into aspects of the experience that were recorded as being the Eighth Division. The Eighth Division is concerned with the weaving together of the different aspects of one's being which have been separated by death. It was only much later that we understood how it had come about that a physical process of restoration was unfolding in our garden.

Following our marriage in 1995, Anna had stripped the whole of our back garden down to bare earth in order to redesign it. This was the preparatory stage for an intense shamanic experience that was deeply moving to witness. For, Anna found that, as she cleared the garden, the Earth itself created patterns which delineated the planting design she had to follow. It took us some time to realize that what had been drawn was a simplified outline of a human head and torso and that, when we acquired the Pan shell, Anna had unconsciously positioned it in the location of the hypothalamus. There was, therefore, an exact correspondence between the design of our garden and our heads.

Anna's experience of being guided by the Earth in conjunction with the descent of the spirit of the gods of Egypt made us aware that our garden had become a living manifestation of the relationship between Heaven, Earth and Man.

By acting upon her impulse to clear our garden and make it a sensual expression of our love – specifically, of our union through marriage – Anna gave material expression to the concept of Love being the original religion. The society of the original religion was profoundly shamanic in its outlook. After following the guidance of the Earth to create the outline of the human form, Anna, through her planting choices (some dictated by dreams), drew to our garden, by means of resonance, the energies needed to restore the function in Nature that is symbolized by the Pan shell. This energy facilitated the healing of the trauma of our having been murdered in our Egyptian lifetime through the restitution in our life of the spirit of Egypt.

The Dream was revealing to us that Anna had, intuitively, followed a tradition she had known in her ancient Egyptian life. Memories of this appeared in a number of Anna's dreams; for example, on 15th June 1997:

> I am a young girl living in ancient Egypt. I am learning about the plants there: being taught how to distinguish between the wild and the cultivated, the native and the foreign.

And, in the same month, she dreamt:

> Anthony and I are living in ancient Egypt. Anthony accompanies me while I plant a palm tree.

In ancient Egypt, "The place where gardens were created was often itself holy and significant as the abode of a deity."[45] Thus, by means

of their gardens, "The Egyptians created sacred landscapes."[46] Royal
gardens demonstrated the power of the pharaoh to provide what the
gods required.[47] The doum-palm was specifically identified with
Thoth;[48] whilst the sycamore fig and papyrus were identified with
Hathor. Significantly, in a dream in March of the following year, 1998,
Anna was provided with knowledge of a similar correspondence for Set:

> It is twilight. I am on the Giza plateau, looking eastwards. The
> full moon rises: it is so beautiful that I gasp. Later, when daylight
> comes, I walk towards the town and come across some pale-lemon
> narcissi with amber-orange centres: these are the flowers of Set.

We later learnt that the Greek god Narcissus was a form of Dionysus[49]
who, as Adonis, was the consort of Venus;[50] and that the six-lobed
narcissus flower formed the sacred hexagram that symbolized the
"union between Goddess and God."[51]

On 16th June 1997, the day after her dream of learning about plants
as a young girl in ancient Egypt, we were shown how successfully the
energetic ambience of ancient Egypt had been realized in our garden,
when Anna dreamt:

> I go out into our garden and find myself in ancient Egypt – in
> our garden there. I walk through our Egyptian garden into a park
> garden beyond.

When viewed from the perspective of ancient Egyptian thought, it will
be seen that many of Anna's dreams in this chapter are linked by the
colour green. Schwaller de Lubicz points out that, if a sagittal section
of the head is placed on a plan of Luxor Temple, the sanctuary devoted
to the olfactory bulb "is exactly at the same height that the uraeus
[the serpent on the royal crown] should occupy on the forehead."[52]
That Serpent, which, in the first dream of her sequence, emerged from
Anna's nose, was a form of Isis named 'Uatch' or 'Wadjet' meaning
the 'Green One'.[53] This theme was developed in Anna's next dream, of
the green jewel, since another meaning of 'uatch' was 'green jewel' or

'green stone' – 'emerald, malachite, feldspar or turquoise'. In addition, there is a reference to green in the image of the dead girl who 'may start to breathe again' because, as I mentioned earlier, that colour was symbolic of resurrection. The dream in which Anna was hit over the head depicted the destruction of her olfactory bulb, where Uatch was located. Then, the dreams situated in our garden were more obviously identified with green, particularly since, for the ancient Egyptians, the colour was "a symbol of growing things and of life itself."[54] The Sceptre of Isis, the symbol of the renewal of life, was called Uatch. Furthermore, the colour green was associated with Hathor,[55] whose sacred stone was the Uatch. In this sequence, Hathor appears as the goddess of the renewal of life – the guardian of those who have embarked upon the process of reincarnation. An ancient Egyptian text reads: "I am she who has the oar of the ship of command. The sovereign of life... The one who guides the... ones who are lost and exhausted on the roads of the reborn... I am Hathor, Queen of the northern sky, Who watches over the reborn."[56]

On 5th October 1997, Anna dreamt:

I am on a dangerous quest. At the end, I am shown that I am the green jewel – the green, dual-pointed crystal.

In Anna's dreams, the transition from her possessing the green jewel to becoming that jewel signified that, as a result of realizing the instruction received through avision, culminating in her fulfilling the summons to the Sphinx, she had become one with the Sothic Mind, of which the green jewel is a symbol. It was the following month that I dreamt that the Grail cup moved into my head. The extent of the correspondence between our two dreams only really became clear to us in 1999 when we learnt that it was said that the Holy Grail was fashioned from an emerald that fell from the crown of Satan as he descended into the Underworld.[57]

Philip Gardiner and Gary Osborn explain that Set's "name 'Set-hen' or 'Sa-tha-ten'... became 'Satan' when the Israelites emigrated [from

Egypt]."[58] In the Middle Ages, it was said of the emerald which fell from the crown of Set: "This stone fell upon earth, and from it was carved a vessel of great beauty, which came, after many ages, into the hands of Joseph of Arimathea. He offered it to the Savior who made use of it in the Last Supper."[59] Jesus celebrated the Last Supper with the cup of Set because, as J. Leibovitch remarked, Set is the "dieu sauveur [saviour god]."[60] In the same vein, H. Te Velde states that "According to the demotic papyrus Leiden I 384, [Set as] the griffin is the shepherd of everything living on earth."[61] Thus, both Set and, later, Jesus, were the Saviour and the Good Shepherd.

As a Semite, nothing would have been more natural than for Jesus to have made a gesture of ritual alignment with Set. Set, who "appeared in the Old Testaments as Seth,"[62] is, as Wake recounts, "the divine ancestor of the Semites" – "the background of their religious consciousness."[63] For the Gnostic sect of Manicheans, "Seth was above all the apostle or saviour who appeared throughout the ages until his mission was fulfilled."[64] In these traditions in which he was the Saviour, Seth was identified as the incarnation of Set. There is reason to think that, in so doing, the Gnostics were maintaining the view of Set which had existed prior to the rise of the Heliopolitan priesthood. But, of course, if Seth's genealogical status as the son of Adam and Eve is stripped of its context within Set's ongoing reincarnation, the net result is that he is merely the human progeny of Adam and Eve rather than a god incarnate. This would then be akin to the rouse by which Horus the Elder was reduced by the Heliopolitan priesthood to being the Child Horus, son of Osiris.

With reference to the Sabeans (the ancient Yemenite people) as the children of the Biblical Seth and the Sabean Manetho's history entitled *Sothis*, Musès wrote (in a handwritten note that is in my possession): "Seth = Sothis ≡ Soter ≡ Saviour (Christos)". Several Gnostic traditions taught of Set's appearance throughout the ages and of "the coming of Seth in the person of Jesus."[65] Doresse stated: "That this cult came to be actually codified is attested by the existence of Egyptian figurines of the god Seth, cast in bronze, which are perfectly appropriate to it. The most significant represent the god walking with the hieratic gait, his body girt with a loin-cloth and surmounted by a head which has not, now, the muzzle of the mythic 'Sethian' animal commonly assigned to Seth in the Pharaonic tradition, but the ass's head much more rarely met with."[66] Here, there is a striking correspondence to the details of Anna's childhood vision, in which ass-headed Set was upright and dressed in a loin-cloth, providing further confirmation of Hornung's statement that the ancient Egyptians did not invent their gods, but experienced them.

Walker points out that the Gnostic view continued to be held in some Christian traditions into Mediaeval times: "Some said Christ was the same as the Jewish ass-god Iao, identified with Set."[67] "Christians of the Middle Ages claimed Iao was Jesus."[68] The tradition that Jesus used a cup carved from an emerald from the crown of Set is consistent with this. In addition, like the Greek Sothic deity Dionysus, Set was the ancient Egyptian god of wine. M.A. Murry argues that Set's name 'Se-tekh' (note the connection with 'tekhi' meaning 'wine cup') meant 'to intoxicate, to cause to be drunken';[69] which "would imply a cult of the same type as that of Bacchus, where drunkenness was regarded as possession by the god."[70] Te Velde recounts that, according to J. Yoyotte, "Seth and Hathor... were tutelar god and goddess of wine."[71] It can be argued, therefore, that when, in the Christian myth, Jesus officiated at the Last Supper, he was observing, not only a characteristically Dionysian, but also a considerably more ancient Setian ritual.

It will be remembered that, in the Dionysian Mysteries, Dionysus was represented by 'that which releases the seed of ideas into existence'. In the Gnostic tradition, Set was described in similar terms. A.F.J. Klijn states: "According to the Apocalypse of Adam, Adam tells Seth that the knowledge they [Adam and Eve] possessed went into 'the seed of the great aeons';"[72] that is, it went into Seth. Klijn provides the crucial explanation that Seth "is the 'seed of this great generation' and for that reason he received his name... Seth [meant] 'another seed'."[73] "In a number of writings, he is the bearer of the divine seed."[74] As the bearer of the divine seed, Seth was both the progenitor of his generation and 'that which releases the seed of ideas into existence'; which is why the descendants of Seth were called by such names as "those to whom the revelation has come."[75] Klijn points out that it is clear, from a description of Seth by Epiphanius, "that Seth was thought to reveal heavenly secrets."[76] The foregoing is entirely in accord with Set being the god of avision.

The common identity of Set and Dionysus is also revealed by the fact that the Dionysian mind finds within the human body "its reflection in the pineal gland (the 'third eye'), which cone-like organ atop the spinal column is represented by the thyrsus, that mysterious Bacchic wand made from a pine-cone fixed to a fennel stalk."[77] The god Set, in the form of the enigmatic griffin, is similarly representative of the pineal gland "which flames from the top of the head ('the knob and stalk of the Greek and Etruscan Griffon being not a bad picture of this gland and its fibres')."[78] (In the next chapter, I shall present a dream of Anna's in which Set, in the form of Mercury – who was the Messenger of the Gods – activated her pineal gland.) The emphasis upon the pineal gland is another demonstration of the sophistication of the sacred science of the ancient world, for this gland has a critical role to play in the physiological process of dreaming. Patrick Holford and Dr. James Braly explain that "Melatonin is perhaps best known for keeping you 'in sync' with nature and the rhythm of day and night and the seasons. Produced in the pineal gland, the 'third eye' in the centre of the head, melatonin levels rise when you sleep, and help to promote sleep and dreaming. All the American astronauts when in orbit take melatonin to sleep, dream and keep their circadian rhythms in check."[79] It is, we believe, for this reason that the ancient Greeks considered the pineal gland to be the 'seat of the soul'.[80]

In ancient times, a powdered gold alloy known as 'shem-an-na' was produced.[81] 'Shem' meant 'highward'[82] and 'an-na' meant 'heavenly stone'.[83] Laurence Gardner explains that shem-an-na was used in pharaonic times to enhance pineal activity and, thereby, to heighten perception and intuition.[84] This effect was achieved because the substance stimulates the production of "super-high levels of melatonin and serotonin."[85] Whilst melatonin, produced by the pineal gland, promotes dreaming, serotonin, which is produced by the pituitary gland, is the chemical messenger that activates this process.[86] "The pineal gland is impregnated by eternal ideas, and gives us the possibility of formulating our own conceptions. It is an organ of thought by means of which we acquire inner perception and can thereby change eternal ideas into earthly conceptions... Yogis believe that the pineal is a receiver and sender of subtle vibrations which carry thoughts and psychic phenomena... The pineal is also known as the 'Eye of Wisdom'... The activities of the pineal gland are directly related to those of the pituitary gland, another small body at the base of the brain. The frontal lobe of the pituitary stimulates the intellectual centres in the frontal lobe of the brain, while the dorsal lobe of the pituitary affects the base of the brain where are situated the centres of poetic inspiration and exalted aspiration... The pituitary gland is the primary radio-receiver, channelling all wave-bands and frequencies. It transmits selected frequencies (through secretions) directly to the pineal gland, which then amplifies certain broadcasts for transmission throughout the body... it is interesting to note that the Pineal Third Eye has been found to contain very fine granular particles, rather like the crystals in a wireless receiving set."[87]

Physiologically, enlightened consciousness is directly associated with the activity of the pineal system. In 2001, Anna and I learnt that, in Taoist symbolism, enlightened consciousness is described as a piece of pure jade. This explained what Lao Tzu had meant when he said: "Therefore the sage, clad in homespun, conceals on his person a priceless piece of jade." We also learnt that, in Taoist religion, the most enlightened beings dwell in a realm called the Palace of Pure Jade, where they are said to have merged with the Tao in its undifferentiated state. Thus, when one's conscious mind is completely at one with the activity of the pineal system, that is, with the part of the body that is concerned with being aligned with the rhythms of Nature and with dreaming, one is said by the Taoists to dwell in the Palace of Pure Jade. Since the Dream is the Tao, to merge with the Tao is to merge with the Dream. Hence, it was only after we had been made aware, through avision, of the significance of the Dream – and particularly after our learning to act upon our dream instructions had culminated in our fulfilling the summons to the Sphinx – that the Grail cup merged with my head and Anna was told she had moved from the position of carrying the green jewel on her person to that of becoming one with it.

Anna came to realize that the different aspects of her being – her different lives – are the myriad facets of the green jewel. Since the green jewel is specifically identified with the pineal system, each facet of the crystal comprises the essence of the pineal experience of the lifetime which that facet represents.

It will be remembered that one of the key insights provided by Lao Tzu is that "Turning back is how the way moves." It will also be remembered that I was instructed that "The Dream is the Tao;" and that I was shown, through the guidance regarding "the superiority of getting one's knowledge directly from Set," that Set is the god of avision. It is entirely consistent with the foregoing that Plutarch stated that one of the meanings of the name 'Set' is 'turning back'. It is also consistent with the machinations of the Heliopolitan priesthood that 'turning back' was twisted into meaning 'to desert' and 'to abandon'.[88] My experience, that Set appeared in my dreams during the time I arrived at the tunnel connected with the ancient Egyptians, confirms for Anna and myself the association of Set with turning back. Supportive of this is Te Velde's informing us that the ancient Egyptian word 'was' meant 'dominion'; and that the 'Was Sceptre' of Set can "be regarded as a symbol of order. Gods often hold it."[89] 'Cosmic Order' and the 'Way' are two different terms for the same phenomenon.

It has been suggested that the Was Sceptre was used to murder Osiris.[90] But it is essential to be aware of the fact that the myth of Osiris, which was conveyed to Plutarch during his sojourn in Egypt, is not consistent with the existing religious texts. Te Velde emphasises that "the Egyptian religious texts contain not a single detailed coherent account of the murder of Osiris by Seth. Neither have any literary texts been preserved dealing with this mythical material."[91] "Kees thinks that the priests of Heliopolis gave the name of Seth to the murderer of Osiris. Lack of material makes it impossible to determine whether, and in how far, the role of Seth in the Osiris myth is secondary."[92] H. Frankfort stated: "the story that Seth dismembered the body of Osiris and that Isis buried the parts where she found them... can hardly have been an original Egyptian belief... The pyramid texts abound in spells in which Isis and Nephthys, Horus or Nut, 'unite' the members of the dead Osiris; they nowhere hint at an earlier wilful dismemberment."[93]

The process of turning back is a chronotopological phenomenon, rather than simply a psychological function. In other words, it is not merely something that happens within one's own psyche, but is, as Lao Tzu taught, a manifestation of how the Way moves. Musès explains that a time wave rolls in exactly the same way that a wave rolls onto a beach. As a time wave proceeds, "there is a continual periodic feedback from future into present, and from present into past... [as well as] from present into future and past into present." As the intensity of a time wave function increases, "there are more intensive and extensive uprushings of normally buried memories into present and current contexts, as well as greater inpourings of anticipation and pulls of as yet unimplemented plans and visions: pulls of the future."[94]

Musès' account corresponds precisely to Anna's and my experience of avision: in Musès' language, as the energy created by the union of Sothis A and B reached its peak and the time waves of that energy broke "on the beach of occurrence," we had increasingly intense upmovings of normally buried memories from our past lives and greater inpourings of future directed plans and visions. Musès stresses that "the words 'past,' 'present' and 'future' betray the deep-seated inadequacy and inapplicability of ordinary analytic, linearly sequential thinking with regard to Time."[95] "time is not intrinsically consecutive but rather... manifesting through apparent cycles... [which are] actually radiating through the ever-present moment... recalling us ineluctably to re-contact our origins, in a prodigious and profound context of what memory means."[96]

Such is the importance of this principle that its practical application was presented to Anna near the outset of her experience of avision, in the form of a poem, in a dream of September 1989:

Following others –
Or parts of ourselves;
Cutting Corners;
Retracing steps.
Our strengths, weaknesses;
Our weaknesses, strengths...
On the move –
Paths through confusion.

The reference to 'others' who are 'parts of ourselves' was the first intimation of the role that our past lives would play in providing the 'paths through confusion'. However, at the time of Anna's dream, we thought that we were being described as following parts of ourselves of this lifetime. It was only when we had assimilated our later dreams concerning reincarnation, that we realized that the 'others – or parts of ourselves' referred to our past lives; hence, our 'retracing steps'.

The theme of 'others' who are 'parts of ourselves' was further developed two months later, in November of 1989, in Anna's first dream of the green jewel. There, she retraced her steps, returning to her old school, within which she encountered a coffin containing the pristine body of a long-dead girl who she realized was herself. Later, in September of 1994, Anna dreamt that she was again in a school, where we were served soup in ancient Egyptian bowls from which we might imbibe food from ancient times. Here, the process of turning back moved us to our life in ancient Egypt, which is, in Musès' terms, "radiating through the ever-present moment... in a prodigious and profound context of what memory means." This dream pointed to our being able to assimilate knowledge from ancient times which we had possessed in our past lives. Other dreams, such as that in which I was told that "Osiris is a false position," have most definitely provided us with the means for 'cutting corners' on our journey along the 'paths through confusion'.

It is the case, too, that we had to learn, sometimes very painfully, that what we had been conditioned to think of as our strengths in this lifetime were actually weaknesses. Conversely, sometimes we were pleasantly surprised when what we had been taught to regard as our weaknesses turned out to be strengths. Often, the greatest progress has been derived from those dreams which have addressed our weaknesses directly; as was the case when Ganesha placed me at the entrance to the school after Anna and I had failed to follow my previous dream instruction from Ganesh.

When, in 1998, we returned to considering the poem that Anna had dreamt, I realized that the sequence of the lines "Retracing steps. Our strengths weaknesses; Our weaknesses strengths..." corresponded precisely to that in the teaching of Lao Tzu: "Turning back is how the way moves; Weakness is the means the way employs."[97]

In practice, the 'parts of ourselves' that we follow are not simply our past lives, but the dreams through which our past lives emerge. There are many people who turn to Lao Tzu for guidance, but one must not forget that Lao Tzu himself turned back to a far more ancient time than his own. In the symbolism of Anna's dream sequence, this meant returning to the time before the Pan shell was smashed. As Oscar Wilde wrote, "O goat-foot god of Arcady! This modern world hath need of thee!"[98]

On 6th October 1997, Anna dreamt of an essential stage in the restoration of the Pan shell:

I am shown Pan being woven into the fabric of things.

Here, it was the energy of Sothis B that Anna was shown being woven into the fabric of material existence.

Later, in May of 1998, Anna's dreams returned to the theme of her death in our ancient Egyptian lifetime:

I am leaving our mansion to be with Anthony. Our two-year-old son (not of this life) remains there with my grandmother (also not of this life). I am stricken to be leaving our child, but I have no choice. As I depart, my grandmother gives out a terrible wail of lament.

In this dream, which is concerned with the events after her death, Anna is shown to have returned to our home for a final glimpse of our child from that life and to have been conscious of her grandmother's terrible distress. Then, on the same night, Anna also had a dream which depicted events preceding the removal of her mummy-wrappings (which she had dreamt of in April of 1997):

> I meet Anthony by some ruins in a rocky, sandy place. We watch as the body of a young woman – perhaps a teenage girl – is brought out of an underground chamber on a stretcher. On first impression, the body has the appearance of being charred – then, I realize it has been mummified and that it is mine.

Here, the body is recovered in similar terrain to that in which Anna was murdered; and it is the body of a young woman, perhaps in her teens, just as in Anna's first dream of the green jewel (in November 1989). The confusion in Anna's mind in that dream about the age of the dead girl – 'I feel she died in her childhood or teens, although she is an adult' – is explained by the fact that, in our ancient Egyptian life, both Anna and I were shorter and slighter in build than we are now.

In a number of Anna's dreams which relate to that lifetime, I am shown to have died before her; for instance, in March of 2001, she dreamt:

> Anthony and I are in Egypt with our small son (not of this life), who is aged between one and two years. Anthony dies suddenly. I am so distraught that I cannot speak. Yet, I know I must carry on to fulfil my purpose.

The Green Jewel

Our son in this dream is the same child who, in the earlier dream, remained in the house with Anna's grandmother. A dream of Anna's from September 1999 had also related to my death:

> Anthony and I are together in Egypt. Then, I find myself alone. Someone comes to tell me that Anthony has died in an accident during an army training exercise, though he was just a bystander. It does not seem to make any sense and I suspect he was murdered. I am devastated, crying terribly with deep sobs.

I was awoken in the night by the sound of Anna's sobbing. When she told me her dream, it immediately brought to mind the first dream that I had after I began to train as a psychotherapist, in January of 1975:

> I am visiting an army training school. I notice that my father is there; and see some recruits engaged in an exercise, which I decide to take part in. I have scarcely done so, when a large, round bomb falls down in front of me and explodes. I am aware that my brain has been blown out of my head and, thinking that this is not acceptable, I rewind the dream to a point before the bomb falls. The dream continues as before, but this time when the bomb makes its appearance I know what is going to happen and search for a means of escape. Suddenly, I find myself floating up into the air. The whole ambience of the dream now changes. I realize that the only solution is for me to conceive myself. I turn into a Christ-like figure and experience a sort of orgasm of self-creation. An extraordinary light glows over the scene, while the 'Sanctus' from Bach's 'Mass in B Minor' fills the air. I carry on rising until I land on top of a cliff – high above where I have come from.

In *Apollo versus the Echomaker* (which I wrote in 1989), I mentioned that this dream had preoccupied me for many years – my fascination being fuelled by the fact that, no matter how much I contemplated it, its true meaning eluded me.

We have now accrued well over a hundred dreams specific to that Egyptian lifetime which are factually informative as well as providing vivid memories of sensory and emotional experience. As a result of some of these dreams, it became apparent that, though, like Anna, I had received a blow to the head, I had not immediately died from that wound. This led me to realize that the 'bombshell' of my dream was intended to be understood metaphorically; and that the detail of my brain being separated from my skull, rather than being the cause of my death, actually referred to the removal of that organ during the process of mummification. The dream being rewound indicates that I had to carry on in this life from the point before the murderous attack on me. It was, therefore, the same message as our being told that 'Anna and I are as connected with the Sphinx now as we were in our Egyptian lifetime so we can just move on from here'. 'Moving on' meant continuing to be aligned with avision and imparting the knowledge received to others. My realizing that the only solution was for me to conceive myself referred to the process of reincarnation and, so, was the first indication provided through our dreams that we are, in essence, the same in each lifetime and, in this regard, are not the product of our biological parents. Since the foregoing diverges radically from conventional psychotherapeutic theory, it is interesting that the Dream was emphatically making these points at the moment that I began my training as a psychotherapist. Yet, I had to wait twenty-six years for the dream of Anna's before I could understand all that my dream was conveying.

My being transformed into a 'Christ-like figure' was, in addition to being symbolic of the process of self-generation that underlies reincarnation, representative of the transformative process that I was to undergo through avision. Thus, as Musès notes, "In his *Tables of Divine Revelation* [the seventeenth century mystic philosopher Jacob] Boehme [who had a profound influence upon figures of the stature of Hegel and Isaac Newton] furnishes an important definition; namely: *With or by the word* Christus *or* Christ *is understood the new man, in the Spirit of Christ, according to the inwardness*, that is, the Christ-consciousness."[99]

By 'Christ-consciousness', Boehme specifically meant the consciousness that arises through gnosis – through divine revelation.

Having recalled and integrated more elements of the experience of her death in her ancient Egyptian lifetime, in January of 1998 Anna also dreamt of her own reincarnation as a process of parthenogenesis:

> I am my own mother – I give birth to myself by flowing out of myself. And I remember having given birth to myself in the same way before.

Incarnating in a human body is only a preparatory stage for the transformation that arises when union with the Cosmic Guiding Fields of Force that emanate from Sothis is attained through the Dream. This process of transformation through a vision was depicted in a dream of Anna's in October of 1997, two weeks after she had been told that she was the green jewel:

> I am sleeping with my writing book, which contains my dreams and poems, clasped to my chest. At the moment of my waking, the writing book and I merge; and I am transformed: I experience this as the coming together within me of two shining discs, like the sun and moon.

Upon waking (this was a dream within a dream), Anna remembered that she had, in a poem, used the sun as a symbol for our present life and the moon as a symbol for our past lives. In this dream, at the moment of the coming together of her past and present lives, Anna woke clutching her writing book in the same way as, in her earlier dream, having encountered herself in a past life, she had awoken clutching the green jewel.

At the time of our ancient Egyptian life, the sun represented the right eye and the moon the left eye of God, symbolizing, and exoterically replacing, the two stars of Sothis. Esoterically, the coming together of sun and moon produces an eclipse, symbolizing the Black Sun, Sothis B. As I mentioned earlier, 'Nesh' was a name of Set; and, in ancient Egyptian, 'neshen' meant 'an eclipse'.[100] The eclipse depicts the replacement of conventional egoic thinking, with its illusion of existing as a separate entity, by the Sothic Mind, the Mind of the Universe.

The guidance contained within her dreams and the insights she had recorded in her poems were shown to have been integrated and to have precipitated a transformation in which Anna and her writing book became one. Both the writing book and the Grail cup are receptacles for Sothic energy – vessels for transformation.

CHAPTER FOURTEEN

The Serpent

To recap, having been told, in October of 1997, that Anna and I had completed one stage to do with the Sphinx and that we were then to begin another, the Dream presented us with the need to focus on the unfolding of the imminent into the manifest – of the evolving of Set into Horus. For myself, the consequence of understanding the relationship between the imminent and the manifest had been that the Grail cup moved from Sothis to the moon and, from there, into my head. The Grail, which in the Hermetic tradition is known to be a receptacle for Sothic energy, had, in my dreams, also been shown to be a vessel within which my past lives and present life were unified. Anna's equivalent experience, following her being shown that she was the green jewel – an ancient Egyptian and Taoist symbol of enlightened consciousness – had been that she had become one with the writing book containing her dreams and poems, also a receptacle for Sothic energy, and had, thereby, been further transformed through the coming together of her past and present lives. Yet another unfolding of the transformational process occurred as Sothis proceeded to raise our understanding of itself and, thereby, of the Egyptian Mysteries, to an altogether higher level. Concomitant with this, were specific instructions about the mental focus required to observe the emergence of the manifest. These themes produced a richly contrapuntal sequence of avision, which began, in December of 1997, with a dream that consisted of my being told:

"There is something about the soul that is not understood."

Since no clues were provided regarding what it was about the soul that was not understood, Anna and I realized that we had to wait for another dream to enlighten us on that matter.

Meanwhile, on 1ˢᵗ February 1998, I dreamt:

I am shown a sheet of writing paper which bears a letter-heading with my name and address on it – and am shocked to see that at the bottom of the page is the hieroglyph of the Winged Disc. I am told that it is my insignia for this lifetime.

The conventional Egyptological view is that the Winged Disc is a "winged sun disc."[1] In contradistinction to this, Anna and I, on the basis of a dream of mine from October 1996 and an examination of the relevant iconography, arrived at the opinion that the Winged Disc is a symbol of the combined energies of Sothis A and B. In the dream:

I see a Horus wing in the heavens. To my surprise, it is a field of radiating energy that is the Mind of God.

Once Anna and I had learnt that the ancient Egyptians identified Sothis as the divine source, it was obvious to us that the beautiful, variegated pattern of energy in my dreams was the efflux from Sothis that emanates as the star 'flies' through the cosmos. "Alan Gardiner argued that the disc represented the 'actual person' of the king syncretized with the sun-god."[2] Again, if one replaces the sun-god with Sothis, Gardiner's understanding of the Winged Disc is entirely in accordance with the central principle of avision conveyed to Anna and myself by the Dream: that one must be 'syncretized' with Sothis.

Musès cites Boehme's commentary upon the Old Testament Joseph: "Yet the right true visions are when man's will resteth in God, and then is God's will manifest in man's will, and the soul seeth with God's eyes from its most inward ground, where it stands in the Word of God. And then the speaking Word goeth into the soul's word... Thus Joseph and also Daniel expressed and expounded... By this figure of Joseph, in that he obtained divine knowledge and skill, and could expound hidden things, we see how the spirit of man turned toward and resigned up into God, when he forsaketh all that is his own, doth attain the divine eye to see and understand; so that he gets much more again than he forsook, and that he is much richer than when he enjoyed his own."[3] This is the best possible account of what is signified by the Winged Disc of my dream.

As has so often been the case, Anna's corresponding dream came several years before my own. In December of 1990, a few days after we began to live together, she dreamt:

I am shown a symbol that is to be mine for this lifetime.

It was not until January of 1999, a year after my dream of the Winged Disc, that Anna discovered by chance that the symbol she had been given was the ancient Egyptian hieroglyph for 'the uterus, symbol of Isis-Hathor', known as the 'Girdle of Hathor'. Anna's dream occurred a few months after she had been provided with her initiatory dream into the Mysteries of Love – "The more intimate, The more infinite." This is particularly relevant because, as I have already mentioned, Venus is the planetary power of Love and Musès recounts that "the power corresponding to Venus was in Ancient Egypt Hathor: a form of the Great Goddess, the name meaning the Place of Horus (i.e. Her Womb)... only when love has become the central priority in one's life, not as mere sentiment but as a universal call and mandate, is one actually ready to begin the path of regenerative metamorphosis." And, so, the symbol that Anna was given in her dream showed that, Love being the central priority in her life, she was a receptacle for the transformative power of Horus.

My dream concerning the Wing of Horus was an exemplification of Anna's earlier dream instruction from April 1992: "Believe in the stars and that they directly affect everything that happens to us." That instruction had been graphically illustrated in a dream of September 1996:

> Anthony and I become aware of lines of light stretching between many parts of our bodies and the stars.

In this dream, we were shown the influence that starlight in general exerts upon us. Then, in July of 1997, Anna had the first dream of ours which specifically focused upon our relationship with Sothis (we had by then learnt that Sothis was the Greek name for Sirius):

> The Arm of Sothis is reaching down to us benignly.

This dream came less than three weeks after the call of the Sphinx – "Come to me. Come to me." – which was itself such a powerful way of Sothis reaching out to us, of the stars directly affecting everything that happens to us. Synesius, whose view was that astronomy is "a science which opens up the way to ineffable theology,"[4] stated: "God, who holds himself afar, comes to you... He presents himself always during your sleep. In sleep, the whole business of initiation is performed."[5]

With regard to the Arm of Sothis reaching down to us, modern physics has established that "distant parts of the universe can be connected instantaneously no matter how far apart."[6] Samanta-Laughton raises the question: "If parts of the universe know what other parts of it are doing, could it be that the universe is actually one?"[7] She then recounts how the physicist David Bohm "believed that the world we see around us, that appears disconnected, is actually a reflection of a much deeper reality. In this deeper reality which he called *the implicate order*, everything is one unified whole. It is the starting point for everything in the universe and actually it still unites everything. It is only our perspective that sees everything as separate."[8] This, it will be remembered, was the view of Synesius.

The ancient Egyptian Uraei (twin serpents on the royal crown) indicated a correspondence between the two hemispheres of the brain and the two stars of Sothis – and the point of interaction between them. Viewed in this light, dreams form an extremely sophisticated two-way feedback mechanism which enables the individual to be both monitored by the Divine Eyes and aligned with the unfolding pattern. Thus, Rudra-Siva, who is "Consciousness itself,"[9] is 'Monitor of the Universe' – "the guardian and Lord of the site on earth." Sothis monitors what is happening in the galaxy in the same way that the human brain monitors the status of the billions of cells and the physiological systems they comprise in the body.

Returning to our sequence of dreams from 1998, towards the end of February, Anna dreamt:

> I read on a piece of paper:
>
> > "The difficulty is in thinking in pairs – 1 and 2.
> > Remember the Black Serpent at the heart of creation."

Despite considerable effort on our part, we found it impossible to decode this cryptic instruction regarding pairs 1 and 2; although a black serpent had previously appeared to Anna in a dream which I shall discuss later in this chapter.

The following month, in March of 1998, I dreamt:

> Anna and I are determinedly leaving an exhibition on Horus that is being held at the British Museum. It has been a very strange exhibition, displaying nothing like the conventional Egyptological notions of Horus. This is because it is about Horus now – in the present. We leave clear that we are only to be interested in the experiences that we are provided with in this lifetime. I am told that, within the whole, the possibilities that can be experienced at any one time are limited – we are not to be concerned with how things might have been.

Key to our being taken back into our Egyptian life was the necessity for us to remember and, thence, to re-establish in this lifetime the complete awareness of the present moment that was the hallmark of the sacerdotal mentality of the pharaonic civilization. This necessity exists because, as André VandenBroeck wrote of contemporary Man, "We see enormous distances into the past, but the moment is a closed book."[10] VandenBroeck describes how, through conversations with Schwaller de Lubicz, he learnt that at the head of the Pharaonic Temple stood "the enlightened priesthood: the perfect identity of science and theology, its main duties *cognition of the present moment*," which Schwaller de Lubicz defined as this "Absolute from which we constantly draw our power."[11]

One can learn a great deal about the way in which avision proceeds by observing how, in order for us to be cognizant of the present moment, Anna and I were taken back to our ancient Egyptian lifetime in which cognition of the present moment was the ideal. Then, in the process of realizing that ideal within ourselves, we were, by the very fact of being cognizant of the present moment, brought back to the present moment (in this lifetime). The instruction that we are not to be concerned with how things might have been is of inestimable value for maintaining balance within a world in which so much that is essential has been lost.

The theme of experiencing Horus now – in the present – was further developed in a dream of Anna's on 3rd April:

> I climb a huge staircase. Each stair is a platform, like a theatre set, containing all my clothes and possessions from a different stage in my past – in this life and previous lives. Time after time, I walk through piles of familiar belongings to reach the next step. At the top, I come to a room in which there are high single beds. Anthony is lying upon one. I choose the one to his left. As I lie there, a baby enveloped in a halo of dazzling light floats towards me and enters my forehead.

In her earlier dream of October 1997, Anna experienced merging with the writing book in which she recorded her dreams and poems as the coming together within her of two shining discs like the sun and moon. Upon waking, she recalled having used the imagery of the sun and moon to symbolize our present and past lives respectively in a poem. Here, that time relationship is depicted as a huge staircase; which was a recognised feature of the ancient Egyptian Mystery tradition. In the *Book of The Coming Forth Into Day*, it is written: *"my mother Sôthis prepares my path and sets up a stairway."*[12] The image of the staircase presents the stages of Anna's past, both of this life and of previous lives, as an integrated whole which proceeds step by step to provide a means of ascent to the present. The single beds indicate that this dream relates to an experience which each must go through alone. The appearance of the baby suggests that the beds are for the purpose of incubation.

Musès shows how 'wt', the root of an ancient Egyptian word meaning 'to embalm', also meant 'to sprout or germinate'; and that the closely related 'sw-t' both referred to the White or 'Hetch' ('brilliant', 'shining') crown and was connected with 'swh-t' which denoted a developing egg, seed or embryo. As I have already mentioned, Musès argued that external mummification was originally a symbol for and, later, became a corruption of an inner regenerative process. He explains that "the entire process... was an inner, metamorphic and transformational super-embryonic process, as both the etymologies and the texts make abundantly clear. Thus, although ancient Egyptians had brought the art of embalming to the highest degree known before or since, yet the oldest meaning of the process their texts recorded refers to life, not death."[13]

There is an obvious correspondence between the brilliant, shining crown associated with the developing embryo in the transformational process and the 'baby enveloped in a halo of dazzling light' which entered Anna's forehead in her dream. In addition, Musès provides key illustrations from sacred texts depicting the super-embryonic process in which the Sacred Stairway is an essential element – a feature, moreover, which he refers to as "a stairway of development."[14]

It was after being shown that her symbol in this lifetime is that of the Womb of Hathor, whose name means 'House or Place of Horus', and our being instructed to focus upon Horus in the present, that the baby enveloped in a halo of dazzling light entered into Anna through her forehead. The significance of the forehead had been emphasised earlier, both by Ganesha, when she brought her forehead into contact with mine, and by the wasp, when it performed the same gesture at the tunnel connected with the ancient Egyptians. We were, thereby, being made aware of the connection between Sothis and the forehead. In Anna's dream, the symbol of the bed indicated that the process she was undergoing was one which takes place during sleep. The pre-condition for her being able to undergo that process was her having merged with the writing book in which she recorded her dreams and poems. There is a direct correspondence between Anna's merging with her writing book, which she experienced as the coming together within her of two shining discs, and the baby enveloped in a halo of dazzling light entering into her.

The coming together of the two shining discs also represented the Divine Union of Sothis A and B. This had originally been presented in Anna's dream of the Dance of Siva as our merging to look as though we were one person. Thus, the act of merging was common to all three dreams. In our sequence of avision, the halo of dazzling light which enveloped the 'baby' identified it as the Divine Child – the product of the Hieros Gamos of Sothis A and B. Synesius defined the gods as "no other than pure Intelligences."[15] Thus, the Divine Child, as pure intelligence, entered into the 'womb' of Anna's mind, thereafter to be nourished by Sa – the blood of Isis – the Spirit of All Intelligence,[16] which is received as avision through the umbilical connection to the heavens. Hence, the pre-condition that Anna became one with her dreams.

The ascent of the staircase and the unification with the Divine Child meant that Anna was then able to complete a task that was presented two weeks later, on 17th April 1998:

Anthony and I enter a hidden chamber of bone and flesh, where a grey wolf god dwells, who is calm and benign. The wolf god is a part of us. Then, the scene changes and we enter a large, old building. The stairs are missing, so we stand on furniture and climb up a balustrade of railings to upper floors. On the top floor, we find a creaking pair of arched, wooden shutters, as large as entrance doors, richly painted in blue with gold designs. I push them open into the brilliant light of a beautiful garden, with the words "I have to do this because my ancestors did it and because my ancestors prophesied it."

It will be remembered that the ancient Egyptian word 'sba' meant both 'star' and 'door' and was a name of Sothis as the Star Door, the Great Door of Heaven. 'Sab' also meant 'door' and was the name of the god Anubis in his wolf-headed or jackal-headed form.[17] Thus, it is Anubis who was the calm and benign wolf god of Anna's dream. Since we were unexpectedly told that Anubis is a part of us, the chamber of bone and flesh in which he dwells is to be found within our own bodies.

Musès, who was, in addition to his other areas of expertise, a world authority in the fields of cybernetics ("The theory or study of communication and control in living organisms or machines"[18]) and the mathematics of morphology ("that branch of biology which is concerned with the form of animals and plants and of their structures... and metamorphoses which govern or influence their form"[19]) explains that human beings "have a regenerative gland associated with the vicinity of the thalamus."[20] This is "the rather 'rusty' neural valve in the brain... that controls the window or lens-opening for a higher light and life energy to pour into us from a higher level of reality."[21] It was this physiological system that was represented by the creaking shutters which Anna's ancestors prophesied she would open to let in the brilliant light, which corresponds to the halo of dazzling light enveloping the baby in her previous dream. Anna's experience was what is described by Musès as "the oldest preserved theurgic [of "divine working"[22]] teachings of the Sacred Way Home – those of ancient Egypt and China... [that] tell of a goddess-inspired, transcendent 'pregnancy'. One that takes place within our still mysterious brain and body (of either sex)."[23] The Sacred Way Home is the Way to Isis-Sothis.

In Anna's dream, her 'ancestors' included her previous incarnations, in which she had succeeded in opening the neural valve. The statement: "I have to do this because my ancestors prophesied it" indicated that it had been known by our ancestors that we would be alive at the time of the Hieros Gamos of Sothis A and B in April of 1994 in order that we could observe and experience "the evolutionary opportunity for humanity" that the synchrony of the Divine Union with solar system dynamics provided.

That the ancient Egyptian priesthood possessed the means to know the future was conveyed to us in a dream of September 2000:

> Anna and I are in a temple in Egypt. An Egyptian priest shows us how a number of stones have been arranged to indicate that we have successfully completed activities during our stay there. At first, we assume that they relate to our recent stay in Egypt; but, gradually, we realize that they represent our completion of future activities, some of which we haven't even planned yet. When we look at the stones, it seems that what is to happen in the future has already happened.

The fact that Anna's ancestors prophesied that she would open the shutters is an indication of the great importance of her so doing and of the enlightenment which that action was to bestow.

In his chapter on the opening of the neural valve that controls the window-lens for a higher light, Musès illustrates the process with a detail from a papyrus which shows Anubis administering restorative Sothic energy.[24] An earlier illustration shows Anubis standing guard as a staircase is ascended.[25] It is entirely consistent with this that, on 21st April 1998, four days after Anna had opened the window shutters, she dreamt:

> I wake and go into the hallway where I see that Anubis is ascending the stairs to the first floor of our house. He has the body of a man with the head of a jackal and is dressed in black.

In this dream within a dream, Anubis – the Guide to the Tuat – was ascending to the part of our house where we sleep and dream, thereby conveying his association with avision. As the Opener of the Ways, Anubis guides one, by means of dreams, through the process of reincarnation and transformation as it unfolds in each lifetime. His identification with avision was such that "During the Graeco-Roman Period Anubis was... related to arcane wisdom as the bringer of light to humanity."[26] As the grey wolf god, Anubis oversaw our ascending to a higher level which, when Anna opened the shutters, looked out onto a garden. Since the ancient Egyptian words 'Aab' and 'aabut' meant 'ancestors', and 'aabt' was 'a garden', the garden in Anna's dream was 'the garden of the ancestors'. The closely related 'aabb' meaning 'love'[27] is, of course, itself associated with the ancestors – Love being the original religion. This association indicates that, following Anna's mounting the staircase of her lives, we were able to ascend further, to the original understanding of the ancestors ("Turning back is how the way moves"), in order that Anna could open the shutters as her ancestors had done. In so doing, we were flooded with the Higher Light that Musès spoke of.

Later in the same month (April 1998), I had a dream which instructed us about that Light:

> I am shown that Horus can be depicted as a pattern of small circles of light radiating from a fixed point.

Having been made aware that Horus is a field of radiating energy that is the Mind of God, we were now told how we were to envisage that energy as it emanated from its energetic source. We were to learn from Musès that ancient Egyptian texts similarly identify the transformational energy with Horus.[28] The fixed point from which Horus radiates is the Hieros Gamos of Sothis A and B. And, so, the light-enveloped baby of Anna's dream – a product of that Divine Union – was one of the circles of radiating light that is Horus. In her earlier dream of the staircase, Anna entered a room in which there were a number of single beds from which other individuals, too, could receive the light of Horus.

Horus is always unfolding as the Imminent moves into the Manifest. The moment of that unfolding recommences every fifty years with the Divine Union of Sothis A and B.

The following month, in May of 1998, I dreamt:

> I am writing about the ram-headed god Khnum.

This dream, where I am writing about the god who symbolizes the Ba soul, was linked to that of the next night, in which we were finally told what it is about the soul that is not understood:

> I am shown that the ba soul needs the Dream.

Pharaoh Merikare said of the ba: "The faculty of transcendence, the *ba*, makes its way to the place that it knows. It will not wander from its habitual path."[29] Taking this statement in conjunction with the instruction that the ba soul needs the Dream, one can see that the ba soul makes its way back to the place that it knows through avision. Its habitual path is, of course, alignment with Sothis, which is the source of avision – the means to that alignment. The ba soul needs the Dream because it is by means of dreams that it is instructed by Sothis. In the words of Synesius: "when asleep, it is from God that the knowledge comes;"[30] and so, sleep necessarily "opens the way to the most perfect inspections of true things to the soul."[31]

In May of 1998, shortly after our being told that the ba soul needs the Dream, Anna dreamt that she herself was in the presence of the divinity Khnum:

> The ram-headed god Khnum is spinning, from a wheel, circles that are ever increasing, as when a pebble is dropped into water. I am standing, facing him, within the circles.

Subsequent to her ascending the stairway of the regenerative process and opening the shutters to allow "a higher light and life energy to pass into us from a higher level of reality," Anna then experienced the "waves of the powers of a higher mode of awareness [which] find their natural development according to each individual's nature."[32] Her dream developed the instruction that Horus can be depicted as a pattern of small circles radiating from a fixed point. However, it did so by demonstrating that the circles are produced by Khnum in his aspect as the Divine Potter. This was somewhat perplexing to us since we had not come across any identification of Khnum with Sothis. We had, again, to wait for further guidance from the Dream.

In September, the month of 'Sept' ('Sothis'),[33] our yearly cycle of avision began with this summation dream of Anna's:

> I am writing about the garden of Eden from the book of *Genesis*. The two trees, of knowledge and of life, are the stars of Sothis. The Serpent is the Dream. Eve is advice that is received through dreams.

Here, the Dream expands upon the theme of the garden of the ancestors and begins to instruct us about the Black Serpent at the heart of creation. Many years later, we learnt from Wake that the Serpent was associated with Khnum: "the ram-headed god from whom the Gnostics are sometimes said to have derived their idea of the *Sophia*. This personification of divine wisdom is undoubtedly represented on Gnostic gems under the form of the serpent."[34] Thus, Anna's dream about Khnum naturally led into her dream about the Serpent in the book of *Genesis*; and her facing Khnum was equivalent to Eve facing the Serpent in the garden of Eden.

The information that the Serpent is the Dream was absolutely essential to our being able to understand a number of our earlier dreams, such as this one of Anna's from October 1997:

> Our parent is a Great Serpent, that we call 'Anuit', who lives in the heavens and whose serpentine body reaches down to us, is in constant contact with us, protecting and caring for us.

We now knew that we had been instructed that our parent is Sothis, who reaches down to us as the Dream.

There are obvious correspondences between Anna's dream of our parent, the Great Serpent Anuit, and that of the Arm of Sothis reaching down to us benignly. For initiates into her Mysteries, Isis-Sothis – the Goddess of avision – is the "Mother of Life"[35] to whom the Platonic philosopher Lucius of Patrae wrote: *"Thou bestowest a mother's tender affections on the misfortunes of unhappy mortals... and stretchest forth the right hand of salavation."*[36]

Despite searching through the literature in our possession, Anna could not find any reference to 'Anuit'. Then, four years later, she came across an ancient Egyptian deity named 'Mesanuit' and discovered that 'mes' meant 'serpent'.[37]

Anna's dream about the garden of Eden makes reference to the passage in the book of *Genesis* where it is written: "And the LORD God commanded the man [Adam], Of every tree of the garden thou mayest freely eat: But of the tree of knowledge of good and evil, thou shalt not eat of it: for in the day that thou eatest thereof thou shalt surely die."(Genesis 2:16-17); "[however,] the serpent said unto the woman [Eve], Ye shall not surely die: For God doth know that in the day ye eat thereof then your eyes shall be opened, and ye shall be as gods, knowing good and evil. And when the woman saw that the tree was good for food, and that it was pleasant to the eyes, and a tree to be desired to make one wise, she took of the fruit thereof, and did eat, and gave also unto her husband with her; and he did eat. And the eyes of both of them were opened."(Genesis 3:4-7) [Here, it is stated that the Serpent had spoken the truth: eating the fruit of the tree of knowledge did indeed make Adam and Eve wise.] "And the LORD God said, Behold the man is become as one of us, to know good and evil: and now, lest he put forth his hand, and take also of the tree of life and eat, and live forever: Therefore the LORD God sent him forth from the garden of Eden."(Genesis 3:22-23)

In the Gnostic text 'The Apocalypse of Adam', it was through Eve "that Adam received perfect gnosis."[38] Walker recounts that "the serpent was worshipped in Palestine long before Yahweh's cult arose. Early Hebrews adopted the serpent-god all their contemporaries revered... Some Jewish Gnostics early in the Christian era maintained that the post-exile Jehovah was no god, but a devil, the usurper of the original Kingdom of the Wise Serpent."[39] As Gardiner and Osborn state, "The Hebrew nation came out of Egypt... and it is widely recognized that they carried with them the secrets of Egypt as well as the image of the popular serpent deity Set (Seth), who later became Satan (Set-Hen)."[40] Walker notes that one form of Set was Sata, the healing serpent god, who dwelt in the Temple of Isis giving oracles, as Python did at Delphi.[41] Set, or Sata, was the consort of the archaic goddess Setet, or Sati, who once ruled Upper Egypt, which was then known as the Land of Sati.[42] It is interesting that, though in *Genesis* the Serpent is not specifically associated with the Dream, this connection is explicitly stated by John Milton in *Paradise Lost*: one reads of Satan "close at the ear of Eve; Assaying by his devilish art to reach The organs of her fancy, and with them forge Illusions as he list, phantasms and dreams."[43] This is a continuation of the teaching of earlier Christian apologists that "a 'tender and susceptible soul which is ignorant of sound teaching' is prey to the irrational fantasies of demons who bedevil the soul in dreams." It is in keeping with the policy of the Catholic Church to undermine the Dream that the Latin 'Diabolus', meaning 'Serpent of the Goddess', came to be used as a name for the Devil.[44]

Gardiner and Osborn point out that "*Philo* means 'love' or 'love of' and *sophy* means 'wisdom' or 'wise serpent'."[45] It will be remembered that, in the *O.E.D.*, the first definition of 'philosopher' is "A lover of wisdom: one who devotes himself to the search of fundamental truth" and the second is "An adept in occult science... a diviner of dreams." Taken together, these definitions concur with Anna's dream instruction. Walker provides confirmation that Eve is advice received through dreams, for she mentions that "Gnostic accounts of the Eden myth used the Aramaic pun identifying Eve, the Teacher, and the Serpent... Hippolytus viewed the serpent as a feminine Logos, 'the wise Word of Eve'. This is the mystery of Eden: this is the river that flows out of Eden."[46]

The combination of the Serpent and flowing water had been presented to us in a dream of Anna's from February 1993 (which I mention at this juncture because we only understood its meaning once we had been instructed that the Serpent is the Dream):

> I am in the old Reading Library/Museum building. In the stairwell hangs an enormous, coiled black serpent. The stairway is being rebuilt. On the wall is an exhibit consisting of a flowing water circuit.

This was the first mention in our dreams of the Black Serpent at the heart of creation. Here, as in Anna's dream of 17th April 1998, the staircase was missing and in need of being rebuilt. In ancient Egyptian, the word 'sep-t' meant 'stairs';[47] whilst (as I have mentioned) 'Sept' was a name of Sothis. Similarly, 'arat' meant 'staircase'; and 'Ara-t' was a name of the uraeus (the serpent on the royal crown).[48] Thus, Anna's dream depicted the link between the staircase and the Serpent that was encoded in the ancient Egyptian language. In her dreams, the Stair-Way – the Star-Way – the Way to Sothis was being rebuilt. The guardian of this process is Anubis – the Dog Star – as the Opener of the Ways. Once we had realized that the stairway is the Way to Sothis, we could see that the transformational process had been depicted in the first dream that I recounted in this book: Anna's dream of the ivory tower. There, we ascended the spiral staircase, at the top of which we encountered Pegasus and the Unicorn. As I discussed earlier, Pegasus and the Unicorn symbolized Sothis A and B respectively.

The Reading Museum houses artefacts and exhibitions pertaining to the history of Reading and the surrounding area. At the time of Anna's dream, it included exhibits dating from pre-historic times. By depicting the Serpent in the museum, the Dream was informing us that the Black Serpent played a significant role in the ancient history of Reading. Knowing that the Serpent is the Dream, we could see that the Black Serpent in the old Reading Library/Museum indicated that an ancient oracle centre had once existed in the Reading area. Since the ancient Egyptian word for 'library', 'per metcha', is comprised of 'per' meaning 'house'[49] and 'metcha' meaning 'god', with 'metcha-t' meaning 'book',[50] it is probable that the original libraries housed the books in which oracular dreams were recorded. This is further supported by the fact that the old English 'lib' was both a noun and a verb meaning 'sleep'.[51]

It has often been thought that there was no Druidic presence in the south-east of England. However, Spence explains that, because they did not leave a written record, "The historical memory of the Druids was entirely at the mercy of their Roman enemies;"[52] and adds that "it must be manifest that if Cæsar does not allude to the existence of Druids in South-Eastern Britain, that he does not do so for political reasons."[53]

Spence notes that the Serpent was a Celtic symbol of the Underworld[54] and that, according to both Pliny and the Welsh bards, the Druids were known as 'Adders'[55] – an indication of their ability to journey into the Underworld. Wood adds that the Serpent is "linked with regeneration" and is "also associated with the acquisition of Otherworld knowledge"[56] – a definition which corresponds with the instruction that the Serpent is the Dream.

At the Sothic dream oracle of Delphi, the personification of "the prophetic spirit" was Python, who was identified with Sol Niger – the Black Sun.[57] In ancient Egypt, Python was known as 'Apep' or 'Apophis' – the Serpent of Darkness.[58] In the Bible, he is 'Apollyon' – "'Spirit of the Pit' (Revelation 9:11);"[59] the 'pit' being the 'abaddon' where people would sleep to dream. Wilkinson writes that Apep "existed from the beginning of time in the waters of primal chaos which preceded creation," being the "embodiment of the powers of... darkness" and the "serpent of rebirth;"[60] whilst Walker relates that "The Pyramid Texts spoke of the serpent as both subterranean and celestial."[61]

As I have mentioned previously, Caversham Bridge links Caversham with the town of Reading, which is situated on the opposite bank of the River Thames. The official explanation is that Reading was named after the Anglo-Saxon Readingas, the followers of Reada, who settled in the area in the fifth or sixth century. Though it is assumed that 'Reada', meaning the 'Red One', was a man, this happens to be one of the titles of Set (whom Anna saw standing in the Thames beside Caversham Bridge in her childhood vision). In the past, other spellings of 'red' were 'read' and 'rede', both of which mean "to make out or discover the meaning or significance of a dream [and] to declare or expound this to another" and "to foresee, foretell and predict."[62] Another meaning of 'rede' is "What is advisable, advantageous and profitable for one; aid, help, succour, remedy;" and it is consistent with the ancient understanding of the Dream that, when applied to God, 'rede' means "to take care or charge of one; to guide, guard or protect"[63] – hence, God redeems. Further, 'rede' means "to make ready" and to "set in order",[64] which corresponds to my dream instruction that Set is concerned with preparation (note that 'ready' is 'read-y'). The different meanings of 'read'/'rede' serve as eloquent testimony of a culture versed in avision.

Rhea, whose name is closely associated with that of Reading, was also known as the 'Red One'.[65] The ancient Greeks held that Rhea was the mother of both Python and Asclepius. As Rhea Lobrine, she was "Goddess of sacred caves."[66] Caves were regarded as the Womb of the Goddess, which is another reason why Rhea and Ar-Themis were associated with the colour red. The followers of Rhea would enter caves so that they could incubate in her womb and, through dreams, be in direct communication with their Great Mother. It was by this means, too, that she issued her laws and was, hence, known as the Lawgiver.[67] One motive for using caves as the location for incubation is that total darkness is required in order for the brain to release serotonin, a neurotransmitter which enables the deepest level of sleep. Euripides was moved to describe dreams as "truth's shadows upfloating from Earth's dark womb."[68]

The town of Reading is built upon caves; and Caversham was so named for its vast cave system. Although, as with so many aspects of

Druidic practice, there are no historical records of mass incubation in Britain, Miranda Green writes: "At the great Celtic healing sanctuaries, professional interpreters of dreams were probably employed, to explain the visions of the sleeping pilgrims."[69] Since Diodorus Siculus explained that the title 'Druid' meant "one who is very knowledgeable" and that "The knowledge he seeks visits him in a dream of revelation... When he awakes, he finds himself in possession of the understanding he sought," I would say it is more than probable that the great Celtic healing sanctuaries of Britain employed dream interpreters.

There is a suggestion of Reading's oracular history surfacing: Daphne Phillips mentions that when the building in Reading of a charitable workhouse for the benefit of poor clothiers was completed, in midsummer of 1628, "For an undiscovered reason it became known by the attractive but mysterious name of The Oracle."[70] Then, in 1999, a shopping centre built in the town was named after the workhouse.

Writing two thousand years ago, Strabo provided a graphic account of incubation, describing how, close to the city of Acharaca, was located the entrance to the Underworld, the Plutonium, comprised of a temple to Pluto and the Maiden, above which was a cave, the Charonium. Those wishing to be healed would come to live for a time with the temple priests in the nearby village. Either the patients were settled in the cave to sleep, or the priests would sleep in the cave on their behalf. Then, their treatments were based upon the dreams they or the priests had been given.[71] Cox Miller states: "It would be difficult, indeed, to overestimate the role played by dreams in the curing of human suffering. In crisis of physical disease and mental distress, many people in the Graeco-Roman era turned to dreams for the healing of their ailments."[72] At that time, this help was particularly sought in the temples of Isis and of the healing god Asclepius, whose symbol was a serpent twined around a rod. The rod of Asclepius was adopted by the medical profession in this country as their emblem in the eighteenth century. It was later replaced by the caduceus – a staff entwined with two serpents (representing the orbital path of Sothis A and B around each other) – the symbol of the messenger god Hermes, which had, in pre-Hellenic Greece, been displayed on the temples of the goddesses Hygeia (Health) and Panacea (All-healing).

It will be remembered that, in his childhood dream, Jung descended into an underground temple which housed a throne bearing a phallus with an eye; and that these symbols correspond to the hieroglyphs for Sothis A and B. Jung mentioned that he had the feeling that the phallus "might at any moment crawl off the throne like a worm." This detail is itself important since the archaic English meaning of 'worm' was 'serpent'. The ancient Egyptians, too, often treated the worm and the serpent as synonymous; thus, Wallis Budge defines 'Hefau' as a name of "the great Worm or serpent... called Apep."[73] Jung's feeling in his dream that the phallus might move in his direction was due to an awareness of the energetic movement of 'that which releases the seed' towards him.

The colour red was a conspicuous feature of Jung's dream: the red carpet and the red cushion upon the throne were reflective of the ancient identification of sovereignty with avision. For instance, in the temple of Angkor Watt in Cambodia, the duration of the king's reign was dependent upon his being embraced by the serpent goddess each night.[74]

Themis, the Mother of Oracles, was, in her virgin form as Ar-Themis, clothed in red. Walker mentions that the dryads – the Druidic priestesses – "were called priestesses of Artemis"[75] and that Themis was also worshipped under the name of the "Goddess-Anna".[76] That the name 'Reading' was derived from 'Reada' – the followers of the Red One, that the Druidic priestesses were priestesses of the Mother of Oracles, who was clothed in red, and that 'read' meant "to make out or discover the meaning or significance of a dream [and] to expound this to another," all point to Reading being the site of an ancient Druidic oracle centre. Such was the importance of Themis that "As Ana or Anu she ruled the Celtic tribes,"[77] which is to say that the Celts were governed by avision. Later, when Christianity became the ruling institution, Themis was Christianized as St. Anne.[78] "Medieval Christians called her Anna of the Angles [Angle being a name of the English race], or Black Annis."[79] The sign of Anna/Annis as the goddess of death, Morg-ana, was the pentacle, which was taken as "the official sigil of St. Anne."[80] A "five-pointed star stood for the underworld in Egyptian hieroglyphs"[81] – this star symbolized Sothis.

The River Thames, the name of which derives from 'Themis', has two sources: one of which is named the 'Isis'; the other being the 'Cherwell'. There is in the name 'Cherwell' evidence of the influence of the Druidic Gauls; since, in French, 'cher' is the adjective denoting a male as 'dear' or 'beloved'. Thus, there is encoded in the landscape of England the powerful symbolic statement that Isis and her beloved companion are the double source of the flow – of the oracles of Themis.

A chapel dedicated to St. Anne, situated at the Caversham end of Caversham Bridge, was a pilgrimage site in the Middle Ages. At the Reading end of the bridge was a chapel dedicated to the Holy Spirit. Walker relates that "Christians adopted the feminine dove as the symbol of the Holy Ghost, originally the Goddess Sophia, representing God's 'Wisdom'."[82] "Sophia once represented God's female soul, source of his power... She was identified with Isis-Hathor."[83] Significantly, with regard to the dream instruction that what we were seeking could only be found in silence, "A Gnostic creation myth said Sophia was born from the primordial female power Sige (Silence)."[84]

Caversham Bridge was constructed to provide access between the major pilgrimage sites of Reading Abbey, founded by Henry I in 1121, (which was six feet longer than St.Peter's in Rome and, I was taught at school, had been built with the intention of being the centre of the Catholic Church) and the shrine of Our Lady of Caversham, which was to be found a hundred yards or so upstream from the bridge. The shrine housed a silver-plated Black Madonna – a form of Black Annis sanctioned by Christianity. For Christians, it was the most important site devoted to the Virgin Mary in southern England. Pagans, under the guise of Christianity, would have had no difficulty in venerating the image of Our Lady of Caversham because, as Wallis Budge explains, "Pictures and sculptures wherein she [Isis] is represented in the act of suckling her child Horus formed the foundation for the Christian figures and paintings of the Madonna and Child. Several of the incidents of the wanderings of the Virgin with the Child in Egypt as recorded in the Apocryphal Gospels reflect scenes in the life of Isis as described in the texts found on the Metternich Stele, and many of the attributes of Isis, the God-mother, the mother of Horus... are identical with those of Mary the Mother of Christ."[85]

For Celts, the shrine of Our Lady of Caversham was the focal point of communion with Black Annis on the river which bore her name of Themis. One can see that it is no easy matter to discern the early Christian from the pagan where Caversham and Reading are concerned – and this was intentionally so. Spence mentions that "The famous bull of Pope Gregory I (A.D. 540-604) permitted the fusion between Keltic and Christian belief which rendered the latter easier of acceptance without altogether destroying the former."[86] "There were masters of mysteries and secret science, whose knowledge, it is claimed, was perpetuated under the shadow of that Church and even within the pale thereof... At a much later period, even in the twelfth century, we have still the indication of perpetuated mysteries... promoted generally by the bards."[87]

Given that Themis is the personification of the oracular power of Sothis, it will come as no surprise that the Black Madonna is frequently identified as a representation of Isis. Ean Begg writes that one "etymology stresses the importance of the syllable 'is', a pre-Celtic word for a holy place where there is a subterranean current of water or telluric energy called a wouivre, which creates special conditions favourable for divinatory and initiatory purposes."[88] This explanation was of particular interest to Anna and myself, since just such a subterranean current of water flows beside our house on its course from the nearby St. Anne's Well (which it used to feed, though the well is now dry) to the River Thames. Famed for its healing waters, St. Anne's

Well was also a pilgrimage site in the Middle Ages. It was common practice for the Catholic Church to usurp pagan sites and rededicate them to St. Anne. According to Begg's view, our ongoing experience of avision has been enhanced by the unique combination of the waters of the ancient underground stream beside our house and the waters of Themis nearby.

Begg suggests that "The ankh [the ancient Egyptian hieroglyph for 'life'] which Isis carries as supreme initiatrix may account for some of the oddly shaped sceptres carried by the Black Virgins who, like Isis, often favour the colour green. Their greenness and blackness point to the beginning of the opus [hence, Anna's early dream of the green jewel] whose secret, according to alchemists, is to be found in 'the sex of Isis'."[89] Jean Markale recounts how in Chartres Cathedral "the sanctuary had been built on the site of a [Druidic] pagan temple in which a mysterious well had been discovered along with a statue depicting a *virgo paritura*, a 'Virgin on the threshold of giving birth';"[90] a representation deeply symbolic of Isis-Sothis, the star-form of the Mother of Creation, giving birth to Horus as a result of the Hieros Gamos. This brings me to the next stage in our dream sequence; on a night in October of 1998, a week after the instruction emphasising the superiority of getting one's knowledge directly from Set, I had numerous dreams in which:

> The importance of being aligned with the start is impressed upon me. The start is represented by Bes.

The start is the Hieros Gamos of Sothis.

Taking these dreams in conjunction with that of the week before, it can be seen that the superiority of getting one's knowledge directly from Set was emphasised because it is by means of avision that one can best be aligned with the start. Here, the start was represented by the dwarf god Bes, the personification of Sothis B, both as 'that which releases the seed' and as the protector of childbirth who facilitates Isis giving birth to Horus. This proposition created difficulties in our understanding of the process in which we were being instructed, because we could not comprehend how it could be equally true that Isis gives birth to Horus, that Set as the imminent becomes Horus as the manifest and that Horus is created by Khnum. It seemed impossible for us to resolve this conundrum; and the fact that it was not within our means to do so was confirmed in another dream in October of 1998, in which I was told:

"Only Apep can do it. Only Apep can put things right."

Only Apep, the Black Serpent at the heart of creation, the Spirit of the Dream that presides over the oracular sites of Themis, can put things right. With this instruction about the Black Serpent, we were brought back to the issue we had been presented with earlier, in February of the same year, concerning the difficulty of thinking in terms of pairs 1 and 2. The answer was finally presented to Anna in December of 1998, when she dreamt:

Anthony and I come to a significant realization about what Ba is. I say: "At one level, pairs 1 and 2 are Isis and Ba, Nephthys and Set."

Anna and I realized that pairs 1 and 2 must comprise the relationship between Yin and Yang. This is supported by Wallis Budge, who states that "Nephthys is the personification of darkness and of all that belongs to it, and... her attributes were rather of a passive than active character. She was the opposite of Isis in every respect; Isis symbolized birth, growth, development and vigour, but Nephthys was the type of death, decay, diminution and immobility. Isis and Nephthys were, however, associated inseparably with each other."[91] We found, in this, confirmation of the conclusion we had arrived at that Sothis A is Yang, while Sothis B is Yin. The difficulty in thinking in terms of pairs 1 and 2 is that each star is itself divided into Yin and Yang. Thus, Isis embodies the Yin aspect and Ba/Khnum the Yang aspect of Sothis A, which is the Yang component of the double star system; whilst Nephthys embodies the Yin aspect and Set the Yang aspect of Sothis B, which is the Yin component.

As I have discussed previously, Anna and I were particularly interested to learn how Schwaller de Lubicz demonstrated that, in ancient Egypt, "the serpent was the symbol for duality, or, more accurately, for the power that results in duality... When it is realized that the serpent bears both a forked tongue and a double penis [or a double vagina], the underlying wisdom of the choice becomes clear." This expounds the relationship between the Black Serpent and the creation of pairs 1 and 2. The process by which these two pairs were created was described by Confucius, in his commentary on the *I Ching*, in the following terms: "there is in the Changes the Great Primal Beginning. This generates the two primary forces. The two primary forces generate the four images. The four images generate the eight trigrams."[92] (Each trigram is comprised of three boken or unbroken lines. A broken line denotes Yin energy; an unbroken line denotes Yang energy. Their different combinations represent the eight transitional states of energy that are fundamental to all processes.) In Chinese thinking, creation is preceded by an infinite expanse of invisible Qi. The Great Primal Beginning was the moment when movement first occurred within that infinite expanse. This may be imagined as the first stirring of the Black Serpent within the primordial waters. Through the act of moving, the Black Serpent brought into existence the two primary forces, Yin and Yang, from which were formed the four images: Isis, Ba/Khnum, Nephthys and Set. The Yin and Yang aspects of the four images form the eight trigrams. (The eight trigrams combine to produce sixty-four hexagrams comprising three hundred and eighty-four lines that represent everything in the cosmos.)

Wallis Budge cites Plutarch as reporting that the ancient Egyptian priesthood differentiated the invisible part of the world, which they called Nephthys, from the visible, to which they gave the name of Isis.[93] This describes the relationship between the imminent and the manifest. Confirmation comes from Wallis Budge, who states: "Isis and Nephthys represent respectively the things which are and the things which are yet to come into being."[94] He also cites a passage which "proves that Nephthys, although a goddess of death, was associated with the coming into existence of the life which springs from death" and, hence, that "she may, generally speaking, be described as the goddess of the death which is not eternal."[95] I have already mentioned that Musès cites an ancient Egyptian text which states that Sopdu (Sothis B) "regulates the pattern of the hours in the Duat." This is what one would expect, since Nephthys and Set, the two aspects of Sothis B, are the deities of death and reincarnation.

It will be remembered that, in Druidism, Annwn (the Underworld) is ruled by the god Gwyddno and the goddess Keridwen; and that, as the Creator, Gwyddno was known as 'Celi', which, since the name meant 'concealing', is closely associated with the ancient Egyptian name for Sothis B: Amun, meaning the Hidden One. Spence also mentions that another name for Keridwen was 'Ced' meaning 'Aid'.[96] That Gwyddno and Keridwen are Set and Nephthys is demonstrated by the fact that they, too, were identified with imminence: "Celi and Keridwen are incomprehensible spirits, but are the originators of crude matter, which came in an embryonic condition from across the [cosmic] ocean, from the source of all elements."[97] One learns that "This essence is feminine and passive in its nature,"[98] which corresponds to the Yin character of Sothis B.

Spence makes reference to the procession of Lady Godiva: "the salient points of Godiva's legend are that she passed through Coventry innocent of any covering save that of abundant golden hair... There is good proof that the ancient Keltic deity, or a woman representing her, appeared in this condition at her annual festival... That Coventry was anciently situated in a district in which Druidical rites were practised is generally conceded. At the village of Southam, hard by, the Godiva procession was formerly celebrated with a faithfulness equal to that evinced in the larger township. But curious variations of the ceremony, even more eloquent of its Druidical character than the rite obtaining at Coventry, were celebrated there... [At Southam, Godiva was] followed by a second Godiva, whose body was *stained black*."[99] Spence adds that the goddess in question was Brigiddu, the same as "the Irish Brigit [who was particularly associated with oracular powers[100]], later Christianized into St. Brigit. She was also known as Danu or Anu, and is undoubtedly identical with... 'Black Annis' [who was represented by] the 'Black Godiva'."[101] It will be remembered that Black Annis was Themis, Mother of Oracles. Thus, the white and black goddesses were Isis and Nephthys. This is supported by Spence, who notes that there are "strong resemblances" between Keridwen and Brigit[102] and states that "The Druidic bards who lived and sang under the Welsh princes unanimously represent Keridwen as presiding over the mysteries of the ancient cult."[103] Thus, it was the dark sister of Isis, Nephthys – Sothis B – that was originally venerated as Black Annis. However, with the loss of knowledge of Sothis B, the identification of Nephthys with Black Annis was displaced onto Isis – Sothis A. Black Annis was of central importance to the Druids because, of all the aspects of Sothis, it is the Yin energy of Nephthys that the Earth is most resonant with.

Tompkins cites "Bede who reports that Pope Gregory I explicitly ordered Bishop Miletus to build churches on pagan shrines."[104] This then became the general practice of the Catholic Church. For instance, as I mentioned earlier, the Mediaeval Cathedral of Chartres "had been built on the site of a Druidic temple and, in Christian times, the cathedral was dedicated to the Black Virgin, a version of the pagan Goddess."[105] Thus, the Black Madonna was the means whereby Druids could continue to worship the goddess of their religion within the forum of the Catholic Church.

That 'pairs 1 and 2 are Isis and Ba, Nephthys and Set' was the first instruction we had been given naming Set as the god of Sothis B. The identification of Set with Sothis is confirmed by Hekekyan Bey, who, in his 'Treatise on the Chronology of Siriadic Monuments', writes of "the star Sirius; the same being known by the appellations of Set, Sothis... and other homophonous words."[106] As a result of this dream of Anna's, we now knew that her childhood vision of ass-headed Set standing in the Thames had been an experience of the personification of the Yang element of Sothis B.

In late Egyptian texts, the dissociation of Set from 'that which releases the seed' was represented as the moment when "Horus wrenched out Set's testicles."[107] In retaliation, "Set tore out Horus' left eye;"[108] this violent imagery symbolizing the detachment of Horus from the Eye star, when he was turned into a solar deity. Mankind's conception of both Set and Horus is shown to have been grievously damaged through the loss of identification with Sothis B.

In the Heliopolitan myth, the solar creator god Atum describes how the Eye – Sothis B – "became enraged against me, when it... saw that I had put another in its place, replacing it with a brighter one."[109] Rundle Clark recounts: "the enraged Eye became a rearing cobra with swollen neck, the uraeus snake. Atum pacified the Eye by binding it – now a snake – around his forehead as the uraeus that guards the crown."[110] Schwaller de Lubicz comments: "Since then, *the solar Eye governs the entire world.*"[111]

The uraeus is (as the aborigines of Australia still hold of the serpent today): "an intermediary between the unmanifest Principle and the realm of matter."[112] The same view is expressed in an early Gnostic text: "Midway between the Father and Matter the Serpent that moves eternally towards the unmoved Father and moved Matter."[113]

Whilst the energy of Reading, situated on the south bank of the Thames, is Yang, that of Caversham, on the north bank, is heavily Yin. Taking into account the fact that, in antiquity, the north was identified with Set, we are of the opinion that the dream oracle centre in Caversham was devoted to communion with Sothis B; that in Reading being devoted to communion with Sothis A.

There is good reason to hold that knowledge of a relationship between Caversham and Set existed in the past. A hundred yards from our home, is the riverside park which I mentioned earlier as being the place where we encountered a heron immediately after Anna had dreamt of it. Within the park, now called Caversham Court, used to stand a large house, known as the Old Rectory, which had been built on the site of the earlier Caversham Priory. Some say that the Black Madonna was originally housed in the Priory; and others that it was kept within the precincts of what is now St. Peter's Church, which is situated on a hill immediately behind where the Priory stood.

In Caversham Court, there are still four flights of steps leading down to the lawn from the area upon which the Priory/Old Rectory (since, demolished) stood. At the top of one of the flights of steps were two magnificent Griffin heads, one on either side, mounted on plinths. In addition, two ancient stone carvings of a stylized human head were positioned facing one another half way down the plinths. These carvings did not merely have an ornamental value; they indicated a link with ancient Egypt, as we discovered when we unexpectedly came across a near identical head in the Memphis Museum. Upon learning that, in Egypt, several animals including "wild asses, and the mythical griffin, were considered Sethian creatures"[114] and that, in western iconography, Set appears in the form of a Griffin, we realized that it could not be a coincidence that representations of the Griffin are to be found less than a hundred yards from the place where Anna saw Set in her vision and an equal distance from our house, where I dreamt of Set in his winged aspect. As if to emphasise the point, 'The Griffin' is the name given to the local pub, whose grounds, which extend to the river, are only a few yards from Caversham Bridge. We arrived at the conclusion that the Griffins in Caversham Court denote a special relationship that was known to exist between Set and the surrounding area – a relationship which manifested itself to us in Anna's childhood vision and our later dreams.

Discussing a representation of Athene – Mistress of Eternal Life – Musès describes the Griffin on her helmet as a "symbol of the great strength of the... power of transhumanization;"[115] that is, of the transformational energy of Sothis B. Athene was known by the ancient Egyptians as Isis Athene.[116] It is, therefore, noteworthy that, amongst the ancient Greeks, Isis as Athene bore the emblem of the Sethian Griffin. Magnificent Griffin heads were a feature of a number of items used at the site of the Delphic Oracle (some of which are still to be seen in the Delphi Museum).

The tree sacred to Sothis is the yew.[117] Within the grounds of Caversham Court are yew trees which are known to be more than two thousand years old (though, their magnificent branch system which formed a grove has recently been removed by the Borough Council). The yew can live for an extraordinary length of time due to its capacity to renew itself through its branches becoming trunks. Being an embodiment of the process of regeneration, the evergreen was a fitting emblem for reincarnation: "priests of the old Celtic religion regarded it as a symbol of immortality and planted it in their sacred groves, where Christian cemeteries were later situated. In this way, the death-and-resurrection connotations of the yew were perpetuated."[118] As a representative of Sothis, the yew witnessed all that was most important in the land: all grave oaths, such as Magna Charta, were sworn in the presence of a yew tree and to break such an oath was to commit treason.

Set was himself identified with the process of reincarnation. Robert Briffault cites a passage from the ancient Egyptian *Book of the Dead* (whose hieroglyphic title is *Book of The Coming Forth Into Day*) where Set presents himself in his aspect as Sata: "I am the serpent Sata, whose years are many, I die and I am born again. I am the serpent Sata which dwelleth in the uttermost parts of the earth. I die and I am born again, and I renew myself, and I grow young each time."[119]

Wood mentions that "Druids impressed Roman visitors with their ability to unlock the patterns of the future."[120] The Druids observed that "Those who wish to predict the future must first be acquainted with the past – which is why Celtic seers... begin their prophecies by looking back in time, not forward. Their experience and learning gives them an 'accurate knowledge of the goodly race', which they use as the basis for their predictions. These gifted souls list their experiences in a litany of past lives, which lends authority to their powers."[121] This approach, akin to the earlier-cited method of Pythagoras, for whom knowledge of one's past lives was the first step in education, is the natural outcome of the experience of avision.

Te Velde cites Egyptologists who have noted that a word meaning 'destiny' was often written over representations of a Set animal. He comments on one such representation at Beni Hasan: "If this Egyptian word for destiny can be determined with the Seth-animal, then the name of the Seth-animal at Beni Hasan might be translated as 'beast of destiny'."[122] Furthermore, Te Velde explains that Set was turned against because, as well as being the beast of destiny, he is also the god of death,[123] or, as those who feared death regarded him, "the destructive demon of death."[124] The people who took this view were, however, left with the prospect that, once dead, they would enter the Underworld where Set has dominion. In an attempt to combat that circumstance, they would incant, or have written on their tombs, such formulas as "I do not die. Seth obtains no power over me."[125] But the main tactic employed by the Heliopolitan priesthood was the substitution of Osiris for Set as the god of the dead. Thus, the Heliopolitan solar deity Atum (who was gradually syncretized with their sun-god Ra[126]) declared: "How perfect is that which I have done for Osiris in contradistinction from all gods. I have given him the realm of the dead and his son Horus as heir upon his throne."[127] The Heliopolitan propaganda continues to determine how a large section of humanity perceives Set and reacts to his appearance in their dreams. In this respect, one would have to say that the Heliopolitan priesthood were remarkably successful in the achievement of their aim.

Turning again to Themis, Jane Harrison observed that "The Greek word *Themis* and the English word *Doom* are, philology tells us, one and the same; and it is curious to note that their development moves on exactly parallel lines. *Doom* is the thing set, fixed, settled [note the repetitive use of Sethian adjectives]."[128] Thus, Themis was the goddess of destiny, of that which is necessarily going to happen and is, hence, unalterable. But Themis is also the divine guidance which enables one to meet one's fate with equanimity. Harrison notes that "Themis is in a sense prophecy incarnate… in the old sense of *prophecy*, utterance, ordinance [direction on how to proceed or act]."[129] From this, one can infer that the dream oracle at Delphi, which was founded by Themis, had been devoted to knowing how to proceed or act. With the usurping of that site by the Apollonian solar cult (which mythologically occurred when Apollo conquered Python, the Black Serpent at the heart of creation), the oracular dream was dispensed with; after which "Apollo's priests used the oracles to create new patriarchal laws."[130] As Briffault said: "to control the oracles was as necessary to a political god as it is to later politicians to control the press or education."[131] With the rise of the solar cult, men sought to be the masters of their own destiny; as a result of which a schism arose between Man and Nature.

Looking back, it was fitting that the dream instructions I received concerning destiny began after a death. That was in January 1990, on the night following the memorial service for Ronnie Laing. The memorial service had been a deeply affecting occasion that marked the end of an era in the world of psychotherapy and psychiatry and the end of my training as a psychotherapist. At that point, a higher educative power imposed itself. I dreamt:

> I am sitting on my bedclothes by the edge of a natural spring at the bottom of the garden of my childhood home contemplating the water in the tranquillity of the beautiful surroundings. Suddenly, a powerful force starts to pull the bedclothes and me with them into the water. After the most desperate effort, I am allowed to pull myself out and retrieve the bedding.

I woke up in a state of terror. As I sat up in bed, wide awake, recovering from the dream and wondering what on earth it could have been about, I sensed and heard a great sheet of water fall from above me and, before I could move out of the way, felt the full impact of its weight upon my head and shoulders. I was stupefied.

The theme of being pulled into a spring was a central element of the Eleusinian Mysteries: in the myth, the goddess Persephone was dragged into a spring by Hades – the Lord of the Underworld, who used the spring as the entrance to his domain – as a result of which she became goddess of the Underworld. It was in this role that Persephone received

232

Orpheus as he searched for his dead wife Eurydice. Kingsley tells how the Pythagorean Zopyrus described "Orpheus descending into the fiery depths of the underworld via a dream oracle at the water crater."[132] There was no actual spring in my childhood garden. However, as I have previously mentioned, Plutarch explained that the water crater at which Orpheus arrived "wanders everywhere throughout mankind in dreams and visions."

In the dream, I felt terrified because I suddenly found myself seemingly being pulled to my death. Then, unlike Persephone, I was allowed to exercise freewill and pull myself out of the spring, only to find that the water I had fought to avoid was immediately manifest in a less terrifying form. I was, as a result, left in no doubt that what is destined will take place and that there is nothing one can do about it.

I was reminded of this experience, with its obvious reference to baptism, when I came across Schwaller de Lubicz's account of "the purifications of the king when he officiates as priest before entering the sanctuary,"[133] during which Thoth and Horus, each holding a vase, pour the contents from above onto the sovereign's head. Schwaller de Lubicz emphasises: "It is not a matter of actually pouring a liquid, be it water or any other fluid, but a gesture of 'influx'."[134] The *O.E.D.* defines 'influx' as "an inflow, as of a physical fluid, water, air, light, heat, spiritual or immaterial influence into the soul."[135] Through experiencing the influx as a physical energy, I was witness to an intermediary stage of the process by which the world of the Dream, which emanates from Sothis, emerges into material reality; my vantage point being the interface between these two areas.

Since life unfolds along a pre-existing sequence of dreams, it is to the Dream that we must turn if we are to be aligned with Life. The dream which led to my identifying Set as the imminent emphasised asking what it is within a dream that will later materialize. Thus, the guidance provided by the Yin element of Sothis B directs one as to how to act; whilst that from the Yang element is more forward looking. Here, I am reminded of a dream of mine from November of 1997:

> I am shown how following the Tao involves being able to see ahead at certain points. A pattern of these points is provided.

Being able to see ahead will necessarily involve perceiving the approach of events both welcome and unwelcome. It will be remembered that Achilles Tatus wrote of dreams which reveal the future: they do so "not that we may contrive a defence to forestall it (for no one can be above fate) but that we may bear it more lightly when it comes." Spence provides the information that "In the native British mysticism the idea of struggle, of evolution, is stressed more as a natural and necessitous course, an act of psychic growth, rather than a definite philosophical path."[136] "There is," he says, "less stress of choice placed on Man in the British system" than upon "the entire cosmic machinery... At the same time we find that a certain amount of contributory action is essential on the part of man."[137] This is exactly the view that Anna and I have arrived at due to the guidance we have received through our dreams.

At the shrine of Our Lady of Caversham, the sense of 'doom' ('destiny') would have been overwhelming for pagan and Christian alike; for, housed within it, was not only the Black Madonna – the pagan personification of doom – but also "the spearhead [the Spear of Destiny] that pierced Christ's side on the Cross, described as the principal relic of the Realm; a piece of the rope with which Judas hanged himself; and the knives that killed Saint-King Edward the Martyr and King Henry VI."[138] From the identification of the site with Themis and the nature of the relics on display, it would seem that Caversham had long been the place in the land to which one came for communion with Destiny in order that one would know how to act. It is well documented that, in the Middle Ages, the shrine was regularly visited by royalty, for whom the sight of the relics housed there must have had a sobering effect.

Returning to ancient Egypt, whereas the Heliopolitan priesthood undermined Set by denigrating him, they undermined Khnum by subsuming him into their solar cult. Briffault, an authority in the field of anthropology, cites Wallis Budge, who says of this policy: "The cult of the sun-god was introduced into Egypt by the priests of Heliopolis under the Vth Dynasty, when they assumed the rule of the country and began to nominate their favourite warriors to the throne of Egypt. The astute theologians, either by force or persuasion, succeeded in making the official classes and priesthood believe that all the indigenous great gods were forms of Rā, and so secured his supremacy."[139] The priesthood which, thus, usurped both temporal and religious power "displayed great ingenuity and tact in absorbing into their form of religion all the older cults of Egypt, together with their magical rites and ceremonies. Apparently, they did not attempt to abolish the old, indigenous gods; on the contrary, they allowed their cults to be continued, provided that the local priesthoods would make their gods subordinate to Rā."[140] With regard to solar worship, Briffault emphatically states of Africa that "primitive cosmic religion has nowhere on that continent been transformed into solar cults"; and, moreover, that "there is no indication in any part of Africa at the present day of any solar cult or cosmology."[141] He cites A. Wiedemann, who states: "The worship of Rā, the sun, as an isolated, almost monotheistically conceived native deity is, in Egypt, found at Heliopolis only."[142] Briffault goes on to point out that "Rā was not even the local god of Heliopolis; nor was he, for that matter, the god of any city or nome in either Lower or Upper Egypt... Rā is in fact never worshipped anywhere in his own name alone, but always in combination with the name of the local god, or of some other god."[143]

Briffault criticizes an Egyptologist who stated the widely held view that "The Egyptians saw in the light of day the image of human life, in night the emblem of death; in the setting of the sun they recognised the prototype of the term of terrestrial existence, in the rising of the luminary, the symbol and token of new birth." To this, he replies that there is "one serious objection to regarding that allegorical account of Egyptian cosmic conceptions as representing their original foundation: the sun does not die, nor does it come to life again, and no uncultured people, ancient or modern, is known to have supposed that it does. The sun is, on the contrary, contrasted by them with the moon on account of its unchanging and undying character. Among the numerous quaint myths and conceptions of uncivilised peoples, with which we are acquainted, there is not in the four quarters of the globe any instance suggesting that it ever entered the head of an unsophisticated human being to regard the setting of the sun, or of the moon, or of any other celestial body, as equivalent to its dying, or its rising as suggesting its rebirth... Primitive conceptions may be crude and puerile as compared with the subtle spiritual similitudes of philosophical theologies, but they have never engendered such a strange monstrosity as the phases of a waxing and waning sun. It was reserved for the ingenuity of more advanced interpreters of cosmic phenomena, and for the meditations of the learned to give birth to such an astronomical curiosity."[144]

Briffault is particularly condemning of the fact that "The cosmological interpretation of ancient Egyptian cult and belief in terms of solar similitudes by the priestly theologians of the Middle and New Kingdoms has been referred to with editorial admiration by learned Egyptologists as both sublime and 'ingenious' or 'subtle'. But it is hard to find in the crude jumble of incongruities and the tissue of self-contradictions presented by those artificial deformations of primitive conceptions anything but a manifestation of phenomenal intellectual clumsiness."[145] He cites Wallis Budge, who concludes that "The confusion and contradictions which appear in the religious texts written under the XXth and following dynasties prove beyond all doubt that the knowledge of the early dynastic religion of Egypt possessed by the priests in general after, let us say 1200 B.C., was extremely vague and uncertain. The result of this was to create in their religion a confusion which is practically unbounded... Such being the case, the information they could impart is almost useless of itself for historical investigations."[146]

The situation described by Wallis Budge is only problematical if one disregards the Dream and, in consequence, suffers the limitation of conventional Egyptology, which is that it views the ancient Egyptian religion from the outside. If one returns to the ancient Egyptian understanding that dreams "serve as a means of communicating the will of the gods" and that one can be instructed into the Mysteries of Sothis by the Dream, one receives from dreams, as Iamblichus explained, "a power and a capacity of knowing which reasons intelligently of the things that were and the things that will be... [and] restores to order many things among men which were discordant and disorderly." Then, there isn't an insuperable problem at all. The instruction regarding Isis and Ba, Nephthys and Set and the Black Serpent at the heart of creation is a present-day experience of the ancient Egyptian religion in its purest form, conveyed to us by the source of that religion.

As I discussed earlier, the conventional Egyptological view is that the *Book of What Is in the Tuat* "describes the journey of the sun god through the twelve hours of the night"[147] and that the book "begins with the entry of the sun god, as a ram-headed *ba* ('soul')."[148] However, through Anna's dream, we were made aware that this is a misrepresentation: the confusion has arisen because the knowledge has been lost or concealed that the ba soul of the sun is located, not within the sun itself, but in Sothis A (as I have explained, Sothis is the central sun of our sun). Thus, it is Ba/Khnum, the Yang element of Sothis A, which makes the journey through the Tuat, the world of the Dream.

Wallis Budge states that Khnum was a very ancient god who existed prior to the rise of Heliopolis.[149] Khnum, therefore, could not originally have been identified as the sun god; though, as the Yang element of Sothis A, he is the god of the sun. Khnum's consort was Sati, or Satet, who Wallis Budge proves was a form of Isis-Sothis;[150] thus confirming the Dream's pairing of Isis and Ba/Khnum.

Khnum was depicted as the potter god because he is that aspect of Sothis which gives shape or form to the imminent as it becomes manifest. The movement of the imminent to the manifest was symbolically designated by the ancient Egyptians as having its source at Elephantine (an island in the Nile located in Upper Egypt), which was the principal cult centre of Khnum. Khnum was, therefore, "regarded as the god of the Nile and of the annual Nile-flood."[151] In this way, Sothis was delineated as the astro-meteorological source of the Nile.

Pinch presents the conventional assessment that "It was probably the fertile mud spread by the inundation that Khnum was thought to use as a 'potter god'."[152] However, this is to overlook the fact that 'Ast', an ancient Egyptian word for clay, was also a name of Isis. That the Yang element of Sothis A was known as the potter god and the Yin element was identified with clay can hardly be a coincidence. Further, when Khnum is represented as seated upon a throne (the symbol for Sothis A) beside his potter's wheel, this wheel upon which the clay is fashioned symbolizes Sothis B – the star described by the Dogon as "spinning." Musès uses the metaphor of the moon reflecting the light of the sun to describe the energetic relationship between the stars of Sothis: the "Super-moon", Sothis B, dispenses "the divine power and light" of the "Super-sun", Sothis A.[153] Though the metaphors differ, it is implicit in the depiction of the Divine Potter that the clay – the energy from Sothis A – is centred upon the wheel – Sothis B; the astrophysical validity of this action being confirmed by Musès. One can then appreciate the profound understanding that the ancient Egyptians were able to encode in such an image. The energy dispensed from Sothis exerts its influence upon the mind of Man through the Dream. In this regard, Khnum is that aspect of the Dream which gives shape to existence; hence, Anna's dream of Khnum creating on his potter's wheel the radiating efflux of Horus.

Wallis Budge states that the name 'Khnemu' (another rendering of 'Khnum') is connected with the root 'Khnem', 'to join, to unite'.[154] This uniting occurred when the Sothic Grail cup moved into my head, becoming one with it, so that the different aspects of my being could be contained therein and coalesce. Those different aspects were my different lives. It will be remembered that Lamy describes the Ba soul as "the soul animating all those beings who... are subject to psychic rebirth." When the Grail cup moved into my head, my ba soul became one with the Ba soul. Khnum, as that which gives form to the imminent as it becomes manifest, is the creator of the Grail, the vessel for the Dream, which is created by the Dream for its own purpose.

The restitution of Khnum as a Sothic, rather than a solar, deity had been anticipated in a pair of dreams of Anna's, on 19th October 1997, the day before I received my instruction about the imminent and the manifest:

> The god Mercury shoots up my nose and into my head, activating my pineal so that I see a fluid light containing the colours of the spectrum.

> Anthony and I are in a tunnel made of smoky quartz. As we look out, in the distance on one side is England, on the other is Egypt. Suddenly, the Great Pyramid appears very close, gleaming gold. Anthony says it is a sign that we are always this close to it. We travel to Elephantine accompanied by two of our children. There, we help to rebuild a temple by finding and replacing red stone or clay discs that some parts of the temple were constructed from. There is a strong oriental influence here – many of the people and the foods are of the Far East.

In the first dream (which occurred before we knew of the fundamental relationship between Sothic energy and the olfactory system), the forward-looking energy of Set entered Anna's olfactory bulb and, from there, her pineal gland. Immediately afterwards, in the second dream, we were in a tunnel from which both England and Egypt were within our view. Suddenly, the Great Pyramid appeared, not in its original white, limestone casing, but gleaming gold. A lingual connection exists between the Great Pyramid and Sothis B; for, in ancient Egyptian, 'Mer' (as well as being a name for Egypt and denoting 'Love') was a name of Set and meant 'pyramid'.[155] Wilkinson discusses the fact that Isis and Nephthys were both associated with gold; and writes of "the close association of the metal with afterlife concerns."[156] This is relevant to the Underworld location of Anna's dream.

An earlier dream of Anna's, which came on the night after the Sphinx confirmed that we were doing everything right, had provided information which would later enable us to determine that the Great Pyramid is resonant with all four aspects of Sothis:

> Anthony and I are in Giza, walking by the pyramids. Anthony says that there is an alignment today which means that a sign will appear in the sky. Suddenly, there is a rushing sound – we look up to see a black stele inscribed with gold symbols and letters immediately above us. The symbols denote four children and the letters read: BOY GIRL BOY GIRL. Anthony says this is a message encoded in the limestone of the pyramids.

It will be noted that, in the dream of Elephantine, while we were in the tunnel between England and Egypt, our seeing the Great Pyramid close by was a sign that we are always close to it; in the same way that, after my dream of being seated beside the tunnel connected with the ancient Egyptians, I was told that Anna and I are as connected with the Sphinx now as we were in our Egyptian lifetime.

It was only after Anna's dream that we learnt that the major cult centre of Khnum was at Elephantine. Our journeying to rebuild the Temple at Elephantine was an indication that we would restore the understanding, which had existed before the rise of the Heliopolitan priesthood, that Khnum (Ba) is the Yang aspect of Sothis A. Our finding and replacing the red stone or clay discs referred to the identification of red/rede with the Dream and of Isis-Sothis with clay (shaped by Ba). The discs, a manifestation of the radiating circles of light that is Horus, were the dreams about Khnum. Anna's dream thereby emphasised the relationship between Khnum, Elephantine and Sothis as the source of the Dream. Confirmation of this is provided by Schwaller de Lubicz, who mentions that the magnificent red granite obelisks which are found outside the great temples of Egypt were quarried on the mainland at Aswan, which is opposite the Island of Elephantine: "granite is so much associated with its place of extraction, that is, the first nome of Upper Egypt, that the name of the metropolis of its nome, *Abu* (meaning 'elephant'), is followed by the distinctive determinative of granite [a determinative depicting a kind of vase]. The word *mat* designates granite in general and perhaps most particularly red granite, because when black granite is meant, the color is usually stipulated. This same word *mat*... means dream."[157]

The strong oriental influence at Elephantine in Anna's dream points to links between ancient Egyptian and ancient Chinese high science. The reference to Far Eastern foods continues the use of food as a metaphor for knowledge, which was first presented to us in Anna's dream of the school (in September of 1994), in which she thought that we may imbibe food from ancient Egypt while consuming soup from ancient Egyptian bowls. Through these references to the Far East, we were being prepared for the forthcoming link that we would have to make between pairs 1 and 2 and the Chinese concept of Yin and Yang. Indeed, once we had been provided with the identity of pairs 1 and 2, a new imperative arose for us to acquire knowledge of Yin and Yang theory. The first intimation that we needed a sophisticated understanding of the practicalities of Yin and Yang had come in a dream of Anna's in July of 1993:

> Anthony and I are preparing a living exhibition of creation. Every exhibit has two corresponding aspects or elements, the passive and the active. These are always complementary; although, if they are not balanced correctly they may appear to be in opposition. Our children help us to assemble the exhibits. When the exhibition is ready, all the exhibits fit together, making one elaborate, harmonious display.

It is worthy of note that Anna's dream of restoring the Temple of Khnum occurred a month after I had been instructed to restore the crane. Both dreams depicted the need to restore a function associated with the Yang aspect of Sothis: in my dream, of Sothis B; in Anna's dream, of Sothis A.

Interestingly, it is an ancient Egyptian dream featuring Khnum and an imperative to restore the Temple at Elephantine which highlights the huge disparity between the social status of the Dream in antiquity and the present day. Carved in rock on the island of Sahal, near Aswan, the Famine Stele, dating from Ptolemaic times, is an account (or a copy thereof) of a royal decree issued by Pharaoh Djoser (2667-2648 B.C.) describing the events that led to the ending of a seven-year famine which had brought Egypt to a state of ruin. Djoser wrote to Mater, the governor of the south of Egypt (the area including Elephantine), requesting information regarding the deity of that region with a view to restoring the Inundation of the Nile. The stele records how Mater went, on behalf of the pharaoh, to Elephantine, where he entered "the secret places" (that is, the inner sanctum of the Temple of Khnum) in order to incubate. Jack Lindsay comments that Mater "would hope for the god to visit him in a dream."[158] This duly happened: "I found the god standing in front of me."[159] Mater was informed by Khnum of the need for the temples that were in a state of disrepair to be restored and told that, if he arranged this, the Inundation would return.

Although some Egyptologists take a sceptical view, believing the Famine Stele to be a means of increasing revenue, through taxes, for the Ptolemaic priesthood, it is, none-the-less, the case that implicit in this account is a conviction that, as Laurens van der Post said, "when life itself feels imperilled, somehow out of it comes the saving element" – that saving element being the Dream.

One cannot be properly aligned with Khnum if he is related to as a solar deity, for there is a considerable difference between the effect of the energy of Sothis upon Mankind and that of the sun. The energy from Sothis is exquisite and, if one is properly aligned, harmonizing. As Sothic energy grows in intensity, it offers increasing possibilities for insight and transformation. The effect of the sun can be altogether more disturbing. Shortly after the First World War, a Russian professor, A.E. Tchijevsky, published the results of his "long and detailed studies of the statistics and histories of seventy-two countries from 500 B.C. to 1922, a period of 2,422 years. He included in his compilations such signs of human unrest and excitability as wars, revolutions, riots, expeditions, and migrations, plus such factors as the number of humans involved, the quality of the event, and the size of area affected. The time when the unrest began and its high point were also reduced to arithmetical values of varying significance. With his volumes of data Professor Tchijevsky constructed a year-by-year Index of Mass Human Excitability that covered the past twenty-four centuries in an amazing panorama of man's emotional moods."[160] Tchijevsky found that there is a correspondence between the greatest times of unrest and the highest levels of sunspot activity.

Modern Man is tossed about by cosmic seas whose existence he is barely aware of. We cannot avoid these forces, we certainly cannot master them in the sense of dominating them, but we can navigate our way through them – master them in the original sense of that word. It is in the nature of a sea journey that the forces of current, wind and storm take one away from one's intended course; and that is how it is in life. Though we chart a straight route, the forces of nature take us where they will. We have then to take stock of our situation – and it is here that mastery is called for. At the heart of 'mastery' is 'aster' meaning 'star'. Mastery involves being able to determine one's position and the direction one must head in using the heavenly bodies as a guide. It is worth pondering that the Greek 'disaster' literally meant 'separation from the stars'.

Towards the end of December 1998, Anna had a dream which vividly conveyed the effect of her having, earlier that month, embraced the instruction concerning Isis and Ba, Nephthys and Set:

> The Pan shell in our garden has become a large, three-tiered, fountain. I am sitting on the top tier. Water is buoying me up and cascading around me. This is both pleasurable and of great significance.

Restoring the temple at Elephantine was a pre-condition for the restoration of the Pan shell. There is, in the ancient Egyptian language, a direct association between the restoration of the Temple of Khnum and the image of the restored Pan shell functioning as a fountain, in that the word 'Khnumit' (or 'Khnemit') meant 'fountain, well and spring'.[161] The Pan shell, which had been smashed and removed in

Anna's dream of September 1997, was now restored, just as her dream had suggested when we felt "that a new Pan shell may grow from the ground." In that dream, the Pan shell had been replaced by three obelisks, which symbolized the subversive influence of the Heliopolitan priesthood. These were now replaced by the three-tiered fountain. We were to learn, from the next dream of Anna's I shall recount, that the three tiers represent the harmonious relationship between Heaven and Man mediated by the Dream. The Heavenly tier is that of Sothis, whose waters buoy Anna up as they cascade to Earth. The flowing fountain demonstrates that the flowing water circuit displayed in Anna's dream of the Black Serpent hanging in the stairwell of the old Reading Library/Museum is fully functioning. The water circuit represents the energy from Sothis flowing down to Earth and, then, being offered, as Maat, back to its source. In the dream of the fountain, the Pan shell has the same function as the Grail cup – it, too, is a vessel for the transformational energy of Sothis.

CHAPTER FIFTEEN

The Temple

᙮

1999 stands out in our memory as being a year in which Anna and I were provided with another extraordinary demonstration of the capacity of the Dream to determine our destiny. The first indication of what was to unfold was presented in a dream of Anna's on the night preceding the summer solstice in June of that year:

> Anthony and I find ourselves in a large, plush building in China. The rooms are spacious and the seating comfortable. We are told that there is a 'Court of Redress' that one can go to in the case of injustice. We watch a puppet theatre that is arranged in a model of a pagoda. The figures are on three levels: gods on the highest level; angels/messengers of the gods on the middle level; humans on the lowest level. Afterwards, we walk through a hall where the wood-work is crimson and the pale blue walls are exquisitely painted with branches of blossom. As we pass through, we overhear a conversation in which a Chinese man says in perfect English that what certain Chinese most appreciate about going to England is the Feng Shui; and that significant people from China are preparing to come to England to assist Anthony and me.

AVISION The Way of the Dream

Here, we were suddenly moved from our preoccupation with our ancient Egyptian life into the Chinese civilization. This was not altogether surprising to us; because, in Anna's dream of our helping to restore the temple at Elephantine, we were shown that a strong oriental influence has existed there: 'many of the people and the foods are of the Far East'. It will be remembered that Musès demonstrated how the Chinese doctrine of transformation reflects that of Egypt. In Anna's earlier dream, we restored the temple with red clay discs, which were symbolic of the Dream. That the 'Court of Redress (Red-ress)' is a function of the Dream – of red/rede – was demonstrated by the puppet theatre depicting the relationship between Heaven and Man as being mediated by 'angels'/'messengers of the gods', which are both synonyms for 'dreams'. A Court of Redress is a court where "reparation of... or compensation" is made "for a wrong sustained or the loss resulting from this." 'Redress' also used to mean a "Remedy for, or relief from, some trouble; assistance, aid, help" and "to set up again, restore, re-establish."[1] We were being shown that the Dream was to provide people from China who would help to remedy a loss we had sustained and that this would involve the relationship between Heaven and Man as mediated by the Dream. There was a strong indication that the people coming to assist us were versed in the ancient Chinese science of geomancy: Feng Shui.

The process of restoring or re-establishing was then directly addressed in another dream of Anna's in August of 1999:

> Anthony and I are able to draw upon any experience in our existence – including that from our other lives – and bring it forth as a reality into the present.

Shortly afterwards, in early September of 1999, this was shown to have been achieved with regard to our ancient Egyptian life when Anna dreamt:

> It is twilight before dawn. Anthony and I are at the back of our garden. Behind us is a standing stone. We are looking towards

the house, through the french-windows, from where shines an exceptional golden light by which we are orienting ourselves. We realize that this is the Light of Egypt.

At the end of September of 1999, a client arrived for a consultation with me directly from a Qigong course he had attended in Switzerland with Dr. Guo, a Chinese Master resident in this country. She had told her students that the leading *I Ching* and Feng Shui Masters in China, Master Shao Aidong and his wife Master Wang Hong, were staying at her home during the first visit of its kind to England; their purpose being to explore the application of the *I Ching* in this country with a view to translating his father's version into English. (In China, this version by Grand Master Shao Weihua, which is completely different from that introduced to the West by Richard Wilhelm, has sold more copies than any other work apart from that of Chairman Mao. The Grand Master's accomplishments are legendary. He was, for instance, consulted by the government of the former Soviet Union in 1984 when their leader Konstantin Chernenko was ill to determine whether or not the illness would be fatal. He predicted that Chernenko would die thirty-six days later; which is what happened.)

The news of the Chinese Masters' visit affected us deeply because of Anna's dream that significant people from China who were, it seemed, versed in Feng Shui were coming to assist us. However, I had been told that the Chinese Masters were almost at the end of their stay; and, so, though we remained hopeful, the possibility of being able to arrange *I Ching* and Feng Shui readings seemed remote. This had occurred on a Tuesday evening. That night, as we were later to learn, Master Shao Aidong was instructed in a dream that he and his wife must cancel their appointment of the following Saturday as something much more important was coming up. So it was that, after I telephoned the next day to see if there was any chance of our having a consultation with them, I was told that they would be travelling (with a translator) from the north of England to our home in Reading that Saturday for a twenty-four hour visit. During the intervening period, they had a number of dreams about Anna and myself which provided all the information they needed for our Life readings (the Life reading is that part of the *I Ching* that concerns one's past and future destiny).

This seminal moment, with its interweaving of life and the Dream, is a striking example, because of its practicality, of avision. It is commendable that Masters Shao Aidong and Wang Hong were prepared to act upon such a dream. I was deeply impressed by this as, though Anna and I had arrived at a position where we were living our life entirely on the basis of instruction received through our dreams, I had not encountered another present-day psychotherapist who would have cancelled an existing appointment because they had been told to do so in a dream. Here, the Dream appeared, not as it is usually viewed in the West – a product of personal conscious or unconscious determinants – but as the central organizing factor of life: entirely purposive; very much to the point; without need of interpretation.

One of the most unexpected features of this process was that the Dream had arranged for Anna and myself to meet a couple we had known in a past life in order that they could, through their dreams, provide us with the information we needed about that life. That information was not unfamiliar to us; since, over the years, elements of it had appeared in our own experience of avision – and it was through these fragmentary references that we were able to confirm the veracity of the Chinese Masters' account.

The Chinese Masters brought back to our memory the unusual circumstances in which Anna and I had met in our Chinese lifetime; and that, after we had fallen in love, a man who had designs upon Anna had orchestrated her death. This was the "wrong sustained" and the "loss resulting from it" which the Court of Redress had to remedy. The description of me in that life given by the Chinese Masters precisely corresponded to my character and appearance in an earlier dream of mine. Similarly, Anna had, through avision, been made aware that she had had a Chinese life; and had also been shown the features of the malevolent man who had arranged her death – although, prior to meeting the Chinese Masters, she had not connected these recollections.

After Anna's death, I, inconsolable, had retreated from the world and devoted the remainder of my life to understanding the forces of destiny through studying the *I Ching* with Masters Shao Aidong and Wang Hong. My Life reading revealed that, as a consequence of this, I was to be, in this lifetime – in nine years time – the *I Ching* Master in the West. When I asked how this would come about, Master Shao replied that it would happen naturally – that it was not necessary for me to undergo any training because the mastery of the *I Ching* which I had attained in my past life would come back to me. Thus, he was describing the process which Anna's dream had instructed us about: that we are able to draw upon an experience from a past life and bring it forth as a reality into the present.

At the time of our meeting the Chinese Masters, I had been using the Wilhelm translation of the Confucian approach to the *I Ching* for twenty-five years. Though it was not necessary for me to study the *I Ching*, I decided I would study with the Chinese Masters because I both welcomed the chance to be able to compare the Confucian approach with theirs and, most importantly, was now provided with the opportunity of studying the *I Ching* and Feng Shui together with Anna – thereby, remedying the effects of the trauma of our separation in our past life.

In the same way that our imbibing food from ancient Egypt out of the soup bowls in Anna's dream of the school had symbolized assimilation of ancient Egyptian knowledge and ideas into our mind or moral system, the 'foods of the Far East' in her dream of our helping to rebuild the temple at Elephantine referred, in this life, to our future study of the *I Ching*, Feng Shui and Qigong. In this way, the Dream ensured that we were provided with a highly sophisticated understanding of Yin and Yang theory, which Anna's dream of pairs 1 and 2 had created the requirement for. Such an understanding was a fundamental element of Egyptian sacred science.

The lineage of which Master Shao is the present-day representative originated with his illustrious ancestor Shao Yung (1011-1077), whose approach to the *I Ching* was later brought to the attention of Gottfried

Liebniz, the inventor of binary arithmetic. Liebniz was profoundly affected by the exact correspondence between the two systems. Subsequently, the binary system was used by Norbert Weiner (with whom Musès co-lectured in a post graduate course on neural-cybernetics) as the mathematical basis of cybernetics. Despite being known in some academic and esoteric circles, the *I Ching* only became the focus of popular interest in the West when Richard Wilhelm's translation was first published in English in 1951; a great deal of that interest having been generated by the foreword Jung wrote for the publication.

In the simplest method for obtaining a reading that Wilhelm mentions, three coins are used: the inscribed surface being given the value of two, denoting Yin, depicted as a broken line; the reverse being given the value of three, denoting Yang, depicted as an unbroken line. When the three coins are thrown, the numbers produced by the upward-facing surface will either be six, representing a Yin line that changes into a Yang line; seven, representing an unchanging Yang line; eight, representing an unchanging Yin line; or nine, representing a Yang line that changes into a Yin line. The coins are thrown six times, producing an ascending pattern of broken or unbroken lines called a 'hexagram'. There are sixty-four hexagrams which, with their changing lines, denote all events in material reality. Central to ancient Chinese thinking was the observation that all events at a given moment in time partake of the qualities of that moment; and, so, the pattern of Yin and Yang lines obtained by throwing the coins embodies the pattern of the moment in which they are thrown. In the Confucian system, judgements are appended both to each hexagram and to the individual changing lines within it, which provide an answer to the question asked.

In the *I Ching* traditions taught to us by Master Shao, no judgement or commentary is appended to the lines. Master Shao described the *I Ching* to us as "the Language of the Universe." Confirmation of this designation was provided by E.H. Grafe, who discovered that there are such astonishing parallels between the *I Ching* and the genetic code that "the two codes fit perfectly into each other."[2] Martin Schönberger, in his exposition and development of Grafe's work, has demonstrated that this correspondence even extends to the Chinese ideogram denoting the '*I Ching*', since it "is at the same time the visual image of the DNA double helix."[3] As Schönberger commented, "Old China grasped this complex of intellect, spirit and body as a unit, and realized it on a scale that is inconceivable for us."[4] It is in this light that one must view the claim of the ancient Chinese that the *I Ching* reveals "a law of universal validity which is not only law, but also said to be the origin of the whole visible world and to be operative in the finest details of its patterns and its turnings of fate – while at the same time constituting a code of conduct for the best possible form of interhuman relationships."[5]

During the period that we studied with Master Shao (2001-2002), I asked him if he would provide me with an *I Ching* reading regarding the publication of this book. At the time of the reading, I mentioned a dream of mine which had answered that question and I was interested to compare his reading with my dream. Master Shao required me to use his personalized coin method to create the hexagram. At the conclusion of my doing so, he explained that the imagery of my dream was identical to that of the *I Ching* reading – that they were one and the same.

Earlier, in February of 2000, I had dreamt:

> Anna and I are walking along a country road. As we do so, we catch sight of a book entitled *The Dreamers* that is placed on an outdoor table. However, when we reach the point where the book should be, it is nowhere to be seen. At first, we carry on walking; but, then, we stop and retrace our steps because we want to know what has happened to the book. We discover that the road we have been following has been created in such a way that only certain people can detect a smaller side-road leading off it. We walk down that smaller road and eventually come across a shop, outside of which is the outdoor table bearing the book we glimpsed earlier. We are told that the shop contains everything a dreamer could need.

At the time of this dream, we had not yet learnt of the shamanic roots of Taoism; that "By the twelfth century BCE... kings and nobles employed shamans as advisers, diviners, and healers;" or that divinational Taoism had its roots in the interpretation of dreams. In the twenty-five years that I had been using the *I Ching*, I had not come across any reference to the Dream having had an influence upon the development of the *I Ching*. It was this situation that my dream was addressing.

My dream of the book entitled *The Dreamers* made reference to a later dream I was to have, in 2002, following a stay in China with the Chinese Masters (during which time they deepened our studies in Feng Shui by taking us to major sites and explaining the geomantic forces operating there). The later dream gave specific details of Anna's and my identity in a still earlier Chinese life from the time of the Dream Masters. It is this that was depicted in Anna's earlier dream as our retracing our steps ("Turning back is how the way moves") until we found 'The Dreamers' – our past selves – outside the shop, which symbolized the community offering 'everything a dreamer could need'. *The Dreamers* being outside the shop represented the traditional location of shamans outside of the community.

At the end of our stay in China, Master Shao again expressed the opinion that I had no need to study the *I Ching*, saying that my understanding of the Dream is such that I can learn everything I need through avision. It was at this point that (whilst we have remained friends) our studies with the Chinese Masters came to an end and we returned to our life of retreat.

In many ways, the most important hexagram in the *I Ching* is the penultimate one, Hexagram 63, which Wilhelm translated as "After Completion;"[6] a rendering Musès described as "misleading."[7] According to Musès, the name of Hexagram 63 – 'Chi Chi' – translates as "after being fulfilled or aided;"[8] a translation of great interest to Anna and myself, since 'aid' is a meaning of 'redress'. In Chinese, 'Chi Chi' literally means "reaching the harmony of the other shore after having crossed over the river."[9] As Musès says, "The conventional Confucian interpretation (spread predominantly throughout the West) of this profound and key hexagram is in serious error... the *I Ching* is essentially Taoist, and it is in the recondite reaches of Taoist teaching that we learn the *Book of Changes*."[10] He demonstrates that Hexagram 63 is linked to the Taoist practice of "perceiving higher light associated with certain stars" which "brought to the adept starry rescue and power."[11] As I have already mentioned, Musès cites Taoist texts which describe the 'controlling centres' of those stars as Sothis A and B, which are approached by the constellation of the Great Bear. In the Confucian literature pertaining to the *I Ching*, it is the complete absence of any reference to the need to be fulfilled or aided by Sothis A and B, through alignment with those stars, that attracted Musès' criticism.

It will be remembered that, in her second dream of the embryological transformational process (in April 1998), Anna and I entered a hidden chamber of bone and flesh where dwelled a calm and benign grey wolf god who was a part of us. In that dream, the stairs, which represent the past in this and previous lives, were missing. Subsequently, the Dream arranged the installation of two of those stairs through our contact with the Chinese Masters. This followed naturally from our encounter with the wolf god because, for the Chinese, the most notable star in the heavens, Sothis, was the 'Wolf Star', as it still is in Tibet. There, the Wolf Star is "the governor of the Tibetan peoples."[12]

Hexagram 63 is comprised of an ascending pattern of alternating Yang and Yin lines. Musès explains that, in the esoteric Taoist tradition, these lines are regarded as "a choreographic encoding of the dance of Yü,"[13] "the ancient demigod ruler of China,"[14] "who walked through the stars to immortality, to the pattern of *Chi Chi*, hexagram number 63."[15] Each pace of the Dance of Yü corresponds to one of the seven stars of the Great Bear that leads to Sothis A and B, which are called the 'Rescuer-Protector' and the 'Sustainer'.[16] As Wong states, "Yü... journeyed frequently to the stars to learn from the celestial spirits."[17] Later, she adds: "In ancient China, the dream was... linked to the shaman's journey to the other realms."[18] Thus, the Dream is a means to travel the path of the Dance of Yü – Hexagram 63. This is because the Dream is the Tao and the Tao is the focus of the *I Ching*.

Such a shamanic journey was described in a poem by the Taoist Master Chen Tuan, who developed an incubatory practice which he called 'Ecstatic Sleep'. Master Chen declared: "I practice the sleep of the perfected," and went on to describe his ascent to the seven stars of the Great Bear and the two stars of Sothis: "Then my spirit leaves to ascend to the Nine Palaces above... I visit the perfected and discuss the principles beyond... This is perfected sleep... You want to know what is in sleep and dream? Its well the highest mystery among men!... Sleep the sleep of all that is perfection; dream the dreams of wide eternity."[19] It is through the Dream that Master Chen 'reached the harmony of the other shore'.

In our experience of avision, the complementary movement, in which the Great Bear comes to us, also takes place. For instance, in a dream of mine in September 1998:

> There is external danger. I realize that in response to this danger a huge bear is going to break through the fabric of our house. It does so and, then, forces its way into our bedroom, where it lays down on our bed and falls asleep. We are safe, for there is no danger once the bear is in the house.

Confirmation that this dream concerned the constellation of the Great Bear came two days later, when I dreamt:

> I am able to recognise concealed astronomical issues.

So, the previous dream had shown the energy of the Great Bear passing through the fabric of our house and coming to rest in the place where we were dreaming.

Anna had a similar dream featuring a bear in December of the same year:

> A great bear has entered the house and approaches us. I say to one of the children that they do not have to move away even though the

bear appears fearsome – they can stay where they are to observe and experience its presence.

Anna woke in the night following this dream and related it to me. We went to the window and observed that the constellation of the Great Bear was immediately above a yew grove at the end of the garden of the house in which we were staying at that time, creating a perfect alignment with our bedroom.

Two dreams of mine, from October of 2000, demonstrate the way in which Anna's and my understanding of the *I Ching* was deepened by the Dream:

> I am shown an *I Ching* reading which reveals the forces operating at the moment. I am required to enter into the reading so that I can see how those forces are affecting everything I do and everything that is happening around me. Finally, I am shown the event they are leading towards.

> I am shown an image, radiating from the heavens, of the hexagram which is operating at the moment. It is then demonstrated to me how the hexagram is manifest within the circumstances of the time. My attention is drawn towards a place of human habitation. Individual details of human behaviour and of natural occurrences are, first, focused in upon, as if I am viewing them through a telescope; and, then, revealed to be directly influenced by the hexagram. In this way, I am repeatedly shown aspects of life and, then, how those aspects emanate from the hexagram.

In addition, the Dream has, on several occasions, provided us with specific hexagrams operative at the time. Our first such dream was given to Anna in late September of 1997:

> Anthony and I are viewing the *I Ching*, which is represented by a series of small, three-dimensional figures of oriental beings, often

in pairs or groups. I say the most significant one for us at this time is number five – a lone figure.

At that time, Anna had not yet read the *I Ching*; and I had disposed of my copy when we went into retreat. Hexagram 5 is concerned with 'waiting', specifically 'waiting when the attainment of one's goal is assured'; the goal being the fulfilment of Hexagram 63: "Waiting is not mere empty hoping. It has the inner certainty of reaching the goal. Such certainty alone gives that light which leads to success. This leads to the perseverance that brings good fortune and bestows power to cross the great water."[20]

In the *I Ching* system practiced by the Chinese Masters, any moment in time can be described in terms of Yin and Yang and the five elements: wood, fire, earth, metal and water. The pattern of those factors can be depicted in the form of a hexagram which represents the determining forces operating at that moment. The character and destiny of an individual are defined by the particular combination of Yin and Yang and the five elements operative at the time of their birth. Thereafter, the pattern of Yin and Yang and the five elements manifest at any moment in time is experienced by the individual as either concordant with, or antagonistic to, the pattern of those factors imprinted on them at the time of their birth. Thus, a moment in time that is nourishing for one person can be devastating for another. It was by applying this understanding that Grand Master Shao Weihua, having been given by the Russian government the details of Chernenko's birth, was able to establish that the forces of Yin and Yang and the five elements would, in thirty-six days time, be so antithetical to the pattern the Soviet leader had acquired at his birth that he would necessarily die. The advantage of Master Shao's *I Ching* system over the Confucian system is that it is capable of determining the timing of events with astonishing accuracy.

When viewed in terms of the movement from the imminent to the manifest, the Dream functions as an indicator of events in exactly the same way as the *I Ching*; which is why "Stoics understood dreams as signs of a reality into which the present would flow. Thus dreams were predictive of the future – not merely predictive but deeply revelatory of the flow in time of configurations embedded in the present." At the same time (and often in the same dream), one's dreaming mind presents a response to the efflux from Sothis and its manifestations, revealing thereby personal or external factors that are concordant or discordant with that flow. (In the process, the dream imagery depicts the same combinations of Yin and Yang and the five elements that are depicted by the *I Ching*.)

As I have outlined, in *I Ching* theory (as in astrology), the character and destiny of an individual are believed to be defined by the particular combination of forces operative at the time of their birth. However, in January of 1994, Anna dreamt:

> I am told by the gods that the zodiacal constellations which affect us most are those at our conception rather than those at our birth.

It is, of course, far more difficult to determine the moment of one's conception than that of one's birth. But, because one's conception is such a significant event, details of that experience will often appear in dreams at the time of its anniversary.

As Musès stated, "the nature of mind or consciousness is reflected in the nature of the cosmos. The ancients... phrased this effectiveness in the maxim, 'As above, so below; as within, so without'. This summary was supposed to have been inscribed by Thoth, the Egyptian divinity presiding over wisdom, on a tablet of emerald, the legend of which was common knowledge in the high days of the great library of Alexandria, and which was transmitted to Europe during the early Renaissance, though it had been well known in Islamic civilization long before, having been handed on with the heritage that passed from Egypt through Greece and then Rome."[21] "no person experiences any constellation of events at given times without there being traceable relations between personality configuration, event types, and the qualities of the occurrence times or periods, as delineated by their macrocosmic or solar system configuration."[22] There is much speculation as to whether or not the fact that "the Maya chose to end their 13-*baktun* calendar on December 21, 2012"[23] signals an event which will energetically enable a transformation of consciousness. (A 'baktun' was a Mayan unit of 5125.36 years, with thirteen baktun constituting a World Age.) It remains to be seen whether there is a clearly discernible pattern of initiatory oneiric events surrounding December 2012 akin to those which Anna and I experienced around the time of the Hieros Gamos of Sothis A and B.

Given the inter-relationship between the genetic code, the *I Ching*, avision and Sothis, Anna and I arrived at the conclusion that DNA-RNA can be reprogrammed by Sothis through the Dream. Support for this possibility was provided by Musès, who wrote: "In a 1962 lecture given before the Cybernetics Group of the Institute for Theoretical Physics of the University of Naples... we voiced the proposition that the *central nervous system* is 'the source of modification of the DNA-RNA through the organism's choice of adaptation to its environment'... In short, decision – deep in the unconscious in most cases – is involved. Six years later, Carl C. Lindgren, professor emeritus of the Biological Research Laboratory of Southern Illinois University, voiced the same proposal: that the brain, by its interaction with the environment, could influence the DNA patterns of the germ cells, resulting in a new kind of pangenesis worked through a feedback control of the nervous system on the germ cells. The recent work of the molecular biologist Thomas H. Jukes and the geneticist R. King at the NASA-sponsored Space Science Laboratories at the University of California at Berkeley now demands mention. Drs. Jukes and King found that there were 'Darwinianly neutral' mutations, formed independently of the process of natural selection and oblivious to its censoring power. Previously, in 1967, under NASA grant NsG-479, Jukes had written that 'a major point in the evolution of the [genetic] code had been played by mutations that are transcribed into the various transfer RNA molecules'. He was referring here to adaptive and non-pathological mutations. It is only time before full verification of the thesis first voiced in 1962 will be established; namely, that the brain (or its lower life-form analogue) – the central organ of environmental interaction – mediates adaptive changes in animal or plant germ plasm via modified RNA... Then a new era in evolutionary theory – now only adumbrated – will be at hand. Awareness, consciousness on some level, is always the touchstone of nature's ways."[24]

I have, again, moved some years away from my narrative and, so, must now return to October of 1999 when, two weeks after meeting the Chinese Masters, I dreamt:

> It is emphasised to me that what matters is existing in this lifetime.

This was a continuation of the instruction in my dream of the Horus exhibition (in March of 1998) that Anna and I are only to be interested in the experiences that we are presented with in this lifetime; though, this instruction was not simply stating that it is always one's present life which matters most. To understand why what matters is existing in this lifetime – at this particular time in history – one has only to turn to Musès' statement regarding the events surrounding the Hieros Gamos of Sothis A and B, that "such timing... occurs but once in some ninety thousand years, giving some inkling of the stunning rarity of the evolutionary opportunity for humanity during the last two decades of the twentieth century."

My being told that 'what matters is existing in this lifetime' developed the message of an earlier dream of mine from July of 1995. I should first explain that I once possessed a pre-dynastic artefact of remarkable beauty and craftsmanship. Known as a 'sept', it came my way when Anna and I visited a fascinating shop in the West Country that Anna had learnt of so that she could buy me a birthday present. Whilst we were looking around, I felt a powerful presence behind a box on the counter and, straining to see what was affecting me so strongly, beheld this extraordinary ritual object. The sept, which was named after Sothis, was carved in the shape of the land of Egypt. As I said, it was in July of 1995, shortly after having been told that things are always as they have to be, that I dreamt:

> I am on Piper's Island [a small island in the River Thames close to Caversham Bridge and to the spot where Anna had her vision of ass-headed Set when she was a child]. Thoth, in human form, appears beside me and says that he will demonstrate the purpose of the sept. We are standing on the bank next to a large tree. Thoth takes the sept into his hand and sits on a thick branch, which begins to extend out across the water, carrying him with it. Before reaching the opposite bank, the branch curves around in a circle, brings him back to where he started and resumes its previous appearance.

Since, at that time, we were not yet aware of the significance that Sothis had had for the ancient Egyptians, we did not appreciate that, because the sept was named after Sothis and represented the land of Egypt, in holding onto it, Thoth was demonstrating that we should hold onto the sacred legacy of ancient Egypt: its relationship to the Sothic system. Nor did we recognise the significance of Thoth demonstrating this to me in the middle of the Thames, whose origins in the Isis and Cherwell designate the stars of Sothis as the source of the flow. In my dream, therefore, the island upon which Thoth and I stood represented the Earth situated within the flow from the stars of Sothis. Thoth – Lord of the Divine Word and Lord of Time – demonstrated that we were to be prepared ('sept' also meaning 'to be prepared'[25]) for the experience of being taken in a cycle of time that moved across the flow (into the memories of our past lives) and, then, returned to the present.

On 1st March 2000, Anna dreamt:

> I cross onto an island in a river. The sun is shining. I walk past the deserted ruins of a building that is partly above and partly below ground. I have a task to carry out. I go into a mansion, to an upper floor at the far end, where there is a sunlit room. From here, I look out of the window and see Anthony at the window of another

mansion on the shore of the mainland. We wave to one another. As I am leaving the island, I realize "This is Elephantine."

That dream was followed by another on 2nd March:

I am told that on Elephantine Island is Star Chamber.

Having returned, once more, to Elephantine (where the ancient Egyptians measured the first indication of how the influx from Sothis was manifest in the Inundation of the Nile) Anna had, again, to make an ascent, as in the dream in which she pushed open the shutters; but, this time, the room she entered was already illuminated. There, she looked out of a window to where she could see me at the window of another mansion on the shore of Aswan. The significance of our looking at and waving to each other from separate locations was then explained in two dreams of mine. In the first, on 7th March:

A polarity of movement is represented by two parallel lines drawn across the sky: by means of the notational device of arrows, in the line furthest away from me, the energy is depicted as travelling from right to left; whilst, in that closest, as travelling from left to right. A horizontal image of the human body is then projected onto the sky so that I can see the parallel lines of energy moving up and down the spine and cranium.

In the second, on 10th March:

Someone is talking to me about the huge physical forces that operate between Sothis A and B as they travel through space: the forces that move them apart and those that hold them together.

As a result of the second dream, Anna and I now knew that the polarity of movement depicted in the first dream represented the huge forces that operate between Sothis A and B. Our attention was drawn to the fact that the first to be mentioned were those forces that move them apart. This, we realized, was due to it being six years since the Sothic stars had come

261

together in their fifty year cycle – their Hieros Gamos – in April of 1994. Whereas their coming together had been depicted in Anna's dream of the Dance of Siva (in June of 1992) as our merging so as to look as though we were one person, the current interplay between Sothis A and B was depicted in her dream of Elephantine (on 1st March 2000) as our looking at and waving to each other from the mansions on different shores.

That 'Star Chamber' was related to the 'hidden chamber of bone and flesh where a grey wolf god dwells' was later revealed to Anna in another dream in September of 2002:

> Anthony and I are on Elephantine Island, at the top of a tower that is open to the sky. It is night and we are gazing at – communicating with – the stars. I feel an intense pressure around my head: it is the force that is welding the two sides of my head together; the left side being human, the right side being canine.

'Canine' was, of course, a reference to Sothis as the Dog or Wolf Star. In this dream, a particular connection between Sothis and the intuitive right side of the brain was being illustrated (hence, the statement in the Pyramid Texts: "Power is exercised thanks to intuitive knowledge."[26]) One can see from this that we were in Elephantine to observe and be aligned with the Sothic pattern; and, thereby, through the offices of 'Star Chamber' – the ancient Egyptian equivalent of the 'Court of Redress' in China – to receive aid in redressing a past life issue.

> "Can you imagine, if it were at all possible, what it would be like to get back to having the mind of a child before there had ever been war?"

This question was presented to me as the opening line of a book in a dream on 9th March 2000, coming between the dream concerning the polarity of movement and that in which I was told about the huge physical forces that operate between Sothis A and B. Its purpose was to get us back to a much earlier life than the Egyptian one I have hitherto been describing; and, so, it provided another illustration of how, as the intensity of experience of a time wave function increases, "there are more intensive and extensive uprushings of normally buried memories into present and current contexts" "recalling us ineluctably to recontact our origins, in a prodigious and profound context of what memory means."

The much earlier life Anna and I were now being presented with pre-dated the "disruption of the old Neolithic cultures in the Near East" that had occurred by the fifth millennium B.C.[27] and the appearance, at the same time, of "the earliest known visual images of Indo-European warrior gods"[28] brought by the invaders of the old culture wherein "the absence of fortifications and weapons attests the peaceful coexistence of this egalitarian civilization."[29] These pacific ancient peoples were the victims of "a strategy for ideological obliteration and takeover"[30] – the consequences of which continue to inform societal 'norms' and academic perspectives to this day. "What we have until now been taught as history is only the history of dominator societies: the record of the male-dominant, authoritarian, and highly violent civilizations that began approximately five thousand years ago. For example, the conventional view is that the beginning of European civilization is marked by the emergence in ancient Greece of the Indo-Europeans. But the new archeological evidence demonstrates that the arrival of the so-called Indo-Europeans actually marks the truncation of European civilization."[31] The instruction that 'Love is the original religion' had been the first instance of the Dream informing us of what had been obliterated.

Eisler notes: "We measure the time we have been taught is human history in centuries. But the span for the earlier segment of a much different kind of history is measured in millennia, or thousands of years. The Paleolithic goes back over 30,000 years. The Neolithic age agricultural revolution was over 10,000 years ago. Catal Huyuk [the largest known Neolithic site in the Near East, built on the plains of Anatolia, now modern Turkey] was founded 8500 years ago. And the civilization of Crete fell only 3200 years ago. For this span of millennia – many times as long as the history we measure on our calendars from the birth of Christ – in most European and Near Eastern societies the emphasis was on technologies that support and enhance the quality of life."³² "But then came the great change – a change so great, indeed, that nothing else in all we know of human cultural evolution is comparable in magnitude... by the fifth millennium B.C.E., or about seven thousand years ago, we begin to find evidence of what Mellaart calls a pattern of disruption of the old Neolithic cultures in the Near East... There is evidence of invasions, natural catastrophes, and sometimes both, causing large-scale destruction and dislocation... Bit by devastating bit, a period of cultural regression and stagnation sets in. Finally, during this time of mounting chaos the development of civilization comes to a standstill... it will be another two thousand years before the civilizations of Sumer and Egypt emerge. In Old Europe the physical and cultural disruption of the Neolithic societies that worshipped the Goddess also seems to begin in the fifth millennium B.C.E."³³

Marija Gimbutas writes that "Thanks to the growing number of radiocarbon dates, it is now possible to trace several migratory waves of steppe pastoralists or 'Kurgan' people that swept across prehistoric Europe."³⁴ Eisler explains: "The Kurgans were of what scholars call Indo-European or Aryan language-speaking stock, a type that was in modern times to be idealized by Nietzsche and then Hitler as the only pure European race. In fact, they were not the original Europeans... Nor were they even originally Indian, for there was another people, the Dravidians, who lived in India before the Aryan invaders conquered them. But the term *Indo-European* has stuck."³⁵ "Ruled by powerful priests and warriors, they brought with them their male gods of war and mountains... they gradually imposed their ideologies and ways of life on the lands and peoples they conquered."³⁶

Walker says of Osiris that "his name came from Ausar or Asar, meaning 'the Asian' just like the Aesir or 'Asian' gods of northern Europe."³⁷ The Aesir were "the Norse gods led by Father Odin, who invaded the lands of the elder deities."³⁸ Walker points out that the "Etruscans also called their ancestral deities Asians... The Asian invaders were aggressive. The *Voluspá* said war occurred 'for the first time in the world' when the Aesir attacked the peace-loving people of the Goddess."³⁹

With regard to the vast age of the earlier civilizations, Schwaller de Lubicz stated that "The ancients considered their prehistory to go back 36,620 years before Menes,"[40] the first Egyptian pharaoh in the historical record to rule over both Upper and Lower Egypt. In addition, Walker points out that "Egyptologists call this person a 'pharaoh'; but the hieroglyphic symbol of Mena [Menes] means both 'moon' and 'milk-giving mother's breast', improbable symbols for a male. More recent scholars admit that this so-called first pharaoh may have been a matriarchal queen, or a titulary king ruling in her name."[41] This issue had been presented to us in a dream of Anna's in March of 1999:

> Anthony and I are in an underground chamber in Egypt, discussing a group of women who were given the erroneous title of 'king' in historical records. They are present in some way – visible to us.

Eisler states: "This new knowledge about a time before divine and temporal power were associated with all-powerful fathers, kings, and lords clearly has important implications for archeologists, students of myth, and religious scholars. But, as was the case with other scientific paradigm shifts, its revolutionary implications are even greater for society at large. It puts at issue the very foundations of a five-thousand-year-old system in which the world was imaged as a pyramid ruled from the top by a male god, with creatures made in his image (men) in turn divinely or naturally ordained to rule over women, children, and the rest of nature: a system marked by chronic warfare and the equation of 'masculinity' with domination and conquest – be it of women, other men, or nature."[42]

As the Egyptian civilization strayed further and further from its foundations, Set was increasingly identified with the drive towards domination and conquest. W.B. Emery was of the opinion "that Seth was, and remained, the god of the original inhabitants of Egypt, whereas the dynastic race who invaded Egypt worshipped Horus."[43] Te Velde explains that, in later Egyptian thinking, "the bipartition of the world may not only be that of Upper and Lower Egypt but also that of home and foreign countries," with Horus being the god of the land which was inundated by the Nile, whilst "Seth was regarded as lord of foreign peoples, of Libyans, Hittites and Semites," functioning in the pantheon as representative of gods who were worshipped abroad.[44] (It would seem that originally worship of Set had been ubiquitous in the Middle East.) Thus, Set was particularly reviled "When Egypt was occupied by Assyrians and afterwards by Persians with their Semitic auxiliaries."[45] As Eisler recounts, "early Semites were a warring people ruled by a caste of warrior-priests (the Levite tribe of Moses, Aaron, and Joshua). Like the Indo-Europeans, they too brought with them a fierce and angry god of war and mountains (Jehovah or Yahweh). And gradually, as we read in the Bible, they too imposed much of their ideology and way of life on the peoples of the lands they conquered. These striking similarities between the Indo-Europeans and the ancient Hebrews have led to some conjecture that there may be some common origins, or at least some elements of cultural diffusion."[46]

It is evident from the book of *Genesis* (22:10), where Abraham prepares to make a sacrifice of his son Isaac to God, that the early Semitic nomads wrongly determined that the Lord of the Dead would most support those who were harbingers of death.

Because Set was identified with such peoples, it came to be thought that "Seth is he who opposes the order of life and death."[47] However, it will be remembered that, as Wallis Budge, said, Set always appears in the much older Pyramid Texts "in the character of a god who is a friend and helper of the dead." Furthermore, Te Velde notes: "There are no cursing-names known composed with Seth;" and he goes on to list names composed with Set which are entirely consistent with Anna's and my experience of avision: " 'Seth is gracious', 'Seth is kind', 'Seth is content', 'Seth gives salvation', 'Seth causes to live'... 'Seth is constant'."[48]

It will be remembered that one of the most outstanding features of Anna's childhood vision of Set was that he had a kind, intelligent face and that, as a result of this experience, Anna was, many years later, able to determine that the identification of Set as an evil god was false. My own dream encounters with Set: in his winged aspect when he landed upon my thigh; as Ganesh; and as the wasp guarding the entrance to the tunnel connected with the ancient Egyptians; all confirmed the understanding Anna had been provided with through avision.

Although the worship of Set was very much older than the Heliopolitan system, the conventional Egyptological view of the god has been heavily determined by the Heliopolitan myth and, thus, by the "strategy for ideological obliteration and takeover" which led to the "truncation of European civilization." Within the context of reincarnation, the very ancient view that Set could be of service to those in the Otherworld accords with our experience through avision. It seems difficult for Egyptologists in general to accept that Set exists independently of any notions that they have about him. As the personification of the Yang aspect of Sothis B, Set really *is* the god of the Otherworld. Set is the Lord of Death and the source of avision: the kind, intelligent god who can be of assistance to the living as well as the dead.

From the foregoing, one can understand the deeper significance of Anna's crossing to Elephantine Island in her dream of 1ˢᵗ March: it embodied the consequence of 'Chi Chi' – "after being fulfilled or aided" – which, it will be remembered, Musès translated as literally meaning "reaching the harmony of the other shore after having crossed over the river." Here, the other shore – the island of Ganesh and Ganesha – represented the harmony that had imbued human existence before the first incursion of violence. Through avision, we were moved from being instructed that 'Love is the original religion' to being presented with the possibility that one could get back to having the mind of a child in the peace-loving world which had existed before 5000 B.C.

For Anna and myself, it was Set, in his aspect of Ganesh, who instructed us in the Law of Maat. Walker recounts that Maat was "the lawgiver of archaic Egypt... [whose] laws were notably benevolent, compared to the harsh commands of later patriarchal gods, backed up by savage threats... An Egyptian was expected to recite [in all truthfulness] the famous Negative Confession in the presence of Maat and Thoth (or Anubis) to show he had obeyed Maat's rules of behaviour:⁴⁹ '*I have not been a man of anger. I have done no evil to mankind. I have not inflicted pain. I have made none to weep. I have done violence to no man. I have not done harm unto animals. I have not robbed the poor. I have not fouled water. I have not trampled fields. I have not behaved with insolence. I have not judged hastily. I have not stirred up strife. I have not made any man to commit murder for me. I have not insisted that excessive work be done for me daily. I have not borne false witness. I have not stolen land. I have not cheated in measuring the bushel. I have allowed no man to suffer hunger. I have not increased my wealth except with such things as are my own possessions. I have not seized wrongfully the property of others. I have not taken milk from the mouths of babes'."*[50] These were the rules of conduct by which one had to abide in the time before 5000 B.C. Walker notes that "African pygmies still know Maat by the name she bore in Sumeria as 'womb' and 'underworld': Matu"[51] – thus, revealing the connection between Maat and Set, the Lord of the Otherworld.

From the instruction of Ganesh regarding Maat, to consider the relation between 'thought' and 'ought', it follows that: one should only act upon a dream instruction if it is in keeping with the Law of Maat.

I have presented the ethos of the pre-patriarchal world, not only because of my dream about the time before war, but also to fulfil the requirement of a dream of Anna's from August 1998:

> I am shown that Anthony and I must write the absolute truth about the male position. Then, our children and, also, other people will naturally be drawn into alignment with this truth.

On 1st May 2000, I dreamt:

> Anna and I suddenly come to the end of our journey and find that we are arriving back into the present.

This was then expanded upon in September of 2000, during a stay in Luxor, in another dream of mine:

> Anna and I negotiate our way along a pathway that is difficult to detect, which emerges inside Karnak Temple: as we exit through

a turnstile, it is stated that we have found our way through the Afterlife.

Finding our way through the Afterlife meant, in the first instance, that the Dream had freed us from the trauma of being murdered and, subsequently, mummified in our later Egyptian life. That having been accomplished, we were then, again by means of avision, guided by Sothis back to our earlier Egyptian life before 5000 B.C. For, it was only by reconnecting with a pre-patriarchal lifetime that we would be able to address the challenges of the future.

Sothis, which, as Musès states, "is the power-source and regenerator"[52] of the transformational process that takes place within the Tuat, is, through avision, the Guide to that domain. On occasion, Sothis provides charts of the Otherworld, as in Anna's dreams depicting the Fifth Division. Musès rightly emphasised: "The charting of the topography of that eschatological realm is one of the major contributions to its culture that the shamanic way can make possible." It is notable that our shamanic journey ended in Egypt, the land of "the most anciently documented Shamanic religion."

On 19th September 2000, the night of our return from Egypt, I dreamt:

> Anna and I are in an Egyptian temple that is the essence of all temples. It has the feeling of an oasis. The temple is comprised of many small integral sections. We find that we have been initiated into the most fundamental section – the foundation of all of them. As we become aware that the sections are areas of understanding, they become circles containing images. These then distil into four circles forming a square with their edges touching. The upper left-hand circle, which represents the fundamental area we have been initiated into, commands our attention to the exclusion of the others. Within this circle is the image of Horus.

The message of this dream was that the understanding we had been provided with through avision, of the movement – from Sothis – of the imminent into the manifest, constituted the foundation of all knowledge in the Egyptian Temple. We were being shown, too, that avision, Nature's way of initiation, remains inviolate, independent of the state of the temples in their material form. "To this day many Indian sects hold that anyone who dreams that he is initiated has in fact been initiated."[53]

On the same night, Anna dreamt:

> Anthony and I are in Egypt, in a vast temple that is of pure, smooth stone – without ornamentation.

This was characteristic of all the temples in our dreams of that time. For instance, on the following night, I dreamt:

> Anna and I are in a temple. As in the temple yesterday, there is no sign of decoration or statuary, but the stone is exquisitely dressed. It is the purest limestone, possessing the most beautiful colour and quality. There is a deep sense of peace.

The description of the temple of our dreams corresponds to that of the Valley Temple in Giza, which is to the side of the Sphinx, and to that of a temple in Abydos, which later became known as the Osireion. These are structures which, as Graham Hancock describes, "bore no resemblance to the typical and well-known products of Ancient Egyptian art and architecture – all copiously decorated, embellished and inscribed."[54] Hancock cites West, who observed that "these desert monuments showed many scientifically unmistakable signs of having been weathered by *water*, an erosive agent they could only have been exposed to in sufficient quantities during the damp 'pluvial' period that accompanied the end of the last Ice Age around the eleventh millennium BC. The implication of this peculiar and extremely distinctive pattern of 'precipitation induced' weathering was that the Osireion, the Sphinx, and other associated structures were built before 10,000 BC."[55] From the pristine condition of the limestone, Anna and I could see that we had been initiated into the teaching of the Temple as it was in at least 10,000 B.C., and probably much earlier than that. Together, we had, at last, reached 'the harmony of the other shore'.

⊗

CHAPTER SIXTEEN

The Present

⊗

In her discussion of pre-patriarchal societies, Eisler observes: "there is overwhelming evidence that while both female and male deities were worshipped in these societies, the highest power in the universe was seen as the feminine power to give and sustain life"[1] and that "the worship of female deities was integral to our most ancient sacred traditions."[2] In his editorial prologue to the book in which Eisler's paper appears, Musès concludes with the magnificent words of John Cowper Powys: "For the great goddess whose forehead is crowned with the Turrets of the Impossible, moves through the generations from one twilight to another; and of her long journeying from revelation to revelation there is no end."[3]

In our lives, as Mankind moved into the New Millennium, and we were being taken back to our pre-patriarchal lifetime, the presence of the Goddess was made known through a dream of Anna's on 1st January 2000:

> Anthony and I are in pleasant conversation with our children in the hallway. Then, I find that the Goddess has left a gift, wrapped in

gold paper, for us on the bottom stair. The parcel is the size of a large tome and is domed. We seem in no hurry to open it. I say that, maybe, we should put it aside for next year, to open on next New Year.

And so, on 2nd January 2001, Anna dreamt:

> Anthony and I open the gift we have been given by the Goddess. It is a serpent housed in a box that is shaped like a small cave, along with a special short pole that has a thick rounded end, which we can use to collect the venom in order that we may vaccinate ourselves. I open the cave, push in the thick end of the pole and stroke the serpent with it; the serpent deposits its venom onto it. Then, I rub the end of the pole against the neck of one of the children – this serves as a protective inoculation. When the cave is open, the serpent could easily escape, but it is choosing to stay with us.

In his exposition upon the esoteric significance of Chi Chi, Musès writes that "just as in Egypt, the ultimate basis for the method [of transformation] is based on the feminine aspect of divinity."[4]

When, in 2005, we obtained a copy of Gardiner and Osborn's recently-published *The Serpent Grail*, we learnt that snake venom possesses powerful medicinal properties. The authors also paint a picture of a shamanic ritual which bears a striking resemblance to Anna's dream: "[The shaman is] standing before his assembled disciples. He is grasping a rattlesnake tightly by the neck. The... audience sits uneasily, gazing intently upon the snake as the poisonous fangs are pressed against the top section of a sacred staff. A thick liquid slowly oozes down the shaft."[5] It is important to note that Anna's dream is characterized by a spirit of co-operation, with the serpent willingly depositing its venom rather than being forced to do so.

It will be remembered that the hieroglyphs denoting 'the Goddess Sirius' can literally be read as 'serpent's tooth'. If one takes this in conjunction with the fact that the ancient Egyptian word 'metu-t', meaning 'venom', was represented by hieroglyphs which included an ejaculating phallus, that 'metut' meant 'seed' and that 'metut neter' was the 'emission of the god',[6] one can see that the image in Anna's dream of the serpent releasing its venom represented the efflux from Sothis. This image linked directly to Anna's dreams of Elephantine, since that was the site where the ancient Egyptians measured the first indication of how the efflux was manifest in the Inundation of the Nile; for, 'met' meant both 'inundation' and 'the emission of the Nile-god'. It also related to my dream about our life before there had been war, because 'metu' meant 'right order' and 'met', like 'maat', meant 'justice'.[7]

Having been told (in Anna's dream of September 1998) that 'the Serpent is the Dream', we summarized the message of her dream of the Serpent venom as conveying that we were to collect the efflux from Sothis and apply it as a means of protecting ourselves and our children in the future. At the end of the dream, the Serpent chose to remain in the cave, which was part of the gift that the Goddess had left for us. What we extracted from that imagery was that the Serpent chose to remain with us in the present (the 'present' being symbolized by the 'gift'). The same pattern had featured in the dream where the Serpent remained in the present because we had put it aside to open the following year. Thus, both dreams were restating the importance of our remaining in the present – 'present' being an anagram of 'serpent'.

These dreams were continuing the message of Anna's dream (from July of 1997) that 'the Arm of Sothis is reaching down to us'; which had then been elaborated upon in another dream (in October of 1997): 'Our parent is a Great Serpent that we call Anuit who lives in the heavens and whose serpentine body reaches down to us, protecting and caring for us'. As an Orphic initiate declared, "I am a child of the earth and the starry heavens, but my race is of heaven alone."[8] Our parent is Sothis, who, in her form of the Great Serpent, is known to us as Anuit. The realization of this relationship with Sothis was *the* essential feature of the Mystery traditions: "my mother Sôthis prepares my path and sets up a stairway."

In Anna's dream of the stairway (in April of 1998), each stair was a platform, like a theatre set, containing all her clothes and possessions from a different stage in her past – in this life or previous lives. By this imagery, her present and previous lives were shown to be one entity extending, serpent-like, through time. Thus, the Egyptian initiate's declaration: "I am the serpent Sata whose years are infinite."

Revelatory for Anna and myself has been the discovery, through avision, that we had continued to be conscious when dead. As Musès stated, "shamanism challenges several basic though unfounded assumptions of the current global technological/agnostic culture, based as it is on the shaky pedestal of what might at best be called secular humanism and, at worst, mere anthropolatry; namely, the current assumptions that the mind requires a brain and the kindred canard that all of anyone's individuality ceases when the physical body ceases to function."[9]

Deploring the abnegation of individual dignity and responsibility in contemporary society, Musès points out that, by contrast, in the Shamanic Way, "answerability for our actions and their consequences are traced to those rarely well-charted realms of experience, now, however, able to be entered upon, felt, and inspected, although ordinarily reachable only upon death. Here, indeed, is a consummation and, we may add, a powerful psychotherapeutic facility, devoutly to be wished. In the shamanic way, that wish finds a womb and is born."[10]

Another ancient Egyptian word for 'venom' was 'men'. 'Men' also meant 'to arrive in port'; whilst 'mena', in addition to 'moon', meant 'harbour or haven' and 'to die'.[11] In our sequence of avision, this concordance presented by the ancient Egyptian language appeared in Anna's dream of the extraction of venom ('men') and mine of the instruction that we had come to the end of our journey ('men'). Associated with this is the Indo-European root 'men', which meant both 'moon' and 'mind'.[12] The moon being the vehicle, by resonance, for the transmission of energy from Sothis, the name of the ruler 'Mena' conveyed that ancient Egypt was governed on the basis of guidance received via the moon from Sothis.

The Present

In ancient Egyptian thought, Thoth was the god of the moon; he was the personification of that aspect of the efflux from Sothis, mediated by the moon, which affects the human heart as the seat of consciousness. As such, Thoth was the god of wisdom and learning. His identification with Sothis B was signified by one of his names, 'Uteth', which meant 'to beget'.[13] Musès points out that another of Thoth's names, 'Tehuti', was derived from 'tekh' meaning 'weight', identifying the god as the Weigher of Questions.[14] As the Lord of the Divine Word, Thoth "is the historical prototype of the Logos [Word] of Plato, Philo and St. John."[15]

Ernest Richardson mentions that Thoth "weighs and records a man's deeds at the final judgement;" and he cites the *Book of The Coming Forth Into Day* in which Thoth declares: "I am Thoth the perfect scribe, whose hands are pure, who opposes every evil deed, who writes down justice... I am the lord of justice, the witness of right before the gods... who taketh the defence of the oppressed."[16] Richardson's heartfelt response was to state: "It is, always has been, and, by the nature of things, everlastingly must be true that learning is the irresistible weapon of the weak against the strong and the strong against the stronger – not learning for itself but learning dominated by a burning zeal for justice and righteousness, the 'two truths' of Thoth. In the present social unrest, economics is not the key word of salvation, but learning bent on justice and righteousness."[17] Though Richardson was writing in 1911, his analysis applies equally to the twenty-first century.

In his aspect as the Lord of Justice and Divine Law, Thoth's consort was Maat. Thoth's declaration continues: "I have come to thee; my hands bring (Truth) Maāt; my heart does not contain any falsehood; I offer the Maāt before thy face; I know her; I swear by her."[18] Richardson comments that this "passion for truth is a constant note in the Egyptian inscriptions and corresponds with the finest spirit of modern science while it points also to the foundation sore of modern social conditions... not of regard for public law, but regard for that law which a man makes for himself by giving his word."[19]

Thoth concludes: "I am Thoth who prepares tomorrow and also foresees what will come afterwards."[20] Richardson summarizes his account of Thoth by saying: "He is, in short, the revealer, the interpreter of the gods to men"[21] who restores consciousness and conscience "through the impartation of truth or knowledge."[22]

On 2nd February 2001, I dreamt:

> Two Egyptian priests of very high rank have installed a personal shrine in the sitting-room of our house and are checking to ensure that all is as it should be. The shrine almost completely fills the sitting-room so that the area in which one stands, situated in front of it, is just large enough for two people. Anna and I have to wait for the priests to finish what they are doing before we can stand in front of the shrine. The priests determine that everything is correct. When they have left, a wonderful sense of peace and a feeling that all is well pervade the house.

Three days later, a further dream of mine revealed the purpose of the shrine and of the priests' preparations:

> Standing in a room in our house, I hear the sound of strange, loud, resonant footsteps in the hallway. As I am wondering what is making this very noticeable, unfamiliar sound, ibis-headed Thoth suddenly walks into the room. Dressed in a vivid red kilt, his appearance is completely like that in illustrated papyri.

The appearance of Thoth was the culmination of a sequence of dreams which had begun in September of 1997 when Anna dreamt that the spirit of Thoth settled at the back of our garden. That dream, too, was pervaded by a deep sense of peace. On the following day, Anna had been shown the interweaving of the gods Hathor, Thoth and Seb through the light and colour of flowers and stars in our garden. Then, two years later, in 1999, also in September, Anna had the dream in which we realized that we could see the Light of Egypt – the Light of Sothis – shining from the back room on the ground floor of our house. It was in this room that the Egyptian priests installed the shrine to Thoth.

As Richardson states, "it is evident and well understood that... the inmost or hindmost part of the temple, the innermost sanctuary, or holy of holies [known as the 'Sept', a name of Sothis]... is the place where the god meets man... It is the place to which man resorts in order to meet his god and to inquire of him. It is, in short, the oracle. This in Egyptian religion... is so often evidenced on monuments as to be a truism." "the oracles were written down as the words of the god residing in the shrine."[23] Ebers remarked that "boxes of writings are often found in Egypt under the feet of the gods."[24] The shrine of Thoth – God of Writing and Lord of the Divine Word – was installed in our sitting-room because that is the place in our house where Anna and I write. Hence, it is the place where I have been writing, and we have been discussing and editing, this account of the Divine Word: *A vision*.

It is noteworthy that, in our dreams, Set landed on my thigh in our bedroom, where we dream; whilst the shrine to Thoth was installed in our sitting-room, where we record, analyse and write about our dreams; and Anubis was on the stairs, which link those two rooms.

It will be remembered that Set, as Seb, was the Egyptian god of Mercury, the messenger planet, with which Thoth, in his Graeco-Egyptian form of Hermes, was identified. Because the functions of Set and Thoth are closely related, Thoth was often substituted for Set in Egyptian iconography. The identification of Thoth with both Mercury and the moon indicates that, in antiquity, it was known that the moon, being resonant with the energy of Mercury, amplifies its transmission to Earth.

The discovery of an archive, compiled by an interpreter of dreams named Hor and his successors, in the ibis galleries at Saqqara has yielded fascinating evidence of how Thoth continued to be consulted as a dream oracle in the late Ptolemaic period. Amongst the texts, is one which speaks of "Isis, lady of the cavern,"[25] and makes reference to a dream in which Isis, accompanied by Thoth, revealed to Hor that Alexandria, which was at that time under threat, would be safe – the content of that oracle having been conveyed to the pharaoh.

Walker notes how "Thoth was often incarnate in a snake"[26] – "the Wise Serpent"[27] – and tells of his "close association with the Great Mother."[28] There is an obvious connection between Isis, lady of the cavern, being accompanied by Thoth, who is often incarnate as the Wise Serpent, and the gift that was left for us by the Goddess of a cave housing the Serpent. In Anna's dream, the Serpent chose to stay with us; and one can see in this an anticipation of the shrine of Thoth being installed in our house, one meaning of 'shrine' being "That... in which something dwells."[29] Anna's two dreams of the gift from the Goddess and mine of the shrine and ibis-headed Thoth were complementary enactments of the same oneiric event, that unfolded in cyclical time within the liminal domain of the imminent, which is itself part of the fabric of Thoth's being.

The shrine of Thoth could only be installed after we had returned to our life before 10,000 B.C.; and it was only after that shrine had been installed that we could, at last, be told what it was that had been regarded as fundamental to the practice of the Buddha that is no longer even mentioned.

In September of 2000, on the first night of a stay in Egypt, I had a dream in which:

> An Egyptian on a camel rides very close to me, leans down and whispers in my ear "You must wait patiently."

Later on the same night, I was told:

> "It is the Buddhist view of the Buddha that is creating the obstacle."

This explained why, in June of 1992, Anna had been shown:

> I am not wired for Buddhism.

Another two years were to pass before, in April of 2002, I dreamt:

> Anna and I each compile an account of our journey through avision. I am shown that we can use these compilations as a means of judging the authenticity of any statement attributed to the Buddha; and that this is so because the original and most sacred teachings of the Buddha were the dream instructions he received over his lifetime. Then, I am told that the sequence of avision about which I am now writing is being completed at the very moment of my having this dream. I notice a resemblance between Anna's and my accounts of our journey through avision and certain notes we took when studying the *I Ching*.

What, then, was the Dream referring to when it stated that it was the Buddhist view of the Buddha that was causing the problem? Angela Sumegi explains that "When the Buddha gave his first teaching and founded an order of monks, he joined a number of other heterodox teachers who were questioning the established religious system based on the authority of the Vedas and the ritual activity of the Brahmin priests."[30] This agenda powerfully influenced the attitude taken towards the Dream by those who, institutionalizing the Buddhist faith, had the political objective of demonstrating that Buddhism transcended the existing religion: because "prognostications drawn from dreams, omens, astrology, and the like were thought to be the business of Brahmins and not considered right livelihood for the Buddhist monastic *saṅgha* (community),"[31] "there is a certain denigration of dreams in Buddhism."[32] This polemical position towards the Dream was very similar to that of the early Christian apologists.

However, co-existing with the Buddhists' politically-determined stance towards the Dream was their experientially-based position. As Sumegi recounts, this led to a situation in which "The world of dream in Tibetan Buddhist narratives occupies a conflicted and ostensibly irresolvable space."[33] Thus, in order to acknowledge orthodoxy, Tibet's great Buddhist practitioner Milarepa is said to have responded to the request of a student for an interpretation of his dreams: "Have you not read the Sūtras and many Tantras? Dreams are unreal and deceptive, as was taught by the Buddha Himself... To collect, supply, and study them will bring little profit" – then, immediately adding: "And yet, your dreams were marvelous – Wondrous omens foretelling things to come. I, the Yogi, have mastered the art of dreams, and will explain their magic to you."[34]

Although Buddhists argue that "enlightened ones do not dream,"[35] since 'enlightened ones' such as Milarepa do dream, they also hold that truly prophetic dreams arise as a consequence of the 'merit' of the dreamer.[36] In addition, "throughout Buddhist history, dreams... appear as signposts of ethical and spiritual progress, and... function as alternate states of consciousness by means of which other worlds and other beings become accessible."[37] Hence, Mahayana Buddhism (the goal of which is liberation for all sentient beings) teaches that "one can receive authentic spiritual instruction, as shamans do through their dreams and trance states."[38] O'Flaherty draws attention to the fact that "the interpretation of dreams to enlighten a king is a recurrent Buddhist motif."[39] "Furthermore, in Buddhist literature the state of buddhahood and the stages of the bodhisattva path [a bodhisattva being a celestial Buddha who has incarnated on Earth for the benefit of humanity] are preceded by stylized dreams whose presence both announces and authenticates the state that has been attained, in much the same way that shamanic cultures accept certain special dreams as the authenticating mark of a shaman's calling."[40]

In Zen Buddhism, there is the example of the thirteenth century Japanese monk Myōe whose daily practice was so stimulated and nourished by his dreams and visions that he was able to inspire the revival of Zen and lead it out of the period of stagnation into which it had descended.[41]

280

"*Buddha* is the past participle of a Sanskrit root *budh* meaning 'to perceive', 'to become cognisant of', also 'to awaken', and 'to recover consciousness'. It signifies one who is spiritually awakened... to the spiritual influence from within or from 'above'."[42] The Sanskrit 'buddhi' means 'intelligence or mind'; whilst 'budha', meaning 'sage', is also a name of the planet Mercury – the son of Soma (the moon).[43] It will be remembered that a Buddhist text stated that the Buddha was the same as the Roman god Mercury – the son of the moon; and that Mercury was the Roman equivalent of the Egyptian Thoth and the Greek Hermes, who, like the Buddha, was an 'enlightened one'. Hence, the close proximity in time of the appearance of Thoth in our house and the revelation about the Buddha. Musès demonstrates that Soma, which "was likened both to a divine water of life and to a divine fire or transforming energy,"[44] is the elixir of transformational energy that emanates from Sothis and enters the earth during the waning cycle of the Moon.[45]

The Dream taught us that it is through avision that one experiences "the Buddhist conception of ultimate realization" whereby "The universe becomes conscious in the individual."[46] In the words of F.D.K. Bosch, "it is not the preaching Buddha who creates the doctrine... there is a pre-existing and ever immutable Dharma [Law of Nature that underpins and supports the Universe], which is the origin of all dharma-preaching Tathāgatas [Buddhas]."[47]

In my dream, it was stated that the sequence of avision about which I was then writing was being completed at the very moment of my having the dream. That was in April of 2002, precisely (as I was later to learn) the month and year which Musès identified as bringing to a close the opportunity for Mankind to benefit from the alignments associated with the Divine Union of Sothis.

Our sequence of Buddhist dreams provided Anna and myself with information about how Buddhism has woven its way through our existence and about the Dream itself. Over a ten year period, those dreams gradually reinstated the Dream into a context from which it had become excluded – that context being the spiritual life of the Buddha after he had attained enlightenment. Our ongoing relationship to the Dream – the bedrock of our existence – was being restored in the same way that a river, if diverted from its path, will always eventually return to its natural course. As Lao Tzu said, "The spirit of the valley never dies."[48]

CHAPTER SEVENTEEN

Conclusion

Pre-eminent amongst the teachings imparted by the shamanic sages of ancient Egypt was the knowledge that, when one's life on Earth has ceased, it is judged on the basis of whether or not one has acted in accordance with the Law of the Universe. This Judgement was symbolically represented as the weighing of the deceased's heart (the seat of consciousness) against the Feather of Maat. The hearts of those who had 'ordered their footsteps by Maat' would, thereby, be seen to be in perfect balance with the Cosmic Order. Through the instruction that 'Dreams are the Law of Nature', Anna and I were made aware that Maat is the Dream and, hence, that, as Synesius expounded in fifth century Alexandria, the Universe is "a well ordered whole"[1] and dreams the means for Mankind to be aligned with the unfolding of events within it. Our experience of avision has been that of an educative process, by means of which we have been taught how to 'order our footsteps by Maat'.

In ancient Egyptian texts, it is Thoth who is represented as recording the result of the weighing of the heart. Musès says of Thoth, as Tehuti, the Weigher of All Questions: "His consort was *Maat*, She Who Measures All Things;" and he goes on to explain: "*Maat* is the measurer of deeds and *Tehuti* of intentions."[2] Of particular importance is an annotation by Musès in his personal copy of Duncan Macnoughton's *A Scheme of Egyptian Chronology*: in a footnote about the role of Sothis in late Babylonian astronomy, Musès has underlined the words "measuring star… equivalent of the Egyptian term 'Sothis' " and written beside them "MAAT"[3] – thereby denoting that Sothis as the measuring star is Maat.

The identification of Sothis with Maat corresponds to that in Hinduism of Rudra with Mahat, the Ordering Intelligence of the Cosmos. However, whereas the Indian civilization has kept that understanding intact, in ancient Egypt the common identity of Sothis and Maat was confounded by Maat being assimilated into the solar religion as the "daughter of Re [the sun]," with Osiris being accorded the title "lord of *maat*."[4] The conventional Egyptological position further confounds matters, as can be seen from Wilkinson's comment that "in later times she [Maat] was subsumed to some extent by Isis."[5] Here, the identification of Maat with Isis-Sothis is interpreted, not as a restitution, but as an incorporation into a later cult. Jacq came closer to the truth in his book *The Living Wisdom of Ancient Egypt*: "Pharaonic Egypt was the country of sages. For more than three thousand years they concerned themselves with the search for spiritual fulfilment through the practice of wisdom which was incarnated in a Goddess, Maat… The Sages of Egypt aimed to open up the spirit and heart with their teachings, making them worthy receptacles for Maat… The term 'Sebayat' or 'Teaching' is formed from the root 'Seba', whose other meanings are 'Door' and 'Star'. Now, these texts really can be seen as doors that open on to the fundamental elements of wisdom and the stars which are destined to guide us on the road of life."[6]

Pharaoh Queen Hatshepsut proclaimed: "I have glorified the Law (Maat) which embraces the Divine Principle. I know that it exists there. Maat is also my bread, I drink her dew, With her I form a complete being."[7] In so saying, Hatshepsut gave expression to the crux of the Mystery tradition: that the highest aspect of Mind is located, not within oneself, but in Sothis; and that it is only through unification with Sothis that one can become a complete being. This is a very different understanding of what it is to be whole than that posited by conventional psychotherapy. It would not be a problem if mainstream psychotherapy acknowledged the distinction between the mundane life and a life lived in accordance with the Mysteries, rather than attempting to reduce the latter to: at best, a forum for merely intra-psychic process; at worst, a manifestation of personal pathology (for example, Irwin cites the neo-Freudian George Devereux who "expressed a remarkable disregard for the religious significance of Native American dreaming by reducing all [their] dreams to compensatory defence mechanisms").

In his paper to the Fourth International Conference on the Study of Shamanism and Alternate Modes of Healing, Musès was rightly critical of anthropologists for "the un-scientific omission of the sacred in their theories."[8] He went on to point out that Freud, Jung and others also "omitted the dimension of the *objectively* deific and numinous from their speculative premises and world view."[9] And that this, in turn, led Jung to unsuccessfully attempt "to quasi-secularly psychologize" "spiritual alchemy".[10] "Jung did realize that psychiatry and religion have deep factors in common but curiously, perhaps because of his father-induced anticlericalism, never saw that the reason the ancient cultures could leave so great a spiritual heritage is precisely that their psychiatries were embedded within their religions and grew from them."[11]

Shortly after the beginning of my psychotherapy training in 1976 (a few months after the dream about my death in my ancient Egyptian lifetime), I had a dream in which:

> I am with a number of people in a museum. We are all searching for the key to the unconscious. Some have been searching for a very long time without success. Suddenly, I find the key. It is lying on bare earth inside an old glass cabinet.

This dream was predictive of my finding the key to the unconscious – that is, the Dream as the key to the Great Door of Heaven, Sothis.

Portraying itself as a museum exhibit that had been long over-looked by all who were in search of it, the Dream revealed that its function as the key to Sothis was no longer held to have any relevance with regard to the practicalities of the modern world. The others searching for the key knew that they were in search of something from antiquity (hence, they were in the museum), but they over-looked the exhibit because of the apparent poverty of its appearance, assuming that something of such cosmic significance would be more commanding of attention. Mankind must again evolve to a level where, in all humility, it takes hold of the key which will enable it to assume its rightful place within the cosmos.

Twenty-six years after my dream of the key, during a stay in Egypt in May of 2002, I dreamt:

> I am shown that there is a need for me to focus on my place: on avision and on my functioning in the world as a guide, through avision, into the Sothic Mysteries.

Through this dream, I was shown that I had to make a transition from practising as a psychotherapist to functioning as a guide to avision and the Sothic Mysteries. By writing this book I fulfil an essential aspect of 'my place'. In antiquity, when Mankind still listened to the Dream, the telling of one's dreams 'renewed life' as it created ever-widening ripples in the community. Thus, it was that the Cretan Epimenides had the ability to heal whole cities as a result of being taught by the gods, by Justice and Truth – Maat – through avision. If I had to choose one phrase to define my place, it is that: I help myself and others to order their footsteps by Maat.

Maat is Sothis; Maat is the Dream; Maat is the Law of Love. As Love, Maat is the "universal symbiotic power of cosmic process." For this reason, a scientist of Musès' stature can refer to "the fundamental reality of love as ultimate power." With regard to the process of transformation, Musès observed: "All loving persons, no matter what their intellectual level... are included by a kind of higher gravitation, on a moving [Sothic] walkway of Light that carries them onward at various speeds. This great Walkway for all beings has different speed-bands, the swiftest being midmost or central. The band on which you are depends on the degree of Love you have developed in your awareness and responses, whether these are initiative or reactive. As your degree of love increases, your band changes to a higher frequency or speed, so to speak; and if that degree should decrease, your speed would decrease correspondingly, and can even reverse... [to the extent that] you would leave the Great Walkway and its Guiding Beams."[12] Hence, our being told at the outset of our experience of avision "The more intimate, The more infinite." and that "Love is the original religion." These simple statements are profound foundational instructions in the Law of Maat.

Schwaller de Lubicz noted that Sothis A and B, a giant star of low density with an incredibly dense dwarf star companion, correspond in equivalence of volume and density to the positron and its diminutive neutron companion which make up an atomic nucleus. In so doing, he made the valuable suggestion that Sothis A and B, as positron and neutron, form the nucleus of our galaxy.[13]

In Anna's sequence of dreams, the message "Believe in the stars and that they directly affect everything that happens to us" was followed by the Dance of Siva. That dance was an enactment of the determining influence which the stars Sothis A and B exert upon us and, hence, of our 'ordering our footsteps by Maat'.

One can equally say that it is because Siva is the God of Love that Love is the original religion. And it is because Siva, as Isi and Isvara, comprises the stars of Love that progress along the Path, which Sothis provides, "depends on the degree of Love you have developed in your awareness and responses".

The instruction from Ganesh in the Law of Maat, which followed the instruction in Love, began with his emphasising that I must tell Anna my dream, as it is through the sharing of our dreams that we could, as a couple, most successfully negotiate the Sothic Path of Love.

Steeped in the culture of ancient Egypt and versed in its literature, Schwaller de Lubicz knew that "Maât in its widest sense is Cosmic

Consciousness."[14] "The Universe is nothing but Consciousness, and in all its appearances reveals nothing but an evolution of Consciousness, from its origin to its end, which is a return to its cause. It is the goal of every 'initiatory' religion to teach the way to this ultimate union."[15] That understanding is supported by the work of Amit Goswami, Professor of Physics at the Institute of Theoretical Sciences at the University of Oregon, who challenges the "unproven assumption", which has dominated science for centuries, that matter is primary and consciousness a secondary phenomenon, positing the reverse: that "everything (including matter) exists in and is manipulated from consciousness."[16] In contrast to the conventional materialist hypothesis which, when applied to the quantum Universe, creates many paradoxes, Goswami's view "provides a paradox-free interpretation of quantum physics that is logical, [and] coherent."[17] By regarding consciousness as fundamental, "our spiritual experiences are acknowledged and validated as meaningful. This philosophy accommodates many of the interpretations of human spiritual experience that have sparked the various world religions. From this vantage point we see that some of the concepts of various religious traditions become as logical, elegant, and satisfying as the interpretation of experiments of quantum physics."[18]

As Cosmic Consciousness, "Maât moves and directs existence."[19] Reiser describes how "Behind our perceived universe of material things in space and time there is a *Cosmic Field of Energy*, infinite, eternal, uncreated, and indestructible. Within this universal ocean of energy there is a Cosmic Imagination which, by way of the *Cosmic Lens* [Divine Eye], acts as a focusing and guiding field of influence controlling the creation and evolution of matter. Thus, high above the local gods of the earth's regional religions, there is a Divinity."[20] The Egyptian Queen Nefertari, wife of Ramses II, the most famous of the Rameside kings, expressed herself in exactly the same terms:

"I follow the Great God,
Who has created Himself.
Who is He?
Energy.

288

The ocean of primordial energy,
The father of the Gods."[21]

In the sacred texts of India, "Rudra in the sky is Sirius, star of stars, most exalted among them... In his most ancient figure he was the Dog Star." Kramrisch relates that the Dog Star "is a fierce watchdog at the gate of the netherworld"[22] and that Rudra is "the power of death"[23] – which links him with Set as the personification of the regions of death. Rudra and Set, both of whom were known as the 'Red One', are synonymous. In view of my dream instruction regarding Set as the imminent, one would expect to find Rudra, too, so identified. Kramrisch describes Rudra as "the guardian of the Uncreate, an indefinable transcendental plenum"[24] – a "state of 'neither nonbeing nor being'."[25] The Uncreate is the state of imminence which preceded the creation of the cosmos. In the Vedas, Rudra prepares "the immortal seed of creation."[26] Rudra/Set existed before creation and, at creation, as the Lord Who Is Half Woman, was realized as Sothis – the material conduit of the movement from the imminent into the manifest.

After landing on my side, Set subsequently took the form of a wasp that was the guardian of the tunnel connected with the ancient Egyptians. In this way, Anna and I were shown that Set, the personification of the regions of death, is the presiding deity of reincarnation. This is consistent with Set being the imminent, since death is the state of imminence out of which new life arises. It, therefore, follows that, in the Vedas, it is said of Rudra that "he is the ferryman. He ferries across to the other shore, into the far beyond of which he is the guardian. He is the liberator, but – paradoxically – he is also the ferryman from death to life."[27]

Precisely how life evolved remains a mystery, but, as Reiser states, "Whatever the final solution of the problem of the origin of life, we know that the cosmic influences do affect the more developed living forms on the earth."[28] The discovery of 'biological clocks' led, at first, to the theory that these involved inner rhythms. Subsequently, it has become clear that, although there is some truth in this theory, "there are external magnetic, electrostatic, and electromagnetic fields of the earth and the solar system that regulate the time-clocks of organisms. These geophysical fields are in turn affected by the movements of the planets, the moon, the sun, and perhaps movements related to the galactic background. Thus cosmic rhythms pace the biological clocks and the timing is not primarily controlled by a built-in heredity."[29] "Astrophysicists know that the interplanetary, intragalactic, and intergalactic spaces are not empty, but filled with fields of force of various kinds. The term 'magnetohydrodynamics' was coined to designate the study of such phenomena of interstellar space. These fields and plasmas mediate a 'running dialogue' between man and the cosmos."[30]

In July of 1995, I had a dream in which:

> I am contemplating the Zen concept of Mu (emptiness or no-thingness). Suddenly, Anna appears in my mind and says: "When you say 'Mu', remember it involves..." – and, then, it is as if she draws back a curtain to reveal the most extraordinary workings of the cosmos, stretching out into the distance and around me in all directions.

In this dream, which came two months after the instruction in the Law of Maat, we were shown that contemplation of the mind must include the workings of the cosmos within which the mind is situated. The curtain is the veil in one's mind formed by mistaken notions of reality that conceals from view the determining impact that the forces at work in the cosmos have upon one's mental processes.

Fortunately, within this welter of cosmic influences, there are, as Dante wrote in the *Divine Comedy*, "footprints of the Eternal Power, which is the end whereto is made the law" by which Mankind may "move onward unto ports diverse o'er the great sea of being... each one with instinct given it."[31] Tellingly, Dante "compares the divine power to a bow [Sothis, the Bow Star] that shoots forth the life impulses of all creatures."[32] As in my sequence of dreams about the Grail cup, in which the Grail moved from Sothis to the moon to myself, Dante describes how the Divine Power, having been released by the 'bow', "bears away the fire towards the moon;" and adds that "this is in mortal hearts the motive power, this binds together and unites the earth."[33]

Significantly, a number of scholars are convinced that the *Divine Comedy* "was inspired by dreams."[34] The prerequisite for deriving the full benefit of avision – the "footprints of the Eternal Power" – was conveyed to me in a dream of August 2001:

> Thoth, in his aspect of Divine Scribe, says to me: "Make sure you record it [the dream] accurately."

Because the primary focus of avision is upon receiving the Divine Word that has issued from Sothis, as Plato said, no detail so imparted should be altered. This condition having been fulfilled, it is, in the words of Iamblichos, "necessary that thou shouldst prefer the true meaning of dreams before thy own notions." Then, one acts in accordance with the Law of Maat, by considering the relation between 'thought' and 'ought'.

In the *Divine Comedy*, Dante is inspired by his love for Beatrice (whose name literally means 'She who makes blessèd'[35]) to attain union with the Divine Mind. Beatrice (whom Dante has, by analogy, compared with Isis-Athene) "controls the great griffon,"[36] the embodiment of Set, that draws the carriage in which she makes her way to meet Dante, who is on the verge of leaving Purgatory, in order to guide him into Paradise. In the Christian myth, Purgatory is the place where a person's soul is cleansed of the mistakes they have made in the conducting of their life.

This brings me to the instruction to 'restore the crane'. In that dream, the mechanical crane, which also functioned as a vehicle, collapsed, trapping a number of people inside. It will be remembered that the crane symbolizes that function of the Dream which corrects a person's understanding, moving them from a mistaken attitude to the appropriate one in order that they are aligned with the unfolding pattern of events and play their part accordingly. Thus, the crane has the same function for the living as, in the Christian myth, Purgatory (less benignly) has for the dead.

The people within the crane are those who are trying to progress by paying attention to their dreams but, due to being trapped by false notions about the Dream, are not able to experience the benefit of avision. One such trap is the acceptance of Freud's dictum that "We must not concern ourselves with what the dream appears to tell us, whether it is intelligible or absurd, clear or confused, since it cannot possibly be the unconscious material we are in search of." Another is the belief that dreams are solely determined by the past experiences of one's present life, including those of the previous day. This involves a failure to recognise that the Dream presents past life issues and is a vehicle for the process of reincarnation; and, also, to perceive that the Dream, being primarily forward looking (not equally so, as Jung proposed), generally only presents one's past experiences of this life insofar as they create an obstacle to meeting the requirements of the future. (Certain experiences of avision in this life are preparations for events in a future life, which may be decades, centuries or millennia ahead.) Yet another trap is the homocentric view of the brain, rather than Sothis, being the source of the Dream; the consequence of which is a failure to recognise the Dream as the Word of God – as the means by which each individual is made aware of what they must address for the benefit of themselves and, consequently, of Life as a whole, as the imminent moves into the manifest. A true science of the human mind must be founded upon an understanding of Man's place within the Universe and of the impact that the rest of the Universe has upon Mankind.

A dream of Anna's from September of 2006 provided invaluable insight into avision as an educative process:

> Anthony and I are at the Rock of the Sibyl in the Delphi Sanctuary. There is a large tray on which are several sack-cloth bags containing variously-shaped objects. The only clue to the identity of the objects is the impression their shapes make upon the bags. I say: "In dreams and visions we are often given clues or partial answers rather than whole answers. This is because we must strive to develop our neuronal connections. Otherwise, it would be like knowing a mathematical formula without understanding the working out. Think of the implications!"

This dream of Anna's was the complement to mine in which Ganesha placed me upon the very spot that Ganesh had instructed us to journey to. In my dream, the message conveyed was that a clear dream instruction – such as the summons to the Sphinx: "Come to me. Come to me." – has to be followed to the letter, whether or not we understand why; whereas, in Anna's dream it was explained that those dreams which provide only clues or partial answers are designed as catalysts for the development of our consciousness. Any loving parent or teacher will be sensitive to the fact that, whilst there are some circumstances in which it is essential that a child obeys a command for their own safety and the safety of others, there are equally times when it is important that the child arrives at a full understanding of an issue or situation through their own effort. Sothis makes such judgements on the basis of both the individual's need and how that individual can best serve humanity and the natural order of the Universe.

In contrast, it was at Delphi that Python, the Spirit of the Dream which emanates from Sothis, was usurped by the patriarchal solar cult of Apollo. Thus, the shadow cast, long before, by the political ambitions of the priests of Heliopolis extended its pall over the mind of Man. I have described how the Heliopolitan suppression of knowledge of Sothis B was followed, at the hands of the Roman Emperor Theodosius, by the criminalization of paganism. That act supported the Christian Church's turning against the Dream, its subsequent outlawing of the truth of reincarnation and its obliteration of ancient wisdom by means of the Inquisition; all of which have inevitably led to a ubiquitous loss of meaning in the life of modern Man. The demonization of Set – the cosmic power which, amongst other functions, seeks to prepare each one of us for the tasks ahead, has made it exceptionally difficult for humanity today to benefit from the instructions and clues which Sothis provides through avision (although, in India and Tibet, it is understood that Set, the Destroyer – as Siva and Kalachakra respectively – is "the Great Destroyer of illusion"[37]).

It is particularly because of his association with destiny and death that Set was regarded as evil. Yet, as the Lord of the Dead, Set will, if allowed, gently prepare us for entrance into his domain so that, in the words of an ancient Egyptian text, one is able to say: "Death has come before me today... like the moment when you finally reach home after a long expedition."[38]

Cox Miller observes that, in antiquity, "dreams were viewed as vehicles of a very material kind of metamorphosis."[39] That metamorphic process (which was depicted in our dreams as our ascending the spiral stair-case) leads, step by step, towards resonance with all four aspects of the Divine Mind – of Sothis, the star form and emanator of the Mind of the Universe. Here, the West has a lot to learn from India; for, as O'Flaherty describes, "In the West, the loss of the sense of self (ego)... is often regarded as a sign of madness, but in India the loss of the sense of Self (*ātman*) as distinct from God (*brahman*) is the key to enlightenment."[40]

Symbolic reference to the metamorphic process appeared in the fifth of Anna's sequence of dreams about the Fifth Division of the Tuat:

> I am inside a pyramid in which there are steps leading up and then down again.

The image of steps leading up and then down again does not appear in the iconography of the Fifth Division. However, several years later, we found that Musès provides an ancient Egyptian illustration of just such a 'Sacred Stairway', in which the top step represents the radiating eye of Sopdu – Sothis B.[41] Thus, Anna's dream was showing us that the pyramid of the Fifth Division is, in part, a chamber for receiving the transformational energy of the Eye Star. For anyone who is interested in the question of the function of the pyramids, this is a priceless piece of information which provides the solution to that enigma. Anna's dream revealed that the pyramids were not (as conventional Egyptology supposes) intended as repositories for the dead, but rather as chambers for the "sacred and secret" process of "gestative regeneration," of which the practice of mummification was a later corruption.[42]

Conclusion

Being the Yang element of Sothis B, Set is Lord of the Dead, Lord of Reincarnation and, as that which releases the seed of ideas into existence, Lord of Avision. Set's Ladder is the Dream as a medium of communication between Sothis and Man.

As the "Dispenser of the Unexpected,"[43] through avision, Sothis eternally provides clues and answers to questions, the solution of which enables life to continue and unfold. Writing of the world of the Dream, the great Sufi mystic Ibn Arabi stated: "There is no world more perfect, since it is the root of the origin of the cosmos... It embodies meanings and changes that which does not subsist in itself into that which does subsist in itself. It gives form to that which has no form. It turns the impossible into the possible."[44]

Cox Miller recounts that, in late antiquity, "apocalyptists [many of whom saw "the dream and the heavenly journey as interconnected phenomena"[45]] presented their views of what is ultimately real as dreams and visions that they had themselves experienced."[46] She adds that they followed "the Graeco-Roman cultural convention that dreams were not the personal property of the dreamers but were rather sent from a divine source" and, so, their own dreams played a significant part in their writings.[47] This book, being founded upon the same understanding, restores that tradition.

I have presented a selection of our dreams with the hope that it will inspire others to see their dreams and the process of dreaming in a new light – the light shed by Sothis. Aristophanes described Sothis as the "light-bringing star of the nocturnal mysteries"[48] and, in certain ancient Greek texts, "Isis, among her other civilizing activities, is seen as the founder of the mysteries throughout the world."[49]

Once the role of avision is appreciated, one can see that there has been too much emphasis by academia upon cross-cultural contact as an explanation for the homogeneity of thought among different civilizations and an absence of recognition of the Dream as their common source of instruction.

To those who are receptive, Sothis speaks of Love; of the Dream; of the workings of the mind, the body and the Universe; of the unfolding pattern of creation; of destiny. Paracelsus, who always paid attention to his dreams,[50] rightly said: *"the power to recognize and to follow the truth cannot be conferred by academical degrees; it comes only from God."*[51] And he warned: *"The highest power of intellect, if not illumined by love... will perish in time."*[52]

There is no such thing as an unimportant dream. All dreams that concern everyday issues are part of the path to avision: the Dream is always presenting the issues which need to be addressed. At the outset, all of your dreams may seem confused. It is often mistakenly thought that such confusion is an inherent feature of the dreaming process; whereas, in truth, the Dream accurately represents the confusion which exists within the dreamer or their social reality. The world of the Dream reveals the world of pattern in space and time. Simply perceiving such patterns in your dreams, even if you do not understand them, has a healing effect that produces a quickening of development.

Those who are unsure of their own judgement regarding avision may feel the need for advice; and, sometimes, the Dream itself requires a person to seek assistance. I have, over the years, assisted a number of people who were specifically instructed in their dreams to consult me.

Then, there are those who, through their dreams, discover that they are suffering from the consequences of past life experiences, which they do not feel able to face alone. For them, as Laing wrote in another context, "there should be some who are guides, who can educt the person from this world and induct him into the other. To guide him in it; and to lead him back again."[53] In existing shamanic societies versed in avision, it is, as it was in antiquity, regarded as essential that such a guide has received their understanding of the territory from the Dream. In this regard, Paracelsus lamented: *"The knowledge which our clergymen possess is not obtained by them from the Father, but they learn it from each other. They... mistake their own opinions for the wisdom of God."*[54]

We have all to free ourselves from the obstacles created by the damage done to us in the past, both in this life and in previous lives, in order that we may realize the cosmic requirement to be fully cognizant of the present moment.

Little by little, all who follow the path of avision will discover that, as Laurens van der Post so beautifully put it, "man is never alone. Acknowledged or unacknowledged, that which dreams through him is always there to support him from within."[55]

An Aztec poet was moved to write: "That we come to this earth to live is untrue. We come but to sleep, to dream."[56] Though I cannot share his view that we do not come to this Earth to live, I wholeheartedly agree that we come here to dream. Since "dreams express the meaning of the Universe, including our relationship to it and each other," if the Dream is undermined, catastrophe will necessarily ensue. If Mankind is to survive, it must recognise that it is here to play its role within the Universe, not to serve the ambitions of those who are driven by their own self-interest.

Lao Tzu wisely counselled: "Hold fast to the way of antiquity In order to keep in control the realm of today. The ability to know the beginning of antiquity Is called the thread running through the way."[57] Musès comments that, worse than the twentieth century's "subjection to fluctuation of scientific fashion, is the attitude of deliberate denigration of the past... Such forced forgetfulness of the past is the antithesis of humanity's unique continuance of cultural memory, the loss of which would eventually be lethal to any civilization or society. And the origin of the word 'lethal' is *Lethe* or the oblivion of forgetfulness."[58]

Traced in the narrative of this book is an ancient portolan re-presented in modern times. The map was created by the Dream, which, as the source of the eternal renewal of meaning, can re-present all that has been lost to those who are ready and willing to receive it. The destination is Sothis. The route by which one travels there is, as I was told in a dream, "a very personal route." The journey is wondrous.

In the words of Synesius, "Then let all of us deliver ourselves to the interpretation of dreams, men and women, young and old, rich and poor... Sleep offers itself to all: it is an oracle always ready, and an infallible and silent counseller."[59]

* * *

We are those who have walked the dark, circuitous passages of our own becoming.[60] By recording, in this book, some of that adventure, Anna and I have fulfilled the requirement, expressed in Utterance 147 of the *Book of The Coming Forth Into Day*, to be able to say: "I have passed on the path created by Anubis... and have protected the Cosmic Law and the Divine Eye."[61] And, in so doing, we have pointed to the way for others to do the same.

In September of 1997, on the night I received the instruction to restore the crane and Anna dreamt that the Sphinx confirmed we were doing everything right, she had a second dream, with which I was later told, through avision, I should conclude my account:

> I pass through a small trap-door and along a very narrow passageway. I find myself in a society where there is a repressive regime. The people of the resistance movement recognise me and ask my help. I tell them that help will come through recognition of their dreams. I relate to them the dream I had in which Anthony gave me the beautiful pack of Tarot cards containing the set of bird cards whose images were raised to appear three-dimensional – of which I was particularly drawn to the heron – and how Anthony and I were given the message: "Believe in the stars and that they directly affect everything that happens to us."

References

Introduction

[1] Laurens van der Post, interview with the author, *International Minds*, Vol.I No.4 p.12 May-July 1990.

[2] Robert J. White, *Oneirocritica* by Artemidorus p.vii, The Banton Press 1992.

[3] Peter Kingsley, *In The Dark Places of Wisdom* pp.247–248, Element Books 1999.

[4] Giorgio de Santillana, *Reflections on Men and Ideas* p.82, Massachusetts Institute of Technology Press 1970.

[5] Peter Kingsley, *In The Dark Places of Wisdom* pp.180-181, Element Books 1999.

[6] Ibid. p.42.

[7] Ibid. p.129.

[8] Ibid. pp.30-31.

[9] Ibid. p.7.

[10] Ibid. p.42.

[11] *The Compact Edition of the Oxford English Dictionary,* edited by Burchfield, p.2154, Oxford University Press 1987.

[12] Dion Chrysostom cited by Lewis Spence, *The Mysteries of Britain* p.57–58, Rider.

[13] Diodorus Siculus cited by Juliette Wood, *The Celtic Book of Living and Dying* pp.98-99, Duncan Baird Publishers 2000.

[14] Tenzin Wangyal Rinpoche, *The Tibetan Yogas of Dream and Sleep* p.23, Snow Lion Publications 1998.

[15] Ibid. p.66.

[16] Peter Kingsley, *Ancient Philosophy, Mystery, and Magic* p.284, Clarendon Paperbacks, Oxford University Press 1996.

17 Iamblichus, *On the Pythagorean Way of Life* – Text, Translation and Notes by John Dylan and Jackson Hershbell p.131, Scholars Press, Atlanta, Georgia 1991.

18 John Strohmeier and Peter Westbrook, *Divine Harmony* p.117, Berkeley Hills Books 2003.

19 Albert Einstein, *Cosmic Religion* p.52, Covici, Friede Inc. 1931.

20 Ibid. p.98.

21 Ibid. p.102.

22 Kelly Bulkeley, *Visions of the Night* p.23, State University of New York Press 1999.

23 John Strohmeier and Peter Westbrook, *Divine Harmony* p.116, Berkeley Hills Books 2003.

24 Peter Kingsley, *In The Dark Places of Wisdom* p.114, Element Books 1999.

25 R.A. Schwaller de Lubicz, *Sacred Science*, translated by André and Goldian VandenBroeck, p.184, Inner Traditions International 1988.

26 Peter Kingsley, *In The Dark Places of Wisdom* p.243, Element Books 1999.

27 *The Compact Edition of the Oxford English Dictionary*, edited by Burchfield, p.147, Oxford University Press 1987.

28 Ibid. p.1837.

29 Ibid. p.147.

30 Joscelyn Godwin, *Mystery Religions in the Ancient World* p.34, Thames and Hudson 1981.

31 Ibid. p.8.

32 Tenzin Wangyal Rinpoche, *The Tibetan Yogas of Dream and Sleep* p.70–71, Snow Lion Publications 1998.

Chapter One

1 Barbara G. Walker, *The Woman's Encyclopedia of Myths and Secrets* p.780, Harper San Francisco, HarperCollins Publishers 1983.

2 Mircea Eliade, *Shamanism* p.467, Princton, N.J.: Bollingen Series 1964, cited by Barbara G. Walker, Ibid. p.780.

3 Wendy Doniger O'Flaherty, *Dreams, Illusion and Other Realities* p.38, University of Chicago Press 1986.

4 Barbara G. Walker, *The Woman's Encyclopedia of Myths and Secrets* p.780, Harper San Francisco, HarperCollins Publishers 1983.

5 E.A. Wallis Budge, *An Egyptian Hieroglyphic Dictionary* p.252, Dover Publications Inc. 1978.

References

[6] A. Leo Oppenheim, *Interpretation of Dreams in the Ancient Near East* p.193, Gorgias Press 2008.

[7] Henry Corbin, *The Dream and Human Societies*, edited by G.E. von Grunebaum and Roger Caillois, p.387, University of California Press 1966.

[8] Sigmund Freud, *The Standard Edition of the Complete Works of Sigmund Freud* Vol.V p.114, Hogarth Press 1961.

[9] Bhikkhu Ñanamoli, *The Life of the Buddha* p.21, Buddhist Publication Society 2006.

[10] Ibid. pp.23-24.

[11] Iamblichus, *On the Pythagorean Way of Life* – Text, Translation and Notes by John Dylan and Jackson Hershbell p.87, Scholars Press, Atlanta, Georgia, 1991.

[12] John J. Winkler, *The Constraints of Desire: The Anthropology of Sex and Gender in Ancient Greece,* New York: Routledge 1990, cited by Patricia Cox Miller, *Dreams in Late Antiquity* pp.81-82, Princeton University Press 1994.

[13] Patricia Cox Miller, Ibid. p.53.

[14] Luther Martin, 'Artemidorus: Dream Theory in Late Antiquity' p.108, *The Second Century* 8 (1991): 97–108, cited by Patricia Cox Miller, Ibid. p.54.

[15] Cicero, *De divinatione,* 2 vols. in one, Ed. A.S. Pease, in *M. Tulli Ciceronis De Divinatione*, New York: Arno Press, repr. 1979, cited by Patricia Cox Miller, Ibid. p.53.

[16] Patricia Cox Miller, Ibid. p.53.

[17] George Steiner, 'The Historicity of Dreams (Two Questions to Freud)', p.13, *Salmagundi* 61 (1983): 6-21, Cited by Patricia Cox Miller, ibid. p.54.

[18] R.T. Rundle Clark, *Myth and Symbol in Ancient Egypt* p.246, Thames and Hudson 1959.

[19] Ibid. p.245.

[20] Ibid. p.84.

[21] Philostratus, *Life of Apollonius of Tyana*, II.XXXVII, cited by Violet MacDermot, *The Cult of the Seer in The Ancient Middle East* p.45, The Wellcome Institute of the History of Medicine 1971.

[22] Dr. Manjir Samanta-Laughton, *Punk Science* p.234, O Books 2006.

[23] Riane Eisler, *The Chalice and the Blade* p.16, HarperCollins Publishers 1995.

[24] Riane Eisler, *In All Her Names,* edited by Joseph Campbell and Charles Musès, p.3, Harper San Francisco 1991.

[25] Riane Eisler, *The Chalice and the Blade* p.xvii, HarperCollins Publishers 1995.

26 Riane Eisler, *In All Her Names,* edited by Joseph Campbell and Charles Musès, pp.9-10, Harper San Francisco 1991.

27 Iamblichos, *Theurgia or The Egyptian Mysteries,* translated by Alexander Wilder, pp.112-113, William Rider and Son 1911/Kessinger.

28 Ibid. p.112.

29 Lao Tzu, *Tao Te Ching,* translated by D.C. Lau , p.47, Penguin Books 1963.

30 Ibid. p.18.

31 Ibid. p.8.

32 Christian Jacq, *The Wisdom of Ptah-Hotep* p.3, Constable and Robinson 2004.

33 Charles Musès, *Destiny and Control in Human Systems* p.158, Note 16, Kluwer-Nijhoff Publishing 1985.

34 Ibid. p.200.

35 Charles Musès, *The Jacob Boehme Society Quarterly,* edited by Charles Musès, Vol.1 No.1 Autumn 1952 p.12.

36 Ibid. pp.17-18.

37 Ibid. p.16.

38 Ibid. p.17.

39 Ibid. p.16.

40 Ibid. p.18.

41 Iamblichos, *Theurgia or The Egyptian Mysteries,* translated by Alexander Wilder, p.111, William Rider and Son 1911/Kessinger.

42 Riane Eisler, *In All Her Names,* edited by Joseph Campbell and Charles Musès, p.18, Harper San Francisco 1991.

43 Ibid. p.19.

Chapter Two

1 *The Compact Edition of the Oxford English Dictionary,* edited by Burchfield, p.1377, Oxford University Press 1987.

2 Barbara G. Walker, *The Woman's Encyclopedia of Myths and Secrets* p.584, Harper San Francisco, HarperCollins Publishers 1983.

3 E.A. Wallis Budge, *An Egyptian Hieroglyphic Dictionary* p.309, Dover Publications Inc. 1978.

4 Ian Shaw and Paul Nicholson, *British Museum Dictionary of Ancient Egypt* p.87, British Museum Press 1995.

5 Ibid. p.164.

References

6 *The Compact Edition of the Oxford English Dictionary*, edited by Burchfield, p.2437, Oxford University Press 1987.

7 Ibid. p.2531.

8 Ian Stevenson, M.D., *Twenty Cases Suggestive of Reincarnation* p.2, University of Virginia Press 1974.

9 Carl Sagan, *The Demon Haunted World* p.302, Random House, New York 1995.

10 Barbara G. Walker, *The Woman's Encyclopedia of Myths and Secrets* p.848, Harper San Francisco, HarperCollins Publishers 1983.

11 Lucie Lamy, *Egyptian Mysteries*, translated by Deborah Lawlor, p.25, Thames and Hudson 1994.

12 Barbara G. Walker, *The Woman's Encyclopedia of Myths and Secrets* p.849, Harper San Francisco, HarperCollins Publishers 1983.

13 Charles Freeman, *AD 381* p.129, Pimlico 2008.

14 Ibid. p.40.

15 Ibid. p.94.

16 Gerard Friell and Stephan Williams, *Theodosius: The Empire at Bay* p.53, B.T. Batsford Ltd. 1994.

17 Charles Freeman, *AD 381* p.1, Pimlico 2008.

18 Ibid. p.27.

19 *The Compact Edition of the Oxford English Dictionary,* edited by Burchfield, p.2052, Oxford University Press 1987.

20 Synesius cited by Charles Freeman, *AD 381* p.xi, Pimlico 2008.

21 *The Compact Edition of the Oxford English Dictionary,* edited by Burchfield, p.1277, Oxford University Press 1987.

22 Barbara G. Walker, *The Woman's Encyclopedia of Myths and Secrets* p.758, Harper San Francisco, HarperCollins Publishers 1983.

23 Charles Freeman, *AD 381* p.124, Pimlico 2008.

24 Charles Freeman, *The Closing of the Western Mind* p.xv, Pimlico 2003.

25 Barbara G. Walker, *The Woman's Encyclopedia of Myths and Secrets* p.252, Harper San Francisco, HarperCollins Publishers 1983.

26 Ibid. p.951.

27 E.A. Wallis Budge, *An Egyptian Hieroglyphic Dictionary* p.831, Dover Publications Inc. 1978.

28 Lee Irwin, *The Dream Seekers* p.164, University of Oklahoma Press 1994.

29 *The Compact Edition of the Oxford English Dictionary,* edited by Burchfield, p.522, Oxford University Press 1987.

[30] Ibid. p.1470.

[31] E.A. Wallis Budge, *An Egyptian Hieroglyphic Dictionary* p.176, Dover Publications Inc.1978.

[32] *I Ching*, The Richard Wilhelm Translation, p.280, Routledge and Kegan Paul 1968.

[33] Lao Tzu, *Tao Te Ching,* translated by D.C. Lau, p.30, Penguin Books 1963.

[34] *I Ching*, The Richard Wilhelm Translation, pp.286-287, Routledge and Kegan Paul 1968.

[35] *The Compact Edition of the Oxford English Dictionary* p.1582, Oxford University Press 1987.

[36] R.D. Laing, *The Politics of Experience* p.117, Penguin Books 1967.

[37] Ibid. p.119.

[38] Ian Shaw and Paul Nicholson, *British Museum Dictionary of Ancient Egypt* p.166, British Museum Press 1997.

[39] Erik Hornung, *Conceptions of God in Ancient Egypt,* translated by John Baines, pp.214-216, Cornell Paperbacks 1996.

[40] R.A. Schwaller de Lubicz, *Sacred Science,* translated by André and Goldian VandenBroeck, p.6, Inner Traditions International 1988.

Chapter Three

[1] C.G. Jung, *Memories, Dreams, Reflections*, edited by Aniela Jaffé, translated by Richard and Clara Winston, p.414, Fontana Press 1995.

[2] Ibid. p.369.

[3] Ibid. p.414.

[4] Peter Kingsley, *In The Dark Places of Wisdom* p.69, Element Books 1999.

[5] Ibid. p.71.

[6] Kelly Bulkeley, *Visions of the Night* p.27, State University of New York Press 1999.

[7] John Anthony West, *Serpent in the Sky* p.1, Quest Books 1993.

[8] Wendy Doniger O'Flaherty, *Dreams, Illusion and Other Realities* p.37, The University of Chicago Press 1984.

[9] Ibid. p.60.

[10] Ibid. p.53.

[11] Ibid. p.59.

[12] Satyajit Layek, *An Analysis of Dream in Indian Philosophy* p.3, Sri Satguru Publications 1990.

References

[13] Wendy Doniger O'Flaherty, *Dreams, Illusion and Other Realities* p.15, The University of Chicago Press 1984.

[14] Ibid. p.53.

[15] Ibid. p.53.

[16] Patricia Cox Miller, *Dreams in Late Antiquity* p.72, Princeton University Press 1994.

[17] Ibid. p.65.

[18] Ibid. p.67.

[19] Kelly Bulkeley, *Visions of the Night* p.5, State University of New York Press 1999.

[20] Dr. Manjir Samanta-Laughton, *Punk Science* p.13, O Books 2006.

[21] Ibid. pp.33-34.

[22] R.A. Schwaller de Lubicz, *Le Temple de l'Homme Apet du Sud à Louqsor,* Paris 1977, cited by Lucie Lamy, *Egyptian Mysteries*, translated by Deborah Lawlor, p.18, Thames and Hudson 1994.

[23] Peter Russell, *From Science to God* p.xii, New World Library 2005.

[24] Charles Musès, *Consciousness and Reality,* edited by Charles Musès and Arthur M. Young, pp.89-90, Outerbridge and Lazard, Inc. 1972.

[25] Ibid. p.89.

[26] Dr. Manjir Samanta-Laughton, *Punk Science* p.198, O Books 2006.

[27] Ibid. pp.178-179.

[28] Hannah Duguid, 'Sleepless at the Serpentine', Viewspaper p.15, *The Independent,* 28th July 2010.

[29] Lee Smolen, *Three Roads to Quantum Gravity*, Phoenix 2001.

[30] C.G. Jung, *Memories, Dreams, Reflections* pp.349-350, Fontana Press 1995.

[31] Jonathan Cott, *The Search for Omm Sety* pp.271-272, Studio 33 Books, Random House 2005.

[32] C.G. Jung, *Memories, Dreams, Reflections,* edited by Aniela Jaffé, translated by Richard and Clara Winston, p.283, Fontana Press 1995.

[33] Achilles Tatius, *Leucippe and Clitophon*, translated by John J. Winkley, p.178, *Collected Greek Novels,* edited by B.P. Reardon, University of California Press 1989.

[34] Laurens van der Post, *Feather Fall*, edited by Jean-Marc Pottiez, p.163, Penguin Books 1995.

[35] Laurens van der Post, *Jung and the Story of Our Time* p.10, The Hogarth Press 1976.

[36] Laurens van der Post, *Feather Fall*, edited by Jean-Marc Pottiez, pp.177-178, Penguin Books 1995.

[37] Laurens van der Post, *Jung and the Story of Our Time* p.42, Penguin Books 1978.

[38] *I Ching*, The Richard Wilhelm Translation, p.354, Routledge and Kegan Paul 1968.

[39] Peter Kingsley, *In The Dark Places of Wisdom* p.147, Element Books 1999.

[40] Patricia Cox Miller, *Dreams in Late Antiquity* p.14, Princeton University Press 1994.

[41] Peter Kingsley, *In The Dark Places of Wisdom* p.114, Element Books 1999.

[42] C.G. Jung, *Psychology and Religion*, translated by R.F.C. Hull, pp.104–105, Pantheon Books 1958.

Chapter Four

[1] *The Compact Edition of the Oxford English Dictionary*, edited by Burchfield, p.2481, Oxford University Press 1987.

[2] E.A. Wallis Budge, *An Egyptian Hieroglyphic Dictionary* p.42, Dover Publications Inc. 1978.

[3] R.A. Schwaller de Lubicz, *Sacred Science*, translated by André and Goldian VandenBroeck, p.14, Inner Traditions International 1988.

[4] Ibid. p.19.

[5] R.A. Schwaller de Lubicz, *The Temple of Man*, translated by Deborah Lawlor and Robert Lawlor, p.376, Inner Traditions International 1998.

[6] John Anthony West, *Serpent in the Sky* p.1, Quest Books 1993.

[7] R.A. Schwaller de Lubicz, *The Temple in Man*, translated by Robert and Deborah Lawlor, p.48, Inner Traditions International 1977.

[8] Ibid. p.52.

[9] Ibid. p.53.

[10] *I Ching*, The Richard Wilhelm Translation, p.169, Routledge and Kegan Paul 1968.

[11] Lao Tzu, *Tao Te Ching*, translated by D.C. Lau, p.20, Penguin Books 1963.

[12] Peter Kingsley, *In The Dark Places of Wisdom* pp.235-236, Element Books 1999.

[13] Ibid. p.235.

Chapter Five

[1] Erik Hornung, *Conceptions of God in Ancient Egypt*, translated by John Baines, p.213, Cornell Paperbacks 1996.

[2] Ibid. p.131.

[3] Peter Kingsley, *Ancient Philosophy, Mystery, and Magic* p.284, Clarendon Paperbacks, Oxford University Press 1996.

References

[4] E.A. Wallis Budge, *The Gods of the Egyptians* Vol.2 p.241, Dover Publications Inc.1969.

[5] Ibid. p.241.

[6] Ibid. p.243.

[7] *The Compact Edition of the Oxford English Dictionary*, edited by Burchfield, p.1914, Oxford University Press 1987.

[8] R.A. Schwaller de Lubicz, *Sacred Science*, translated by André and Goldian VandenBroeck, p.189, Inner Traditions International 1988.

[9] Christian Jacq, *The Living Wisdom of Ancient Egypt* p.156, Simon and Schuster U.K. Ltd. 1999.

[10] Lucie Lamy, *Egyptian Mysteries*, translated by Deborah Lawlor, p.89, Thames and Hudson 1994.

Chapter Six

[1] *The Compact Edition of the Oxford English Dictionary* edited by Burchfield, p.1889, Oxford University Press 1987.

[2] *Encyclopedia of World Mythology* p.11, Octopus Books Ltd. 1975.

[3] Laurens van der Post, *Jung and the Story of Our Time* p.19, Penguin Books 1978.

[4] C.G. Jung, *Memories, Dreams, Reflections*, edited by Aniela Jaffé, translated by Richard and Clara Winston, p.373, Fontana Press 1995.

[5] Erik Hornung, *Conceptions of God in Ancient Egypt*, translated by John Baines, p.203, Cornell Paperbacks 1996.

[6] Patricia Cox Miller, *Dreams in Late Antiquity* p.61, Princeton University Press 1994.

[7] Rosalie David, *Egyptian Magic* by C. Jacq, translated by Janet M. Davis, p.ix, Aris and Phillips 1985.

[8] Dr. Manjir Samanta-Laughton, *Punk Science* p.33, O Books 2006.

[9] R.A. Schwaller de Lubicz, *Sacred Science*, translated by André and Goldian VandenBroeck, p.8, Inner Traditions International 1988.

[10] Patricia Cox Miller, *Dreams in Late Antiquity* pp.52-53, Princeton University Press 1994.

[11] E.A. Wallis Budge, *A History of Egypt* Vol.4 p.80, Oxford 1902.

[12] Ian Shaw and Paul Nicholson, *British Museum Dictionary of Ancient Egypt* p.87, British Museum Press 1997.

[13] Erik Hornung, *Conceptions of God in Ancient Egypt*, translated by John Baines, p.251, Cornell Paperbacks 1996.

Chapter Seven

[1] Alexandre Piankoff, *The Tomb of Ramses VI*, Bollingen Series XL·1, p.261, Pantheon Books 1954.

[2] Selim Hassan, *Excavations at Giza* p.265, Government Press 1946, cited by Robert Bauval and Graham Hancock, *Keeper of Genesis* p.156, Arrow Books 1997.

[3] Ibid. p.265.

[4] Robert Bauval and Adrian Gilbert, *The Orion Mystery* p.123, Arrow Books 1994.

[5] E.A. Wallis Budge, *The Egyptian Heaven and Hell* Vol.I p.86, Dover Publications Inc. 1996.

[6] Patricia Cox Miller, *Dreams in Late Antiquity* pp.54-55, Princeton University Press 1994.

[7] Erik Hornung, *The Ancient Egyptian Books of the Afterlife*, translated by David Lorton, p.27, Cornell University Press 1999.

[8] Lucie Lamy, *Egyptian Mysteries*, translated by Deborah Lawlor, p.25, Thames and Hudson 1994.

[9] Ibid. p.25.

[10] Ibid. p.25.

[11] Ibid. pp.24-25.

[12] Erik Hornung, *The Ancient Egyptian Books of the Afterlife*, translated by David Lorton, p.41, Cornell University Press 1999.

[13] R.A. Schwaller de Lubicz, *Sacred Science*, translated by André and Goldian VandenBroeck, p.132, Inner Traditions International 1988.

[14] Ibid. p.133.

[15] Charles Musès, *Proceedings of the Fourth International Conference on the Study of Shamanism and Alternate Modes of Healing* p.180, Independent Scholars of Asia 1988.

[16] Ibid. p.179.

[17] Livio Strecchini cited by Robert K.G. Temple, *The Sirius Mystery* fig.14 p.146, Destiny Books 1987.

[18] Peter Kingsley, *Ancient Philosophy, Mystery, and Magic* p.138, Clarendon Paperbacks, Oxford University Press 1996.

[19] Ibid. pp.140-141.

[20] Ibid. pp.137-138.

[21] Charles Musès, *Proceedings of the Fourth International Conference on the Study of Shamanism and Alternate Modes of Healing* p.184, Independent Scholars of Asia 1988.

References

22 Ibid. p.187.
23 Ibid. p.190.
24 Ibid. p.179.
25 Ibid. p.179.
26 Lucie Lamy, *Egyptian Mysteries*, translated by Deborah Lawlor, p.29, Thames and Hudson 1994.
27 Ibid. p.30.
28 Ibid. p.30.
29 Ibid. p.30.
30 Ibid. p.30.

Chapter Eight

1 E.A. Wallis Budge, *An Egyptian Hieroglyphic Dictionary* p.896, Dover Publications Inc. 1978.
2 Ibid. p.896.
3 Ananda Coomaraswamy cited by F.D.K. Bosch, *The Golden Germ* p.192. Munshiram Manoharlal Publishers 1994.
4 *The Compact Edition of the Oxford English Dictionary*, edited by Burchfield, p.683, Oxford University Press 1987.
5 Patricia Cox Miller, *Dreams in Late Antiquity* p.55, Princeton University Press 1994.
6 *The Compact Edition of the Oxford English Dictionary*, edited by Burchfield, p.683, Oxford University Press 1987.
7 Plato, *Timaeus,* translated by R.G. Bury, *Plato* Vol.9 p.187, Harvard University Press 1929.
8 Patricia Cox Miller, *Dreams in Late Antiquity* p.55, Princeton University Press 1994.
9 William Shakespeare, *The Tempest*, *The New Penguin Shakespeare* p.120, Penguin Books 1996.
10 Patricia Cox Miller, *Dreams in Late Antiquity* p.55, Princeton University Press 1994.
11 Ibid. p.55.
12 Ibid. pp.58-59.
13 Athenagoras, *Legatio* 27, translated by Cyril Richardson, p.330, in *Library of Christian Classics* Vol.1: *Early Christian Fathers*, Philadelphia: Westminster Press, 1953, and Clement of Alexandria, *Protrepticus* 1.3.2. and 2.11.2-3, edited

311111111

11111

and translated by Claude Mondésert, pp. 55, 67-68, in *Clément d'Alexandrie: Le Protreptique.* Sources Chrétiennes 2, Paris: Les Editions du Cerf, 2nd ed., 1949, cited by Patricia Cox Miller, ibid. p.64.

[14] Violet Macdermot, *The Cult of the Seer in the Ancient Middle East* pp.46-47, The Wellcome Institute of the History of Medicine 1971.

[15] *The Septuagint Bible*, translated by Charles Thomson; edited, revised and enlarged by Charles Musès, Shekinah Enterprises.

[16] Dr. Paul Carus, *History of the Devil and the Idea of Evil* p.307, Kessinger Publishing.

[17] Louis M. Savary, Patricia H. Berne and Strephon Kaplan Williams, *Dreams and Spiritual Growth* p.28, Paulist Press 1984.

[18] Ibid. p.1.

[19] Ibid. p.35.

[20] Ibid. p.36.

[21] Andrew Welburn, *The Beginnings of Christianity* p.84, Floris Books 2007.

[22] Louis M. Savary, Patricia H. Berne and Strephon Kaplan Williams, *Dreams and Spiritual Growth* p.1, Paulist Press 1984.

[23] G.E. von Grunebaum, *The Dream and Human Societies,* edited by G.E. von Grunebaum and Roger Caillois, p.6, University of California Press 1966.

[24] Ibid. pp.6-7.

[25] Ibid. p.20.

[26] Ibid. p.7.

[27] Aldous Huxley, *Themes and Variations* p.259, Chatto and Windus 1950.

[28] Roger Caillois, *The Dream and Human Societies,* edited by G.E. von Grunebaum and Roger Caillois, p.27, University of California Press 1966.

[29] Synesius, *The Essays and Hymns of Synesius of Cyrene* translated by Augustine Fitzgerald p.343, Oxford University Press 1930.

[30] Ibid. p.343.

[31] Ibid. pp.343-344.

[32] Synesius, *On Dreams,* translated by Isaac Myer (1888), p.23, Kessinger Publishing.

Chapter Nine

[1] Marcel Griaule and Germaine Dieterlen, *African Worlds*, edited by Daryll Forde, pp.83-110, Oxford University Press 1954, cited by Robert K.G. Temple, *The Sirius Mystery* p.2, Destiny Books 1987.

[2] Ibid. p.3.

[3] Ibid. p.1.

310

References

[4] Giorgio Piccardi cited by Edward R. Dewey, *Cycles* p.159, Hawthorn Books Inc. 1971.

[5] Professor George Wald, 'Evolution of the Earth's Atmosphere', Lloyd V. Berkner Memorial Symposium, *Science,* 157, 1957, 1466, cited by Oliver L. Reiser, *Cosmic Humanism and World Unity* p.111, Interface/Gordon and Breach 1975.

[6] Oliver L. Reiser. Ibid. p.111.

[7] David Bohm and B. Hiley, 'On the Intuitive Understanding of Nonlocality as Implied by Quantum Theory', *Foundations of Physics* Vol.5 1975.

[8] Fred Hoyle, *Frontiers of Astronomy* p.304, Heinemann, London 1970 .

[9] Lucie Lamy, *Egyptian Mysteries*, translated by Deborah Lawlor, p.18, Thames and Hudson 1994.

[10] Ibid. p.18.

[11] Edward R. Dewey, *Cycles* p.9, Hawthorn Books Inc. 1971.

[12] Oliver L. Reiser, *Cosmic Humanism and World Unity* p.137, Interface/Gordon and Breach 1975.

[13] Charles Musès, *Destiny and Control in Human Systems* p.219, Kluwer-Nijhoff Publishing 1985.

[14] Ibid. p.174.

[15] Ibid. pp.190-191.

[16] Ibid. p.40.

[17] Ibid. p.40.

[18] Ibid. p.40.

[19] Ibid. p.51.

[20] Ibid. p.41.

[21] Ibid. pp.50-51.

[22] Louis M. Savary, Patricia H. Berne and Strephon Kaplan Williams, *Dreams and Spiritual Growth* p.40, Paulist Press 1984.

[23] Jay Bregman, *Synesius of Cyrene* p.146, University of California Press 1982.

[24] Thomas Cleary, *The Essential Tao* p.1, Harper Collins 1993.

[25] D.C. Lau, *Tao Te Ching* by Lao Tzu, translated by D.C. Lau, p.xv, Penguin Books 1963.

[26] Fung Yu-Lan, *A Short History of Chinese Philosophy*, edited by Derk Bodde, p.3, The Free Press, a division of Simon and Schuster 1997.

[27] Wing-Tsit Chan, *A Source Book in Chinese Philosophy* p.136, Princeton University Press 1963.

28 Oliver L. Reiser, *Cosmic Humanism and World Unity* p.20, Interface/Gordon and Breach 1975.

29 *The Compact Edition of the Oxford English Dictionary,* edited by Burchfield, p.3719, Oxford University Press 1987.

30 Joseph Needham, *Science and Civilisation in China* p.36, Cambridge University Press 1996.

31 Eva Wong, *The Shambhala Guide to Taoism* p.14, Shambhala 1997.

32 Ibid. p.3.

33 Ibid. p.15.

34 Ibid. p.5.

35 Ibid. p.17.

36 Ibid. p.18.

37 Charles Musès, *In All Her Names*, edited by Joseph Campbell and Charles Musès, p.142, Harper San Francisco 1991.

38 Ibid. p.142.

39 Ibid. p.139.

40 Deng Ming-Dao, *The Wandering Taoist, Chronicles of Tao* p.142, HarperCollins Publishers 1993.

41 Ibid. pp.115-116.

42 Chen Kaiguo and Zheng Shunchao, *Opening the Dragon Gate*, translated by Thomas Cleary, p.141, Tuttle Publishing 1996.

43 Ibid. p.276.

44 Ibid. p.276.

45 Ibid. p.142.

46 Oliver L. Reiser, *Cosmic Humanism and World Unity* p.167, Interface/Gordon and Breach 1975.

47 Ibid. pp.167-168.

48 R.A. Schwaller de Lubicz, *Sacred Science*, translated by André and Goldian VandenBroeck, p.28, Inner Traditions International 1988.

49 Rodney Collin, *The Theory of Celestial Influence* pp.18-19, Mercury Publications, Inc. 2006.

50 Musaios (Dr. Charles Musès), *The Lion Path* p.63, Golden Sceptre Publishing 1988.

51 Marcel Griaule and Germaine Dieterlen, *Le Renard Pâle,* an English translation commissioned and cited by Robert K.G. Temple, *The Sirius Mystery* p.30, Destiny Books 1987.

References

[52] Ibid. p.66.

[53] Sir Monier Monier-Williams, *A Sanskrit-English Dictionary* p.171, Motilal Banarsidass Publishers 2005.

[54] Stella Kramrisch, *The Presence of Śiva* p.23, Princeton University Press 1992.

[55] Ibid. p.440.

[56] Ibid. pp.439-440.

[57] Ibid. p.332.

[58] Ibid. p.261.

[59] *Liṅga Purāṇa* cited by Stella Kramrisch, ibid. p.246.

[60] Musaios (Dr. Charles Musès), *The Lion Path* p.38, Golden Sceptre Publishing 1988.

[61] Ibid. p.22.

[62] Sir Monier Monier-Williams, *A Sanskrit-English Dictionary* p.1074, Motilal Banarsidass Publishers 2005.

[63] *The Compact Edition of the Oxford English Dictionary,* edited by Burchfield, p.142, Oxford University Press 1987.

[64] Ibid. p.1986.

[65] Ibid. p.35.

[66] Ibid. p.1056.

[67] Ibid. p.2813.

[68] Ibid. p.3641.

[69] Ibid. p.3794.

[70] Stella Kramrisch, *The Presence of Śiva* p.7, Princeton University Press 1992.

[71] Ibid. p.57.

[72] Ibid. p.18.

[73] Ibid. p.44.

[74] Ibid. p.31.

[75] Ibid. p.80.

[76] Sir Monier Monier-Williams, *A Sanskrit-English Dictionary* p.794, Motilal Banarsidass Publishers 2005.

[77] Ibid. p.794.

[78] Kenneth Demarest, *Consciousness and Reality*, edited by Charles Musès and Arthur M. Young, p.379, Outerbridge and Lazard, Inc. 1972.

[79] Ibid. p. 379.

[80] Stella Kramrisch, *The Presence of Śiva* p.90, Princeton University Press 1992.

[81] Robert K.G. Temple, *The Sirius Mystery* p.62, Destiny Books 1987.

[82] Musaios (Dr. Charles Musès), *The Lion Path* p.67, Golden Sceptre Publishing 1988.

[83] Ibid. p.43.

[84] Robert K.G. Temple , The Sirius Mystery p.48, Destiny Books 1987.

[85] Stella Kramrisch, *The Presence of Siva* p.57, Princeton University Press 1992.

[86] Ibid. p.434.

[87] Ibid. p.331.

[88] Ibid. p.439.

[89] E.A. Wallis Budge, *An Egyptian Hieroglyphic Dictionary* p.163, Dover Publications Inc. 1978.

[90] Ibid. p.161.

[91] Oliver L. Reiser, *Cosmic Humanism and World Unity* p.26, Interface/Gordon and Breach 1975.

[92] Ibid. p.26.

[93] Ibid. p.44.

[94] Ibid. p.34.

[95] Ibid. p.180.

[96] Ibid. pp.59-60.

[97] Ibid. p.258.

[98] Dr. Harold S. Burr cited by Linda Goodman, *Sun Signs* p.542, George G. Harrap and Co. Ltd. 1968.

[99] Charles Musès, *Consciousness and Reality*, edited by Charles Musès and Arthur M. Young, p.118, Outerbridge and Lazard, Inc. 1972.

[100] Charles Musès, *Destiny and Control in Human Systems* p.63, Kluwer-Nijhoff Publishing 1985.

[101] Barbara Watterson, *Gods of Ancient Egypt* p.184, Sutton Publishing 1996.

[102] Geraldine Pinch, *Egyptian Mythology* p.210, Oxford University Press 2002.

[103] E.A. Wallis Budge, *The Gods of the Egyptians* Vol.1 p.402, Dover Publications Inc. 1969.

[104] Ibid. p.407.

[105] Richard Wilhelm, *Tao Te Ching* by Lao Tzu, translated by Richard Wilhelm, p.74, Arcana 1989.

[106] E.A. Wallis Budge, *Osiris and the Egyptian Resurrection*, 2 vols. London, 1911, Vol.1, pp.389-90, cited by Robert K.G. Temple, *The Sirius Mystery* p.179, Destiny Books 1987.

References

[107] Richard Wilhelm, *Tao Te Ching* by Lao Tzu, translated by Richard Wilhelm, p.69, Arcana 1989.

[108] Wendy Doniger O'Flaherty, *Dreams, Illusion and Other Realities* p.16, University of Chicago Press 1986.

[109] Musaios (Dr. Charles Musès), *The Lion Path* p.18, Golden Sceptre Publishing 1988.

[110] Ibid. pp.21-22.

[111] Ibid. p.22.

[112] Barbara G. Walker, *The Woman's Encyclopedia of Myths and Secrets* p.1027, Harper San Francisco, HarperCollins Publishers 1983.

[113] Ibid. p.780.

[114] Ibid. p.780.

[115] Charles Musès *Proceedings of the Fourth International Conference on the Study of Shamanism and Alternate Modes of Healing* p.186, Independent Scholars of Asia 1988.

[116] Musaios (Dr. Charles Musès), *The Lion Path* p.31, Golden Sceptre Publishing 1988.

[117] Ibid. p.31.

[118] Walter Burkert, *Ancient Mystery Cults* p.10, Harvard University Press 1987.

[119] Oliver L. Reiser, *Cosmic Humanism and World Unity* p.258, Interface/Gordon and Breach 1975.

[120] Charles Musès, *Consciousness and Reality*, edited by Charles Musès and Arthur M. Young, p.120, Outerbridge and Lazard Inc. 1972.

[121] R.T. Wallis, *Neo-Platonism* p.107, Charles Scribner's Sons 1972.

[122] Ibid. p.146.

[123] Barbara G. Walker, *The Woman's Encyclopedia of Myths and Secrets* p.74, Harper San Francisco, HarperCollins Publishers 1983.

[124] Musaios (Dr. Charles Musès), *The Lion Path* p.64, Golden Sceptre Publishing 1988.

[125] Charles Musès, *Destiny and Control in Human Systems* p.136, Kluwer-Nijhoff Publishing 1985.

[126] Ibid. p.135.

[127] Musaios (Dr. Charles Musès), *The Lion Path* p.122, Golden Sceptre Publishing 1988.

[128] Charles Musès, *Destiny and Control in Human Systems* p.156, Kluwer-Nijhoff Publishing 1985.

[129] *The Compact Edition of the Oxford English Dictionary*, edited by Burchfield, pp.3719-3720, Oxford University Press 1987.

[130] Musaios (Dr. Charles Musès), *The Lion Path* p.113, Golden Sceptre Publishing 1988.

Chapter Ten

[1] Robert K.G. Temple, *The Sirius Mystery* p.171, Destiny Books 1987.

[2] Ibid. p.170.

[3] Ibid. p.175.

[4] E.A. Wallis Budge, *An Egyptian Hieroglyphic Dictionary* p.723, Dover Publications Inc. 1978.

[5] Ibid. p.815.

[6] Ibid. p.cxxv.

[7] Musaios (Dr. Charles Musès), *The Lion Path* p.97, Golden Sceptre Publishing 1988.

[8] Hans Cousto, *The Cosmic Octave* p.40, Life Rhythm Publication 2000.

[9] John Anthony West, *Serpent in the Sky* pp.97-98, Quest Books 1993.

[10] Oliver L. Reiser, *Cosmic Humanism and World Unity* pp.257-258, Interface/Gordon and Breach 1975.

[11] Ibid. p.260.

[12] Sir Monier Monier-Williams, *A Sanskrit-English Dictionary* p.858, Motilal Banarsidass Publishers 2005.

[13] Ibid. p.858.

[14] Stella Kramrisch, *The Presence of Śiva* pp.459-460, Princeton University Press 1992.

[15] Robert K.G. Temple, *The Sirius Mystery* p.163, Destiny Books 1987.

[16] Ajit Mookerjee, *Yoga Art* p.25, Thames and Hudson 1975.

[17] Ibid. p.26.

[18] Ibid. p.30.

[19] Ibid. p.33.

[20] Ibid. p.43.

[21] Pliny, 9.58. Cf. Aristotle, *Historia Animalium* 8.15.559B-600, cited by Giorgio de Santillana and Hertha von Dechend, *Hamlet's Mill* p.215, Godine 2005.

[22] Giorgio de Santillana and Hertha von Dechend, ibid. p.358.

[23] Ibid. p.215.

[24] Ibid. p.358.

References

[25] Ibid. p.358.

[26] Dr. F. Batmanghelidj, *Your Body's Many Cries for Water* p.15, The Tagman Press 2000.

[27] *I Ching*, The Richard Wilhelm Translation p.371, Routledge and Kegan Paul 1968.

[28] Ibid. p.386.

[29] Ibid. p.386.

[30] Ibid. p.12.

[31] Alfred Huang, *The Complete I Ching* p.38, Inner Traditions International 1998.

[32] *I Ching*, The Richard Wilhelm Translation p.11, Routledge and Kegan Paul 1968.

[33] *Kūrma Puraṇa* cited by Stella Kramrisch, *The Presence of Śiva* pp.248–249, Princeton University Press 1992.

[34] Stella Kramrisch, ibid. pp.162-163.

[35] Ibid. p.170.

[36] Ibid. p.165.

[37] Ibid. p.163.

[38] *Liṅga Purāṇa* cited by Stella Kramrisch, ibid. p.246.

[39] *Śaunaka Saṁhitā* cited by Satyajit Layek, *An Analysis of Dream in Indian Philosophy* p.12, Sri Satguru Publications 1990.

[40] Stella Kramrisch, *The Presence of Śiva* p.161, Princeton University Press 1992.

[41] Carl Kerényi, *Dionysos* translated by Ralph Manheim p.30, Princeton University Press 1976.

[42] Ibid. p.77.

[43] Ibid. p.78-79.

[44] Ibid. pp.162-163.

[45] Ibid. pp.164-165.

[46] Ibid. pp.167.

[47] Joscelyn Godwin, *Mystery Religions in the Ancient World* p.133, Thames and Hudson 1981.

[48] Stella Kramrisch, *The Presence of Śiva* p.171, Princeton University Press 1992.

[49] Ibid. p.479.

[50] Ibid. p.167.

[51] Carl Kerényi, *Dionysos* translated by Ralph Manheim p.205, Princeton University Press 1976.

[52] Ibid. p.206.

[53] Ibid. p.207.

[54] Ibid. p.210.

[55] Ibid. pp.207-208.

[56] Ibid. p.211.

[57] Oliver L. Reiser, *Cosmic Humanism and World Unity* p.156, Interface/Gordon and Breach 1975.

[58] Ibid. p.156-157.

[59] Musaios (Dr. Charles Musès), *The Lion Path* p.35, Golden Sceptre Publishing 1988.

[60] Ian Shaw and Paul Nicholson, *British Museum Dictionary of Ancient Egypt* p.54, British Museum Press 1997.

[61] Barbara Watterson, *Gods of Ancient Egypt* p.118, Sutton Publishing 1996.

[62] Richard H. Wilkinson, *The Complete Gods and Goddesses of Ancient Egypt* p.102, Thames and Hudson 2003.

[63] E.A. Wallis Budge, *The Gods of the Egyptians* Vol.1 p.498, Dover Publications 1969.

[64] Richard H. Wilkinson, *The Complete Gods and Goddesses of Ancient Egypt* p.103, Thames and Hudson 2003.

[65] Ibid. p.103.

[66] E.A. Wallis Budge, *An Egyptian Hieroglyphic Dictionary,* p.586, Dover Publications Inc. 1978.

[67] Barbara G. Walker, *The Woman's Encyclopedia of Myths and Secrets* p.874, Harper, San Francisco, HarperCollins Publishers 1983.

[68] Stephen Quirke, *Ancient Egyptian Religion* p.122, British Museum Press 2000.

[69] Ibid. p.31.

[70] Charles Musès, *Destiny and Control in Human Systems* p.59, Kluwer-Nijhoff Publishing 1985.

[71] Ibid. p.57.

[72] Ibid. p.57.

[73] E.A. Wallis Budge, *An Egyptian Hieroglyphic Dictionary* p.752, Dover Publications Inc. 1978.

[74] Ibid. p.753.

[75] R.A. Schwaller de Lubicz, *Sacred Science,* translated by André and Goldian VandenBroeck, p.156, Inner Traditions International 1982.

[76] Sir Monier Monier-Williams, *A Sanskrit-English Dictionary* p.1074, Motilal Banarsidass Publishers 2005.

[77] Plutarch cited by Barbara Watterson, *Gods of Ancient Egypt* p.51, Sutton Publishing 1996.

[78] Geraldine Pinch, *Egyptian Mythology* p.152, Oxford University Press 2002.

[79] Ibid. p.152.

[80] Ibid. p.152.

[81] Richard H. Wilkinson, *The Complete Gods and Goddesses of Ancient Egypt* p.230, Thames and Hudson 2003.

[82] E.A. Wallis Budge, *The Gods of the Egyptians* Vol.1 p.294, Dover Publications 1969.

Chapter Eleven

[1] Roger Caillois, *The Dream and Human Societies,* edited by G.E. von Grunebaum and Roger Caillois, p.38, University of California Press 1966.

[2] Musaios (Dr. Charles Musès), *The Lion Path* p.35, Golden Sceptre Publishing 1988.

[3] Kenneth Demarest, *Consciousness and Reality,* edited by Charles Musès and Arthur M. Young, p.354, Outerbridge and Lazard, Inc. 1972.

[4] *The Compact Edition of the Oxford English Dictionary*, edited by Burchfield, p.3731, Oxford University Press 1987.

[5] Basil Cottle, *The Penguin Dictionary of Surnames* p.227, Penguin Books 1987.

[6] Juliette Wood, *The Celtic Book of Living and Dying* p.92, Duncan Baird Publishers Ltd. 2000.

[7] Ibid. p.92.

[8] Ibid. p.120.

[9] Ibid. p.121.

[10] Lewis Spence, *The Mysteries of Britain* p.17, Rider.

[11] Ibid. p.156.

[12] Ibid. p.235.

[13] Ibid. p.203.

[14] Ibid. p.216.

[15] Ibid. p.203.

[16] Andrew Collins, *The Cygnus Mystery* p.285, Watkins Publishing 2006.

[17] Robert Graves, *The Greek Myths* p.67, Penguin Books 1960.

[18] Barbara G. Walker, *The Woman's Encyclopedia of Myths and Secrets,* p.396, Harper San Francisco, HarperCollins Publishers 1983.

[19] Ibid. p.398.

[20] Ibid. p.398.

[21] Ibid. p.42.

[22] Richard Payne Knight, *The Symbolical Language of Ancient Art and Mythology* p.113, J.W. Bouton 1892.

[23] Barbara G. Walker, *The Woman's Encyclopedia of Myths and Secrets* p.43, Harper San Francisco, HarperCollins Publishers 1983.

[24] Stella Kramrisch, *The Presence of Śiva* p.48, Princeton University Press 1992.

[25] Barbara G. Walker, *The Woman's Encyclopedia of Myths and Secrets* p.356, Harper San Francisco, HarperCollins Publishers 1983.

[26] Ibid. p.398.

[27] Ibid. p.794.

[28] Michael Harrison, *The Roots of Witchcraft* p.210, Frederick Muller 1973.

[29] Ian Shaw and Paul Nicholson, *British Museum Dictionary of Ancient Egypt* p.32, British Museum Press 1997.

[30] Barbara G. Walker, *The Woman's Encyclopedia of Myths and Secrets* p.397, Harper San Francisco, HarperCollins Publishers 1983.

[31] Ibid. p.545.

[32] Ibid. p.545.

[33] Ibid. p.397.

[34] Charles Musès, *Consciousness and Reality,* edited by Charles Musès and Arthur M. Young, p.15, Outerbridge and Lazard, Inc. 1972.

[35] Barbara G. Walker, *The Woman's Encyclopedia of Myths and Secrets* p.395, Harper San Francisco, HarperCollins Publishers 1983.

[36] Ibid. p.395.

[37] Kenneth Demarest, *Consciousness and Reality,* edited by Charles Musès and Arthur M. Young, p.419 Outerbridge and Lazard, Inc. 1972.

[38] Ibid. p.425.

[39] Ibid. p.419.

[40] Ibid. p.434.

[41] Barbara G. Walker, *The Woman's Encyclopedia of Myths and Secrets* p.455, Harper San Francisco, HarperCollins Publishers 1983.

[42] Kenneth Demarest, *Consciousness and Reality,* edited by Charles Musès and Arthur M. Young, p.436, Outerbridge and Lazard, Inc. 1972.

[43] Barbara G. Walker, *The Woman's Encyclopedia of Myths and Secrets* p.935, Harper San Francisco, HarperCollins Publishers 1983.

References

[44] Richard H. Wilkinson, *The Complete Gods and Goddesses of Ancient Egypt* p.217, Thames and Hudson 2003.

[45] Ibid. p.215.

[46] Kenneth Demarest, *Consciousness and Reality,* edited by Charles Musès and Arthur M. Young, p.421, Outerbridge and Lazard, Inc. 1972.

[47] C.G. Jung, *Memories, Dreams, Reflections,* edited by Aniela Jaffé, translated by Richard and Clara Winston, p.26, Fontana Press 1995.

[48] Ibid. pp.26-28.

[49] Ibid. p.29.

[50] Barbara G. Walker, *The Woman's Encyclopedia of Myths and Secrets* p.901, Harper San Francisco, HarperCollins Publishers 1983.

[51] C.G. Jung, *Memories, Dreams, Reflections,* edited by Aniela Jaffé, translated by Richard and Clara Winston, pp.42-43, Fontana Press 1995.

[52] Ibid. pp.58-59.

[53] Ibid. p.58.

[54] Ibid. p.389.

[55] Ibid. p.65.

[56] Walter Burkert, *Ancient Mystery Cults* p.89, Harvard University Press 1987.

[57] Ibid. p.90.

[58] Ibid. p.90.

[59] Ibid. p.93.

[60] Ibid. p.95.

[61] Ibid. p.96.

[62] Carl Kerényi, *Eleusis* p.57, Princeton University Press 1967.

[63] *The Compact Edition of the Oxford English Dictionary,* edited by Burchfield, p.2818, Oxford University Press 1987.

[64] J. Bregman, *Synesius of Cyrene* p.32, University of California Press 1982.

Chapter Twelve

[1] E.A. Wallis Budge, *An Egyptian Hieroglyphic Dictionary* p.697, Dover Publications Inc. 1978.

[2] Richard H. Wilkinson, *The Complete Gods and Goddesses of Ancient Egypt* p.166, Thames and Hudson 2003.

[3] Richard H. Wilkinson, *Reading Egyptian Art* p.47, Thames and Hudson 2003.

[4] C.G. Jung, *Symbols of Transformation, The Collected Works* Vol.5, translated by R.F.C. Hull, p.234, Routledge 2004.

[5] Ibid. p.239.

[6] Ibid. p.251.

[7] Musaios (Dr. Charles Musès), *The Lion Path* p.41, Golden Sceptre Publishing 1988.

[8] Ibid. p.42.

[9] Ibid. p.42.

[10] Richard H. Wilkinson, *The Complete Gods and Goddesses of Ancient Egypt* p.118, Thames and Hudson 2003.

[11] R.T. Rundle Clark, *Myth and Symbol in Ancient Egypt* p.98, Thames and Hudson 1959.

[12] Richard H. Wilkinson, *The Complete Gods and Goddesses of Ancient Egypt* pp.118-119, Thames and Hudson 2003.

[13] E.A. Wallis Budge, *An Egyptian Hieroglyphic Dictionary* p.395, Dover Publications Inc. 1978.

[14] *I Ching*, The Richard Wilhelm Translation, p.237, Routledge and Kegan Paul 1968.

[15] Ibid. p.386.

[16] Ibid. pp.237-238.

[17] E.A. Wallis Budge, *An Egyptian Hieroglyphic Dictionary* p.842, Dover Publications Inc. 1978.

[18] Carl Kerényi, *Dionysos*, translated by Ralph Manheim, p.75, Princeton University Press 1976.

[19] Ibid. p.55.

[20] E.A. Wallis Budge, *An Egyptian Hieroglyphic Dictionary* pp.654-655, Dover Publications Inc. 1978.

[21] Carl Kerényi, *Dionysos*, translated by Ralph Manheim, p.258, Princeton University Press 1976.

[22] Ibid. p.257.

[23] Barbara G. Walker, *The Woman's Encyclopedia of Myths and Secrets*, p.236, Harper San Francisco, HarperCollins Publishers 1983.

[24] Arthur Edward Waite, *The Hidden Church of the Holy Grail* p.7, Fredonia Books 2002.

[25] Barbara G. Walker, *The Woman's Encyclopedia of Myths and Secrets*, p.352, Harper San Francisco, HarperCollins Publishers 1983.

[26] Ibid. p.353.

References

[27] Peter Kingsley, *Ancient Philosophy, Mystery, and Magic* pp.133-134, Oxford University Press 1996.

[28] Ibid. p.133.

[29] Ibid. p.135.

[30] Charles Musès, *The Jacob Boehme Society Quarterly*, edited by Charles Musès, Vol.I No.3 Spring 1953 p.24.

[31] W. Wynn Westcott, *The Divine Pymander,* translated by Dr. Everard in 1650, edited by W. Wynn Westcott, p.91, Theosophical Publishing Society 1894.

[32] Ibid. p.91.

[33] Plutarch cited by Peter Kingsley, *Ancient Philosophy, Mystery, and Magic* p.138, Clarendon Paperbacks, Oxford University Press 1996.

[34] Lewis Spence, *The Mysteries of Britain* p.146, Rider.

[35] R.A. Schwaller de Lubicz, *The Temple of Man,* translated by Deborah Lawlor and Robert Lawlor, p.730, Inner Traditions International 1998.

[36] Ibid. p.61.

[37] E.A. Wallis Budge, *An Egyptian Hieroglyphic Dictionary* p.326, Dover Publications Inc. 1978.

[38] *The Compact Edition of the Oxford English Dictionary,* edited by Burchfield, p.1380, Oxford University Press 1987.

[39] *I Ching*, The Richard Wilhelm Translation, p.lvii, Routledge and Kegan Paul 1968.

[40] Ibid. p.lvii.

[41] R.A. Schwaller de Lubicz, *Sacred Science,* translated by André and Goldian VandenBroeck, p.33, Inner Traditions International 1988.

[42] Ibid. p.33.

[43] Oliver L. Reiser, *Cosmic Humanism and World Unity* p.47, Interface/Gordon and Breach 1975.

[44] C.G. Jung, *The Psychogenesis of Mental Disease, The Collected Works* Vol. 3, translated by R.F.C. Hull, p.185, Routledge 2000.

[45] Ibid. p.182.

[46] Ibid. p.185.

[47] Oliver L. Reiser, *Cosmic Humanism and World Unity* p.45, Interface/Gordon and Breach 1975.

[48] Richard H. Wilkinson, *The Complete Gods and Goddesses of Ancient Egypt* p.200, Thames and Hudson 2003.

[49] Ibid. p.201.

[50] Barbara Watterson, *Gods of Ancient Egypt,* p.106, Sutton Publishing 1996.

[51] Stella Kramrisch, *The Presence of Śiva* p.151, Princeton University Press 1992.

[52] Ibid. p.482.

[53] Carl Kerényi, *Dionysos,* translated by Ralph Manheim, p.225, Princeton University Press 1976.

[54] Ian Shaw and Paul Nicholson, *British Museum Dictionary of Ancient Egypt* p.214, British Museum Press 1997.

[55] Erik Hornung, *Conceptions of God in Ancient Egypt,* translated by John Baines, p.210, Cornell Paperbacks 1996.

[56] R.T. Rundle Clark, *Myth and Symbol in Ancient Egypt* p.17, Thames and Hudson 1959.

[57] Ibid. p.109.

[58] Ibid. p.200.

[59] Ibid. p.110.

[60] E.A. Wallis Budge, *The Gods of the Egyptians* Vol.1 p.3, Dover Publications 1969.

[61] J.P. Seaton, *The Shambhala Anthology of Chinese Poetry,* translated and edited by J.P. Seaton, p.3, Shambhala Publications Inc. 2006.

[62] E.A. Wallis Budge, *The Egyptian Heaven and Hell* Vol.III p.4, Dover Publications 1996.

[63] R.T. Rundle Clark, *Myth and Symbol in Ancient Egypt* pp.28-29, Thames and Hudson 1959.

[64] Ibid. pp.138-139.

[65] Ian Shaw and Paul Nicholson, *British Museum Dictionary of Ancient Egypt* p.265, British Museum Press 1997.

[66] Dr. Paul Carus, *History of the Devil and the Idea of Evil* p.28, Kessinger Publishing.

[67] R.A. Schwaller de Lubicz, *The Temple of Man,* translated by Deborah Lawlor and Robert Lawlor, p.1018, Inner Traditions International 1998.

[68] Ian Shaw and Paul Nicholson, *British Museum Dictionary of Ancient Egypt* p.87, British Museum Press 1997.

[69] C.G. Jung, *Aion, The Collected Works* Vol.9 Part II, translated by R.F.C. Hull, p.99, Routledge 2004.

[70] Ibid. p.76.

[71] Charles Musès, *Destiny and Control in Human Systems* p.135, Kluwer-Nijhoff Publishing 1985.

[72] Musaios (Dr. Charles Musès), *The Lion Path* p.76, Golden Sceptre Publishing 1988.

References

[73] Manley P. Hall cited by Peter Tompkins, *Secrets of the Great Pyramid* p.61, Harper and Row, HarperCollins Publishers 1971.

[74] R.A. Schwaller de Lubicz, *Sacred Science,* translated by André and Goldian VandenBroeck, p.147, Inner Traditions International 1988.

[75] Ibid. p.238.

[76] R.A. Schwaller de Lubicz, *The Temple of Man,* translated by Deborah Lawlor and Robert Lawlor, plate 101, Inner Traditions International 1998.

[77] R.A. Schwaller de Lubicz, *Sacred Science,* translated by André and Goldian VandenBroeck, p.237, Inner Traditions International 1988.

[78] Ibid. p.237.

[79] Wing-Tsit Chan, *A Source Book in Chinese Philosophy,* p.139, Princeton University Press 1973.

[80] Richard H. Wilkinson, *The Complete Gods and Goddesses of Ancient Egypt* p.83, Thames and Hudson 2003.

[81] Ted J. Kaptchuk, *Chinese Medicine* p.44, Rider 2000.

[82] Tu Wei-ming cited by Ted J. Kaptchuk, ibid. p.69.

[83] Ibid. p.50.

[84] R.A. Schwaller de Lubicz, *Sacred Science,* translated by André and Goldian VandenBroeck, p.160, Inner Traditions International 1988.

[85] Ibid. p.160.

[86] Richard H. Wilkinson, *The Complete Gods and Goddesses of Ancient Egypt* p.83, Thames and Hudson 2003.

[87] Bisong Guo and Andrew Powell, *Listen to Your Body* pp.18-21, University of Hawai'i Press 2001.

[88] Ted J. Kaptchuk, *Chinese Medicine* pp.7-8, Rider 2000.

[89] Ibid. p.8.

[90] Ibid. p.8.

[91] Dr. Paul Carus, *History of the Devil and the Idea of Evil* p.18, Kessinger Publishing.

[92] R.A. Schwaller de Lubicz, *Sacred Science,* translated by André and Goldian VandenBroeck, p.192, Inner Traditions International 1988.

[93] Ibid. p.192.

[94] Ibid. p.237.

[95] H. Te Velde, *Seth, God of Confusion* p.68, E.J. Brill 1977.

[96] Ibid. pp.68-69.

[97] Ibid. p.71.

[98] Ibid. p.73.

[99] Christian Jacq, *The Living Wisdom of Ancient Egypt* p.143, Simon and Schuster U.K. Ltd. 1999.
[100] Musaios (Dr. Charles Musès), *The Lion Path* p.138, Golden Sceptre Publishing 1988.
[101] Ibid. p.83.
[102] Ibid. p.89.
[103] Ibid. p.84.
[104] Richard H. Wilkinson, *The Complete Gods and Goddesses of Ancient Egypt* p.215, Thames and Hudson 2003.
[105] Carl Kerényi, *Dionysos*, translated by Ralph Manheim, p.200, Princeton University Press 1976.
[106] Ibid. p.179.
[107] Ibid. p.xxxii.
[108] Ibid. p.xxxiv.
[109] Ibid. p.xxxv.
[110] Musaios (Dr. Charles Musès), *The Lion Path* p.44, Golden Sceptre Publishing 1988.
[111] Kenneth Demarest, *Consciousness and Reality*, edited by Charles Musès and Arthur M. Young, p.434, Outerbridge and Lazard Inc. 1972.

Chapter Thirteen
[1] John Baldwin, *Serpent and Siva Worship and Mythology in Central America, Africa and Asia and The Origin of Serpent Worship*, edited by Alexander Wilder M.D., pp.xvii-xviii, J.W. Bouton, New York 1877.
[2] James Fergusson, *Tree and Serpent Worship* p.2, Brampton: Ballantrae, Facsimile of the 1868 London edition.
[3] Alexander Wilder, *Serpent and Siva Worship and Mythology in Central America, Africa and Asia and The Origin of Serpent Worship* edited by Alexander Wilder M.D., p.iii, J.W. Bouton, New York 1877.
[4] Ibid. p.vi.
[5] Ibid. p.vi.
[6] Ibid. p.vi.
[7] Ibid. p.28.
[8] Ibid. p.28.
[9] Ibid. p.xvii.
[10] Ibid. p.xvii.

References

[11] Ibid. p.27.

[12] James Fergusson cited by C. Staniland Wake, ibid. p.36.

[13] Ibid. pp.36-37.

[14] C. Staniland Wake, ibid. pp.37-38.

[15] Ibid. p.39.

[16] E.A. Wallis Budge, *An Egyptian Hieroglyphic Dictionary* pp.260-261, Dover Publications Inc. 1978.

[17] Ibid. p.36.

[18] Ibid. p.39.

[19] Arthur Lillie, *India in Primitive Christianity* p.281, Kegan Paul, Trench, Trübner and Co. Ltd. 1909.

[20] Andrew Welburn, *The Beginnings of Christianity* p.130, Floris Books 2007.

[21] Ibid. p.131.

[22] Jean Doresse, *The Secret Books of the Egyptian Gnostics* p.264, M.J.F. Books 1986.

[23] Ibid. p84.

[24] Arthur Lillie, *India in Primitive Christianity* p.281, Kegan Paul, Trench, Trübner and Co. Ltd. 1909.

[25] Patrice Chaplin, *City of Secrets* p.261, Quest Books 2008.

[26] Andrew Welburn, *The Beginnings of Christianity* p.130, Floris Books 2007.

[27] Lao Tzu, *Tao Te Ching,* translated by D.C. Lau, p.77, Penguin Books 1963.

[28] Richard H. Wilkinson, *Symbol and Magic in Egyptian Art* p.108, Thames and Hudson 1994.

[29] Michael A. Cremo, *Human Devolution* p.428, Torchlight Publishing 2003.

[30] John Strohmeier and Peter Westbrook, *Divine Harmony* p.58, Berkeley Hills Books 2003.

[31] R.A. Schwaller de Lubicz, *The Temple of Man,* translated by Deborah Lawlor and Robert Lawlor, p.458, Inner Traditions International 1998.

[32] Ibid. p.458.

[33] Ibid. p.696.

[34] Ibid. p.467.

[35] Laurence Gardner, *Genesis of the Grail Kings* p.187, Bantam Books 2005.

[36] R.A. Schwaller de Lubicz, *The Temple of Man,* translated by Deborah Lawlor and Robert Lawlor, p.459, Inner Traditions International 1998.

[37] Laurence Gardner, *Genesis of the Grail Kings* p.185, Bantam Books 2005.

[38] R.A. Schwaller de Lubicz, *The Temple of Man,* translated by Deborah Lawlor and Robert Lawlor, p.458, Inner Traditions International 1998.

[39] Ibid. p.461.

[40] E.A. Wallis Budge, *An Egyptian Hieroglyphic Dictionary* p.652, Dover Publications Inc. 1978.

[41] Barbara G. Walker, *The Woman's Encyclopedia of Myths and Secrets* p.236, Harper San Francisco, HarperCollins Publishers 1983.

[42] Ian Shaw and Paul Nicholson, *British Museum Dictionary of Ancient Egypt* p.208, British Museum Press 1997.

[43] Musaios (Dr. Charles Musès), *The Lion Path* p.63, Golden Sceptre Publishing 1988.

[44] E.A. Wallis Budge, *The Egyptian Heaven and Hell* Vol.I pp.172, 173, 179, Dover Publications Inc. 1996.

[45] Alix Wilkinson, *The Garden in Ancient Egypt* p.2, The Rubicon Press 1998.

[46] Ibid. p.2.

[47] Ibid. p.3.

[48] Ibid. p.3.

[49] Barbara G. Walker, *The Woman's Encyclopedia of Myths and Secrets* p.718, Harper San Francisco, HarperCollins Publishers 1983.

[50] Barbara G. Walker, *The Woman's Dictionary of Symbols and Sacred Objects* p.430, Harper San Francisco, HarperCollins Publishers 1988.

[51] Ibid. p.430.

[52] R.A. Schwaller de Lubicz, *The Temple of Man*, translated by Deborah Lawlor and Robert Lawlor, p.461, Inner Traditions International 1998.

[53] Richard H. Wilkinson, *Symbol and Magic in Egyptian Art* p.108, Thames and Hudson 1994.

[54] Ibid. p.108.

[55] Ibid. p.109.

[56] Christian Jacq, *The Living Wisdom of Ancient Egypt* p.147, Simon and Schuster U.K. Ltd. 1999.

[57] Barbara G. Walker, *The Woman's Dictionary of Symbols and Sacred Objects* p.510, Harper San Francisco, HarperCollins Publishers 1988.

[58] Philip Gardiner with Gary Osborn, *The Serpent Grail* p.118, Watkins Publishing 2005.

[59] H.A. Guerber, *Legends of the Middle Ages* p.211, BiblioBazaar 2006.

[60] J. Liebovitch cited by H. Te Velde, *Seth, God of Confusion* p.21, E.J. Brill 1977.

[61] H. Te Velde, ibid. p.21.

References

[62] Barbara G. Walker, *The Woman's Encyclopedia of Myths and Secrets* p.910, Harper San Francisco, HarperCollins Publishers 1983.

[63] C. Staniland Wake, *Serpent and Siva Worship and Mythology in Central America, Africa and Asia and The Origin of Serpent Worship*, edited by Alexander Wilder, p.45, J.W. Bouton 1877.

[64] A.F.J. Klijn, *Seth in Jewish, Christian and Gnostic Literature* pp.109-110, E.J. Brill 1977.

[65] Ibid. p.83.

[66] Jean Doresse, *The Secret Books of the Egyptian Gnostics* p.105, M.F.J. Books 1986.

[67] Barbara G. Walker, *The Woman's Encyclopedia of Myths and Secrets* p.69, Harper San Francisco, HarperCollins Publishers 1983.

[68] Ibid. p.424.

[69] M.A. Murry cited by H. Te Velde, *Seth, God of Confusion* p.6, E.J. Brill 1977.

[70] Ibid. p.6.

[71] H. Te Velde, ibid. p.7.

[72] A.F.J. Klijn, *Seth in Jewish, Christian and Gnostic Literature* p.92, E.J. Brill 1977.

[73] Ibid. p.92.

[74] Ibid. p.113.

[75] Ibid. p.113.

[76] Ibid. p.89.

[77] Joscelyn Godwin, *Mystery Religions in the Ancient World* p.133, Thames and Hudson 1981.

[78] Elizabeth Leader cited by Oliver L. Reiser, *This Holyest Erthe* p.96, Perennial Books 1974.

[79] Patrick Holford and James Braly, *The H. Factor* pp.213-214, Piatkus, a division of Little, Brown Book Club 2003.

[80] Laurence Gardner, *Genesis of the Grail Kings* p.178, Bantam Books 2005.

[81] Ibid. p.120.

[82] Ibid. p.119.

[83] Ibid. p.120.

[84] Ibid. p.194.

[85] Ibid. p.197.

[86] Ibid. pp.184-185.

[87] Ibid. pp.185-187.

[88] H. Te Velde, *Seth, God of Confusion* pp.5-6, E.J. Brill 1977.

[89] Ibid. p.90.

[90] Ibid. p.90.

[91] Ibid. pp.83-84.

[92] Ibid. p.85.

[93] H. Frankfort cited by H. Te Velde, ibid. p.91.

[94] Charles Musès, *Destiny and Control in Human Systems* pp.65-66, Kluwer-Nijhoff Publishing 1985.

[95] Ibid. p.69.

[96] Ibid. p.89 Note 24.

[97] Lao Tzu, *Tao Te Ching,* translated by D.C. Lau, p.47, Penguin Books 1963.

[98] Oscar Wilde cited by Barbara G. Walker, *The Woman's Encyclopedia of Myths and Secrets* p.766, Harper San Francisco 1983.

[99] Charles Musès, 'Jacob Boehme – Philosopher', *The Jacob Boehme Society Quarterly* Vol.I No.1 Autumn 1952 p.11.

[100] E.A. Wallis Budge, *An Egyptian Hieroglyphic Dictionary* p.395, Dover Publications Inc. 1978.

Chapter Fourteen

[1] Richard H. Wilkinson, *Reading Egyptian Art* p.101, Thames and Hudson 2003.

[2] Alan Gardiner cited by Ian Shaw and Paul Nicholson, *British Museum Dictionary of Ancient Egypt* p.305, British Museum Press 1997.

[3] Jacob Boehme cited by Charles Musès,'Excerpts from The Way of a Pilgrim', *The Jacob Boehme Society Quarterly* Vol.I No.2 Winter 1952–3 p.18.

[4] Synesius cited by J. Bregman, *Synesius of Cyrene* p.21, University of California Press 1982.

[5] Synesius, *On Dreams,* translated by Isaac Myer (1888) pp.20–21, Kessinger Publishing.

[6] Dr. Manjir Samanta-Laughton, *Punk Science* pp.74–75, O Books 2006.

[7] Ibid. p.75.

[8] Ibid. pp.75-76.

[9] Stella Kramrisch, *The Presence of Śiva* p.250, Princeton University Press 1992.

[10] André VandenBroeck, *Al-Kemi* p.8, Lindisfarne Press 1987.

[11] Ibid. p.43.

[12] Musaios (Dr. Charles Musès), *The Lion Path* p.113, Golden Sceptre Publishing 1988.

[13] Ibid. pp.43-44.

[14] Ibid. p.57.

References

[15] Synesius, *On Dreams,* translated by Isaac Myer (1888) p.2, Kessinger Publishing.

[16] Barbara G. Walker, *The Woman's Encyclopedia of Myths and Secrets* p.874, Harper San Francisco, HarperCollins Publishers 1983.

[17] E.A. Wallis Budge, *An Egyptian Hieroglyphic Dictionary* p.588, Dover Publications Inc. 1978.

[18] *The Supplement to the Compact Edition of the Oxford English Dictionary,* edited by Burchfield, p.180, Oxford University Press 1987.

[19] *The Compact Edition of the Oxford English Dictionary,* edited by Burchfield, p.1852, Oxford University Press 1987.

[20] Musaios (Dr. Charles Musès), *The Lion Path* p.91, Golden Sceptre Publishing 1988.

[21] Ibid. p.83.

[22] Charles Musès, *In All Her Names,* edited by Joseph Campbell and Charles Musès, p.131, Harper San Francisco 1991.

[23] Ibid. p.131.

[24] Musaios (Dr. Charles Musès), *The Lion Path* p.93, Golden Sceptre Publishing 1988.

[25] Ibid. p.57.

[26] Richard H. Wilkinson, *The Complete Gods and Goddesses of Ancient Egypt* p.188, Thames and Hudson 2003.

[27] E.A. Wallis Budge, *An Egyptian Hieroglyphic Dictionary* p.19, Dover Publications Inc., 1978.

[28] Musaios (Dr. Charles Musès), *The Lion Path* p.8, Golden Sceptre Publishing 1988.

[29] Christian Jacq, *The Living Wisdom of Ancient Egypt* p.143, Simon and Schuster U.K. Ltd. 1999.

[30] Synesius, *On Dreams,* translated by Isaac Myer (1888), p.8, Kessinger Publishing.

[31] Ibid. p.7.

[32] Musaios (Dr. Charles Musès), *The Lion Path* pp.91–92, Golden Sceptre Publishing 1988.

[33] E.A. Wallis Budge, *An Egyptian Hieroglyphic Dictionary* p.664, Dover Publications Inc. 1978.

[34] C. Staniland Wake, *Serpent and Siva Worship and Mythology in Central America, Africa and Asia and The Origin of Serpent Worship* p.39, J.W. Bouton 1877.

[35] Barbara G. Walker, *The Woman's Encyclopedia of Myths and Secrets* p.454, Harper San Francisco, HarperCollins Publishers 1983.

[36] Ibid. p.453.

37 E.A. Wallis Budge, *An Egyptian Hieroglyphic Dictionary* pp.323–324, Dover Publications Inc. 1978.

38 A.J.F. Klijn, *Seth in Jewish, Christian and Gnostic Literature* p.98, E.J. Brill 1977.

39 Barbara G. Walker, *The Woman's Encyclopedia of Myths and Secrets* p.905, Harper San Francisco, HarperCollins Publishers 1983.

40 Philip Gardiner with Gary Osborn, *The Serpent Grail* p.231, Watkins 2005.

41 Barbara G. Walker, *The Woman's Encyclopedia of Myths and Secrets* p.895, Harper San Francisco, HarperCollins Publishers 1983.

42 Ibid. pp.894-895.

43 John Milton, *Paradise Lost, The Major Works* p.440, Oxford University Press 2003.

44 Barbara G. Walker, *The Woman's Encylopedia of Myths and Secrets* p.232, Harper San Francisco, HarperCollins Publishers 1983.

45 Philip Gardiner with Gary Osborn, *The Serpent Grail* p.138, Watkins 2005.

46 Barbara G. Walker, *The Woman's Encyclopedia of Myths and Secrets* p.906, Harper San Francisco, HarperCollins Publishers 1983.

47 E.A. Wallis Budge, *An Egyptian Hieroglyphic Dictionary* p.596, Dover Publications Inc. 1978.

48 Ibid. p.130.

49 Ibid. pp.237-238.

50 Ibid. p.337.

51 *The Compact Edition of the Oxford English Dictionary,* edited by Burchfield, p.1612, Oxford University Press 1987.

52 Lewis Spence, *The Mysteries of Britain* p.43, Rider.

53 Ibid. p.43.

54 Ibid. p.50.

55 Ibid. p.86.

56 Juliette Wood, *The Celtic Book of Living and Dying* p.56, Duncan Baird Publishers 2000.

57 Barbara G. Walker, *The Woman's Encyclopedia of Myths and Secrets* p.46, Harper San Francisco, HarperCollins Publishers 1983.

58 Ibid. p.46.

59 Ibid. p.2.

60 Richard H. Wilkinson, *The Complete Gods and Goddesses of Ancient Egypt* p.221, Thames and Hudson 2003.

References

[61] Barbara G. Walker, *The Woman's Encyclopedia of Myths and Secrets* p.908, Harper San Francisco, HarperCollins Publishers 1983.

[62] *The Compact Edition of the Oxford English Dictionary,* edited by Burchfeild, p.2427, Oxford University Press 1987.

[63] Ibid. p.2453.

[64] *The New Shorter Oxford English Dictionary,* edited by Brown, p.2513, Oxford University Press 1993.

[65] Barbara G. Walker, *The Woman's Encyclopedia of Myths and Secrets* p.856, Harper, San Francisco, HarperCollins Publishers 1983.

[66] Ibid. p.201.

[67] Ibid. p.856.

[68] Euripides cited by Patricia Cox Miller, *Dreams in Late Antiquity* p.217, Princeton University Press 1994.

[69] Miranda J. Green, *Dictionary of Celtic Myth and Legend* p.166, Thames and Hudson 1997.

[70] Daphne Phillips, *The Story of Reading* p.54, Countryside Books 2004.

[71] Peter Kingsley, *In The Dark Places of Wisdom* pp.91-92, Element Books 1999.

[72] Patricia Cox Miller, *Dreams in Late Antiquity* p.106, Princeton University Press 1994.

[73] E.A. Wallis Budge, *An Egyptian Hieroglyphic Dictionary* p.480, Dover Publications Inc. 1978.

[74] Barbara G. Walker, *The Woman's Encyclopedia of Myths and Secrets* p.903, Harper San Francisco, HarperCollins Publishers 1983.

[75] Ibid. p.256.

[76] Ibid. p.58.

[77] Ibid. p.39.

[78] Ibid. p.39.

[79] Ibid. p.39.

[80] Ibid. p.39.

[81] Ibid. p.39.

[82] Ibid. p.253.

[83] Ibid. p.951.

[84] Ibid. p.951.

[85] E.A. Wallis Budge, *The Gods of the Egyptians* Vol.2 p.220, Dover Publications 1969.

[86] Lewis Spence, *The Mysteries of Britain* p.94, Rider.

[87] Arthur Edward Waite, *The Hidden Church of the Holy Grail* pp.176-177, Fredonia Books 2002, cited by Lewis Spence, ibid. pp.140-141.

[88] Ean Begg, *The Cult of the Black Virgin* p.64, Chiron Publications 2006.

[89] Ibid. pp.62-63.

[90] Jean Markale, *Cathedral of the Black Madonna* p.13, Inner Traditions International 2004.

[91] E.A. Wallis Budge, *The Gods of the Egyptians* Vol.2 p.258, Dover Publications 1969.

[92] *I Ching*, The Richard Wilhelm Translation, p.318, Routledge and Kegan Paul 1968.

[93] E.A. Wallis Budge, *The Gods of the Egyptians* Vol.II p.264, London 1904.

[94] E.A. Wallis Budge, *The Gods of the Egyptians* Vol.2 p.258, Dover Publications 1969.

[95] Ibid. p.258.

[96] Lewis Spence, *The Mysteries of Britain* p.216, Rider.

[97] Ibid. p.216.

[98] Ibid. p.216.

[99] Ibid. pp.172-173.

[100] Miranda J. Green, *Dictionary of Celtic Myth and Legend* p.166, Thames and Hudson 1997.

[101] Lewis Spence, *The Mysteries of Britain* p.174, Rider.

[102] Ibid. p.247.

[103] Ibid. p.237.

[104] Peter Tompkins, *Secrets of the Great Pyramid* pp.139-140, Harper and Row, HarperCollins Publishers 1971.

[105] Michael Howard, *The Occult Conspiracy* p.89, Destiny Books 1989.

[106] Hekekyan Bey, *On Egyptian Chronology* p.v, printed by Taylor and Francis for private circulation, London 1863.

[107] R.T. Rundle Clark, *Myth and Symbol in Ancient Egypt* p.109, Thames and Hudson 1993.

[108] Ibid. p109.

[109] Ibid. p.91.

[110] Ibid. p.90.

[111] R.A. Schwaller de Lubicz, *Sacred Science,* translated by André and Goldian VandenBroeck, p. 151, Inner Traditions International 1988.

[112] James Cowan, *Aborigine Dreaming* p.18, Thorsons 1992.

References

[113] Ibid. p.18.

[114] Geraldine Pinch, *Egyptian Mythology* p.192, Oxford University Press 2002.

[115] Kenneth Demarest, *Consciousness and Reality,* edited by Charles Musès and Arthur M. Young, p.377, Outerbridge and Lazard Inc. 1972.

[116] Barbara G. Walker, *The Woman's Encyclopedia of Myths and Secrets* p.74, Harper San Francisco, HarperCollins Publishers 1983.

[117] Giorgio de Santillana and Hertha von Dechend, *Hamlet's Mill* p.447, Godine 2005.

[118] Barbara G. Walker, *The Woman's Dictionary of Symbols and Sacred Objects* p.476, Harper San Francisco, HarperCollins Publishers 1988.

[119] Robert Briffault, *The Mothers* Vol.II p.649, Macmillan, New York 1927.

[120] Juliette Wood, *The Celtic Book of Living and Dying* p.85, Duncan Baird Publishers 2000.

[121] Ibid. p.86.

[122] H. Te Velde, *Seth, God of Confusion* p.21, E.J. Brill 1977.

[123] Ibid. p.25.

[124] Ibid. p.94.

[125] Ibid. p.92.

[126] Ian Shaw and Paul Nicholson, *British Museum Dictionary of Ancient Egypt* p.45, British Museum Press 1997.

[127] H. Te Velde, *Seth, God of Confusion* p.81, E.J. Brill 1977.

[128] Jane Ellen Harrison, *Epilegomena to the Study of Greek Religion and Themis* p.483, University Books 1927.

[129] Ibid. pp.481-482.

[130] Barbara G. Walker, *The Woman's Encyclopedia of Myths and Secrets* p.46, Harper San Francisco, HarperCollins Publishers 1983.

[131] Robert Briffault, *The Mothers* Vol.III p.154, Macmillan, New York 1927.

[132] Peter Kingsley, *Ancient Philosophy, Mystery, and Magic* p.283, Clarendon Paperbacks, Oxford University Press 1996.

[133] R.A. Schwaller de Lubicz, *Sacred Science,* translated by André and Goldian VandenBroeck, p.145, Inner Traditions International 1988.

[134] Ibid. p.145.

[135] *The Compact Edition of the Oxford English Dictionary,* edited by Burchfield, p.1431, Oxford University Press 1987.

[136] Lewis Spence, *The Mysteries of Britain* p.242, Rider.

[137] Ibid. pp.242-243.

[138] Gillian Clark, *Down by the River* p.3, Two Rivers Press 2009.

[139] E.A. Wallis Budge, *Osiris and the Egyptian Resurrection* Vol.I p.xv, New York 1911.

[140] E.A. Wallis Budge, *The Gods of the Egyptians* Vol.I p.333, London 1904.

[141] Robert Briffault, *The Mothers* Vol.II p.762, Macmillan, New York 1927.

[142] A. Wiedemann, *Agyptische Geschichte,* Vol.I, pp.44 sq., cited by Robert Briffault, ibid. p.765.

[143] Robert Briffault, ibid. p.765.

[144] Ibid. pp.770-771.

[145] Ibid. pp.772-773.

[146] E.A. Wallis Budge, *Osiris and the Egyptian Resurrection* Vol.I p.p.viii and xv, cited by Robert Briffault, ibid. p.773.

[147] Erik Hornung, *The Ancient Egyptian Books of the Afterlife* p.33, Cornell University Press 1999.

[148] Ibid. p.34.

[149] E.A. Wallis Budge, *The Gods of the Egyptians* Vol.2 p.49, Dover Publications 1969.

[150] Ibid. p.55.

[151] Ibid. p.50.

[152] Geraldine Pinch, *Egyptian Mythology* p.154, Oxford University Press 2002.

[153] Musaios (Dr. Charles Musès), *The Lion Path* p.40, Golden Sceptre Publishing 1988.

[154] E.A. Wallis Budge, *The Gods of the Egyptians* Vol.2 p.50, Dover Publications 1969.

[155] E.A. Wallis Budge, *An Egyptian Hieroglyphic Dictionary* p.314, Dover Publications Inc. 1978.

[156] Richard H. Wilkinson, *Symbol and Magic in Egyptian Art* pp.83-84, Thames and Hudson 1984.

[157] R.A. Schwaller de Lubicz, *Sacred Science,* translated by André and Goldian VandenBroeck, p.99, Inner Traditions International 1988.

[158] Jack Lindsay, *Men and Gods on the Roman Nile* p.73, Frederick Muller 1968.

[159] Ibid. p.73.

[160] Edward R. Dewey, *Cycles* p.58, Hawthorn Books Inc. 1971.

[161] E.A. Wallis Budge, *An Egyptian Hieroglyphic Dictionary,* p.579, Dover Publications Inc. 1978.

Chapter Fifteen

[1] *The Compact Edition of the Oxford English Dictionary,* edited by Burchfield, p.2456, Oxford University Press 1987.

References

[2] Dr. Martin Schönberger, *The I Ching and the Genetic Code* p.75, Aurora Press 1992.

[3] Ibid. p.92.

[4] Ibid. p.94.

[5] Ibid. p.29.

[6] *I Ching*, The Richard Wilhelm Translation, p.244, Routledge and Kegan Paul 1968.

[7] Charles Musès, *In All Her Names*, edited by Joseph Campbell and Charles Musès, p.143, Harper San Francisco 1991.

[8] Ibid. p.143.

[9] Ibid. p.143.

[10] Ibid. p.143.

[11] Ibid. p.143.

[12] Edward H. Schafer, *Pacing the Void* p.53, Floating World Editions 2005.

[13] Charles Musès, *In All Her Names*, edited by Joseph Campbell and Charles Musès, p.148, Harper San Francisco 1991.

[14] Ibid. p.143.

[15] Ibid. p.148.

[16] Ibid. p.149.

[17] Eva Wong, *The Shambala Guide to Taoism* p.12, Shambala 1997.

[18] Ibid. p.15.

[19] Livia Kohn, *The Taoist Experience* pp.271-276, State University of New York Press 1993.

[20] *I Ching*, The Richard Wilhelm Translation, pp.24-25, Routledge and Kegan Paul 1968.

[21] Charles Musès, *Consciousness and Reality,* edited by Charles Musès and Arthur M. Young, pp.128-129, Outerbridge and Lazard Inc. 1972.

[22] Charles Musès, *Astrologia* Vol.1 No.1 1974 p.21.

[23] John Major Jenkins, *Galactic Alignment* p.2, Bear and Company 2002.

[24] Charles Musès, *Consciousness and Reality,* edited by Charles Musès and Arthur M. Young, pp.92-93, Outerbridge and Lazard Inc. 1972.

[25] E.A. Wallis Budge, *An Egyptian Hieroglyphic Dictionary* p.663, Dover Publications Inc. 1978.

[26] Christian Jacq, *The Living Wisdom of Ancient Egypt* p.99, Simon and Schuster U.K. Ltd. 1999.

[27] Riane Eisler, *The Chalice and the Blade* p.43, HarperCollins Publishers 1987.

[28] Marija Gimbutas, 'Beginning of the Bronze Age' p.201, cited by Riane Eisler, ibid. p.49.

[29] Ibid. p.48.

[30] Riane Eisler, ibid. p.51.

[31] Riane Eisler, *In All Her Names*, edited Joseph Campbell and Charles Musès, p.13, Harper San Francisco 1991.

[32] Riane Eisler, *The Chalice and the Blade* p.42, HarperCollins Publishers 1987.

[33] Ibid. pp.43-44.

[34] Marija Gimbutas, 'The First Wave of Eurasian Steppe Pastoralists into Copper Age Europe', *Journal of Indo-European Studies* 5 (Winter 1977): 277, cited by Riane Eisler, ibid. p.44.

[35] Riane Eisler, ibid. p.44.

[36] Ibid. p.44.

[37] Barbara G. Walker, *The Woman's Encyclopedia of Myths and Secrets* p.751, Harper San Francisco, HarperCollins Publishers 1983.

[38] Ibid. p.12.

[39] Ibid. p.12.

[40] R.A. Schwaller de Lubicz, *Sacred Science*, translated by André and Goldian VandenBroeck, p.86, Inner Traditions International 1988.

[41] Barbara G. Walker, *The Woman's Encyclopedia of Myths and Secrets* p.632, Harper San Francisco, HarperCollins Publishers 1983.

[42] Riane Eisler, *In All Her Names*, edited by Joseph Campbell and Charles Musès, p.4, Harper San Francisco 1991.

[43] H. Te Velde, *Seth, God of Confusion* p.77, E.J. Brill 1977.

[44] Ibid. p.62.

[45] Ibid. p.147.

[46] Riane Eisler, *The Chalice and the Blade* pp.44-45, HarperCollins Publishers 1987.

[47] H. Te Velde, *Seth, God of Confusion* p.95, E.J. Brill 1977.

[48] Ibid. p.138.

[49] Barbara G. Walker, *The Woman's Encyclopedia of Myths and Secrets* p.561, Harper San Francisco, HarperCollins Publishers 1983.

[50] E.A. Wallis Budge, *Dwellers on the Nile* p.254, Dover Publications Inc. 1977, cited by Barbara G. Walker, ibid. pp.561-562.

[51] Barbara G. Walker, ibid. p.562.

[52] Musaios (Dr. Charles Musès), *The Lion Path* p.39, Golden Sceptre Publishing 1988.

References

[53] Wendy Doniger O'Flaherty, *Dreams, Illusion and Other Realities* p.142, The University of Chicago Press 1986.

[54] Graham Hancock, *Fingerprints of the Gods* p.361, Century Books 2001.

[55] Ibid. p.377.

Chapter Sixteen

[1] Riane Eisler, *In All Her Names,* edited by Joseph Campbell and Charles Musès, p.4, Harper San Francisco 1991.

[2] Ibid. p.5.

[3] John Cowper Powys cited by Charles Musès, ibid. p.2.

[4] Charles Musès, ibid. p.139.

[5] Philip Gardiner with Gary Osborn, *The Serpent Grail* p.297, Watkins Publishing 2005.

[6] E.A. Wallis Budge, *An Egyptian Hieroglyphic Dictionary* pp.331-332, Dover Publications Inc. 1978.

[7] Ibid. p.332.

[8] Musaios (Dr.Charles Musès), *The Lion Path* p.20, Golden Sceptre Publishing 1988.

[9] Charles Musès, 'The Shamanic Way in Ancient Egypt', *Proceedings of the Fourth International Conference on the Study of Shamanism and Alternate Modes of Healing* p.180, Independent Scholars of Asia 1988.

[10] Ibid. p.180.

[11] E.A. Wallis Budge, *An Egyptian Hieroglyphic Dictionary* p.300, Dover Publications Inc. 1978.

[12] Barbara G. Walker, *The Woman's Encyclopedia of Myths and Secrets* p.670, Harper San Francisco, HarperCollins Publishers 1983.

[13] E.A. Wallis Budge, *An Egyptian Hieroglyphic Dictionary* p.189, Dover Publications Inc. 1978.

[14] Charles Musès, *Consciousness and Reality,* edited by Charles Musès and Arthur M. Young, p.128, Outerbridge and Lazard Inc. 1972.

[15] Ernest Cushing Richardson, *Old Egyptian Librarians* p.15, Princeton University Press 1911.

[16] Ibid. pp.15-17.

[17] Ibid. p.17.

[18] Ibid. p.17.

[19] Ibid. pp.17-18.

20 Ibid. p.18.

21 Ibid. p.65.

22 Ibid. p.63.

23 Ibid. pp.76-77.

24 Ibid. p.80.

25 J.D. Ray, *The Archive of Hor* p.18, Egypt Exploration Society 1976.

26 Barbara G. Walker, *The Woman's Encyclopedia of Myths and Secrets* p.904, Harper San Francisco, HarperCollins Publishers 1983.

27 Ibid. p.996.

28 Ibid. p.996.

29 *The Compact Edition of the Oxford English Dictionary*, edited by Burchfield, p.2807, Oxford University Press 1987.

30 Angela Sumegi, *Dream Worlds of Shamanism and Tibetan Buddhism* p.49, State University of New York Press 2008.

31 Ibid. p.57.

32 Ibid. p.57.

33 Ibid. p.2.

34 *The Hundred Thousand Songs of Milarepa*, translated by Garma C.C. Chang ,Vol.2 p.483-484, Shambhala Publications 1977.

35 Angela Sumegi, *Dream Worlds of Shamanism and Tibetan Buddhism* p.57, State University of New York Press 2008.

36 Ibid. p.57.

37 Ibid. p.67.

38 Ibid. p.68.

39 Wendy Doniger O'Flaherty, *Dreams, Illusion and Other Realities* p. 37, University of Chicago 1986.

40 Angela Sumegi, *Dream Worlds of Shamanism and Tibetan Buddhism* p.68, State University of New York Press 2008.

41 George J. Tanabe Jr., *Myōe the Dreamkeeper*, The Council on East Asian Studies, Harvard University 1992

42 G. de Purucker, *Occult Glossary* pp.33-34, Rider and Co. 1933.

43 Sir Monier Monier-Williams, *A Sanskrit-English Dictionary* p.734, Motilal Banarsidass Publishers 2005.

44 Kenneth Demarest, *Consciousness and Reality*, edited by Charles Musès and Arthur M. Young, p.373, Outerbridge and Lazard Inc. 1973.

45 Ibid. p.361.

References

[46] Lama Anagarika Govinda, *Foundations of Tibetan Mysticism* p.81, Rider and Co. 1959.
[47] F.D.K. Bosch, *The Golden Germ* p.123, Munshiram Manoharlal Publishers 1994.
[48] Lao Tzu, *Tao Te Ching*, translated by D.C. Lau, p.10, Penguin Books 1963.

Chapter Seventeen

[1] Synesius, *On Dreams*, translated by Isaac Myer (1888) p.5, Kessinger Publishing.
[2] Charles Musès, *Consciousness and Reality*, edited by Charles Musès and Arthur M. Young, p.128, Outerbridge and Lazard Inc. 1972.
[3] Duncan Macnoughton, *A Scheme of Egyptian Chronology* p.29, Luzac and Co. 1932 (Charles Musès' copy in possession of the author).
[4] Richard H. Wilkinson, *The Complete Gods and Goddesses of Ancient Egypt* p.150, Thames and Hudson 2003.
[5] Ibid. p.150.
[6] Christian Jacq, *The Living Wisdom of Ancient Egypt* pp.11-12, Simon and Schuster U.K. Ltd. 1999.
[7] Ibid. p.23.
[8] Charles Musès, *Proceedings of the Fourth International Conference on the Study of Shamanism and Alternate Modes of Healing* p.189, Independent Scholars of Asia 1988.
[9] Ibid. p.189.
[10] Ibid. p.187.
[11] Ibid. p.187.
[12] Musaios (Dr. Charles Musès), *The Lion Path* p.118, Golden Sceptre Publishing 1988.
[13] R.A. Schwaller de Lubicz, *Sacred Science*, translated by André and Goldian VandenBroeck, p.28, Inner Traditions International 1988.
[14] Lucie Lamy, *Egyptian Mysteries*, translated by Deborah Lawlor, p.17, Thames and Hudson 1994.
[15] R.A. Schwaller de Lubicz cited by Lucie Lamy, ibid. p.18.
[16] Amit Goswami, *The Self-Aware Universe* p.10, Jeremy P. Tarcher/Putnam 1995.
[17] Ibid. p.11.
[18] Ibid. p.11.
[19] Lucie Lamy, *Egyptian Mysteries*, translated by Deborah Lawlor, p.17, Thames and Hudson 1994.
[20] Oliver L. Reiser, *Cosmic Humanism and World Unity* p.43, Interface/Gordon and Breach 1975.

21 Christian Jacq, *The Living Wisdom of Ancient Egypt* p.51, Simon and Schuster U.K. Ltd. 1999.

22 Stella Kramrisch, *The Presence of Śiva* p.44, Princeton University Press 1992.

23 Ibid. p.34.

24 Ibid. p.20.

25 Ibid. p.20.

26 Ibid. p.90.

27 Ibid. p.75.

28 Oliver L. Reiser, *Cosmic Humanism and World Unity* p.112, Interface/Gordon and Breach 1975.

29 Ibid. pp.114-115.

30 Ibid. p.113.

31 Dante, *The Divine Comedy,* translated by Longfellow, cited by Kenneth Demarest, *Consciousness and Reality,* edited by Charles Musès and Arthur M. Young, p.433, Outerbridge and Lazard Inc. 1972.

32 Kenneth Demarest, ibid. p.433.

33 Dante, *The Divine Comedy,* translated by Longfellow, cited by Kenneth Demarest, ibid. p.433.

34 Raymond de Becker, *The Understanding of Dreams* p.105, Hawthorn Books 1968.

35 Kenneth Demarest, *Consciousness and Reality,* edited by Charles Musès and Arthur M. Young, p.432, Outerbridge and Lazard Inc. 1972.

36 Ibid. p.432.

37 Ajit Mookerjee, *Yoga Art* p.73, Thames and Hudson 1975.

38 Christian Jacq, *The Living Wisdom of Ancient Egypt* p.153, Simon and Schuster U.K. Ltd. 1999.

39 Patricia Cox Miller, *Dreams in Late Antiquity* p.113, Princeton University Press 1994.

40 Wendy Doniger O'Flaherty, *Dreams, Illusion and Other Realities* p.121, University of Chicago Press 1986.

41 Musaios (Dr. Charles Musès), *The Lion Path* p.57, Golden Sceptre Publishing 1988.

42 Ibid. p.44.

43 Ibid. p.31.

44 Ibn Arabi cited by Peter Lamborn Wilson, *'Shower of Stars' Dream and Book* p.49, Autonomedia 1996.

References

[45] Patricia Cox Miller, *Dreams in Late Antiquity* p.62, Princeton University Press 1994.

[46] Ibid. p.62.

[47] Ibid. p.62.

[48] Carl Kerényi, *Dionysos* p.79, Princeton University Press 1996.

[49] Walter Burket, *Ancient Mystery Cults* p.41, Harvard University Press 1987.

[50] Raymond de Becker, *The Understanding of Dreams* pp.172-173, Hawthorn Books 1968.

[51] Paracelsus, *De Fundamento Sapientiae*, *The Jacob Boehme Society Quarterly* Vol.I No.1 p.32, Autumn 1952.

[52] Ibid. p32.

[53] R.D. Laing, *The Politics of Experience* p.114, Penguin Books 1967.

[54] Paracelsus, *De Fundamento Sapientiae*, *The Jacob Boehme Society Quarterly* Vol.I No.1 p.32, Autumn 1952.

[55] Laurens van der Post, *Jung and the Story of Our Time* p.9, Penguin Books 1978.

[56] Joseph Campbell, *The Mythic Image* p.1, Princeton University Press 1990.

[57] Lao Tzu, *Tao Te Ching,* translated by D.C. Lau, p.18, Penguin Books 1963.

[58] Charles Musès, *Destiny and Control in Human Systems* pp.54-55, Kluwer-Nijhoff Publishing 1985.

[59] Synesius, *On Dreams,* translated by Isaac Myer (1888), p.23, Kessinger Publishing.

[60] Free rendition from the Ancient Egyptian *Book of the Dead,* translated by Normandi Ellis, cited by Robert Bauval and Graham Hancock, *Keeper of Genesis* p.283, Arrow Books 1997.

[61] Musaios (Dr. Charles Musès), *The Lion Path* p.43, Golden Sceptre Publishing 1988.

343

Acknowledgements

Every effort has been made to trace the copyright holders of material reproduced in this book where required. Should any error or omission in acknowledgement have been made, the author offers his apologies.

Permission to reprint from the following works is gratefully acknowledged:

From *Myth and Symbol in Ancient Egypt* by R.T. Rundle Clark. © 1978. Reprinted by kind permission of Thames & Hudson Ltd.
From *Egyptian Mysteries* by Lucie Lamy. © 1981 Lucie Lamy. Reprinted by kind permission of Thames & Hudson Ltd.
From *Mystery Religions in the Ancient World* by Joscelyn Godwin. © 1981 Thames & Hudson Ltd., London. Reprinted by kind permission of Thames & Hudson Ltd.
From *The Complete Gods and Goddesses of Ancient Egypt* by Richard H. Wilkinson. © Text 2003 Richard H. Wilkinson. Reprinted by kind permission of Thames & Hudson Ltd.
From *Symbol and Magic in Ancient Egypt* by Richard H. Wilkinson. © 1994 Thames & Hudson Ltd., London. Reprinted by kind permission of Thames & Hudson Ltd.
From *Dictionary of Celtic Myth and Legend* by Miranda J. Green. © 1992 Thames & Hudson Ltd., London. Reprinted by kind permission of Thames & Hudson Ltd.
From *Yoga Art* by Ajit Mookerjee. © 1975 Thames & Hudson Ltd., London. Reprinted by kind permission of Thames & Hudson Ltd.
From *Chinese Medicine* by Ted J. Kaptchuk, published by Rider. Reprinted by permission of The Random House Group Ltd.

Acknowledgements

From *The Search for Omm Sety* by Jonathan Cott, published by Rider. Reprinted by permission of The Random House Group Ltd.

From *The Closing of the Western Mind* by Charles Freeman, published by Pimlico. Reprinted by permission of The Random House Group Ltd.

From *AD 381* by Charles Freeman, published by Pimlico. Reprinted by permission of The Random House Group Ltd. (Copyright © Charles Freeman, 2008) Reprinted by kind permission of A.M. Heath & Co. Ltd.

From *The Fingerprints of the Gods* by Graham Hancock, published by William Heinemann. Reprinted by permission of The Random House Group Ltd. (Copyright © Graham Hancock, 1995) Reprinted by kind permission of A.M. Heath & Co. Ltd.

From *The Standard Edition of the Complete Psychological Works of Sigmund Freud,* translated and edited by James Strachey, published by The Hogarth Press. Reprinted by permission of The Random House Group Ltd.

From *Jung and the Story of Our Time* by Laurens van der Post, published by The Hogarth Press. Reprinted by permission of The Random House Group Ltd.

From *Feather Fall* by Laurens van der Post, edited by Jean-Marc Pottiez, published by The Hogarth Press. Reprinted by permission of The Random House Group Ltd.

From *Genesis of the Grail Kings* by Laurence Gardner, published by Bantam Books. Reprinted by permission of The Random House Group Ltd.

From *Egyptian Magic* by Christian Jacq, translated by Janet M. Davis, published by Aris & Phillips 1985. Copyright © C. Jacq 1985. Reprinted by permission of Aris & Phillips.

From *Opening the Dragon Gate* by Chen Kaiguo and Zeng Shunchao, translated by Thomas Cleary, Tuttle Publishing 1996. Reprinted with the express permission of Tuttle Publishing.

From *Dreams, Illusion and Other Realities* by Wendy Doniger O'Flaherty. Copyright © 1984 by the University of Chicago. Reprinted by permission of the University of Chicago.

From *British Museum Dictionary of Ancient Egypt* by Ian Shaw and Paul Nicholson. Copyright © British Museum Press 1995. Reprinted by permission of the British Museum Press and the Trustees of the British Museum.

From *Serpent in the Sky* by John Anthony West. Copyright © 1993 Quest Books. This material was reproduced by permission of Quest Books, the imprint of The Theosophical Publishing House. www.questbooks.net.

Acknowledgements

The Temple in Man by R.A. Schwaller de Lubicz, Rochester, VT © 1977 Inner Traditions/Bear & Co., originally published in France © 1949. Reprinted by permission of Inner Traditions/Bear & Co.

Cathedral of the Black Madonna by Jean Markale, Rochester, VT © 2004 Inner Traditions/Bear & Co., originally published © 1988 Éditions Pygmalion/Gérard Watelet. Reprinted by permission of Inner Traditions/Bear & Co.

The Complete I Ching translated by Taoist Master Alfred Huang, Rochester, VT © 1998, 2004 Inner Traditions/Bear & Co. Reprinted by permission of Inner Traditions/ Bear & Co.

Galactic Alignment by John Major Jenkins, Bear & Company, Rochester, VT © 2002 Inner Traditions/Bear & Co. Reprinted by permission of Inner Traditions/Bear & Co.

The Secret Books of the Egyptian Gnostics by Jean Doresse, Rochester, VT © 1986 Inner Traditions/Bear & Co., originally published © 1958 Librairie Plon. Reprinted by permission of Inner Traditions/Bear & Co.

Sacred Science by R.A. Schwaller de Lubicz, translated by André and Goldian VandenBroeck. English translation © 1982 by Inner Traditions International, originally published © 1961 by Flammarion. Reprinted by permission of Inner Traditions/Bear & Co.

G.E. von Grunebaum, Roger Caillois and Henry Corbin, *The Dream and Human Societies,* edited by G.E. von Grunebaum and R. Caillois. © University of California Press 1966. Reprinted by permission of University of California Press.

J. Bregman, *Synesius of Cyrene.* © University of California Press 1982. Reprinted by permission of University of California Press.

Leucippe and Clitophon by Achilles Tatius, translated by John J. Winkley, from *Collected Greek Novels,* edited by B.P. Reardon. © University of California Press 1989. Reprinted by permission of University of California Press.

Kramrisch, Stella; *The Presence of Śiva.* © 1981 Princeton University Press. Reprinted by permission of Princeton University Press.

Kerenyi, C.; *Dionysos.* © 1976 Princeton University Press. 2004 renewed P.U.P. Reprinted by permission of Princeton University Press.

Miller, Patricia Cox; *Dreams in Late Antiquity.* © 1994 Princeton University Press. Reprinted by permission of Princeton University Press.

Reprinted by permission of the publisher from *Ancient Mystery Cults* by Walter Burkert, Cambridge, Mass.: Harvard University Press. Copyright © 1987 by the President and Fellows of Harvard College.

CPSIA information can be obtained at www.ICGtesting.com
Printed in the USA
BVOW012238190213

313724BV00011B/234/P